Cambridge Tracts in Theoretical Computer Science 52

Advanced Topics in Bisimulation and Coinduction

Coinduction is a method for specifying and reasoning about infinite data types and automata with infinite behaviour. In recent years, it has come to play an ever more important role in the theory of computing. It is studied in many disciplines, including process theory and concurrency, modal logic and automata theory. Typically, coinductive proofs demonstrate the equivalence of two objects by constructing a suitable bisimulation relation between them.

This collection of surveys is aimed at both researchers and Master's students in computer science and mathematics, and deals with various aspects of bisimulation and coinduction, with an emphasis on process theory. Seven chapters cover the following topics: history; algebra and coalgebra; algorithmics; logic; higher-order languages; enhancements of the bisimulation proof method; and probabilities. Exercises are also included to help the reader master new material.

DAVIDE SANGIORGI is Full Professor in Computer Science at the University of Bologna, Italy, and Head of the University of Bologna/INRIA team 'Focus'.

JAN RUTTEN is a senior researcher at Centrum Wiskunde & Informatica (CWI) in Amsterdam and Professor of Theoretical Computer Science at the Radboud University Nijmegen.

Cambridge Tracts in Theoretical Computer Science 52

Editorial Board

Titles in the series

A complete list of books in the series can be found at
www.cambridge.org/mathematics.
Recent titles include the following:

Advanced Topics in Bisimulation and Coinduction

Edited by

DAVIDE SANGIORGI
University of Bologna (Italy)
and INRIA (France)

JAN RUTTEN
Centrum Wiskunde & Informatica (CWI), Amsterdam
and the Radboud University Nijmegen

CAMBRIDGE
UNIVERSITY PRESS

Shaftesbury Road, Cambridge CB2 8EA, United Kingdom

One Liberty Plaza, 20th Floor, New York, NY 10006, USA

477 Williamstown Road, Port Melbourne, VIC 3207, Australia

314–321, 3rd Floor, Plot 3, Splendor Forum, Jasola District Centre, New Delhi – 110025, India

103 Penang Road, #05–06/07, Visioncrest Commercial, Singapore 238467

Cambridge University Press is part of Cambridge University Press & Assessment, a department of the University of Cambridge.

We share the University's mission to contribute to society through the pursuit of education, learning and research at the highest international levels of excellence.

www.cambridge.org
Information on this title: www.cambridge.org/9781107004979

© Cambridge University Press & Assessment 2012

First published 2012

A catalogue record for this publication is available from the British Library

ISBN   978-1-107-00497-9   Hardback

Additional resources for this publication at www.cs.unibo.it/~sangio/Book_Bis_Coind.html

Contents

Contributors

Luca Aceto
School of Computer Science, Reykjavik University, Menntavegur 1,
101 Reykjavik, Iceland.
email: luca@ru.is
web: www.ru.is/faculty/luca/

Anna Ingolfsdottir
School of Computer Science, Reykjavik University, Menntavegur 1,
101 Reykjavik, Iceland.
email: annai@ru.is
web: www.ru.is/faculty/annai/

Bart Jacobs
Institute for Computing and Information Sciences (ICIS), Radboud University
Nijmegen, Heyendaalseweg 135, 6525 AJ Nijmegen, The Netherlands.
email: bart@cs.ru.nl
web: www.cs.ru.nl/B.Jacobs/

Prakash Panangaden
McGill University, 3480 rue University, Room 318 Montreal, Quebec,
H3A 2A7 Canada.
email: prakash@cs.mcgill.ca
web: www.cs.mcgill.ca/~prakash/

Andrew M. Pitts
University of Cambridge, Computer Laboratory, William Gates Building,
15 JJ Thomson Ave, Cambridge CB3 0FD, UK.
email: Andrew.Pitts@cl.cam.ac.uk
web: www.cl.cam.ac.uk/~amp12/

Damien Pous
CNRS, Team Sardes, INRIA Rhône-Alpes, 655, avenue de l'Europe,
Montbonnot, 38334 Saint Ismier, France.
email: Damien.Pous@inria.fr
web: http://sardes.inrialpes.fr/~pous/

Jan Rutten
CWI, P.O. Box 94079, 1090 GB Amsterdam, The Netherlands.
Also: Radboud University Nijmegen.
email: janr@cwi.nl
web: http://homepages.cwi.nl/~janr/

Davide Sangiorgi
Università di Bologna/INRIA Team Focus, Dipartimento di Scienze
dell'Informazione, Università di Bologna, Mura Anteo Zamboni, 7 40126
Bologna, Italy.
email: Davide.Sangiorgi@cs.unibo.it
web: www.cs.unibo.it/~sangio/

Jiri Srba
Department of Computer Science, University of Aalborg, Selma Lagerlöfs Vej
300, 9220 Aalborg East, Denmark.
email: srba@cs.aau.dk
web: www.brics.dk/~srba/

Colin Stirling
School of Informatics, Edinburgh University, Informatics Forum, 10 Crichton
Street, Edinburgh EH8 9AB.
email: cps@staffmail.ed.ac.uk
web: http://homepages.inf.ed.ac.uk/cps/

Preface

This book is about bisimulation and coinduction. It is the companion book of the volume *An Introduction to Bisimulation and Coinduction*, by Davide Sangiorgi (Cambridge University Press, 2011), which deals with the basics of bisimulation and coinduction, with an emphasis on labelled transition systems, processes, and other notions from the theory of concurrency.

In the present volume, we have collected a number of chapters, by different authors, on several advanced topics in bisimulation and coinduction. These chapters either treat specific aspects of bisimulation and coinduction in great detail, including their history, algorithmics, enhanced proof methods and logic. Or they generalise the basic notions of bisimulation and coinduction to different or more general settings, such as coalgebra, higher-order languages and probabilistic systems. Below we briefly summarise the chapters in this volume.

- *The origins of bisimulation and coinduction, by Davide Sangiorgi*

    In this chapter, the origins of the notions of bisimulation and coinduction are traced back to different fields, notably computer science, modal logic, and set theory.

- *An introduction to (co)algebra and (co)induction, by Bart Jacobs and Jan Rutten*

    Here the notions of bisimulation and coinduction are explained in terms of coalgebras. These mathematical structures generalise all kinds of infinite-data structures and automata, including streams (infinite lists), deterministic and probabilistic automata, and labelled transition systems. Coalgebras are formally dual to algebras and it is this duality that is used to put both induction and coinduction into a common perspective. This generalises the treatment in the companion introductory volume, where induction and coinduction were explained in terms of least and greatest fixed points.

- *The algorithmics of bisimilarity, by Luca Aceto, Anna Ingolfsdottir and Jiří Srba*

  This chapter gives an overview of the solutions of various algorithmic problems relating bisimilarity and other equivalences and preorders on labelled transition systems. Typical questions that are addressed are: How can one compute bisimilarity? What is the complexity of the algorithms? When is bisimilarity decidable?

- *Bisimulation and logic, by Colin Stirling*

  This chapter discloses the strong and beautiful ties that relate bisimulation and modal logics. Various logical characterisations of bisimilarity are discussed. The main results are the characterisations of bisimilarity via a simple modal logic, the Hennessy–Milner logic, and the characterisation of this modal logic as the fragment of first-order logic that is bisimulation invariant. The results are then extended to modal logic with fixed points and to second-order logic.

- *Howe's Method for higher-order languages, by Andrew Pitts*

  In programming languages, an important property of bisimulation-based equivalences is whether they are a congruence, that is, compatible with the language constructs. This property may be difficult to prove if such languages involve higher-order constructs, that is, ones permitting functions and processes to be data that can be manipulated by functions and processes. This chapter presents a method for establishing compatibility of coinductively defined program equalities, originally due to Howe.

- *Enhancements of the bisimulation proof method, by Damien Pous and Davide Sangiorgi*

  This chapter discusses enhancements of the bisimulation proof method, with the goal of facilitating the proof of bisimilarity results. The bisimulation proof method is one of the main reasons for the success of bisimilarity. According to the method, to establish the bisimilarity between two given objects one has to find a bisimulation relation containing these objects as a pair. This means proving a certain closure property for each pair in the relation. The amount of work needed in proofs therefore depends on the size of the relation. The enhancements of the method in the chapter allow one to reduce such work by using relations that need only be *contained* in bisimulation relations. The chapter shows that it is possible to define a whole theory of enhancements, which can be very effective in applications.

- *Probabilistic bisimulation, by Prakash Panangaden*

  Here notions of bisimulation are introduced for probabilistic systems. These differ from non-deterministic ones in that they take quantitative data into account on the basis of which they make quantitative predictions about a system's behaviour. The chapter first discusses the basic example of discrete systems, called labelled Markov chains. After a rapid introductory section on measure theory, the more general continuous case, of so-called labelled Markov processes, is treated. For both the discrete and the continuous case, logical characterisations of bisimilarity are given.

The chapters on probabilities and higher-order linguistic constructs deal with two important refinements of bisimulation. While these are certainly not the only interesting refinements of bisimulation (one could mention, for instance, the addition of time or of space constraints), probabilities and higher-order constructs have strong practical relevance (e.g. in distributed systems and other complex systems such as biological systems, and in programming languages) and offer technical challenges that make them one of the most active research topics in the area of coinduction and bisimulation.

Each chapter is a separate entity, therefore notations among chapters may occasionally differ. We are very grateful to the colleagues who contributed the chapters for the time, effort, and enthusiasm that they put into this book project.

We recall the Web page with general information and auxiliary material about the two volumes, including solutions to exercises in some of the chapters. At the time of writing, the page is

`www.cs.unibo.it/~sangio/Book_Bis_Coind.html`

Davide Sangiorgi and Jan Rutten

1

Origins of bisimulation and coinduction

DAVIDE SANGIORGI

1.1 Introduction

In this chapter, we look at the origins of bisimulation. We show that bisimulation has been discovered not only in computer science, but also – and roughly at the same time – in other fields: philosophical logic (more precisely, modal logic), and set theory. In each field, we discuss the main steps that led to the discovery, and introduce the people who made these steps possible.

In computer science, philosophical logic, and set theory, bisimulation has been derived through refinements of notions of morphism between algebraic structures. Roughly, morphisms are maps (i.e. functions) that are 'structure-preserving'. The notion is therefore fundamental in all mathematical theories in which the objects of study have some kind of structure, or algebra. The most basic forms of morphism are the *homomorphisms*. These essentially give us a way of embedding a structure (the source) into another one (the target), so that all the relations in the source are present in the target. The converse, however, need not be true; for this, stronger notions of morphism are needed. One such notion is *isomorphism*, which is, however, extremely strong – isomorphic structures must be essentially the same, i.e. 'algebraically identical'. It is a quest for notions in between homomorphism and isomorphism that led to the discovery of bisimulation.

The kind of structures studied in computer science, philosophical logic, and set theory were forms of rooted directed graphs. On such graphs bisimulation is coarser than graph isomorphism because, intuitively, bisimulation allows us to observe a graph only through the movements that are possible along its edges. By contrast, with isomorphisms the identity of the nodes is observable too. For instance, isomorphic graphs have the same number of nodes, which need not be the case for bisimilar graphs (bisimilarity on two graphs indicates that their roots are related in a bisimulation).

1

The independent discovery of bisimulation in three different fields suggests that only limited exchanges and contacts among researchers existed at the time. The common concept of bisimulation has somehow helped to improve this situation. An example of this are the advances in set theory and computer science derived from Aczel's work.

Bisimilarity and the bisimulation proof method represent examples of a coinductive definition and the coinduction proof method, and as such are intimately related to fixed points, in particular greatest fixed points. We therefore also discuss the introduction of fixed points, and of coinduction. In this case, however, with a more limited breadth: we only consider computer science – fixed points have a much longer history in mathematics – and we simply discuss the main papers in the introduction of coinduction and fixed-point theory in the field. We conclude with some historical remarks on the main fixed-point theorems that underpin the theory of induction and coinduction presented in [San12].

In each section of the chapter, we focus on the origins of the concept dealt with in that section, and do not attempt to follow the subsequent developments. The style of presentation is generally fairly informal, but – we hope – technical enough to make the various contributions clear, so that the reader can appreciate them.

I believe that examining the developments through which certain concepts have come to light and have been discovered is not a matter of purely intellectual curiosity, but it also useful to understand the concepts themselves (e.g. problems and motivations behind them, relationship with other concepts, alternatives, etc.). Further, the chapter offers the opportunity of discussing bisimulation in set theory, where nowadays the role of bisimulation is well recognised. Set theory is not considered in other chapters of the book.

Structure of the chapter In Sections 1.2–1.4 we examine the origins of bisimulation and bisimilarity in modal logic, computer science, and set theory. We report on the introduction of coinduction and fixed points in computer science in Section 1.5, and, in Section 1.6, we discuss the fixed-point theorems.

This chapter is extracted from [San09]; I refer to this for further details on the topic. Solutions to most of the exercises can be found in [San09] and in the Web pages for the book.

Acknowledgements I am very grateful to the following people who helped me to find relevant papers and materials or helped me in tracing back bits of history: L. Aceto, P. Aczel, G. Boudol, J. van Benthem, E. Clarke, Y. Deng, R. Hinnion, F. Honsell, J.-P. Katoen, A. Mazurkiewicz, Y. N. Moschovakis, L.

Moss, R. Milner, U. Montanari, P. Panangaden, W.P. de Roever, W. Thomas, M. Tofte.

1.2 Bisimulation in modal logic

1.2.1 Modal logics

Philosophical logic studies and applies logical techniques to problems of interest to philosophers, somewhat similarly to what mathematical logic does for problems that interest mathematicians. Of course, the problems do not only concern philosophers or mathematicians; for instance, nowadays both philosophical and mathematical logics have deep and important connections with computer science.

Strictly speaking, in philosophical logic a modal logic is any logic that uses *modalities*. A modality is an operator used to qualify the truth of a statement, that is, it creates a new statement that makes an assertion about the truth of the original statement.

For the discussion below we use the 'full propositional logic' introduced in [Sti12], to which we refer for explanations and the interpretation of the formulas:

$$\phi \stackrel{\text{def}}{=} p \mid \neg\phi \mid \phi_1 \wedge \phi_2 \mid \langle\mu\rangle\phi \mid \bot$$

where p is a proposition letter. We recall that *Labelled Transition Systems (LTSs) with a valuation*, also called *Kripke models*, are the models for the logic. In the examples we will give, when we do not mention proposition letters it is intended that no proposition letters hold at the states under consideration.

1.2.2 From homomorphism to p-morphism

Today, some of the most interesting results in the expressiveness of modal logics rely on the notion of bisimulation. Bisimulation is indeed discovered in modal logic when researchers begin to investigate seriously issues of expressiveness for the logics, in the 1970s. For this, important questions tackled are: When is the truth of a formula preserved when the model changes? Or, even better, under which model constructions are modal formulas invariant? Which properties of models can modal logics express? (When moving from a model $\mathcal{M}$ to another model $\mathcal{N}$, preserving a property means that if the property holds in $\mathcal{M}$ then it holds also when one moves to $\mathcal{N}$; the property being invariant means that also the converse is true, that is, the property holds in $\mathcal{M}$ iff it holds when one moves to $\mathcal{N}$.)

To investigate such questions, it is natural to start from the most basic structure-preserving construction, that of *homomorphism*. A homomorphism from a model $\mathcal{M}$ to a model $\mathcal{N}$ is a function F from the points of $\mathcal{M}$ to the points of $\mathcal{N}$ such that

- whenever a proposition letter holds at a point P of $\mathcal{M}$ then the same letter also holds at $F(P)$ in $\mathcal{N}$;
- whenever there is a μ-transition between two points P, P' in $\mathcal{M}$ then there is also a μ-transition between $F(P)$ and $F(P')$ in $\mathcal{N}$.

Thus, contrasting homomorphism with bisimulation, we note that

(i) homomorphism is a functional, rather than relational, concept;
(ii) in the definition of homomorphism there is no back condition; i.e. the reverse implication, from transitions in $\mathcal{N}$ to those in $\mathcal{M}$, is missing.

It is easy to see that homomorphisms are too weak to respect the truth of modal formulas:

Exercise 1.2.1 Show, by means of a counterexample, that modal formulas are not preserved by homomorphisms.   □

That is, a homomorphism H from a model $\mathcal{M}$ to a model $\mathcal{N}$ does not guarantee that if a formula holds at a point Q of $\mathcal{M}$ then the same formula also holds at $H(Q)$ in $\mathcal{N}$.

The culprit for the failure of homomorphisms is the lack of a back condition. We can therefore hope to repair the invariance by adding some form of reverse implication. There are two natural ways of achieving this:

(1) turning the 'implies' of the definition of homomorphism into an 'iff' (that is, a propositional letter holds at P in $\mathcal{M}$ iff it holds at $F(P)$ in $\mathcal{N}$; and $P \xrightarrow{\mu} P'$ in $\mathcal{M}$ iff $F(P) \xrightarrow{\mu} F(P')$ in $\mathcal{N}$, for any P and P');
(2) explicitly adding back conditions (that is, if a propositional letter holds at $F(P)$ in $\mathcal{N}$ then it also holds at P in $\mathcal{M}$; and if in $\mathcal{N}$ there is a transition $F(P) \xrightarrow{\mu} Q$, for some point Q, then in $\mathcal{M}$ there exists a point P' such that $P \xrightarrow{\mu} P'$ and $Q = F(P')$.

Solution (1) is the requirement of *strong homomorphisms*. Solution (2) is first formalised by Krister Segerberg in his famous dissertation [Seg71], as the requirement of *p-morphisms*.

Segerberg starts the study of morphisms between models of modal logics that preserve the truth of formulas in [Seg68]. Initially, p-morphisms are called *pseudo-epimorphims* [Seg68], and are indeed surjective mappings. Later

[Seg70, Seg71], the term is shortened to p-morphisms, and thereafter used to denote also non-surjective mappings. A notion similar to p-morphisms had also occurred earlier, in a work of Jongh and Troelstra [JT66], for certain surjective mappings on partial orders that were called *strongly isotone*. Sometimes, today, p-morphisms are called *bounded morphisms*, after Goldbatt [Gol89]. The p-morphisms can be regarded as the natural notion of homomorphism in LTSs or Kripke models; indeed other reasons make p-morphisms interesting for modal logics, for instance they are useful in the algebraic semantics of modal logics (e.g. when relating modal algebras).

With either of the additions in (1) or (2), the invariance property holds: modal formulas are invariant both under surjective strong homomorphisms and under p-morphisms. (The surjective condition is necessary for strong homomorphisms, but not for p-morphisms.)

Exercise 1.2.2

(1) Exhibit a surjective p-morphism that is not a surjective strong homomorphism.
(2) Show that the invariance property does not hold for non-surjective strong homomorphisms. □

As far as invariance is concerned, the surjective strong homomorphism condition is certainly a very strong requirement – we are not far from isomorphism, in fact (the only difference is injectivity of the function, but even when functions are not injective only states with essentially the 'same' transitions can be collapsed, that is, mapped onto the same point). In contrast, p-morphisms are more interesting. Still, they do not capture all situations of invariance. That is, there can be states s of a model $\mathcal{M}$ and t of a model $\mathcal{N}$ that satisfy exactly the same modal formulas and yet there is no p-morphisms that take s into t or vice versa (Exercise 1.2.3).

1.2.3 Johan van Benthem

The next step is made by Johan van Benthem in his PhD thesis [Ben76] (the book [Ben83] is based on the thesis), who generalises the directional relationship between models in a p-morphism (the fact that a p-morphism is a function) to a symmetric one. This leads to the notion of bisimulation, which van Benthem calls *p-relation*. (Later [Ben84] he renames p-relations as *zigzag relations*.) On Kripke models, a p-relation between models $\mathcal{M}$ and $\mathcal{N}$ is a total relation $\mathcal{S}$ on the states of the models (the domain of $\mathcal{S}$ are the states of $\mathcal{M}$ and the codomain the states of $\mathcal{N}$) such that whenever $P \mathcal{S} Q$ then: a propositional letter holds at

P iff it holds at Q; for all P' with $P \xrightarrow{\mu} P'$ in $\mathcal{M}$ there is Q' such that $Q \xrightarrow{\mu} Q'$ in $\mathcal{N}$ and $P' \mathcal{S} Q'$; the converse of the previous condition, on the transitions from Q.

Exercise 1.2.3 Find an example of points in two models that are in a p-relation but no p-morphism can be established between them. □

Van Benthem defines p-relations while working on *correspondence theory*, precisely the relationship between modal and classical logics. Van Benthem's objective is to characterise the fragment of first-order logic that 'corresponds' to modal logic – an important way of measuring expressiveness. He gives a sharp answer to the problem, via a theorem that is today called the 'van Benthem characterisation theorem'. In nowadays's terminology, van Benthem's theorem says that a first-order formula A containing one free variable is equivalent to a modal formula iff A is invariant for bisimulations. That is, modal logic is the fragment of first-order logic whose formulas have one free variable and are invariant for bisimulation. We refer to [Sti12] for discussions on this theorem.

The original proof of the theorem is also interesting. The difficult implication is the one from right to left. A key part of the proof is to show that a point P in a model $\mathcal{M}$ and a point Q in a model $\mathcal{N}$ satisfy the same modal formulas if there are extensions $\mathcal{M}'$ and $\mathcal{N}'$ of the models $\mathcal{M}$ and $\mathcal{N}$ in which P and Q are bisimilar. The extensions are obtained as the limits of appropriate elementary chains of models, starting from the original models. Further, the embedding of the original models into the limits of the chains preserves modal formulas. The reason why it is necessary to move from the original models $\mathcal{M}$ and $\mathcal{N}$ to the extended models $\mathcal{M}'$ and $\mathcal{N}'$ is that on arbitrary models two points may satisfy the same set of formulas without being bisimilar. This may occur if the models are not finitely branching. By contrast, the extended models $\mathcal{M}'$ and $\mathcal{N}'$ are 'saturated', in the sense that they have 'enough points'. On such models, two points satisfy the same modal formulas iff they are bisimilar. As all finitely branching models are saturated, van Benthem's construction also yields the familiar Hennessy–Milner theorem for modal logics [HM85] (an earlier version is [HM80]): on finitely branching models, two points are bisimilar iff they satisfy the same modal formulas. Saturated models need not be finitely branching, however, thus van Benthem's construction is somewhat more general. Note that the need for saturation also would disappear if the logic allowed some infinitary constructions, for instance infinite conjunction. In modern textbooks, such as [BRV01], the proof is sometimes presented in a different way, by directly appealing to the existence of saturated models; however, elementary chains are employed to show the existence of such saturated models. Again, for details on the above proof and on the characterisation of bisimulation via modal logic, we refer to [Sti12].

After van Benthem's theorem, bisimulation has been used extensively in modal logic, for instance, to analyse the expressive power of various dialects of modal logics, to understand which properties of models can be expressed in modal logics, and to define operations on models that preserve the validity of modal formulas.

1.2.4 Discussion

In philosophical logic we see, historically, the first appearance of the notion of bisimulation. We do not find here, however, coinduction, at least not in an explicit way. Thus total relations between models that represent bisimulations are defined – the p-relations – but there is no explicit definition and use of bisimilarity. Similarly no links are made to fixed-point theory.

In retrospect, today we could say that bisimulation, as a means of characterising equivalence of modal properties, 'was already there' in the *Ehrenfeucht–Fraïssé games*. In the 1950s, Roland Fraïssé [Fra53] gave an algebraic formulation, as a weak form of isomorphism, of indistinguishability by formulas of first-order logic. Andrzej Ehrenfeucht [Ehr61] then extended the result and gave it a more intuitive game-theoretic formulation, in what is now called the Ehrenfeucht–Fraïssé games. Such games are today widely used in computer science, notably in logic, finite model theory, but also in other areas such as complexity theory, following Immerman [Imm82]. It is clear that the restriction of the Ehrenfeucht–Fraïssé games to modal logic leads to game formulations of bisimulation. However, such a connection has been made explicit only after the discovery of bisimulation. See, for instance, Thomas [Tho93].

1.3 Bisimulation in computer science

1.3.1 Algebraic theory of automata

In computer science, the search for the origins of bisimulation takes us back to the algebraic theory of automata, well-established in the 1960s. A good reference is Ginzburg's book [Gin68]. Homomorphisms can be presented on different forms of automata. We follow here *Mealy automata*. In these automata, there are no initial and final states; however, an output is produced whenever an input letter is consumed. Thus Mealy automata can be compared on the set of output strings produced. Formally, a Mealy automaton is a 5-tuple $(W, \Sigma, \Theta, \mathcal{T}, \mathcal{O})$ where

- W is the finite set of *states*;
- Σ is the finite set of *inputs*;
- Θ is a finite set of *outputs*;
- T is the *transition function*, that is a set of partial functions $\{T_a \mid a \in \Sigma\}$ from W to W;
- $\mathcal{O}$ is the *output function*, that is, a set of partial functions $\{\mathcal{O}_a \mid a \in \Sigma\}$ from W to Θ.

The output string produced by a Mealy automaton is the *translation* of the input string with which the automaton was fed; of course the translation depends on the state on which the automaton is started. Since transition and output functions of a Mealy automaton are partial, not all input strings are consumed entirely.

Homomorphism is defined on Mealy automata following the standard notion in algebra, e.g. in group theory: a mapping that commutes with the operations defined on the objects of study. Below, if A is an automaton, then W^A is the set of states of A, and similarly for other symbols. As we deal with partial functions, it is convenient to view these as relations, and thereby use for them relational notations. Thus fg is the composition of the two function f and g where f is used first (that is, $(fg)(a) = g(f(a))$); for this, one requires that the codomain of f be included in the domain of g. Similarly, $f \subseteq g$ means that whenever f is defined then so is g, and they give the same result.

A *homomorphism* from the automaton A to the automaton B is a surjective function F from W^A to W^B such that for all $a \in \Sigma$:

(1) $T_a^A F \subseteq F T_a^B$ (condition on the states); and
(2) $\mathcal{O}_a^A \subseteq F \mathcal{O}_a^B$ (condition on the outputs).

(We assume here for simplicity that the input and output alphabets are the same, otherwise appropriate coercion functions would be needed.)

At the time (the 1960s), homomorphism and similar notions are all expressed in purely algebraic terms. Today we can make an operational reading of them, which for us is more enlightening. Writing $P \xrightarrow[b]{a} Q$ if the automaton, on state P and input a, produces the output b and evolves into the state Q, and assuming for simplicity that $\mathcal{O}_a^A$ and T_a^A are undefined exactly on the same points, the two conditions above become:

- for all $P, P' \in W^A$, if $P \xrightarrow[b]{a} P'$ then also $F(P) \xrightarrow[b]{a} F(P')$.

Homomorphisms are used in that period to study a number of properties of automata. For instance, minimality of an automaton becomes the condition that the automaton has no proper homomorphic image. Homomorphisms are also used to compare automata. Mealy automata are compared using the notion of *covering* (written ≤): $A \leq B$ (read 'automaton B covers automaton A') if B can do, statewise, at least all the translations that A does. That is, there is a total function ψ from the states of A to the states of B such that, for all states P of A, all translations performed by A when started in P can also be performed by B when started in $\psi(P)$. Note that B can however have states with a behaviour completely unrelated to that of any state of A; such states of B will not be the image of states of A. If both $A \leq B$ and $B \leq A$ hold, then the two automata are deemed *equivalent*.

Homomorphism implies covering, i.e. if there is a homomorphism from A to B then $A \leq B$. The converse result is (very much) false. The implication becomes stronger if one uses *weak homomorphisms*. These are obtained by relaxing the functional requirement of homomorphism into a relational one. Thus a weak homomorphism is a total relation $\mathcal{R}$ on $W^A \times W^B$ such that for all $a \in \Sigma$:

(1) $\mathcal{R}^{-1} \mathcal{T}_a^A \subseteq \mathcal{T}_a^B \mathcal{R}^{-1}$ (condition on the states); and
(2) $\mathcal{R}^{-1} \mathcal{O}_a^A \subseteq \mathcal{O}_a^B$ (condition on the outputs)

where relational composition, inverse, and inclusion are defined in the usual way for relations [San12, section 0.5], and again functions are taken as special forms of relations. In an operational interpretation as above, the conditions give:

- whenever $P \mathcal{R} Q$ and $P \overset{a}{\underset{b}{\to}} P'$ hold in A, then there is Q' such that $Q \overset{a}{\underset{b}{\to}} Q'$ holds in B and $P' \mathcal{R} Q'$.

(On the correspondence between the algebraic and operational definitions, see also Remark 1.3.1 below.) Weak homomorphism reminds us of the notion of simulation (see [San12]). The former is however stronger, because the relation $\mathcal{R}$ is required to be *total*. (Also, in automata theory, the set of states and the sets of input and output symbols are required to be finite, but this difference is less relevant.)

Remark 1.3.1 To understand the relationship between weak homomorphisms and simulations, we can give an algebraic definition of simulation on LTSs, taking these to be triples $(W, \Sigma, \{\mathcal{T}_a \mid a \in \Sigma\})$ whose components have the same interpretation as for automata. A simulation between two LTSs A and B becomes a relation $\mathcal{R}$ on $W^A \times W^B$ such that, for all $a \in \Sigma$, condition (1) of weak homomorphism holds, i.e.

- $\mathcal{R}^{-1} \mathcal{T}_a^A \subseteq \mathcal{T}_a^B \mathcal{R}^{-1}$.

This is precisely the notion of simulation (as defined operationally in [San12]). Indeed, given a state $Q \in W^B$ and a state $P' \in W^A$, we have $Q \, \mathcal{R}^{-1} \, \mathcal{T}_a^A \, P'$ whenever there is $P \in W^A$ such that $P \stackrel{a}{\to} P'$. Then, requiring that the pair (Q, P') is also in $\mathcal{T}_a^B \mathcal{R}^{-1}$ is the demand that there is Q' such that $Q \stackrel{a}{\to} Q'$ and $P' \, \mathcal{R} \, Q'$.   □

Exercise 1.3.2 Suppose we modified the condition on states of weak homomorphism as follows:

- $\mathcal{T}_a^A \mathcal{R} \subseteq \mathcal{R} \mathcal{T}_a^B$,

and similarly for the condition on outputs. Operationally, what would this mean? What is the relationship to simulations?   □

Exercise 1.3.3 Suppose we strengthen the condition in Remark 1.3.1 by turning the inclusion $\subseteq$ into an equality. What would it mean, operationally? Do we obtain bisimulations? Do we obtain relations included in bisimilarity? How can bisimulation (on LTSs) be formulated algebraically?   □

As homomorphisms, so weak homomorphisms imply covering. The result for weak homomorphism is stronger as the homomorphisms are strictly included in the weak homomorphisms.

Exercise 1.3.4 Find an example of a weak homomorphism that is not a homomorphism.   □

Exercise 1.3.5 Show that there can be automata B and A with $A \leq B$ and yet there is no weak homomorphism between A and B. (Hint: use the fact that the relation of weak homomorphism is total.)   □

In conclusion: in the algebraic presentation of automata in the 1960s we find concepts that remind us of bisimulation, or better, simulation. However, there are noticeable differences, as we have outlined above. But the most important difference is due to the fact that the objects are deterministic. To see how significant this is, consider the operational reading of weak homomorphism, namely 'whenever $P \, \mathcal{R} \, Q$ ... then there is Q' such that ....'. As automata are deterministic, the existential in front of Q' does not play a role. Thus the alternation of universal and existential quantifiers – a central aspect of the definitions of bisimulation and simulation – does not really show up on deterministic automata.

1.3.2 Robin Milner

Decisive progress towards bisimulation is made by Robin Milner in the 1970s. Milner transplants the idea of weak homomorphism into the study of the behaviour of programs in a series of papers in the early 1970s ([Mil70, Mil71a, Mil71b], with [Mil71b] being a synthesis of the previous two). He studies programs that are sequential, imperative, and that may not terminate. He works on the comparisons among such programs. The aim is to develop techniques for proving the correctness of programs, and for abstracting from irrelevant details so that it is clear when two programs are realisations of the same algorithm. In short, the objective is to understand when and why two programs can be considered 'intensionally' equivalent.

To this end, Milner proposes – appropriately adapting it to his setting – the algebraic notion of weak homomorphism that we have described in Section 1.3.1. He renames weak homomorphism as *simulation*, a term that better conveys the idea of the application in mind. Although the definition of simulation is still algebraic, Milner now clearly spells out its operational meaning. But perhaps the most important contribution in his papers is the proof technique associated to simulation that he strongly advocates. This techniques amounts to exhibiting the set of pairs of related states, and then checking the simulation clauses on each pair. The strength of the technique is precisely the *locality* of the checks that have to be made, in the sense that we only look at the immediate transitions that emanate from the states (as opposed to, say, trace equivalence where one considers sequences of transitions, which may require examining states other than the initial one of a sequence). The technique is proposed to prove not only results of simulation, but also results of input/output correctness for programs, as a simulation between programs implies appropriate relationships on their inputs and outputs. Besides the algebraic theory of automata, other earlier works that have been influential for Milner are those on program correctness, notably Floyd [Flo67], Manna [Man69], and Landin [Lan69], who pioneers the algebraic approach to programs.

Formally, however, Milner's simulation remains the same as weak homomorphism and as such it is not today's simulation. Programs for Milner are deterministic, with a total transition function, and these hypotheses are essential. Non-deterministic and concurrent programs or, more generally, programs whose computations are trees rather than sequences, are mentioned in the conclusions for future work. It is quite possible that if this challenge had been quickly taken up, then today's notion of simulation (or even bisimulation) would have been discovered much earlier.

Milner himself, later in the 1970s, does study concurrency very intensively, but under a very different perspective: he abandons the view of parallel programs as objects with an input/output behaviour akin to functions, in favour of the view of parallel programs as *interactive* objects. This leads Milner to develop a new theory of processes and a calculus – CCS – in which the notion of behavioural equivalence between processes is fundamental. Milner however keeps, from his earlier works, the idea of 'locality' – an equivalence should be based outcomes that are local to states.

The behavioural equivalence that Milner puts forward, and that is prominent in the first book on CCS [Mil80], is inductively defined. It is the stratification of bisimilarity $\sim_\omega \overset{\text{def}}{=} \bigcap_n \sim_n$ presented in [San12, section 2.10]. Technically, in contrast with weak homomorphisms, $\sim_\omega$ has also the reverse implication (on the transitions of the second components of the pairs in the relation), and can be used on non-deterministic structures. The addition of a reverse implication was not obvious. For instance, a natural alternative would have been to maintain an asymmetric basic definition, possibly refine it, and then take the induced equivalence closure to obtain a symmetric relation (if needed). Indeed, among the main behavioural equivalences in concurrency – there are several of them, see [Gla93, Gla90] – bisimulation is the only one that is not naturally obtained as the equivalence-closure of a preorder.

With Milner's advances, the notion of bisimulation is almost there: it remained to turn an inductive definition into a coinductive one. This will be David Park's contribution.

It is worth pointing out that, towards the end of the 1970s, homomorphisms-like notions appear in other attempts at establishing 'simulations', or even 'equivalences', between concurrent models – usually variants of Petri nets. Good examples are John S. Gourlay, William C. Rounds, and Richard Statman [GRS79] and Kurt Jensen [Jen80], which develop previous work by Daniel Brand [Bra78] and Y.S. Kwong [Kwo77]. Gourlay, Rounds, and Statman's homomorphisms (called *contraction*) relate an abstract system with a more concrete realisation of it – in other words, a specification with an implementation. Jensen's proposal (called *simulation*), which is essentially the same as Kwong's *strict reduction* [Kwo77], is used to compare the expressiveness of different classes of Petri nets. The homomorphisms in both papers are stronger than today's simulation or bisimulation; for instance they are functions rather than relations. Interestingly, in both cases there are forms of 'reverse implications' on the correspondences between the transitions of related states. Thus these homomorphisms, but especially those in [GRS79], remind us of bisimulation, at least in the intuition behind it. In [GRS79] and [Jen80], as well as other similar works of that period, the homomorphisms are put forward because they represent conditions sufficient to preserve certain important properties (such as Church–Rosser and deadlock freedom). In contrast with Milner, little emphasis is given to the proof technique based on local checks that they bear upon. For instance the definitions of the homomorphisms impose correspondence on *sequences* of actions from related states.

1.3.3 David Park

In 1980, Milner returns to Edinburgh after a six-month appointment at Aarhus University, and completes his first book on CCS. Towards the end of that year, David Park begins a sabbatical in Edinburgh, and stays at the top floor of Milner's house.

Park is one of the top experts in fixed-point theory at the time. He makes the final step in the discovery of bisimulation precisely guided by fixed-point theory. Park notices that the inductive notion of equivalence that Milner is using for his CCS processes is based on a monotone functional over a complete lattice. And by adapting an example by Milner, he sees that Milner's equivalence ($\sim_\omega$) is not a fixed point for the functional, and that therefore the functional is not cocontinuous. He then defines bisimilarity as the greatest fixed point of the functional, and derives the bisimulation proof method from the theory of greatest fixed points. Further, Park knows that, to obtain the greatest fixed point of the functional in an inductive way, the ordinals and transfinite induction, rather then the naturals and standard induction, are needed [San12, theorem 2.8.8]. Milner immediately and enthusiastically adopts Park's proposal. Milner knew that $\sim_\omega$ is not invariant under transitions. Indeed he is not so much struck by the difference between $\sim_\omega$ and bisimilarity as behavioural equivalences, as the processes exhibiting such differences can be considered rather artificial. What excites him is the coinductive proof technique for bisimilarity. Both bisimilarity and $\sim_\omega$ are rooted in the idea of locality, but the coinductive method of bisimilarity further facilitates proofs. In the years to come Milner makes bisimulation popular and the cornerstone of the theory of CCS [Mil89].

In computer science, the standard reference for bisimulation and the bisimulation proof method is Park's paper 'Concurrency on automata and infinite sequences' [Par81a] (one of the most quoted papers in concurrency). However, Park's discovery is only partially reported in [Par81a], whose main topic is a different one, namely omega-regular languages (extensions of regular languages containing also infinite sequences) and operators for fair concurrency. Bisimulation appears at the end, as a secondary contribution, as a proof technique for trace equivalence on automata. Bisimulation is first given on finite automata, but only as a way of introducing the concept on the Büchi-like automata investigated in the paper. Here, bisimulation has additional clauses that make it non-transitive and different from the definition of bisimulation we know today. Further, bisimilarity and the coinduction proof method are not mentioned in the paper.

Indeed, Park never writes a paper to report on his findings about bisimulation. It is possible that this does not appear to him a contribution important enough to warrant a paper: he considers bisimulation a variant of the earlier notion of simulation by Milner [Mil70, Mil71b]; and it is not in Park's style to write many papers. A good account of Park's discovery of bisimulation and bisimilarity are the summary and the slides of his talk at the 1981 Workshop on the Semantics of Programming Languages [Par81b].

1.3.4 Discussion

In computer science, the move from homomorphism to bisimulation follows a somewhat opposite path with respect to modal logic: first homomorphisms are made relational, then they are made symmetric, by adding a reverse implication.

It remains puzzling why bisimulation has been discovered so late in computer science. For instance, in the 1960s weak homomorphism is well-known in automata theory and, as discussed in Section 1.3.1, this notion is not that far from simulation. Another emblematic example, again from automata theory, is given by the algorithm for minimisation of deterministic automata, already known in the 1950s [Huf54, Moo56] (also related to this is the Myhill–Nerode theorem [Ner58]). The aim of the algorithm is to find an automaton equivalent to a given one but minimal in the number of states. The algorithm proceeds by progressively constructing a relation S with all pairs of non-equivalent states. It roughly goes as follows. First step (a) below is applied, to initialise S; then step (b), where new pairs are added to S, is iterated until a fixed point is reached, i.e. no further pairs can be added:

(a) For all states P, Q, if P final and Q is not, or vice versa, then $P \, S \, Q$.
(b) For all states P, Q such that $\neg(P \, S \, Q)$: if there is a such that $T_a(P) \, S$ $T_a(Q)$ then $P \, S \, Q$.

The final relation gives all pairs of non-equivalent states. Then its complement, say $\overline{S}$, gives the equivalent states. In the minimal automaton, the states in the same equivalence class for $\overline{S}$ are collapsed into a single state.

The algorithm strongly reminds us of the partition refinement algorithms for computing bisimilarity and for minimisation modulo bisimilarity, discussed in [AIS12]. Indeed, the complement relation $\overline{S}$ that one wants to find has a natural coinductive definition, as a form of bisimilarity, namely the largest relation R such that

(1) if $P \mathcal{R} Q$ then either both P and Q are final or neither is;

(2) for each a, if $P \mathcal{R} Q$ then $\mathcal{T}_a(P) \mathcal{R} \mathcal{T}_a(Q)$.

Further, any relation $\mathcal{R}$ that satisfies the conditions (1) and (2) – that is, any bisimulation – only relates pairs of equivalent states and can therefore be used to determine equivalence of specific states.

The above definitions and algorithm are for deterministic automata. Bisimulation would have been interesting also on non-deterministic automata. Although on such automata bisimilarity does not coincide with trace equivalence – the standard equality on automata – at least bisimilarity implies trace equivalence and the algorithms for bisimilarity have a better complexity (P-complete, rather than PSPACE-complete; see [AIS12]).

Lumpability in probability theory An old concept in probability theory that today may be viewed as somehow reminiscent of bisimulation is Kemeny and Snell's *lumpability* [KS60]. A lumping equivalence is a partition of the states of a continuous-time Markov chain. The partition must satisfy certain conditions on probabilities guaranteeing that related states of the partition can be collapsed (i.e. 'lumped') into a single state. These conditions, having to do with sums of probabilities, are rather different from the standard one of bisimulation. (Kemeny and Snell's lumpability roughly corresponds to what today is called bisimulation for continuous-time Markov chains in the special case where there is only one label for transitions.)

The first coinductive definition of behavioural equivalence, as a form of bisimilarity, that takes probabilities into account appears much later, put forward by Larsen and Skou [LS91]. This paper is the initiator of a vast body of work on coinductive methods for probabilistic systems in computer science. Larsen and Skou were not influenced by lumpability. The link with lumpability was in fact noticed much later [Buc94].

In conclusion: in retrospect we can see that Kemeny and Snell's lumpability corresponds to a very special form of bisimulation (continuous-time Markov chains, only one label). However, Kemeny and Snell's lumpability has not contributed to the discovery of coinductive concepts such as bisimulation and bisimilarity.

1.4 Set theory

In mathematics, bisimulation and concepts similar to bisimulation are formulated in the study of properties of extensionality of models. Extensionality guarantees that equal objects cannot be distinguished within the given model.

When the structure of the objects, or the way in which the objects are supposed to be used, are non-trivial, the 'correct' notion of equality may be non-obvious. This is certainly the case for non-well-founded sets, as they are objects with an infinite depth, and indeed most of the developments in set theory towards bisimulation are made in a line of work on the foundations of theories of non-well-founded sets. Bisimulation is derived from the notion of isomorphism (and homomorphism), intuitively with the objective of obtaining relations coarser than isomorphism but still with the guarantee that related sets have 'the same' internal structure.

Bisimulation is first introduced by Forti and Honsell and, independently, by Hinnion, around the same time (the beginning of the 1980s). It is recognised and becomes important with the work of Aczel and Barwise. Some earlier constructions, however, have a clear bisimulation flavour, notably Mirimanoff's isomorphism at the beginning of the twentieth century.

1.4.1 Non-well-founded sets

Non-well-founded sets are, intuitively, sets that are allowed to contain themselves. As such they violate the *axiom of foundation*, according to which the membership relation on sets does not give rise to infinite descending sequences

$$\ldots A_n \in A_{n-1} \in \ldots \in A_1 \in A_0 \, .$$

For instance, a set Ω which satisfies the equation $\Omega = \{\Omega\}$ is circular and as such non-well-founded. A set can also be non-well-founded without being circular; this can happen if there is an infinite membership chain through a sequence of sets all different from each other.

If the axiom of foundation is used, the sets are *well-founded*. On well-founded sets the notion of equality is expressed by Zermelo's *extensionality axiom*: two sets are equal if they have exactly the same elements. In other words, a set is precisely determined by its elements. This is very intuitive and naturally allows us to reason on equality proceeding by (transfinite) induction on the membership relation. For instance, we can thus establish that the relation of equality is unique. Non-well-founded sets, by contrast, may be infinite in depth, and therefore inductive arguments may not be applicable. For instance, consider the sets A and B defined via the equations $A = \{B\}$ and $B = \{A\}$. If we try to establish that they are equal via the extensionality axiom we end up with a tautology ('A and B are equal iff A and B are equal') that takes us nowhere.

Different formulations of equality on non-well-founded sets appear during the twentieth century, together with proposals for *axioms of anti-foundation*.

1.4.2 The stratified approach to set theory

The first axiomatisation of set theory by Ernst Zermelo in 1908 [Zer08] has seven axioms, among which is the axiom of extensionality. However, it has no axioms of foundation, and the possibility of having circular sets is in fact left open (page 263, op. cit.).

In the same years, Bertrand Russell strongly rejects all definitions that can involve forms of circularity ('whatever involves all of a collection must not be one of the collection', in one of Russell's formulations [Rus08]). He favours a *theory of types* that only allows *stratified* constructions, where objects are hereditarily constructed, starting from atoms or primitive objects at the bottom and then iteratively moving upward through the composite objects. A preliminary version of the theory is announced by Russell already in 1903 [Rus03, Appendix B]; more complete and mature treatments appear in 1908 [Rus08] and later, in 1910, 1912, 1913, in the monumental work with Alfred North Whitehead [RW13].

Russell's approach is followed by the main logicians of the first half of the twentieth century, including Zermelo himself, Abraham Fraenkel, Thoralf Skolem, Johann von Neumann, Kurt Gödel, Paul Bernays. Their major achievements include the formulation of the axiom of foundation, and the proofs of its consistency and independence. An axiom of foundation is deemed necessary so as to have a 'canonical' universe of sets. Without foundation, different interpretations are possible, some including circular sets. This possibility is clearly pointed out as a weakness by Skolem [Sko23], and by Fraenkel [Fra22], where circular sets (precisely, Mirimanoff's 'ensembles extraordinaires', see below) are labelled as 'superfluous'. It will be formally proved by Bernays only in 1954 [Ber54] that the existence of circular sets does not lead to contradictions in the Zermelo–Fraenkel system without the axiom of foundation.

Remark 1.4.1 The axiom of foundation forces the universe of sets in which the other axioms (the basic axioms) should be interpreted to be the smallest possible one; i.e. to be an 'inductive universe'. By contrast, axioms of anti-foundation lead to the largest possible universe, i.e. a 'coinductive universe'. Indeed, referring to the algebraic/coalgebraic interpretation of induction/coinduction, the foundation axiom can be expressed as a requirement that the universe of sets should be an *initial algebra* for a certain powerset functor, whereas anti-foundation (as in Forti and Honsell, Aczel, and Barwise) can be expressed as a requirement that the universe should be a *final coalgebra* for the same functor. The former is an inductive definition of the universe, whereas the latter is a coinductive one. □

The motivations for formalising and studying the stratified approach advocated by Russell were strong at the beginning of the twentieth century. The discovery of paradoxes such as Burali-Forti's and Russell's had made the set theory studied by Cantor and Frege shaky, and circularity – with no distinction of cases – was generally perceived as the culprit for these as well as for paradoxes known in other fields. Further, the stratified approach was in line with common sense and perception (very important in Russell's conception of science), which denies the existence of circular objects.

The stratified approach remains indeed *the only* approach considered (in logics and set theory), up to roughly the 1960s, with the exception of Mirimanoff and Finsler that we discuss below. The stratified approach has also inspired – both in the name and in the method – type theory in computer science, notably in the works of Church, Scott, and Martin-Löf. It will be first disputed by Jean-Yves Girard and John Reynolds, in the 1970s, with the introduction of impredicative polymorphism.

1.4.3 Non-well-founded sets and extensionality

Dimitry Mirimanoff first introduces in 1917 the distinction between well-founded and non-well-founded sets, the 'ensembles *ordinaires* et *extraordinaires*' in Mirimanoff's words [Mir17a] (on the same topic are also the two successive papers [Mir17b] and [Mir20]). Mirimanoff realises that Zermelo's set theory admitted sophisticated patterns of non-well-foundedness, beyond the 'simple' circularities given by self-membership as in the purely reflexive set $\Omega = \{\Omega\}$. In [Mir17b], Mirimanoff also tries to give an intuition for the non-well-founded sets; he recalls the cover of a children's book he had seen, with the image of two children looking at the cover of a book, which in turn had the image of two children, in a supposedly infinite chain of nested images.

Mirimanoff defines an interesting notion of isomorphism between sets, that we report in Section 1.4.8. Mirimanoff does not however go as far as proposing an axiom of extensionality more powerful than Zermelo's. This is first attempted by Paul Finsler, in 1926 [Fin26]. Finsler presents three axioms for a universe of sets equipped with the membership relation. The second one is an extensionality axiom, stipulating that isomorphic sets are equal. Finsler's notion of isomorphism between two sets X and Y – which is different from Mirimanoff's – is, approximately, a bijection between the transitive closures of X and Y (more precisely, the transitive closures of the unit sets $\{X\}$ and $\{Y\}$; the precise meaning of isomorphism for Finsler can actually be debated, for it appears in different forms in his works).[1] Finsler uses graph theory to explain the properties and structure of sets, something that later Aczel will make more rigorous and at the heart of his theory of non-well-founded sets.

Mirimanoff's and Finsler's works are remarkable: they go against the standard approach to set theory at the time; and against common sense according to which objects are stratified and circular sets are 'paradoxical'. For Mirimanoff and Finsler, not all circular definitions are dangerous, and the challenge is to isolate the 'good' ones.

The attempts by Mirimanoff and Finsler remain little known. We have to wait till around the 1960s with, e.g. Specker [Spe57] and Scott [Sco60], to see a timid revival of interest in non-well-founded structures, and the late 1960s, and then the 1970s and 1980s, for a wider revival, with Boffa (with a number of papers, including [Bof68, Bof69, Bof72]) and many others. New proposals for anti-foundation axioms are thus made, and with them, new interpretations of extensionality on non-well-founded sets, notably from Scott [Sco60], and Forti and Honsell [FH83]. Forti and Honsell obtain bisimulation; their work is then developed by Aczel and Barwise. We discuss the contributions of Forti and Honsell, Aczel, and Barwise's. On the history of non-well-founded sets, the reader may also consult Aczel [Acz88, appendix A].

1.4.4 Marco Forti and Furio Honsell

Marco Forti's and Furio Honsell's work on non-well-founded sets [Hon81, FH83] (and various papers thereafter) is spurred by Ennio De Giorgi, a well-known analyst who, in the 1970s and 1980s, organises regular weekly meetings at the Scuola Normale Superiore di Pisa, on logics and foundations of Mathematics. In some of these meetings, De Giorgi proposes constructions that could yield infinite descending chains of membership on sets, that Forti and Honsell then go on to elaborate and develop.

The most important paper is [FH83]. Here Forti and Honsell study a number of anti-foundation axioms, derived from a 'Free Construction Principle' proposed by De Giorgi. They include axioms that already appeared in the literature (such as Scott's [Sco60]), and a new one, called X_1, that gives the strongest extensionality properties, in the sense that it equates more sets. (We recall X_1 in the next section, together with Aczel's version of it.) The main objective of the

---

[1] A set A is transitive if each set B that is an element of A has the property that all the elements of B also belong to A; that is, all composite elements of A are also subsets of A. The transitive closure of a set C is the smallest transitive set that contains C. Given C, its transitive closure is intuitively obtained by copying at the top level all sets that are elements of C, and then recursively continuing so with the new top-level sets.

paper is to compare the axioms, and define models that prove their consistency. Bisimulations and similar relations are used in the constructions to guarantee the extensionality of the models.

Forti and Honsell use, in their formulation of bisimulation, functions $f : A \mapsto \wp(A)$ from a set A to its powerset $\wp(A)$. Bisimulations are called *f-conservative* relations and are defined along the lines of the fixed-point interpretation of bisimulation in [San12, section 2.10]. We can make a state-transition interpretation of their definitions, for a comparison with today's definition. If f is the function from A to $\wp(A)$ in question, then we can think of A as the set of the possible states, and of f itself as the (unlabelled) transition function; so that $f(x)$ indicates the set of possible 'next states' for x. Forti and Honsell define the fixed-point behaviour of f on the relations on A, via the functional F defined as follows.[2] If $\mathcal{R}$ is a relation on A, and $P, Q \in A$, then $(P, Q) \in F(\mathcal{R})$ if:

- for all $P' \in f(P)$ there is $Q' \in f(Q)$ such that $P' \mathcal{R} Q'$;
- the converse, i.e. for all $Q' \in f(Q)$ there is $P' \in f(P)$ such that $P' \mathcal{R} Q'$.

A reflexive and symmetric relation $\mathcal{R}$ is *f-conservative* if $\mathcal{R} \subseteq F(\mathcal{R})$; it is *f-admissible* if it is a fixed point of F, i.e. $\mathcal{R} = F(\mathcal{R})$. The authors note that F is monotone over a complete lattice, hence it has a greatest fixed point (the largest *f-admissible* relation). They also prove that such a greatest fixed point can be obtained as the union over all *f-conservative* relations (the coinduction proof principle), and also, inductively, as the limit of a sequence of decreasing relations over the ordinals that starts with the universal relation $A \times A$ (akin to the characterisation in [San12, theorem 2.8.8]). The main difference between *f-conservative* relations and today's bisimulations is that the former are required to be reflexive and symmetric.

However, while the bisimulation proof method is introduced, as derived from the theory of fixed points, it remains rather hidden in Forti and Honsell's works, whose main goal is to prove the consistency of anti-foundation axioms. For this the main technique uses the *f-admissible* relations.

1.4.5 Peter Aczel

In mathematics, bisimulation and non-well-founded sets are made popular by Peter Aczel, notably with his book [Acz88]. Aczel is looking for mathematical foundations of processes, prompted by the work of Milner on CCS and his way of equating processes with an infinite behaviour via a bisimulation quotient. Aczel reformulates Forti and Honsell's anti-foundation axiom X_1. In Forti and

---

[2] We use a notation different from Forti and Honsell here.

Fig. 1.1. Sets as graphs.

Honsell [FH83], the axiom says that from every relational structure there is a unique homomorphism onto a transitive set (a relational structure is a set equipped with a relation on its elements; a set A is transitive if each set B that is an element of A has the property that all the elements of B also belong to A; that is, all composite elements of A are also subsets of A). Aczel calls the axiom AFA and expresses it with the help of graph theory, in terms of graphs whose nodes are decorated with sets. For this, sets are thought of as (pointed) graphs, where the nodes represent sets, the edges represent the converse membership relation (e.g. an edge from a node x to a node y indicates that the set represented by y is a member of the set represented by x), and the root of the graph indicates the starting point, that is, the node that represents the set under consideration. For instance, the sets $\{\emptyset, \{\emptyset\}\}$ and $D = \{\emptyset, \{D\}\}$ naturally correspond to the graphs of Figure 1.1 (where for convenience nodes are named) with nodes 2 and c being the roots. The graphs for the well-founded sets are those without infinite paths or cycles, such as the graph on the left in Figure 1.1. AFA essentially states that each graph represents a unique set. This is formalised via the notion of *decoration*. A decoration for a graph is an assignment of sets to nodes that respects the structure of the edges; that is, the set assigned to a node is equal to the set of the sets assigned to the children of the node. For instance, the decoration for the graph on the left of Figure 1.1 assigns $\emptyset$ to node 0, $\{\emptyset\}$ to node 1, and $\{\emptyset, \{\emptyset\}\}$ to node 2, whereas that for the graph on the right assigns $\emptyset$ to a, $\{D\}$ to b, and $\{\emptyset, \{D\}\}$ to c. Axiom AFA stipulates that *every graph has a unique decoration*. (In Aczel, the graph plays the role of the relational structure in Forti and Honsell, and the decoration the role of the homomorphism into a transitive set.) In this, there are two important facts: the existence of the decoration, and its uniqueness. The former tells us that the non-well-founded sets we need do exist. The latter tell us what is equality for them. Thus two sets are equal if they can be assigned to the same node of a graph. For instance the sets A and B in Section 1.4.1 and Ω in Section 1.4.3 are equal because the graph

has a decoration in which both nodes receive Ω, and another decoration in which the node on the left receives A and that on the right B. Bisimulation comes out when one tries to extract the meaning of equality. A bisimulation relates sets A and B such that

- for all $A_1 \in A$ there is $B_1 \in B$ with A_1 and B_1 related; and the converse, for the elements of B_1.

Two sets are equal precisely if there is a bisimulation relating them. The bisimulation proof method can then be used to prove equalities between sets, for instance the equality between the sets A and B above. This equality among sets is the most generous, or coarsest, equality that is compatible with the membership structure of sets: two sets are different only if there they present some genuine, observable, structural difference.

Exercise 1.4.2 AFA postulates that graphs have unique decoration. Show that the converse is false, i.e. there are (non-well-founded) sets that decorate different graphs.   □

Aczel formulates AFA towards the end of 1983; he does not publish it immediately having then discovered the earlier work of Forti and Honsell and the equivalence between AFA and X_1. Instead, he goes on developing the theory of non-well-founded sets, mostly through a series of lectures in Stanford between January and March 1985, which leads to the book [Acz88]. Aczel shows how to use the bisimulation proof method to prove equalities between non-well-founded sets, and develops a theory of coinduction that sets the basis for the coalgebraic approach to semantics (final semantics).

Up to Aczel's book [Acz88], all the works on non-well-founded sets had remained outside the mainstream. This changes with Aczel, for two main reasons: the elegant theory that he develops, and the concrete motivations for studying non-well-founded sets that he brings up.

Something that influences the developments of non-well-founded sets, and that is manifest in Aczel's work, is *Mostowski's collapse lemma* (proved probably sometime in the 1940s and today recognised as fundamental in the study of models of set theory). The original statement of the lemma talks about well-founded relations; roughly it says that given any such relation there is a unique set that faithfully represents the relation in its membership structure. Aczel reformulates the collapse on graphs. It becomes the assertion that every well-founded graph has a unique decoration. Axiom AFA is then obtained by removing the well-foundedness hypothesis (of course now, on the non-well-founded sets, it is an axiom, whereas Mostowski's collapse on the well-founded sets is a lemma). The collapse is also fundamental for the formal representation of sets as graphs, as it allows us to conclude that we can associate a unique set to each pointed graph, via the decoration. When Finsler writes his 1926 paper [Fin26], the collapse construction is not known and indeed Finsler's use of graph theory remains informal.

Exercise 1.4.3 Using AFA, show that a graph has a decoration in which all nodes are mapped to Ω iff all nodes of the graphs have a child. □

1.4.6 Jon Barwise

Aczel's original motivation for the study on non-well-founded sets is to provide set-theoretic models for CCS. Jon Barwise brings up other applications, notably the study of paradoxes such as the liar paradox in philosophical logic and more broadly the study of meaning in natural (i.e. human spoken) languages [BE87].

Further, Barwise develops a theory of non-well-founded sets that is not based on the relationship between sets and graph theory as Aczel, but, instead, on systems of equations. The axiom AFA becomes a requirement that appropriate systems of equations have a unique solution. To understand this point consider that, as the purely reflexive set Ω can be seen as the solution to the equation $x = \{x\}$, so all non-well-founded sets arise from systems of equations with variables on the left-hand side, and well-founded sets possibly containing such variables on the right-hand side. In Aczel [Acz88] this is expressed as the 'solution lemma'. Barwise makes it the base assumption from which all the theory of sets is derived. For more details, the reader may consult Barwise's excellent book with Lawrence Moss [BM96].

1.4.7 Extensionality quotients: Roland Hinnion and others

More or less at the same time as Forti and Honsell, and independently of them, bisimulation-like relations are used by Roland Hinnion [Hin80, Hin81] (a related, but later, paper is also [Hin86]). Hinnion follows Mostowski's collapse; Mostowski's construction allows one to obtain, from a well-founded relational structure, a model of set theory in which Zermelo's axiom of extensionality holds. Hinnion aims at generalising this to arbitrary (i.e. not necessarily well-founded) structures. Thus he defines forms of bisimulation on relational structures, as usual the 'transitions' of the bisimulation game being dictated by the relation on the structure. He considers two such forms. The *final equivalences* (later [Hin86] called *increasing*) are the bisimulations that are also equivalences. The *contractions* are the final equivalences whose quotient on the original structure satisfies the extensionality axiom. Roughly we can think of contractions as bisimulation equivalences that are also congruences, in that they are preserved by the operators of the model, i.e. by the addition of external structure.

Hinnion does not formulate axioms of anti-foundation. Thus while imposing the AFA axiom makes equality the only possible bisimulation for any structure, Hinnion uses bisimulations to define new structures, via a quotient.

Although Hinnion points out that final equivalences and contractions form a complete lattice, he does not put emphasis on the maximal ones. The equalities obtained via his quotients can indeed be finer than the equality that the AFA axiom yields (which corresponds to the quotient with bisimilarity, the maximal bisimulation). Consequently, he also does not put emphasis on the coinduction proof principle associated to bisimulation.

Constructions similar to Hinnion's, that is, uses of relations akin to bisimulation to obtain extensional quotient models, also appear in works by Harvey Friedman [Fri73] and Lev Gordeev [Gor82]. In this respect, however, the first appearance of a bisimulation relation I have seen is in a work by Jon Barwise, Robin O. Gandy, and Yiannis N. Moschovakis [BGM71], and used in the main result about the characterisation of the structure of the next admissible set A^+ over a given set A. (Admissible sets form a set theory weaker than Zermelo–Fraenkel's in the principles of set existence; it was introduced in the mid-1960s by Saul Kripke and Richard Platek with the goal of generalising ordinary recursion theory on the integers to ordinals smaller than a given 'well-behaved' one.) A stronger version of the result is found in Moschovakis's book [Mos74] (where the main result is theorem 9E.1, in chapter 9, and the bisimulation relation is used in the proof of lemma 9). As with most of the results we have mentioned in set theory, so the Barwise–Gandy–Moschovakis theorem is inspired by Mostowski's collapse lemma. While the papers [BGM71, Fri73, Gor82] make use of specific bisimulation-like relations, they do not isolate or study the concept.

1.4.8 Discussion

It may appear surprising that also in mathematics it takes so long for the notion of bisimulation to appear. This is partly explained by the limited attention to non-well-founded structures up to the 1980s, as discussed in Section 1.4.2.

It is fair to say, however, that some of the very early constructions already had a definite bisimulation flavour. An enlightening example is Mirimanoff's pioneering work on non-well-founded sets. Mirimanoff [Mir17a] defines a notion of isomorphism for sets that have atoms (often called urelements), i.e. elements that cannot be decomposed and that are not the empty set. Two such sets E and E' are deemed *isomorphic* when the two conditions below hold:

(1) The sets E and E' are equivalent; that is, a perfect correspondence can be established between the elements of E and E'.

(2) Further, the above correspondence can be established in such a way that each atom e in E corresponds to an atom e' in E' and conversely; and each element-set F of E corresponds to an element-set F' of E' (an element-set of a set G is an element of G that is a set). The perfect correspondence between F and F' can then be established in such a way that each atom in F corresponds to an atom in F', and each element-set of F corresponds to an element-set of F'; and so forth.

Although today we would give this definition in a different way, its meaning is clear. Mirimanoff's isomorphism abstracts from the nature and identity of the atoms. His intention – clearly stated in [Mir17b] – is to relate sets with the same tree structure, as determined by the membership relation. (In other words, if we think of sets as trees, along the lines of the representation of sets as graphs mentioned in Section 1.4.5, then Mirimanoff's isomorphism is essentially an isomorphism between such trees.)

Mirimanoff's isomorphism is not far from the equality on sets given by Finsler's and Scott's anti-foundation axioms. These equalities too, indeed, are based on notions of isomorphism. The peculiarity of Mirimanoff's definition is that it is built on the idea of equating potentially infinite objects by decomposing, or observing, them top-down, from a composite object to its constituents. This idea is also at the heart of the definition of bisimulation (where, for instance, decomposing a process is observing its transitions). The 'perfect correspondence' used by Mirimanoff is however a bijection between the components of the sets, rather than a relation, and as such the resulting notion of equality is finer than bisimilarity. For instance, consider the purely reflexive set Ω and the set $U = \{\Omega, U\}$. It is easy to see that they are bisimilar. However they are not isomorphic for Mirimanoff as their trees, in Figure 1.2, are quite different. (The two sets are also different under Finsler's and Scott's equalities; bisimilarity is indeed strictly coarser than Finsler's and Scott's equalities, see [Acz88].)

What really makes Mirimanoff's isomorphism different from bisimulation is that Mirimanoff fails to promote isomorphism to equality for sets. For instance, the sets $A = \{B\}$ and $B = \{A\}$ are isomorphic but not equal, hence the set $\{A, B\}$ has two elements and is not isomorphic to the set $\{A\}$ or to the set $\{B\}$, which have only one element. To identify isomorphism and equality, the clause of isomorphism, in establishing the 'perfect correspondence' between the elements of two isomorphic sets, should take into account the collapse given by isomorphism itself. This can be easily obtained by weakening the requirements of injectivity and surjectivity in the correspondences, for instance making the

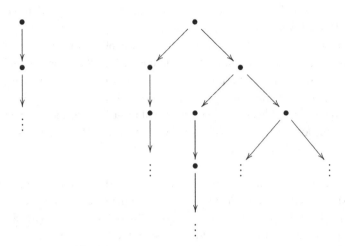

Fig. 1.2. Tree unfolding of the sets Ω and U.

correspondences total relations – i.e. making them bisimulations. In conclusion, had Mirimanoff investigated the impact of isomorphism on extensionality, while retaining the spirit of his definition, he would have probably discovered bisimulation.

However, Mirimanoff pays little attention to extensionality. His main interest, motivated by Burali–Forti and Russell's paradoxes, is understanding what are the conditions for the existence of a set of objects. And his main results are theorems asserting – using modern terminology – that certain classes are not sets. In set theory, even more than in modal logic or computer science, the move from the 'functional' concepts of homomorphism and isomorphism to the 'relational' concept of bisimulation will take time.

1.5 The introduction of fixed points in computer science

Bisimulation and the bisimulation proof method, as coinductive concepts, are intimately related to fixed points. We have seen the characterisation of bisimulation via greatest fixed points in [San12, section 2.10]. We therefore also examine coinduction and fixed points. We do not attempt, however, to trace the general history of fixed-point theory – in mathematics this is a story stretching far back in time. Instead, we concentrate on computer science, and recall some papers that well witness the introduction of coinduction and fixed-point theory for the design and analysis of programming languages. The Fixed-Point

Theorem 2.3.21 in [San12], about the existence of a least and greatest fixed point for a monotone function on a complete lattice, or variations of this such as Theorem 2.8.5 in the same volume, are the starting point for all the works we mention.

The earliest uses of fixed points in computer science, in the form of least fixed points, can be found in recursive function theory, see for instance Rogers's book [Rog67] and references therein, and formal language theory, as in the work of Arden [Ard60] and Ginsburg and Rice [GR62]. However, distinguishing computer science from recursive function theory, the importance of fixed points in computer science really comes up only at the end of the 1960s, with four independent papers, roughly at the same time, by Dana Scott and Jaco de Bakker [SdB69], Hans Bekič [Bek69], David Park [Par69], and Antoni Muzurkiewicz [Maz71] (however [Maz71] does not make explicit reference to fixed-point theory). Although [Maz71] is published in 1971, it is already made available, as a working paper, in December 1969 to the IFIP Working Group 2.2, whose members included some of the most influential researchers on programming language concepts at that time; this paper also had an impact on the discovery of continuations in denotational semantics, see [Rey93]. It might sound surprising that [SdB69] and [Bek69] should be considered 'independent', given that both appear as manuscripts from the same place, the Vienna IBM Laboratory. The reason is that Bekič's work is mainly carried out during a one-year visit (November 1968–November 1969) to Queen Mary College, London, where Bekič stays in Peter Landin's group (indeed Landin has a strong influence on [Bek69]). Thus when Scott and de Bakker's work is presented at the Vienna IBM Laboratory in August 1969, Bekič – who is a member of the Laboratory – is still in London. The first time when the two works can be discussed and compared is the IFIP Working Group 2.2 meeting in Colchester in September 1969.

The above four papers bring out the importance of least fixed points for the semantics of programs, the relevance of lattice theory and the Fixed-Point Theorem, and propose various rules for reasoning about least fixed points. Programs take the form of recursive function definitions or of flowcharts. Further, [SdB69] paves the way for the fundamental work on denotational semantics by Scott and Strachey in Oxford in the 1970s, where least fixed points, and continuity of functions, are essential. Influential on the above four papers are earlier works on program correctness and on uses of the 'paradoxical combinator' Y of the λ-calculus, notably papers by Landin such as [Lan64], by McCarthy such as [McC61, McC63], and by Floyd such as [Flo67]. For instance, McCarthy [McC61, McC63] proposes the first method for proving properties of recursive programs, called *recursion induction*; variants and stronger versions of the method are formulated in [SdB69], [Bek69], and [Par69]. Also, the fixed-point properties of the Y combinator of the λ-calculus had been known for a long time (used for instance by Curry, Feys, Landin, and Strachey), but the precise mathematical meaning of Y as fixed point remains unclear until Scott works out his theory of reflexive domains, at the end of 1969 [Sco69b, Sco69a]; see [Par70]. (Another relevant paper is [Sco69c], in which fixed points appear but which precedes the discovery of reflexive domains. We may also recall James H. Morris, who earlier [Mor68] had proved a minimal fixed-point property for the Y combinator; in the same document, Morris had considered the relationship between least fixed points and functions computed by first-order recursive definitions of programs.)

During the 1970s, further fixed-point techniques and rules are put forward. A number of results on fixed points and induction rules, and the basic theory of continuous functions, are due to Scott, e.g. [Sco72b, Sco72a, Sco76]. On uses of least fixed points in semantics and in techniques for program correctness, we should also mention the work of de Bakker and his colleagues in The Netherlands, e.g. [BR73, Bak75, Bak71]; the Polish school, with Mazurkiewicz, Blikle, and colleagues, e.g. [Maz71, Maz73, Bli77]; and the work of Ugo Montanari and colleagues in Pisa, such as [GM76] that contains notions of observations and equivalence of representations in abstract data types that today we recognise as related to fixed points via the concept of finality. Other references to the early works on fixed points can be found in Zohar Manna's textbook [Man74].

The above works all deal with least fixed points. Greatest fixed points, and related coinductive techniques, begin to appear as well in the 1970s. It is hard to tell what is the first appearance. One reason for this is that the rules for greatest fixed points are not surprising, being the dual of rules for least fixed points that had already been studied. I would think however that the first to make explicit and non-trivial use of greatest fixed points is David Park, who, throughout the 1970s, works intensively on fairness issues for programs that may contain constructs for parallelism and that may not terminate. The fixed-point techniques he uses are rather sophisticated, possibly involving alternation of least and greatest fixed points. Park discusses his findings in several public presentations. A late overview paper is [Par79]; we already pointed out in Section 1.3.3 that Park did not publish much.

Other early interesting uses of greatest fixed points are made by the following authors. Mazurkiewicz [Maz73] studies properties of computations from processes, where processes are modelled via forms of LTSs; the properties studied include divergence and termination. The way in which Mazurkiewicz defines divergent states (i.e. the states from which a computation may not terminate) and the technique proposed to prove divergence of states are coinductive, though – as in his earlier paper [Maz71] – there is no explicit reference to fixed-point theory.

Edmund Clarke [Cla77] shows that the correctness proofs for Floyd–Hoare axiom systems – deductive systems for partial correctness based on invariance assertions intensively investigated in the 1970s – could be elegantly formalised by means of fixed-point theory, whereby: program invariants become greatest fixed points; completeness of a system becomes the proof of the existence of a fixed point for an appropriate functional; and soundness is derived from the maximality of such a fixed point. Thus soundness is a coinductive proof. Willem-Paul de Roever [dR77] strongly advocates the coinduction principle as a proof technique (he calls it 'greatest fixed-point induction'). De Roever uses the technique to reason about divergence, bringing up the duality between this technique and inductive techniques that had been proposed previously to reason on programs.

Coinduction and greatest fixed points are implicit in a number of earlier works in the 1960s and 1970s. Important examples, with a wide literature, are the works on unification, for instance on structural equivalence of graphs, and the works on invariance properties of programs. Fixed points are also central in *stream processing* systems (including *data flow* systems). The introduction of streams in computer science is usually attributed to Peter Landin, in the early 1960s (see [Lan65a, Lan65b] where Landin discusses the semantics of Algol 60 as a mapping into a language based on the λ-calculus and Landin's SECD machine [Lan64], and historical remarks in [Bur75]). However, fixed points are explicitly used to describe stream computations only after Scott's theory of domain, with the work of Gilles Kahn [Kah74].

1.6 Fixed-point theorems

We conclude with a few remarks on the main fixed-point theorems in [San12]. The Fixed-Point Theorem 2.3.21 is usually called the 'Knaster–Tarski fixed-point theorem'. The result was actually obtained by Tarski, who, in a footnote to [Tar55] (footnote 2, page 286), where the result appears as theorem 1, explains its genesis:

> In 1927 Knaster and the author [i.e. Tarski] proved a set-theoretical fixed point theorem by which every function on and to the family of all subsets of a set, which is increasing under set-theoretical inclusion has at least one fixed point; see [Kna28] where some applications of this result in set theory [...] and topology are also mentioned. A generalisation of this result is the lattice-theoretical fixed point

theorem stated above as Theorem 1. The theorem in its present form and its various applications and extensions were found by the author in 1939 and discussed it in a few public lectures in 1939–1942. (See, for example, a reference in the American Mathematical Monthly 49(1942), 402.) An essential part of Theorem 1 was included in [Bir48, p. 54]; however the author was informed by Professor Garret Birkhoff that a proper historical reference to this result was omitted by mistake.

Tarski first properly publishes the theorem in 1955 [Tar55], together with a few related results, proofs, and applications to boolean algebras and topology. He had anticipated a summary of [Tar55] in 1949, as [Tar49]. Credit for the theorem is also given to Bronislaw Knaster because of the following result in [Kna28]:

> If F is monotone function over sets such that $(*)$
> there is a set Pr with $F(Pr) \subseteq Pr$ then
> there is a subset Q of Pr such that $F(Q) = Q$.

While the fixed-point theorem describes the structure of the fixed points for a function, the result $(*)$ only asserts the existence of at least one fixed point. Moreover the fixed-point theorem is on arbitrary lattices, whereas we can think of $(*)$ as being on the special lattices given by the powerset construction. [Kna28] is actually a very short note – about one page – in which the lemma is used to derive, as a special case, a theorem on monotone functions over sets. The note itself confirms that the results presented had been obtained by Knaster together with Tarski.

It would not be so surprising if the fixed-point theorem had been obtained around the same period also by Stephen C. Kleene or Leonid V. Kantorovich, although the writings from these authors that we have today only deal with constructive proofs of the existence of least and greatest fixed points along the lines of the Continuity/Cocontinuity Theorem 2.8.5 in [San12] (see below). (Leonid Vitalyevich Kantorovich [1912–1986] was a Russian mathematician who obtained the Nobel Prize for Economics in 1975 for his work on the allocation and optimisation of resources, in which he pioneers the technique of linear programming.)

In computer science, the Continuity/Cocontinuity Theorem is often called the 'Kleene fixed-point theorem', with reference to Kleene's first recursion theorem [Kle52], and often presented on pointed complete partial orders and for least fixed points. The first recursion theorem is obtained by Kleene around the end of the 1930s, as reported in [Kle52, Kle70]. Around that time, or anyhow before the 1950s, the Continuity/Cocontinuity Theorem is independently known to other authors, first of all Tarski and Kantorovich (for instance theorem I in [Kan39] is similar to the Continuity/Cocontinuity Theorem), but possibly others – see also the discussion in [CC79, page 56]. It is indeed unclear who should be credited for the theorem. Lassez, Nguyen, and Sonenberg [LNS82] consider the origins of this theorem (as well as of the other fixed-point theorems) and conclude that it should be regarded as a 'folk theorem'. The ordinal characterisation in [San12, theorem 2.8.8] is from Hitchcock and Park [HP73]. Similar versions are also given by Devidé [Dev63], Pasini [Pas74], Cadiou [Cad72], Cousot and Cousot [CC79]. A related theorem also appears in Bourbaki [Bou50].

Bibliography

[Acz88] P. Aczel. *Non-Well-Founded Sets*. CSLI Lecture Notes, no. 14, 1988.

[AIS12] L. Aceto, A. Ingolfsdottir, and J. Srba. The algorithmics of bisimilarity. Chapter 3 of this volume.

[Ard60] D.N. Arden. Delayed logic and finite state machines. In *Theory of Computing Machine Design*, pages 1–35. University of Michigan Press, 1960.

[Bak71] J.W. de Bakker. *Recursive Procedures*. Mathematical Centre Tracts 24, Mathematisch Centrum, Amsterdam, 1971.

[Bak75] J.W. de Bakker. The fixed-point approach in semantics: theory and applications. In J.W. de Bakker, editor, *Foundations of Computer Science*, pages 3–53. Mathematical Centre Tracts 63, Mathematisch Centrum, Amsterdam, 1975.

[BE87] J. Barwise and J. Etchemendy. *The Liar: an Essay in Truth and Circularity*. Oxford University Press, 1987.

[Bek69] H. Bekič. Definable operations in general algebras and the theory of automata and flowcharts. Unpublished Manuscript, IBM Lab. Vienna 1969. Also appeared in [Jon84].

[Ben76] J. van Benthem. *Modal correspondence theory*. PhD thesis, Mathematish Instituut & Instituut voor Grondslagenonderzoek, University of Amsterdam, 1976.

[Ben83] J. van Benthem. *Modal Logic and Classical Logic*. Bibliopolis, 1983.

[Ben84] J. van Benthem. Correspondence theory. In D.M. Gabbay and F. Guenthner, editors, *Handbook of Philosophical Logic*, volume 2, pages 167–247. Reidel, 1984.

[Ber54] P. Bernays. A system of axiomatic set theory–Part VII. *Journal of Symbolic Logic*, **19**(2):81–96, 1954.

[BGM71] J. Barwise, R.O. Gandy, and Y.N. Moschovakis. The next admissible set. *Journal of Symbolic Logic*, **36**:108–120, 1971.

[Bir48] G. Birkhoff. *Lattice Theory (Revised Edition)*. Volume 25 of American Mathematical Society Colloquium Publications. American Mathematical Society, 1948.

[Bli77] A. Blikle. A comparative review of some program verification methods. In Jozef Gruska, editor, *6th Symposium on Mathematical Foundations of*

Computer Science (MFCS'77), volume 53 of *Lecture Notes in Computer Science*, pages 17–33. Springer, 1977.

[BM96] J. Barwise and L. Moss. *Vicious Circles: On the Mathematics of Non-Wellfounded Phenomena*. CSLI (Center for the Study of Language and Information), 1996.

[Bof68] M. Boffa. Les ensembles extraordinaires. *Bulletin de la Société Mathématique de Belgique*, **XX**:3–15, 1968.

[Bof69] M. Boffa. Sur la théorie des ensembles sans axiome de fondement. *Bulletin de la Société Mathématique de Belgique*, **XXXI**:16–56, 1969.

[Bof72] M. Boffa. Forcing et negation de l'axiome de fondement. *Académie Royale de Belgique, Mémoires de la Classe des Sciences, 2e série*, **XL**(7):1–53, 1972.

[Bou50] N. Bourbaki. Sur le théorème de Zorn. *Archiv der Mathematik*, **2**:434–437, 1950.

[BR73] J.W. de Bakker and W.P. de Roever. A calculus for recursive program schemes. In M. Nivat, editor, *Proceedings of the IRIA Symposium on Automata, Languages and Programming*, Paris, France, July, 1972, pages 167–196. North-Holland, 1973.

[Bra78] D. Brand. Algebraic simulation between parallel programs. Research Report RC 7206, Yorktown Heights, NY, 39 pp., June 1978.

[BRV01] P. Blackburn, M. de Rijke, and Y. Venema. *Modal Logic*. Cambridge University Press, 2001.

[Buc94] P. Buchholz. Markovian process algebra: composition and equivalence. In U. Herzog and M. Rettelbach, editors, *Proceedings of the 2nd Workshop on Process Algebras and Performance Modelling*, pages 11–30. Arbeitsberichte des IMMD, Band 27, Nr. 4, 1994.

[Bur75] W.H. Burge. Stream processing functions. *IBM Journal of Research and Development*, **19**(1):12–25, 1975.

[Cad72] J.M. Cadiou. *Recursive definitions of partial functions and their computations*. PhD thesis, Computer Science Department, Stanford University, 1972.

[CC79] P. Cousot and R. Cousot. Constructive versions of Tarski's fixed point theorems. *Pacific Journal of Mathematics*, **81**(1):43–57, 1979.

[Cla77] E.M. Clarke. Program invariants as fixed points (preliminary reports). In *FOCS*, pages 18–29. IEEE, 1977. Final version in *Computing*, **21**(4):273–294, 1979. Based on Clarke's PhD thesis, *Completeness and Incompleteness Theorems for Hoare-like Axiom Systems*, Cornell University, 1976.

[Dev63] V. Devidé. On monotonous mappings of complete lattices. *Fundamenta Mathematicae*, **LIII**:147–154, 1963.

[dR77] W.P. de Roever. On backtracking and greatest fixpoints. In Arto Salomaa and Magnus Steinby, editors, *Fourth Colloquium on Automata, Languages and Programming (ICALP)*, volume 52 of *Lecture Notes in Computer Science*, pages 412–429. Springer, 1977.

[Ehr61] A. Ehrenfeucht. An application of games to the completeness problem for formalized theories. *Fundamenta Mathematicae*, **49**:129–141, 1961.

[FH83] M. Forti and F. Honsell. Set theory with free construction principles. *Annali Scuola Normale Superiore, Pisa, Serie IV*, **X**(3):493–522, 1983.

[Fin26] P. Finsler. Über die Grundlagen der Mengenlehre. *I. Math. Zeitschrift*, **25**:683–713, 1926.

[Flo67] R.W. Floyd. Assigning meaning to programs. In *Proceeding of Symposia in Applied Mathematics*, volume 19, pages 19–32. American Mathematical Society, 1967.

[Fra22] A. Fraenkel. Zu den Grundlagen der Cantor-Zermeloschen Mengenlehre. *Mathematische Annalen*, **86**:230–237, 1922.

[Fra53] R. Fraïssé. *Sur quelques classifications des systèmes de relations*. PhD thesis, University of Paris, 1953. Also in *Publications Scientifiques de l'Université d'Alger, series A*, **1**, 35–182, 1954.

[Fri73] H. Friedman. The consistency of classical set theory relative to a set theory with intuitionistic logic. *Journal of Symbolic Logic*, **38**:315–319, 1973.

[Gin68] A. Ginzburg. *Algebraic Theory of Automata*. Academic Press, 1968.

[Gla90] R.J. van Glabbeek. The linear time-branching time spectrum (extended abstract). In J.C.M. Baeten and J.W. Klop, editors, *First Conference on Concurrency Theory (CONCUR'90)*, volume 458 of *Lecture Notes in Computer Science*, pages 278–297. Springer, 1990.

[Gla93] R.J. van Glabbeek. The linear time–branching time spectrum II (the semantics of sequential systems with silent moves). In E. Best, editor, *Fourth Conference on Concurrency Theory (CONCUR'93)*, volume 715, pages 66–81. Springer, 1993.

[GM76] F. Giarratana, V. Gimona and U. Montanari. Observability concepts in abstract data type specification. In A. Mazurkievicz, editor, *5th Symposium on Mathematical Foundations of Computer Science*, volume 45 of *Lecture Notes in Computer Science*, pages 576–587. Springer, 1976.

[Gol89] R. Goldblatt. Varieties of complex algebras. *Annals of Pure and Applied Logic*, **44**:173–242, 1989.

[Gor82] L. Gordeev. Constructive models for set theory with extensionality. In A.S. Troelstra and D. van Dalen, editors, *The L.E.J. Brouwer Centenary Symposium*, pages 123–147, 1982.

[GR62] S. Ginsburg and H. Gordon Rice. Two families of languages related to algol. *Journal of the ACM*, **9**(3):350–371, 1962.

[GRS79] J.S. Gourlay, W.C. Rounds, and R. Statman. On properties preserved by contraction of concurrent systems. In G. Kahn, editor, *International Symposium on Semantics of Concurrent Computation*, volume 70 of *Lecture Notes in Computer Science*, pages 51–65. Springer, 1979.

[HE67] J. van Heijenoort, editor. *From Frege to Gödel: A Source Book in Mathematical Logic 1879–1931*. Harvard University Press, 1967.

[Hin80] R. Hinnion. Contraction de structures et application à NFU. *Comptes Rendus Académie des Sciences de Paris*, Sér. A **290**:677–680, 1980.

[Hin81] R. Hinnion. Extensional quotients of structures and applications to the study of the axiom of extensionality. *Bulletin de la Société Mathématique de Belgique*, **XXXIII** (Fas. II, Sér. B):173–206, 1981.

[Hin86] R. Hinnion. Extensionality in Zermelo–Fraenkel set theory. *Zeitschrift für Mathematische Logik und Grundlagen Mathematik*, **32**:51–60, 1986.

[HM80] M. Hennessy and R. Milner. On observing nondeterminism and concurrency. In J.W. de Bakker and J. van Leeuwen, editors, *Proc. 7th Colloquium Automata, Languages and Programming*, volume 85 of *Lecture Notes in Computer Science*, pages 299–309. Springer, 1980.

[HM85] M. Hennessy and R. Milner. Algebraic laws for nondeterminism and concurrency. *Journal of the ACM*, **32**:137–161, 1985.

[Hon81] F. Honsell. *Modelli della teoria degli insiemi, principi di regolarità e di libera costruzione*. Tesi di Laurea, Università di Pisa, 1981.

[HP73] P. Hitchcock and D. Park. Induction rules and termination proofs. In M. Nivat, editor, *Proceedings of the IRIA Symposium on Automata, Languages and Programming, Paris, France, July, 1972*, pages 225–251. North-Holland, 1973.

[Huf54] D.A. Huffman. The synthesis of sequential switching circuits. *Journal of the Franklin Institute (Mar. 1954) and (Apr. 1954)*, **257**(3–4):161–190 and 275–303, 1954.

[Imm82] N. Immerman. Upper and lower bounds for first order expressibility. *Journal of Computer and System Science*, **25**(1):76–98, 1982.

[Jen80] K. Jensen. A method to compare the descriptive power of different types of petri nets. In P. Dembinski, editor, *Proc. 9th Mathematical Foundations of Computer Science 1980 (MFCS'80), Rydzyna, Poland, September 1980*, volume 88 of *Lecture Notes in Computer Science*, pages 348–361. Springer, 1980.

[Jon84] C.B. Jones, editor. *Programming Languages and Their Definition – Hans Bekic (1936–1982)*, volume 177 of *Lecture Notes in Computer Science*. Springer, 1984.

[JT66] D.H.J. de Jongh and A.S. Troelstra. On the connection of partially ordered sets with some pseudo-Boolean algebras. *Indagationes Mathematicae*, **28**:317–329, 1966.

[Kah74] G. Kahn. The semantics of simple language for parallel programming. In *IFIP Congress*, pages 471–475. North-Holland, 1974.

[Kan39] L.V. Kantorovich. The method of successive approximations for functional equations. *Acta Mathematica*, **71**:63–97, 1939.

[Kle52] S.C. Kleene. *Introduction to Metamathematics*. Van Nostrand, 1952.

[Kle70] S.C. Kleene. The origin of recursive function theory. In *20th Annual Symposium on Foundations of Computer Science*, pages 371–382. IEEE, 1970.

[Kna28] B. Knaster. Un théorème sur les fonctions d'ensembles. *Annales de la Société Polonaise de Mathématique*, **6**:133–134, 1928.

[KS60] J. Kemeny and J.L. Snell. *Finite Markov Chains*. Van Nostrand, 1960.

[Kwo77] Y.S. Kwong. On reduction of asynchronous systems. *Theoretical Computer Science*, **5**(1):25–50, 1977.

[Lan64] P.J. Landin. The mechanical evaluation of expressions. *The Computer Journal*, **6**(4):308–320, 1964.

[Lan65a] P.J. Landin. Correspondence between ALGOL 60 and Church's Lambda-notation: Part I. *Communications of the ACM*, **8**(2):89–101, 1965.

[Lan65b] P.J. Landin. A correspondence between ALGOL 60 and Church's Lambda-notations: Part II. *Communications of the ACM*, **8**(3):158–167, 1965.

[Lan69] P. Landin. A program-machine symmetric automata theory. *Machine Intelligence*, **5**:99–120, 1969.

[LNS82] J.-L. Lassez, V.L. Nguyen, and L. Sonenberg. Fixed point theorems and semantics: A folk tale. *Information Processing Letters*, **14**(3):112–116, 1982.

[LS91] K.G. Larsen and A. Skou. Bisimulation through probabilistic testing. *Information and Computation*, **94**(1):1–28, 1991. Preliminary version in POPL'89, 344–352, 1989.

[Man69] Z. Manna. The correctness of programs. *Journal of Computer and System Sciences*, **3**(2):119–127, 1969.

[Man74] Z. Manna. *Mathematical Theory of Computation*. McGraw-Hill, 1974.

[Maz71] A.W. Mazurkiewicz. Proving algorithms by tail functions. *Information and Control*, 18(3):220–226, 1971.

[Maz73] A. Mazurkiewicz. Proving properties of processes. Technical report 134, Computation Center of Polish Academy of Sciences, Warsaw, 1973. Also in *Algorytmy*, **11**, 5–22, 1974.

[McC61] J. McCarthy. A basis for a mathematical theory of computation. In *Proceedings of the Western Joint Computer Conference*, volume 19, pages 225–238. Spartan Books, 1961. Reprinted, with corrections and an added tenth section, in *Computer Programming and Formal Systems*, P. Braffort and D. Hirschberg, editors, pages 33–70, North-Holland, 1963.

[McC63] J. McCarthy. Towards a mathematical science of computation. In *Proceedings of IFIP Congress 62*, pages 21–28. North-Holland, 1963.

[Mil70] R. Milner. A formal notion of simulation between programs. Memo 14, Computers and Logic Research Group, University College of Swansea, UK, 1970.

[Mil71a] R. Milner. Program simulation: an extended formal notion. Memo 17, Computers and Logic Research Group, University College of Swansea, UK, 1971.

[Mil71b] R. Milner. An algebraic definition of simulation between programs. In *Proceedings of the 2nd International Joint Conferences on Artificial Intelligence*. British Computer Society, London, 1971.

[Mil80] R. Milner. *A Calculus of Communicating Systems*, volume 92 of *Lecture Notes in Computer Science*. Springer, 1980.

[Mil89] R. Milner. *Communication and Concurrency*. Prentice Hall, 1989.

[Mir17a] D. Mirimanoff. Les antinomies de Russell et de Burali-Forti et le problème fondamental de la théorie des ensembles. *L'Enseignement Mathématique*, **19**:37–52, 1917.

[Mir17b] D. Mirimanoff. Remarques sur la théorie des ensembles et les antinomies cantoriennes I. *L'Enseignement Mathématique*, **19**:209–217, 1917.

[Mir20] D. Mirimanoff. Remarques sur la théorie des ensembles et les antinomies cantoriennes II. *L'Enseignement Mathématique*, **21**:29–52, 1920.

[Moo56] E.F. Moore. Gedanken experiments on sequential machines. *Automata Studies, Annals of Mathematics Series*, **34**:129–153, 1956.

[Mor68] J.H. Morris. *Lambda-calculus models of programming languages*. PhD thesis, MIT, project MAC, Dec. 1968.

[Mos74] Y.N. Moschovakis. *Elementary Induction on Abstract Structures*, volume 77 of *Studies in Logic and the Foundations of Mathematics*. North-Holland, Amsterdam, 1974.

[Ner58] A. Nerode. Linear automaton transformations. In *Proceedings of the American Mathematical Society*, **9**, 541–544, 1958.

[Par69] D. Park. Fixpoint induction and proofs of program properties. In B. Meltzer and D. Michie, editors, *Machine Intelligence 5*, pages 59–78. Edinburgh University Press, 1969.

[Par70]   D. Park. The Y-combinator in Scott's lambda-calculus models. *Symposium on Theory of Programming*, University of Warwick, unpublished (A revised version: Research Report CS-RR-013, Department of Computer Science, University of Warwick, June 1976), 1970.

[Par79]   D. Park. On the semantics of fair parallelism. In *Proceedings of Abstract Software Specifications, Copenhagen Winter School*, Lecture Notes in Computer Science, pages 504–526. Springer, 1979.

[Par81a]   D. Park. Concurrency on automata and infinite sequences. In P. Deussen, editor, *Conference on Theoretical Computer Science*, volume 104 of *Lecture Notes in Computer Science*, pages 167–183. Springer, 1981.

[Par81b]   D. Park. A new equivalence notion for communicating systems. In G. Maurer, editor, *Bulletin EATCS*, volume 14, pages 78–80, 1981. Abstract of the talk presented at the *Second Workshop on the Semantics of Programming Languages*, Bad Honnef, March 16–20 1981. Abstracts collected in the Bulletin by B. Mayoh.

[Pas74]   A. Pasini. Some fixed point theorems of the mappings of partially ordered sets. *Rendiconti del Seminario Matematico della Università di Padova*, 51:167–177, 1974.

[Rey93]   J.C. Reynolds. The discoveries of continuations. *Lisp and Symbolic Computation*, 6(3–4):233–248, 1993.

[Rog67]   H. Rogers. *Theory of Recursive Functions and Effective Computability*. McGraw Hill, 1967. Reprinted, MIT Press, 1987.

[Rus03]   B. Russell. *Principles of Mathematics*. Cambridge University Press, 1903.

[Rus08]   B. Russell. Mathematical logic as based on the theory of types. *American Journal of Mathematics*, 30:222–262, 1908. Also in [HE67], pages 153–168.

[RW13]   B. Russell and A.N. Whitehead. *Principia Mathematica*, 3 vols. Cambridge University Press, 1910, 1912, 1913.

[San09]   D. Sangiorgi. On the origins of bisimulation and coinduction. *ACM Transactions on Programming Languages and Systems*, 31(4), 2009.

[San12]   D. Sangiorgi. *An Introduction to Bisimulation and Coinduction*. Cambridge University Press, 2012.

[Sco60]   D. Scott. A different kind of model for set theory. Unpublished paper, given at the 1960 *Stanford Congress of Logic, Methodology and Philosophy of Science*, 1960.

[Sco69a]   D. Scott. Models for the λ-calculus. Manuscript, draft, Oxford, December 1969.

[Sco69b]   D. Scott. A construction of a model for the λ-calculus. Manuscript, Oxford, November 1969.

[Sco69c]   D. Scott. A type-theoretical alternative to CUCH, ISWIM, OWHY. Typed script, Oxford. Also appeared as [Sco93], October 1969.

[Sco72a]   D. Scott. Continuous lattices. In E. Lawvere, editor, *Toposes, Algebraic Geometry and Logic*, volume 274 of *Lecture Notes in Mathematics*, pages 97–136. Springer, 1972.

[Sco72b]   D. Scott. The lattice of flow diagrams. In E. Engeler, editor, *Symposium of Semantics of Algorithmic Languages*, volume 188 of *Lecture Notes in Mathematics*, pages 311–366. Springer, 1972.

[Sco76] D. Scott. Data types as lattices. *SIAM Journal on Computing*, **5**:522–587, 1976. A manuscript with the same title was written in 1972.

[Sco93] D.S. Scott. A type-theoretical alternative to ISWIM, CUCH, OWHY. *Theoretical Computer Science*, **121**(1&2):411–440, 1993.

[SdB69] D. Scott and J.W. de Bakker. A theory of programs. Handwritten notes. IBM Lab., Vienna, Austria, 1969.

[Seg68] K. Segerberg. Decidability of S4.1. *Theoria*, **34**:7–20, 1968.

[Seg70] K. Segerberg. Modal logics with linear alternative relations. *Theoria*, **36**:301–322, 1970.

[Seg71] K. Segerberg. An essay in classical modal logic. Filosofiska Studier, Uppsala, 1971.

[Sko23] T. Skolem. Einige Bemerkungen zur Axiomatischen Begründung der Mengenlehre. In *Proceedings of the 5th Scandinavian Mathematics Congress, Helsinki, 1922*, pages 217–232. Akademiska Bokhandeln, Helsinki, 1923. English translation, 'Some remarks on axiomatized set theory', in [HE67], pages 290–301.

[Spe57] E. Specker. Zur Axiomatik der Mengenlehre. *Zeitschrift für Mathematische Logik und Grundlagen der Mathematik*, **3**(3):173–210, 1957.

[Sti12] C. Stirling. Bisimulation and Logic. Chapter 4 of this volume.

[Tar49] A. Tarski. A fixpoint theorem for lattices and its applications (preliminary report). *Bulletin of the American Mathematical Society*, **55**:1051–1052 and 1192, 1949.

[Tar55] A. Tarski. A lattice-theoretical fixpoint theorem and its applications. *Pacific Journal of Mathematics*, **5**:285–309, 1955.

[Tho93] W. Thomas. On the Ehrenfeucht–Fraïssé game in theoretical computer science. In M.-C. Gaudel and J.-P. Jouannaud, editors, *TAPSOFT*, volume 668 of *Lecture Notes in Computer Science*, pages 559–568. Springer, 1993.

[Zer08] E. Zermelo. Untersuchungen über die Grundlagen der Mengenlehre I. *Mathematische Annalen*, **65**:261–281, 1908. English translation, 'Investigations in the foundations of set theory', in [HE67], pages 199–215.

2

An introduction to (co)algebra and (co)induction

BART JACOBS AND JAN RUTTEN

2.1 Introduction

Algebra is a well-established part of mathematics, dealing with sets with operations satisfying certain properties, like groups, rings, vector spaces, etc. Its results are essential throughout mathematics and other sciences. *Universal* algebra is a part of algebra in which algebraic structures are studied at a high level of abstraction and in which general notions like homomorphism, subalgebra, congruence are studied in themselves, see e.g. [Coh81, MT92, Wec92]. A further step up the abstraction ladder is taken when one studies algebra with the notions and tools from category theory. This approach leads to a particularly concise notion of what is an algebra (for a functor or for a monad), see for example [Man74]. The conceptual world that we are about to enter owes much to this categorical view, but it also takes inspiration from universal algebra, see e.g. [Rut00].

In general terms, a program in some programming language manipulates data. During the development of computer science over the past few decades it became clear that an abstract description of these data is desirable, for example to ensure that one's program does not depend on the particular representation of the data on which it operates. Also, such abstractness facilitates correctness proofs. This desire led to the use of algebraic methods in computer science, in a branch called *algebraic specification* or *abstract data type theory*. The objects of study are data types in themselves, using notions and techniques which are familiar from algebra. The data types used by computer scientists are often generated from a given collection of (constructor) operations. The same applies in fact to programs, which themselves can be viewed as data too. It is for this reason that 'initiality' of algebras plays such an important role in computer science (as first clearly emphasised in [GTW78]). See for example [EM85, Wir90, Wec92] for more information.

38

Standard algebraic techniques have proved useful in capturing various essential aspects of data structures used in computer science. But it turned out to be difficult to algebraically describe some of the inherently dynamical structures occuring in computing. Such structures usually involve a notion of state, which can be transformed in various ways. Formal approaches to such state-based dynamical systems generally make use of automata or transition systems, see e.g. [Plo81, Par81, Mil89] as classical early references. During the last decade the insight gradually grew that such state-based systems should not be described as algebras, but as so-called coalgebras. These are the formal duals of algebras, in a way which will be made precise in this chapter. The dual property of initiality for algebras, namely finality, turned out to be crucial for such coalgebras. And the logical reasoning principle that is needed for such final coalgebras is not induction but coinduction.

These notions of coalgebra and coinduction are still relatively unfamiliar, and it is our aim in this chapter to explain them in elementary terms. Most of the literature already assumes some form of familiarity either with category theory, or with the (dual) coalgebraic way of thinking (or both).

Before we start, we should emphasise that there is no new (research) material in this chapter. Everything that we present is either known in the literature, or in the folklore, so we do not have any claims to originality. Also, our main concern is with conveying ideas, and not with giving a correct representation of the historical developments of these ideas. References are given mainly in order to provide sources for more (background) information.

Also, we should emphasise that we do not assume any knowledge of category theory on the part of the reader. We shall often use the diagrammatic notation which is typical of category theory, but only in order to express equality of two composites of functions, as often used also in other contexts. This is simply the most efficient and most informative way of presenting such information. But in order to fully appreciate the underlying duality between algebra and induction on the one hand, and coalgebra and coinduction on the other, some elementary notions from category theory are needed, especially the notions of *functor* (homomorphism of categories), and of *initial* and *final* (also called *terminal*) object in a category. Here we shall explain these notions in the concrete set-theoretic setting in which we are working, but we definitely encourage the interested reader who wishes to further pursue the topic of this chapter to study category theory in greater detail. Among the many available texts on category theory, [Pie91, Wal91, AM75, Awo06] are recommended as easy-going starting points, [BW90, Cro93, LS86] as more substantial texts, and [Lan71, Bor94] as advanced reference texts.

This chapter starts with some introductory expositions in Sections 2.2–2.4. The technical material in the subsequent sections is organised as follows.

(1) The starting point is ordinary induction, both as a definition principle and as a proof principle. We shall assume that the reader is familiar with induction, over natural numbers, but also over other data types, say of lists, trees or (in general) of terms. The first real step is to reformulate ordinary induction in a more abstract way, using initiality (see Section 2.5). More precisely, using initiality for 'algebras of a functor'. This is something which we do not assume to be familiar. We therefore explain how signatures of operations give rise to certain functors, and how algebras of these functors correspond to algebras (or models) of the signatures (consisting of a set equipped with certain functions interpreting the operations). This description of induction in terms of algebras (of functors) has the advantage that it is highly generic, in the sense that it applies in the same way to all kinds of (algebraic) data types. Further, it can be dualised easily, thus giving rise to the theory of coalgebras.

(2) The dual notion of an algebra (of a functor) is a coalgebra (of a functor). It can also be understood as a model consisting of a set with certain operations, but the direction of these operations is not as in algebra. The dual notion of initiality is finality, and this finality gives us coinduction, both as a definition principle and as a reasoning principle. This pattern is as in the previous point, and is explained in Section 2.6.

(3) In Section 2.7 we give an alternative formulation of the coinductive reasoning principle (introduced in terms of finality) which makes use of bisimulations. These are relations on coalgebras which are suitably closed under the (coalgebraic) operations; they may be understood as duals of congruences, which are relations which are closed under algebraic operations. Bisimulation arguments are used to prove the equality of two elements of a final coalgebra, and require that these elements are in a bisimulation relation.

(4) In Section 2.8 we present a coalgebraic account of transition systems and a simple calculus of *processes*. The latter will be defined as the elements of a final coalgebra. An elementary language for the construction of processes will be introduced and its semantics will be defined coinductively. As we shall see, this will involve the mixed occurrence of both algebraic and coalgebraic structures. The combination of algebra and coalgebra will also play a central role in Section 2.9, where a coalgebraic description is given of trace semantics.

In a first approximation, the duality between induction and coinduction that we intend to describe can be understood as the duality between least and greatest fixed points (of a monotone function), see Exercise 2.10.3. These notions generalise to least and greatest fixed points of a functor, which are suitably described as initial algebras and final coalgebras. The point of view mentioned in (1) and (2) above can be made more explicit as follows – without going into technicalities yet. The abstract reformulation of induction that we will describe is:

$$\boxed{\text{induction} \ = \ \text{use of initiality for algebras.}}$$

An algebra (of a certain kind) is *initial* if for an arbitrary algebra (of the same kind) there is a unique homomorphism (structure-preserving mapping) of algebras:

$$\begin{pmatrix} \text{initial} \\ \text{algebra} \end{pmatrix} - \underset{\text{homomorphism}}{\overset{\text{unique}}{- - - - - - - \!\!\!\!\!>}} \begin{pmatrix} \text{arbitrary} \\ \text{algebra} \end{pmatrix}. \qquad (2.1)$$

This principle is extremely useful. Once we know that a certain algebra is initial, by this principle we can define functions acting on this algebra. Initiality involves unique existence, which has two aspects:

Existence This corresponds to (ordinary) *definition* by induction.

Uniqueness This corresponds to *proof* by induction. In such uniqueness proofs, one shows that two functions acting on an initial algebra are the same by showing that they are both homomorphisms (to the same algebra).

The details of this abstract reformulation will be elaborated as we proceed.

Dually, coinduction may be described as:

$$\boxed{\text{coinduction} \ = \ \text{use of finality for coalgebras.}}$$

A coalgebra (of some kind) is *final* if for an arbitrary coalgebra (of the same kind), there is a unique homomorphism of coalgebras as shown:

$$\begin{pmatrix} \text{arbitrary} \\ \text{coalgebra} \end{pmatrix} - \underset{\text{homomorphism}}{\overset{\text{unique}}{- - - - - - - \!\!\!\!\!>}} \begin{pmatrix} \text{final} \\ \text{coalgebra} \end{pmatrix}. \qquad (2.2)$$

Again we have the same two aspects: existence and uniqueness, corresponding this time to definition and proof by coinduction.

The initial algebras and final coalgebras which play such a prominent role in this theory can be described in a canonical way: an initial algebra can be obtained from the closed terms (i.e. from those terms which are generated by iteratively applying the algebra's constructor operations), and the final coalgebra can be obtained from the pure observations. The latter is probably not very familiar, and will be illustrated in several examples in Section 2.2.

History of this chapter An earlier version of this chapter was published as '*A tutorial on (co)algebras and (co)induction*', in *EATCS Bulletin* **62** (1997), pp. 222–259. More than 10 years later, the present version has been updated. Notably, two sections have been added that are particularly relevant for the context of the present book: processes coalgebraically (Section 2.8), and trace semantics coalgebraically (Section 2.9). In both these sections both initial algebras and final coalgebras arise in a natural combination. In addition, the references to related work have been brought up-to-date.

Coalgebra has by now become a well-established part of the foundations of computer science and (modal) logic. In the last decade, much new coalgebraic theory has been developed, such as so-called universal coalgebra [Rut00, Gum99], in analogy to universal algebra, and coalgebraic logic, generalising in various ways classical modal logic, see for instance [Kur01, Kur06, CP07, Kli07] for an overview. But there is much more, none of which is addressed in any detail here. Much relevant recent work and many references can be found in the proceedings of the workshop series CMCS: *Coalgebraic Methods in Computer Science* (published in the ENTCS series) and CALCO: *Conference on Algebra and Coalgebra in Computer Science* (published in the LNCS series). The aim of this chapter is in essence still the same as it was 10 years ago: to provide a brief introduction to the field of coalgebra.

2.2 Algebraic and coalgebraic phenomena

The distinction between algebra and coalgebra pervades computer science and has been recognised by many people in many situations, usually in terms of data versus machines. A modern, mathematically precise way to express the difference is in terms of algebras and coalgebras. The basic dichotomy may be described as *construction* versus *observation*. It may be found in process theory [Mil89], data type theory [GGM76, GM82, AM82, Kam83] (including the theory of classes and objects in object-oriented programming [Rei95, HP95, Jac96b, Jac96a]), semantics of programming languages [MA86] (denotational versus operational [RT94, Tur96, BV96]) and of lambda-calculi [Pit94, Pit96, Fio96, HL95], automata theory [Par81], system theory [Rut00], natural language theory [BM96, Rou96] and many other fields.

We assume that the reader is familiar with definitions and proofs by (ordinary) induction. As a typical example, consider for a fixed dataset A, the set $A^* = \text{list}(A)$ of finite sequences (lists) of elements of A. One can inductively define a length function $\text{len} \colon A^* \to \mathbb{N}$ by the two clauses:

$$\text{len}(\langle\rangle) = 0 \qquad \text{and} \qquad \text{len}(a \cdot \sigma) = 1 + \text{len}(\sigma)$$

for all $a \in A$ and $\sigma \in A^*$. Here we have used the notation $\langle\rangle \in A^*$ for the empty list (sometimes called nil), and $a \cdot \sigma$ (sometimes written as $\text{cons}(a, \sigma)$) for the list obtained from $\sigma \in A^*$ by prefixing $a \in A$. As we shall see later, the definition of this length function $\text{len} \colon A^* \to \mathbb{N}$ can be seen as an instance of the above initiality diagram (2.1).

A typical induction proof that a predicate $P \subseteq A^*$ holds for all lists requires us to prove the induction assumptions

$$P(\langle\rangle) \qquad \text{and} \qquad P(\sigma) \Rightarrow P(a \cdot \sigma)$$

for all $a \in A$ and $\sigma \in A^*$. For example, in this way one can prove that $\text{len}(\sigma \cdot a) = 1 + \text{len}(\sigma)$ by taking $P = \{\sigma \in A^* \mid \forall a \in A. \ \text{len}(\sigma \cdot a) = 1 + \text{len}(\sigma)\}$. Essentially, this induction proof method says that A^* has no proper subalgebras. In this (algebraic) setting we make use of the fact that all finite lists of elements of A can be constructed from the two operations $\text{nil} \in A^*$ and $\text{cons} \colon A \times A^* \to A^*$. As above, we also write $\langle\rangle$ for nil and $a \cdot \sigma$ for $\text{cons}(a, \sigma)$.

Next we describe some typically coalgebraic phenomena, by sketching some relevant examples. Many of the issues that come up during the description of these examples will be explained in further detail in later sections.

(i) Consider a black-box machine (or process) with one (external) button and one light. The machine performs a certain action only if the button is pressed. And the light goes on only if the machine stops operating (i.e. has reached a final state); in that case, pressing the button has no effect any more. A client on the outside of such a machine cannot directly observe the internal state of the machine, but (s)he can only observe its behaviour via the button and the light. In this simple (but paradigmatic) situation, all that can be observed directly about a particular state of the machine is whether the light is on or not. But a user may iterate this experiment, and record the observations after a change of state caused by pressing the button.[1] In this situation, a user can observe how many times (s)he has to press the button to make the light go on. This may be zero times (if the light is already on), $n \in \mathbb{N}$ times, or infinitely many times (if the machine keeps on operating and the light never goes on).

---

[1] It is assumed that such actions of pressing a button happen instantaneously, so that there is always an order in the occurrence of such actions.

Mathematically, we can describe such a machine in terms of a set X, which we understand as the unknown state space of the machine, on which we have a function

$$\text{button}: X \longrightarrow \{*\} \cup X$$

where $*$ is a new symbol not occurring in X. In a particular state $s \in X$, applying the function button – which corresponds to pressing the button – has two possible outcomes: either $\text{button}(s) = *$, meaning that the machine stops operating and that the light goes on, or $\text{button}(s) \in X$. In the latter case the machine has moved to a next state as a result of the button being pressed. (And in this next state, the button can be pressed again.) The above pair $(X, \text{button}: X \to \{*\} \cup X)$ is an example of a coalgebra.

The observable behaviour resulting from iterated observations as described above yields an element of the set $\overline{\mathbb{N}} = \mathbb{N} \cup \{\infty\}$, describing the number of times the button has to be pressed to make the light go on. Actually, we can describe this behaviour as a function $\text{beh}: X \to \overline{\mathbb{N}}$. As we shall see later, it can be obtained as an instance of the finality diagram (2.2).

(ii) Let us consider a slightly different machine with two buttons: value and next. Pressing the value button results in some visible indication (or attribute) of the internal state (e.g. on a display), taking values in a dataset A, without affecting the internal state. Hence pressing value twice consecutively yields the same result. By pressing the next button the machine moves to another state (the value of which can be inspected again). Abstractly, this new machine can be described as a coalgebra

$$\langle \text{value}, \text{next} \rangle : X \longrightarrow A \times X$$

on a state space X. The behaviour that we can observe of such machines is the following: for all $n \in \mathbb{N}$, read the value after pressing the next button n times. This results in an infinite sequence $(a_0, a_1, a_2, \ldots) \in A^{\mathbb{N}}$ of elements of the dataset A, with element a_i describing the value after pressing next i times. Observing this behaviour for every state $s \in X$ gives us a function $\text{beh}: X \to A^{\mathbb{N}}$.

The set $A^{\mathbb{N}}$ of infinite sequences, in computer science also known as streams, carries itself a coalgebra structure

$$\langle \text{head}, \text{tail} \rangle : A^{\mathbb{N}} \to A \times A^{\mathbb{N}}$$

given, for all $\alpha = (a_0, a_1, a_2, \ldots) \in A^{\mathbb{N}}$, by

$$\text{head}(\alpha) = a_0 \qquad \text{tail}(\alpha) = (a_1, a_2, a_3, \ldots).$$

This coalgebra is final and the behaviour function beh: $X \to A^{\mathbb{N}}$ can thus be seen as an instance of (2.2).

(iii) The previous example is leading us in the direction of a coalgebraic description of classes in object-oriented languages. Suppose we wish to capture the essential aspects of the class of points in a (real) plane that can be moved around by a client. In this situation we certainly want two attribute buttons first: $X \to \mathbb{R}$ and second: $X \to \mathbb{R}$ which tell us, when pushed, the first and second coordinate of a point belonging to this class. As before, the X plays the role of a hidden state space, and elements of X are seen as objects of the class (so that an object is identified with a state). Further we want a button (or method, in object-oriented terminology) move: $X \times (\mathbb{R} \times \mathbb{R}) \to X$ which requires two parameters (corresponding to the change in first and second coordinate). This move operation allows us to change a state in a certain way, depending on the values of the parameters. The move method can equivalently be described as a function move: $X \to X^{(\mathbb{R} \times \mathbb{R})}$ taking the state as single argument, and yielding a function $(\mathbb{R} \times \mathbb{R}) \to X$ from parameters to states.

As a client of such a class we are not interested in the actual details of the implementation (what the state space X exactly looks like) as long as the behaviour is determined by the following two equations:

$$\text{first}(\text{move}(s, (d1, d2))) = \text{first}(s) + d1$$
$$\text{second}(\text{move}(s, (d1, d2))) = \text{second}(s) + d2.$$

These describe the first and second coordinates after a move in terms of the original coordinates and the parameters of the move. Such equations can be seen as constraints on the observable behaviour.

An important aspect of the object-oriented approach is that classes are built around a hidden state space, which can only be observed and modified via certain specified operations. A user is not interested in the details of the actual implementation, but only in the behaviour that is realised. This is why our black-box description of classes with an unknown state space X is appropriate.

The three buttons of such a class (as abstract machine) can be combined into a single function

$$\langle \text{first}, \text{second}, \text{move} \rangle : X \longrightarrow \mathbb{R} \times \mathbb{R} \times X^{(\mathbb{R} \times \mathbb{R})}$$

which forms a coalgebra on the state space X. The observable behaviour is very simple in this case. It consists of the values of the first and second coordinates, since if we know these values, then we know the future observable behaviour: the only change of state that we can bring about is through the move button; but its observable effect is determined by the above two equations. Thus what we can observe about a state is obtained by direct observation, and repeated observations do not produce new information. Hence our behaviour function takes the form beh: $X \to \mathbb{R} \times \mathbb{R}$, and is again an instance of (2.2).[2] In automata-theoretic terms one can call the space $\mathbb{R} \times \mathbb{R}$ the minimal realisation (or implementation) of the specified behaviour.

In the above series of examples of coalgebras we see each time a state space X about which we make no assumptions. On this state space a function is defined of the form

$$f : X \to \boxed{ X }$$

where the box on the right is some expression involving X again. Later this will be identified as a *functor*. The function f often consists of different components, which allow us either to observe some aspect of the state space directly, or to move on to next states. We have limited access to this state space in the sense that we can only observe or modify it via these specified operations. In such a situation all that we can describe about a particular state is its behaviour, which arises by making successive observations. This will lead to the notion of bisimilarity of states: it expresses of two states that we cannot distinguish them via the operations that are at our disposal, i.e. that they are 'equal as far as we can see'. But this does not mean that these states are also identical as elements of X. Bisimilarity is an important, and typically coalgebraic, concept.

The above examples are meant to suggest the difference between construction in algebra, and observation in coalgebra. This difference will be described more formally below. In practice it is not always completely straightforward to distinguish between algebraic and coalgebraic aspects, for the following two reasons.

(1) Certain abstract operations, like $X \times A \to X$, can be seen as both algebraic and coalgebraic. Algebraically, such an operation allows us to build new elements in X starting from given elements in X and parameters in A. Coalgebraically, this operation is often presented in the equivalent from $X \to X^A$ using function types. It is then seen as acting on the state space X, and yielding for each state a function from A to X which produces for each parameter element in A a next state. The context should make clear which view is prevalent. But operations of the form $A \to X$ are definitely algebraic (because they gives us information about how to put elements in X), and operations of the form $X \to A$ are coalgebraic (because they give us observable attribute values holding for elements of X). A

---

[2] To be precise, for coalgebras of a comonad.

further complication at this point is that on an initial algebra X one may have operations of the form $X \to A$, obtained by initiality. An example is the length function on lists. Such operations are derived, and are not an integral part of the (definition of the) algebra. Dually, one may have derived operations $A \to X$ on a final coalgebra X.

(2) Algebraic and coalgebraic structures may be found in different hierarchic layers. For example, one can start with certain algebras describing one's application domain. On top of these one can have certain dynamical systems (processes) as coalgebras, involving such algebras (e.g. as codomains of attributes). And such coalgebraic systems may exist in an algebra of processes.

A concrete example of such layering of coalgebra on top of algebra is given by Plotkin's so-called structural operational semantics [Plo81]. It involves a transition system (a coalgebra) describing the operational semantics of some language, by giving the transition rules by induction on the structure of the terms of the language. The latter means that the set of terms of the language is used as (initial) algebra. See Section 2.8 and [RT94, Tur96] for a further investigation of this perspective. Hidden sorted algebras, see [GM94, GD94, BD94, GM96, Mal96], can be seen as other examples: they involve 'algebras' with 'invisible' sorts, playing a (coalgebraic) role of a state space. Coinduction is used to reason about such hidden state spaces, see [GM96].

2.3 Inductive and coinductive definitions

In the previous section we have seen that 'constructor' and 'destructor/observer' operations play an important role for algebras and coalgebras, respectively. Constructors tell us how to generate our (algebraic) data elements: the empty list constructor nil and the prefix operation cons generate all finite lists. And destructors (or observers, or transition functions) tell us what we can observe about our data elements: the head and tail operations tell us all about infinite lists: head gives a direct observation, and tail returns a next state.

Once we are aware of this duality between constructing and observing, it is easy to see the difference between inductive and coinductive definitions (relative to given collections of constructors and destructors):

> In an *inductive definition* of a function f,
> one defines the value of f on all constructors.

And:

> In a *coinductive definition* of a function f,
> one defines the values of all destructors on each outcome $f(x)$.

Such a coinductive definition determines the observable behaviour of each $f(x)$.

We shall illustrate inductive and coinductive definitions in some examples involving finite lists (with constructors nil and cons) and infinite lists (with destructors head and tail) over a fixed dataset A, as in the previous section. We assume that inductive definitions are well-known, so we only mention two trivial examples: the (earlier mentioned) function len from finite lists to natural numbers giving the length, and the function empty? from finite lists to booleans {true, false} telling whether a list is empty or not:

$$\begin{cases} \text{len(nil)} = 0 \\ \text{len(cons}(a, \sigma)) = 1 + \text{len}(\sigma). \end{cases} \qquad \begin{cases} \text{empty?(nil)} = \text{true} \\ \text{empty?(cons}(a, \sigma)) = \text{false}. \end{cases}$$

Typically in such inductive definitions, the constructors on the left-hand side appear 'inside' the function that we are defining. The example of empty? above, where this does not happen, is a degenerate case.

We turn to examples of coinductive definitions (on infinite lists, say of type A). If we have a function $f: A \rightarrow A$, then we would like to define an extension ext(f) of f mapping an infinite list to an infinite list by applying f componentwise. According to the above coinductive definition scheme we have to give the values of the destructors head and tail for a sequence ext(f)(σ). They should be:

$$\begin{cases} \text{head(ext}(f)(\sigma)) = f(\text{head}(\sigma)) \\ \text{tail(ext}(f)(\sigma)) = \text{ext}(f)(\text{tail}(\sigma)). \end{cases}$$

Here we clearly see that on the left-hand side, the function that we are defining occurs 'inside' the destructors. At this stage it is not yet clear if ext(f) is well-defined, but this is not our concern at the moment.

Alternatively, we can write the definition of ext(f) as:

$$\frac{\sigma \xrightarrow{a} \sigma'}{\text{ext}(f)(\sigma) \xrightarrow{f(a)} \text{ext}(f)(\sigma')}.$$

Suppose next, that we wish to define an operation even which takes an infinite list, and produces a new infinite list which contains (in order) all the elements occurring in evenly numbered places of the original list. That is, we would like the operation even to satisfy

$$\text{even}(\sigma(0), \sigma(1), \sigma(2), \ldots) = (\sigma(0), \sigma(2), \sigma(4), \ldots). \qquad (2.3)$$

A little thought leads to the following definition clauses:

$$\begin{cases} \text{head}(\text{even}(\sigma)) = \text{head}(\sigma) \\ \text{tail}(\text{even}(\sigma)) = \text{even}(\text{tail}(\text{tail}(\sigma))). \end{cases} \qquad (2.4)$$

Or, in the transition relation notation:

$$\frac{\sigma \xrightarrow{a} \sigma' \xrightarrow{a'} \sigma'}{\text{even}(\sigma) \xrightarrow{a} \text{even}(\sigma')}.$$

Let us convince ourselves that this definition gives us what we want. The first clause in (2.4) says that the first element of the list even(σ) is the first element of σ. The next element in even(σ) is head(tail(even(σ))), and can be computed as

$$\text{head}(\text{tail}(\text{even}(\sigma))) = \text{head}(\text{even}(\text{tail}(\text{tail}(\sigma)))) = \text{head}(\text{tail}(\text{tail}(\sigma))).$$

Hence the second element in even(σ) is the third element in σ. It is not hard to show for $n \in \mathbb{N}$ that head(tail$^{(n)}$(even(σ))) is the same as head(tail$^{(2n)}$(σ)).

In a similar way one can coinductively define a function odd which keeps all the oddly listed elements. But it is much easier to define odd as: odd = even $\circ$ tail.

As another example, we consider the merge of two infinite lists σ, τ into a single list, by taking elements from σ and τ in turn, starting with σ, say. A coinductive definition of such a function merge requires the outcomes of the destructors head and tail on merge(σ, τ). They are given as:

$$\begin{cases} \text{head}(\text{merge}(\sigma, \tau)) = \text{head}(\sigma) \\ \text{tail}(\text{merge}(\sigma, \tau)) = \text{merge}(\tau, \text{tail}(\sigma)). \end{cases}$$

In transition system notation, this definition looks as follows.

$$\frac{\sigma \xrightarrow{a} \sigma'}{\text{merge}(\sigma, \tau) \xrightarrow{a} \text{merge}(\tau, \sigma')}.$$

Now one can show that the n-th element of σ occurs as the $2n$-th element in merge(σ, τ), and that the n-th element of τ occurs as the $(2n + 1)$-th element of merge(σ, τ):

$$\text{head}(\text{tail}^{(2n)}(\text{merge}(\sigma, \tau))) = \text{head}(\text{tail}^{(n)}(\sigma))$$
$$\text{head}(\text{tail}^{(2n+1)}(\text{merge}(\sigma, \tau))) = \text{head}(\text{tail}^{(n)}(\tau)).$$

One can also define a function $\mathsf{merge}_{2,1}(\sigma, \tau)$ which takes two elements of σ for every element of τ (see Exercise 2.10.6).

An obvious result that we would like to prove is: merging the lists of evenly and oddly occuring elements in a list σ returns the original list σ. That is: $\mathsf{merge}(\mathsf{even}(\sigma), \mathsf{odd}(\sigma)) = \sigma$. From what we have seen above we can easily compute that the n-th elements on both sides are equal:

$$
\begin{aligned}
&\mathsf{head}(\mathsf{tail}^{(n)}(\mathsf{merge}(\mathsf{even}(\sigma), \mathsf{odd}(\sigma)))) \\
&= \begin{cases} \mathsf{head}(\mathsf{tail}^{(m)}(\mathsf{even}(\sigma))) & \text{if } n = 2m \\ \mathsf{head}(\mathsf{tail}^{(m)}(\mathsf{odd}(\sigma))) & \text{if } n = 2m + 1 \end{cases} \\
&= \begin{cases} \mathsf{head}(\mathsf{tail}^{(2m)}(\sigma)) & \text{if } n = 2m \\ \mathsf{head}(\mathsf{tail}^{(2m+1)}(\sigma)) & \text{if } n = 2m + 1 \end{cases} \\
&= \mathsf{head}(\mathsf{tail}^{(n)}(\sigma)).
\end{aligned}
$$

There is however a more elegant coinductive proof technique, which will be presented later: in Example 2.6.3 using uniqueness – based on the finality diagram (2.2) – and in the beginning of Section 2.7 using bisimulations.

2.4 Functoriality of products, coproducts and powersets

In the remainder of this chapter we shall put the things we have discussed so far in a general framework. Doing so properly requires a certain amount of category theory. We do not intend to describe the relevant matters at the highest level of abstraction, making full use of category theory. Instead, we shall work mainly with ordinary sets. That is, we shall work in the universe given by the category of sets and functions. What we do need is that many operations on sets are 'functorial'. This means that they not act only on sets, but also on functions between sets, in an appropriate manner. This is familiar in the computer science literature, not in categorical terminology, but using a 'map' terminology. For example, if $\mathsf{list}(A) = A^\star$ describes the set of finite lists of elements of a set A, then for a function $f: A \to B$ one can define a function $\mathsf{list}(A) \to \mathsf{list}(B)$ between the corresponding sets of lists, which is usually called[3] $\mathsf{map\_list}(f)$. It sends a finite list $(a_1, \ldots, a_n)$ of elements of A to the list $(f(a_1), \ldots, f(a_n))$ of elements of B, by applying f elementwise. It is not hard to show that this $\mathsf{map\_list}$ operation preserves identity functions and composite functions, i.e. that $\mathsf{map\_list}(id_A) = id_{\mathsf{list}(A)}$ and $\mathsf{map\_list}(g \circ f) = \mathsf{map\_list}(g) \circ \mathsf{map\_list}(f)$. This preservation of identities and compositions is the appropriateness that we mentioned above. In this section we concentrate

---

[3] In the category theory literature one uses the same name for the actions of a functor on objects and on morphisms; this leads to the notation $\mathsf{list}(f)$ or $f^\star$ for this function $\mathsf{map\_list}(f)$.

on such functoriality of several basic operations, such as products, coproducts (disjoint unions) and powersets. It will be used in later sections.

We recall that for two sets X, Y the Cartesian product $X \times Y$ is the set of pairs

$$X \times Y = \{(x, y) \mid x \in X \quad \text{and} \quad y \in Y\}.$$

There are then obvious projection functions $\pi \colon X \times Y \to X$ and $\pi' \colon X \times Y \to Y$ by $\pi(x, y) = x$ and $\pi'(x, y) = y$. Also, for functions $f \colon Z \to X$ and $g \colon Z \to Y$ there is a unique 'pair function' $\langle f, g \rangle \colon Z \to X \times Y$ with $\pi \circ \langle f, g \rangle = f$ and $\pi' \circ \langle f, g \rangle = g$, namely $\langle f, g \rangle(z) = (f(z), g(z)) \in X \times Y$ for $z \in Z$. Notice that $\langle \pi, \pi' \rangle = id \colon X \times Y \to X \times Y$ and that $\langle f, g \rangle \circ h = \langle f \circ h, g \circ h \rangle \colon W \to X \times Y$, for functions $h \colon W \to Z$.

Interestingly, the product operation $(X, Y) \mapsto X \times Y$ not only applies to sets, but also to functions: for functions $f \colon X \to X'$ and $g \colon Y \to Y'$ we can define a function $X \times Y \to X' \times Y'$ by $(x, y) \mapsto (f(x), g(y))$. One writes this function as $f \times g \colon X \times Y \to X' \times Y'$, whereby the symbol $\times$ is overloaded: it is used both on sets and on functions. We note that $f \times g$ can be described in terms of projections and pairing as $f \times g = \langle f \circ \pi, g \circ \pi' \rangle$. It is easily verified that the operation $\times$ on functions satisfies

$$id_X \times id_Y = id_{X \times Y} \qquad \text{and} \qquad (f \circ h) \times (g \circ k) = (f \times g) \circ (h \times k).$$

This expresses that the product $\times$ is *functorial*: it not only applies to sets, but also to functions; and it does so in such a way that identity maps and composites are preserved.

Many more operations are functorial. Also the coproduct (or disjoint union, or sum) $+$ is. For sets X, Y we write their disjoint union as $X + Y$. Explicitly:

$$X + Y = \{\langle 0, x \rangle \mid x \in X\} \cup \{\langle 1, y \rangle \mid y \in Y\}.$$

The first components 0 and 1 serve to force this union to be disjoint. These 'tags' enable us to recognise the elements of X and of Y inside $X + Y$. Instead of projections as above we now have 'coprojections' $\kappa \colon X \to X + Y$ and $\kappa' \colon Y \to X + Y$ going in the other direction. One puts $\kappa(x) = \langle 0, x \rangle$ and $\kappa'(y) = \langle 1, y \rangle$. And instead of tupleing we now have 'cotupleing' (sometimes called 'source tupleing'): for functions $f \colon X \to Z$ and $g \colon Y \to Z$ there is a unique function $[f, g] \colon X + Y \to Z$ with $[f, g] \circ \kappa = f$ and $[f, g] \circ \kappa' = g$. One defines $[f, g]$ by case distinction:

$$[f, g](w) = \begin{cases} f(x) & \text{if } w = \langle 0, x \rangle \\ g(y) & \text{if } w = \langle 1, y \rangle. \end{cases}$$

Notice that $[\kappa, \kappa'] = id$ and $h \circ [f, g] = [h \circ f, h \circ g]$.

This is the coproduct $X + Y$ on sets. We can extend it to functions in the following way. For $f: X \to X'$ and $g: Y \to Y'$ there is a function $f + g: X + Y \to X' + Y'$ defined by

$$(f + g)(w) = \begin{cases} \langle 0, f(x) \rangle & \text{if } w = \langle 0, x \rangle \\ \langle 1, g(y) \rangle & \text{if } w = \langle 1, y \rangle. \end{cases}$$

Equivalently, we could have defined: $f + g = [\kappa \circ f, \kappa' \circ g]$. This operation $+$ on functions preserves identities and composition:

$$id_X + id_Y = id_{X+Y} \quad \text{and} \quad (f \circ h) + (g \circ k) = (f + g) \circ (h + k).$$

We should emphasise that this coproduct $+$ is very different from ordinary union $\cup$. For example, $\cup$ is idempotent: $X \cup X = X$, but there is not an isomorphism between $X + X$ and X (if $X \neq \emptyset$).

For a fixed set A, the assignment $X \mapsto X^A = \{ f \mid f \text{ is a function } A \to X \}$ is functorial: a function $g: X \to Y$ yields a function $g^A: X^A \to Y^A$ sending $f \in X^A$ to $(g \circ f) \in Y^A$. Clearly, $id^A = id$ and $(h \circ g)^A = h^A \circ g^A$.

Another example of a functorial operation is powerset: $X \mapsto \mathcal{P}(X)$. For a function $f: X \to X'$ one defines $\mathcal{P}(f): \mathcal{P}(X) \to \mathcal{P}(X')$ by

$$U \mapsto \{ f(x) \mid x \in U \}.$$

Then $\mathcal{P}(id_X) = id_{\mathcal{P}(X)}$ and $\mathcal{P}(f \circ h) = \mathcal{P}(f) \circ \mathcal{P}(h)$. We shall write $\mathcal{P}_{\text{fin}}(-)$ for the (functorial) operation which maps X to the set of its *finite* subsets.

Here are some trivial examples of functors. The identity operation $X \mapsto X$ is functorial: it acts on functions as $f \mapsto f$. And for a constant set C we have a constant functorial operation $X \mapsto C$; a function $f: X \to X'$ is mapped to the identity function $id_C: C \to C$.

Once we know these actions on functions, we can define functorial operations (or: *functors*, for short) merely by giving their actions on sets. We will often say things like: consider the functor

$$T(X) = X + (C \times X).$$

The action on sets is then $X \mapsto X + (C \times X)$. And for a function $f: X \to X'$ we have an action $T(f)$ of the functor T on f as a function $T(f): T(X) \to T(X')$. Explicitly, $T(f)$ is the function

$$f + (id_C \times f): X + (C \times X) \longrightarrow X' + (C \times X')$$

given by:

$$w \mapsto \begin{cases} \langle 0, f(x) \rangle & \text{if } w = \langle 0, x \rangle \\ \langle 1, (c, f(x)) \rangle & \text{if } w = \langle 1, (c, x) \rangle. \end{cases}$$

The only functors that we shall use in the sequel are such 'polynomial' functors T, which are built up with constants, identity functors, products, coproducts and also (finite) powersets. We describe these functors by only giving their actions on sets. Mostly, the functors in this chapter will be of the sort *Set* $\to$ *Set*, acting on sets and functions between them, with the exception of Section 2.9 on trace semantics where we shall use functors *Rel* $\to$ *Rel*, acting on sets with relations between them as morphisms.

There is a more general notion of functor $\mathbb{C} \to \mathbb{D}$ as mapping from one 'category' $\mathbb{C}$ to another $\mathbb{D}$, see e.g. [Awo06]. Here we are only interested in these polynomial functors, going from the category *Set* of sets and functions to itself (or from *Rel* to *Rel*). But much of the theory applies to more general situations.

We shall write $1 = \{*\}$ for a singleton set, with typical inhabitant $*$. Notice that for every set X there is precisely one function $X \to 1$. This says that 1 is *final* (or *terminal*) in the category of sets and functions. And functions $1 \to X$ correspond to elements of X. Usually we shall identify the two. Thus, for example, we sometimes write the empty list as nil : $1 \to A^\star$ so that it can be cotupled with the function cons : $A \times A^\star \to A^\star$ into the algebra

$$[\text{nil}, \text{cons}] \colon 1 + (A \times A^\star) \to A^\star$$

that will be studied more deeply in Example 2.5.6.

We write 0 for the empty set. For every set X there is precisely one function $0 \to X$, namely the empty function. This property is the *initiality* of 0. These sets 1 and 0 can be seen as the empty product and coproduct.

We list some useful isomorphisms.

$$X \times Y \cong Y \times X \qquad\qquad X + Y \cong Y + X$$
$$1 \times X \cong X \qquad\qquad 0 + X \cong X$$
$$X \times (Y \times Z) \cong (X \times Y) \times Z \quad X + (Y + Z) \cong (X + Y) + Z$$
$$X \times 0 \cong 0 \qquad\qquad X \times (Y + Z) \cong (X \times Y) + (X \times Z).$$

The last two isomorphisms describe the distribution of products over finite coproducts. We shall often work 'up-to' the above isomorphisms, so that we can simply write an n-ary product as $X_1 \times \cdots \times X_n$ without bothering about bracketing.

2.5 Algebras and induction

In this section we start by showing how polynomial functors – as introduced in the previous section – can be used to describe signatures of operations. Algebras of such functors correspond to models of such signatures. They consist of a carrier set with certain functions interpreting the operations. A general notion of homomorphism is defined between such algebras of a functor. This allows us to define initial algebras by the following property: for an arbitrary algebra there is precisely one homomorphism from the initial algebra to this algebra. This turns out to be a powerful notion. It captures algebraic structures which are generated by constructor operations, as will be shown in several examples. Also, it gives rise to the familiar principles of definition by induction and proof by induction.

We start with an example. Let T be the polynomial functor $T(X) = 1 + X + (X \times X)$, and consider for a set U a function $a \colon T(U) \to U$. Such a map a may be identified with a 3-cotuple $[a_1, a_2, a_3]$ of maps $a_1 \colon 1 \to U$, $a_2 \colon U \to U$ and $a_3 \colon U \times U \to U$ giving us three separate functions going into the set U. They form an example of an algebra (of the functor T): a set together with a (cotupled) number of functions going into that set. For example, if one has a group G, with unit element $e \colon 1 \to G$, inverse function $i \colon G \to G$ and multiplication function $m \colon G \times G \to G$, then one can organise these three maps as an algebra $[e, i, m] \colon T(G) \to G$ via cotupling.[4] The shape of the functor T determines a certain signature of operations. Had we taken a different functor $S(X) = 1 + (X \times X)$, then maps (algebras of S) $S(U) \to U$ would capture pairs of functions $1 \to U, U \times U \to U$ (e.g. of a monoid).

Definition 2.5.1 Let T be a functor. An *algebra* of T (or, a *T-algebra*) is a pair consisting of a set U and a function $a \colon T(U) \to U$.

We shall call the set U the *carrier* of the algebra, and the function a the *algebra structure*, or also the *operation* of the algebra.

For example, the zero and successor functions $0 \colon 1 \to \mathbb{N}$, $S \colon \mathbb{N} \to \mathbb{N}$ on the natural numbers form an algebra $[0, S] \colon 1 + \mathbb{N} \to \mathbb{N}$ of the functor $T(X) = 1 + X$. And the set of A-labelled finite binary trees $\mathsf{Tree}(A)$ comes with functions $\mathsf{nil} \colon 1 \to \mathsf{Tree}(A)$ for the empty tree, and $\mathsf{node} \colon \mathsf{Tree}(A) \times A \times \mathsf{Tree}(A) \to \mathsf{Tree}(A)$ for constructing a tree out of two (sub)trees and a (node) label. Together, nil and node form an algebra $1 + (\mathsf{Tree}(A) \times A \times \mathsf{Tree}(A)) \to \mathsf{Tree}(A)$ of the functor $S(X) = 1 + (X \times A \times X)$.

We illustrate the link between signatures (of operations) and functors with further details. Let Σ be a (single-sorted, or single-typed) signature, given by a finite collection Σ of operations σ, each with an arity $\mathrm{ar}(\sigma) \in \mathbb{N}$. Each $\sigma \in \Sigma$

---

[4] Only the group's operations, and not its equations, are captured in this map $T(G) \to G$.

will be understood as an operation

$$\sigma: \underbrace{X \times \cdots \times X}_{\text{ar}(\sigma) \text{ times}} \longrightarrow X$$

taking $\text{ar}(\sigma)$ inputs of some type X, and producing an output of type X. With this signature Σ, say with set of operations $\{\sigma_1, \ldots, \sigma_n\}$ we associate a functor

$$T_\Sigma(X) = X^{\text{ar}(\sigma_1)} + \cdots + X^{\text{ar}(\sigma_n)},$$

where for $m \in \mathbb{N}$ the set X^m is the m-fold product $X \times \cdots \times X$. An algebra $a: T_\Sigma(U) \to U$ of this functor T_Σ can be identified with an n-cotuple $a = [a_1, \ldots a_n]: U^{\text{ar}(\sigma_1)} + \cdots + U^{\text{ar}(\sigma_n)} \to U$ of functions $a_i: U^{\text{ar}(\sigma_i)} \to U$ interpreting the operations σ_i in Σ as functions on U. Hence algebras of the functor T_Σ correspond to models of the signature Σ. One sees how the arities in the signature Σ determine the shape of the associated functor T_Σ. Notice that as a special case when an arity of an operation is zero we have a constant in Σ. In a T_Σ-algebra $T_\Sigma(U) \to U$ we get an associated map $U^0 = 1 \to U$ giving us an element of the carrier set U as interpretation of the constant. The assumption that the signature Σ is finite is not essential for the correspondence between models of Σ and algebras of T_Σ; if Σ is infinite, one can define T_Σ via an infinite coproduct, commonly written as $T_\Sigma(X) = \coprod_{\sigma \in \Sigma} X^{\text{ar}(\sigma)}$.

Polynomial functors T built up from the identity functor, products and coproducts (without constants) have algebras which are models of the kind of signatures Σ described above. This is because by the distribution of products over coproducts one can always write such a functor in 'disjunctive normal form' as $T(X) = X^{m_1} + \cdots + X^{m_n}$ for certain natural numbers n and $m_1, \ldots, m_n$. The essential role of the coproducts is to combine multiple operations into a single operation.

The polynomial functors that we use are not only of this form $T(X) = X^{m_1} + \cdots + X^{m_n}$, but may also involve constant sets. This is quite useful, for example, to describe for an arbitrary set A a signature for lists of A's, with function symbols nil: $1 \to X$ for the empty list, and cons: $A \times X \to X$ for prefixing an element of type A to a list. A model (interpretation) for such a signature is an algebra $T(U) \to U$ of the functor $T(X) = 1 + (A \times X)$ associated with this signature.

We turn to 'homomorphisms of algebras', to be understood as structure-preserving functions between algebras (of the same signature, or functor). Such a homomorphism is a function between the carrier sets of the algebras which commutes with the operations. For example, suppose we have two algebras $\ell_1: 1 \to U_1$, $c_1: A \times U_1 \to U_1$ and $\ell_2: 1 \to U_2$, $c_2: A \times U_2 \to U_2$ of the above list signature. A homomorphism of algebras from the first to the second consists of a function $f\colon U_1 \to U_2$ between the carriers with $f \circ \ell_1 = \ell_2$ and $f \circ c_1 = c_2 \circ (id \times f)$. In two diagrams:

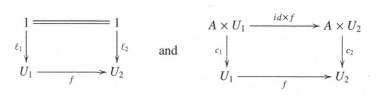

Thus, writing $n_1 = \ell_1(*)$ and $n_2 = \ell_2(*)$, these diagrams express that $f(n_1) = n_2$ and $f(c_1(a, x)) = c_2(a, f(x))$, for $a \in A$ and $x \in U_1$.

These two diagrams can be combined into a single diagram:

$$
\begin{array}{ccc}
1 + (A \times U_1) & \xrightarrow{\ id + (id \times f)\ } & 1 + (A \times U_2) \\
{\scriptstyle [\ell_1, c_1]}\downarrow & & \downarrow{\scriptstyle [\ell_2, c_2]} \\
U_1 & \xrightarrow{\quad f \quad} & U_2
\end{array}
$$

i.e., for the list-functor $T(X) = 1 + (A \times X)$,

$$
\begin{array}{ccc}
T(U_1) & \xrightarrow{\ T(f)\ } & T(U_2) \\
{\scriptstyle [\ell_1, c_1]}\downarrow & & \downarrow{\scriptstyle [\ell_2, c_2]} \\
U_1 & \xrightarrow{\quad f \quad} & U_2
\end{array}
$$

The latter formulation is entirely in terms of the functor involved. This motivates the following definition.

Definition 2.5.2 Let T be a functor with algebras $a\colon T(U) \to U$ and $b\colon T(V) \to V$. A *homomorphism of algebras* (also called a *map of algebras*, or an *algebra map*) from (U, a) to (V, b) is a function $f\colon U \to V$ between the carrier sets which commutes with the operations: $f \circ a = b \circ T(f)$ in

$$
\begin{array}{ccc}
T(U) & \xrightarrow{\ T(f)\ } & T(V) \\
{\scriptstyle a}\downarrow & & \downarrow{\scriptstyle b} \\
U & \xrightarrow{\quad f \quad} & V
\end{array}
$$

As a triviality we notice that for an algebra $a\colon T(U) \to U$ the identity function $U \to U$ is an algebra map $(U, a) \to (U, a)$. And we can compose algebra maps as functions: given two algebra maps

$$\left(T(U) \xrightarrow{a} U\right) \xrightarrow{f} \left(T(V) \xrightarrow{b} V\right) \xrightarrow{g} \left(T(W) \xrightarrow{c} W\right)$$

then the composite function $g \circ f : U \to W$ is an algebra map from (U, a) to (W, c). This is because $g \circ f \circ a = g \circ b \circ T(f) = c \circ T(g) \circ T(f) = c \circ T(g \circ f)$, see the following diagram:

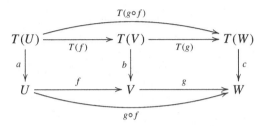

Thus: algebras and their homomorphisms form a category.

Now that we have a notion of homomorphism of algebras we can formulate the important concept of 'initiality' for algebras.

Definition 2.5.3 An algebra $a : T(U) \to U$ of a functor T is *initial* if for each algebra $b : T(V) \to V$ there is a unique homomorphism of algebras from (U, a) to (V, b). Diagrammatically we express this uniqueness by a dashed arrow, call it f, in

$$
\begin{array}{ccc}
T(U) & \dashrightarrow{\;T(f)\;} & T(V) \\
{\scriptstyle a}\downarrow & & \downarrow{\scriptstyle b} \\
U & \dashrightarrow{\;f\;} & V
\end{array}
$$

We shall sometimes call this f the 'unique mediating algebra map'.

We emphasise that unique existence has two aspects, namely *existence* of an algebra map out of the initial algebra to another algebra, and *uniqueness*, in the form of equality of any two algebra maps going out of the initial algebra to some other algebra. Existence will be used as an (inductive) definition principle, and uniqueness as an (inductive) proof principle.

As a first example, we shall describe the set $\mathbb{N}$ of natural numbers as initial algebra.

Example 2.5.4 Consider the set $\mathbb{N}$ of natural number with its zero and successor function $0 : 1 \to \mathbb{N}$ and $S : \mathbb{N} \to \mathbb{N}$. These functions can be combined into a single function $[0, S] : 1 + \mathbb{N} \to \mathbb{N}$, forming an algebra of the functor

$T(X) = 1 + X$. We will show that this map $[0, S]: 1 + \mathbb{N} \to \mathbb{N}$ is the initial algebra of this functor T. And this characterises the set of natural numbers (up to isomorphism), by Lemma 2.5.5(ii) below.

To prove initiality, assume we have an arbitrary set U carrying a T-algebra structure $[u, h]: 1 + U \to U$. We have to define a 'mediating' homomorphism $f: \mathbb{N} \to U$. We try iteration:

$$f(n) = h^{(n)}(u)$$

where we simply write u instead of $u(*)$. That is,

$$f(0) = u \quad \text{and} \quad f(n + 1) = h(f(n)).$$

These two equations express that we have a commuting diagram

$$
\begin{array}{ccc}
1 + \mathbb{N} & \xrightarrow{\;id + f\;} & 1 + U \\
{\scriptstyle [0,S]}\Big\downarrow & & \Big\downarrow{\scriptstyle [u,h]} \\
\mathbb{N} & \xrightarrow{\quad f \quad} & U
\end{array}
$$

making f a homomorphism of algebras. This can be verified easily by distinguishing for an arbitrary element $x \in 1 + \mathbb{N}$ in the upper-left corner the two cases $x = (0, *) = \kappa(*)$ and $x = (1, n) = \kappa'(n)$, for $n \in \mathbb{N}$. In the first case $x = \kappa(*)$ we get

$$f([0, S](\kappa(*))) = f(0) = u = [u, h](\kappa(*)) = [u, h]((id + f)(\kappa(*))).$$

In the second case $x = \kappa'(n)$ we similarly check:

$$
\begin{aligned}
f([0, S](\kappa'(n))) &= f(S(n)) = h(f(n)) = [u, h](\kappa'(f(n))) \\
&= [u, h]((id + f)(\kappa'(n))).
\end{aligned}
$$

Hence we may conclude that $f([0, S](x)) = [u, h]((id + f)(x))$, for all $x \in 1 + \mathbb{N}$, i.e. that $f \circ [0, S] = [u, h] \circ (id + f)$.

This looks promising, but we still have to show that f is the only map making the diagram commute. If $g: \mathbb{N} \to U$ also satisfies $g \circ [0, S] = [u, h] \circ (id + g)$, then $g(0) = u$ and $g(n + 1) = h(g(n))$, by the same line of reasoning followed above. Hence $g(n) = f(n)$ by induction on n, so that $g = f: \mathbb{N} \to U$.

We shall give a simple example showing how to use this initiality for inductive definitions. Suppose we wish to define by induction the function $f(n) = 2^{-n}$ from the natural numbers $\mathbb{N}$ to the rational numbers $\mathbb{Q}$. Its defining equations are:

$$f(0) = 1 \quad \text{and} \quad f(n + 1) = \tfrac{1}{2} f(n).$$

In order to define this function $f \colon \mathbb{N} \to \mathbb{Q}$ by initiality, we have to put an algebra structure $1 + \mathbb{Q} \to \mathbb{Q}$ on the set of rational numbers $\mathbb{Q}$, see the above definition. This algebra on $\mathbb{Q}$ corresponds to the right-hand side of the two defining equations of f, given as two functions

$$
\begin{array}{lll}
1 \xrightarrow{\ 1\ } \mathbb{Q} & \qquad & \mathbb{Q} \xrightarrow{\ \frac{1}{2}(-)\ } \mathbb{Q} \\[2mm]
* \longmapsto 1 & \qquad & x \longmapsto \tfrac{1}{2}x
\end{array}
$$

(where we use '1' both for the singleton set $1 = \{*\}$ and for the number $1 \in \mathbb{Q}$) which combine into a single function

$$
1 + \mathbb{Q} \xrightarrow{\ [1, \frac{1}{2}(-)]\ } \mathbb{Q}
$$

forming an algebra on $\mathbb{Q}$. The function $f(n) = 2^{-n}$ is then determined by initiality as the unique function making the following diagram commute.

$$
\begin{array}{ccc}
1 + \mathbb{N} & \xrightarrow{\ id+f\ } & 1 + \mathbb{Q} \\[2mm]
{\scriptstyle [0,S]} \downarrow & & \downarrow {\scriptstyle [1, \frac{1}{2}(-)]} \\[2mm]
\mathbb{N} & \xrightarrow[\ f\ ]{} & \mathbb{Q}
\end{array}
$$

This shows how initiality can be used to define functions by induction. It requires that one puts an appropriate algebra structure on the codomain (i.e. the range) of the intended function, corresponding to the induction clauses that determine the function.

We emphasise that the functor T is a parameter in Definitions 2.5.2 and 2.5.3 of 'homomorphism' and 'initiality' for algebras, yielding uniform notions for all functors T (representing certain signatures). It turns out that initial algebras have certain properties, which can be shown for all functors T at once. Diagrams are convenient in expressing and proving these properties, because they display information in a succinct way. And they are useful both in existence and uniqueness arguments.

Lemma 2.5.5 *Let T be a functor.*

(i) *Initial T-algebras, if they exist, are unique, up-to-isomorphism of algebras. That is, if we have two initial algebras $a \colon T(U) \to U$ and $a' \colon T(U') \to$*

U' of T, then there is a unique isomorphism $f : U \xrightarrow{\cong} U'$ of algebras:

$$
\begin{array}{ccc}
T(U) & \xrightarrow[\cong]{T(f)} & T(U') \\
{\scriptstyle a}\big\downarrow & & \big\downarrow{\scriptstyle a'} \\
U & \xrightarrow[\cong]{f} & U'
\end{array}
$$

(ii) *The operation of an initial algebra is an isomorphism: if $a : T(U) \to U$ is an initial algebra, then a has an inverse $a^{-1} : U \to T(U)$.*

The first point tells us that a functor can have (essentially) at most one initial algebra.[5] Therefore, we often speak of *the* initial algebra of a functor T. And the second point – which is due to Lambek – says that an initial algebra $T(U) \to U$ is a fixed point $T(U) \cong U$ of the functor T. Initial algebras may be seen as generalisations of least fixed points of monotone functions, since they have a (unique) map into an arbitrary algebra, see Exercise 2.10.3.

Proof (i) Suppose both $a : T(U) \to U$ and $a' : T(U') \to U'$ are initial algebras of the functor T. By initiality of a there is a unique algebra map $f : U \to U'$. Similarly, by initiality of a' there is a unique algebra map $f' : U' \to U$ in the other direction:

$$
\begin{array}{ccc}
T(U) & \dashrightarrow^{T(f)} & T(U') \\
{\scriptstyle a}\big\downarrow & & \big\downarrow{\scriptstyle a'} \\
U & \dashrightarrow_{f} & U'
\end{array}
\qquad
\begin{array}{ccc}
T(U') & \dashrightarrow^{T(f')} & T(U) \\
{\scriptstyle a'}\big\downarrow & & \big\downarrow{\scriptstyle a} \\
U' & \dashrightarrow_{f'} & U
\end{array}
$$

Here we use the existence parts of initiality. The uniqueness part gives us that the two resulting algebra maps $(U, a) \to (U, a)$, namely $f \circ f'$ and id in:

$$
\begin{array}{ccccc}
T(U) & \xrightarrow{T(f)} & T(U') & \xrightarrow{T(f')} & T(U) \\
{\scriptstyle a}\big\downarrow & & {\scriptstyle a'}\big\downarrow & & \big\downarrow{\scriptstyle a} \\
U & \xrightarrow{f} & U' & \xrightarrow{f'} & U
\end{array}
\quad \text{and} \quad
\begin{array}{ccc}
T(U) & \xrightarrow{T(id)} & T(U) \\
{\scriptstyle a}\big\downarrow & & \big\downarrow{\scriptstyle a} \\
U & \xrightarrow{id} & U
\end{array}
$$

must be equal, i.e. that $f' \circ f = id$. Uniqueness of algebra maps $(U', a') \to (U', a')$ similarly yields $f \circ f' = id$. Hence f is an isomorphism of algebras.

(ii) Let $a : T(U) \to U$ be an initial T-algebra. In order to show that the function a is an isomorphism, we have to produce an inverse function $U \to$

[5] This is a more general property of initial objects in a category.

$T(U)$. Initiality of (U, a) can be used to define functions out of U to arbitrary algebras. Since we seek a function $U \to T(U)$, we have to put an algebra structure on the set $T(U)$. A moment's thought yields a candidate, namely the result $T(a)\colon T(T(U)) \to T(U)$ of applying the functor T to the function a. This function $T(a)$, by initiality of $a\colon T(U) \to U$, gives rise to a function $a'\colon U \to T(U)$ with $T(a) \circ T(a') = a' \circ a$ in:

$$
\begin{array}{ccc}
T(U) & \xdashrightarrow{\;T(a')\;} & T(T(U)) \\
\Big\downarrow{\scriptstyle a} & & \Big\downarrow{\scriptstyle T(a)} \\
U & \xdashrightarrow[\;a'\;]{} & T(U)
\end{array}
$$

The function $a \circ a'\colon U \to U$ is an algebra map $(U, a) \to (U, a)$:

$$
\begin{array}{ccccc}
T(U) & \xrightarrow{\;T(a')\;} & T(T(U)) & \xrightarrow{\;T(a)\;} & T(U) \\
\Big\downarrow{\scriptstyle a} & & \Big\downarrow{\scriptstyle T(a)} & & \Big\downarrow{\scriptstyle a} \\
U & \xrightarrow[\;a'\;]{} & T(U) & \xrightarrow[\;a\;]{} & U
\end{array}
$$

so that $a \circ a' = id$ by uniqueness of algebra maps $(U, a) \to (U, a)$. But then

$$
\begin{aligned}
a' \circ a &= T(a) \circ T(a') && \text{by definition of } a' \\
&= T(a \circ a') && \text{since } T \text{ preserves composition} \\
&= T(id) && \text{as we have just seen} \\
&= id && \text{since } T \text{ preserves identities.}
\end{aligned}
$$

Hence $a\colon T(U) \to U$ is an isomorphism with a' as its inverse. $\qquad\square$

From now on we shall often write an initial T-algebra as a map $a\colon T(U) \xrightarrow{\cong} U$, making this isomorphism explicit.

Example 2.5.6 Let A be a fixed set and consider the functor $T(X) = 1 + (A \times X)$ that we used earlier to capture models of the list signature $1 \to X$, $A \times X \to X$. We claim that the initial algebra of this functor T is the set $A^\star = \mathsf{list}(A) = \bigcup_{n \in \mathbb{N}} A^n$ of finite sequences of elements of A, together with the function (or element) $1 \to A^\star$ given by the empty list $\mathsf{nil} = (\ )$, and the function $A \times A^\star \to A^\star$ which maps an element $a \in A$ and a list $\alpha = (a_1, \ldots, a_n) \in A^\star$ to the list $\mathsf{cons}(a, \alpha) = (a, a_1, \ldots, a_n) \in A^\star$, obtained by prefixing a to α. These two functions can be combined into a single function $[\mathsf{nil}, \mathsf{cons}]\colon 1 + (A \times A^\star) \to A^\star$, which, as one easily checks, is an isomorphism. But this does not yet mean that it is the initial algebra. We will check this explicitly.

For an arbitrary algebra $[u, h]\colon 1 + (A \times U) \to U$ of the list-functor T we have a unique homomorphism $f\colon A^\star \to U$ of algebras:

$$
\begin{array}{ccc}
1 + (A \times A^\star) & \xrightarrow{\ id + (id \times f)\ } & 1 + (A \times U) \\
{\scriptstyle [\mathsf{nil},\mathsf{cons}]}\Big\downarrow & & \Big\downarrow{\scriptstyle [u,h]} \\
A^\star & \xrightarrow[\qquad f \qquad]{} & U
\end{array}
$$

namely

$$
f(\alpha) = \begin{cases} u & \text{if } \alpha = \mathsf{nil} \\ h(a, f(\beta)) & \text{if } \alpha = \mathsf{cons}(a, \beta). \end{cases}
$$

We leave it to the reader to verify that f is indeed the unique function $A^\star \to U$ making the diagram commute.

Again we can use this initiality of $A^\star$ to define functions by induction (for lists). As an example we take the length function $\mathsf{len}\colon A^\star \to \mathbb{N}$, described already in the beginning of Section 2.2. In order to define it by initiality, it has to arise from a list-algebra structure $1 + A \times \mathbb{N} \to \mathbb{N}$ on the natural numbers $\mathbb{N}$. This algebra structure is the cotuple of the two functions $0\colon 1 \to \mathbb{N}$ and $S \circ \pi'\colon A \times \mathbb{N} \to \mathbb{N}$. Hence len is determined as the unique function in the following initiality diagram.

$$
\begin{array}{ccc}
1 + (A \times A^\star) & \xrightarrow{\ id + (id \times \mathsf{len})\ } & 1 + (A \times \mathbb{N}) \\
{\scriptstyle [\mathsf{nil},\mathsf{cons}]}\Big\downarrow{\scriptstyle \cong} & & \Big\downarrow{\scriptstyle [0,\,S \circ \pi']} \\
A^\star & \xrightarrow[\qquad \mathsf{len} \qquad]{} & \mathbb{N}
\end{array}
$$

The algebra structure that we use on $\mathbb{N}$ corresponds to the defining clauses $\mathsf{len}(\mathsf{nil}) = 0$ and $\mathsf{len}(\mathsf{cons}(a, \alpha)) = S(\mathsf{len}(\alpha)) = S(\mathsf{len}(\pi'(a, \alpha))) = S(\pi'(id \times \mathsf{len})(a, \alpha))$.

We proceed with an example showing how proof by induction involves using the uniqueness of a map out of an initial algebra. Consider therefore the 'doubling' function $d\colon A^\star \to A^\star$ which replaces each element a in a list α by two consecutive occurrences a, a in $d(\alpha)$. This function is defined as the unique one making the following diagram commute.

$$
\begin{array}{ccc}
1 + (A \times A^\star) & \xrightarrow{\ id + (id \times d)\ } & 1 + (A \times A^\star) \\
{\scriptstyle [\mathsf{nil},\mathsf{cons}]}\Big\downarrow{\scriptstyle \cong} & & \Big\downarrow{\scriptstyle [\mathsf{nil},\,\lambda(a,\alpha).\,\mathsf{cons}(a,\mathsf{cons}(a,\alpha))]} \\
A^\star & \xrightarrow[\qquad d \qquad]{} & A^\star
\end{array}
$$

That is, d is defined by the induction clauses $d(\mathsf{nil}) = \mathsf{nil}$ and $d(\mathsf{cons}(a, \alpha)) = \mathsf{cons}(a, \mathsf{cons}(a, d(\alpha)))$. We wish to show that the length of the list $d(\alpha)$ is twice the length of α, i.e. that

$$\mathsf{len}(d(\alpha)) = 2 \cdot \mathsf{len}(\alpha).$$

The ordinary induction proof consists of two steps:

$$\mathsf{len}(d(\mathsf{nil})) = \mathsf{len}(\mathsf{nil}) = 0 = 2 \cdot 0 = 2 \cdot \mathsf{len}(\mathsf{nil})$$

and

$$
\begin{aligned}
\mathsf{len}(d(\mathsf{cons}(a, \alpha))) &= \mathsf{len}(\mathsf{cons}(a, \mathsf{cons}(a, d(\alpha)))) \\
&= 1 + 1 + \mathsf{len}(d(\alpha)) \\
&\overset{(\mathrm{IH})}{=} 2 + 2 \cdot \mathsf{len}(\alpha) \\
&= 2 \cdot (1 + \mathsf{len}(\alpha)) \\
&= 2 \cdot \mathsf{len}(\mathsf{cons}(a, \alpha)).
\end{aligned}
$$

The 'initiality' induction proof of the fact $\mathsf{len} \circ d = 2 \cdot (-) \circ \mathsf{len}$ uses uniqueness in the following manner. Both $\mathsf{len} \circ d$ and $2 \cdot (-) \circ \mathsf{len}$ are homomorphism from the (initial) algebra $(A^\star, [\mathsf{nil}, \mathsf{cons}])$ to the algebra $(\mathbb{N}, [0, S \circ S \circ \pi'])$, so they must be equal by initiality. First we check that $\mathsf{len} \circ d$ is an appropriate homomorphism by inspection of the following diagram:

The rectangle on the left commutes by definition of d. And commutation of the rectangle on the right follows easily from the definition of len. Next we check that $2 \cdot (-) \circ \mathsf{len}$ is also a homomorphism of algebras:

The square on the left commutes by definition of len. Commutation of the upper square on the right follows from an easy computation. And the lower square on the right may be seen as defining the function $2 \cdot (-) \colon \mathbb{N} \to \mathbb{N}$ by the clauses: $2 \cdot 0 = 0$ and $2 \cdot (S(n)) = S(S(2 \cdot n))$, which we took for granted in the earlier 'ordinary' proof.

We conclude our brief discussion of algebras and induction with a few remarks.

(1) Given a number of constructors one can form the carrier set of the associated initial algebra as the set of 'closed' terms (or 'ground' terms, not containing variables) that can be formed with these constructors. For example, the zero and successor constructors $0 \colon 1 \to X$ and $S \colon X \to X$ give rise to the set of closed terms,

$$\{0, S(0), S(S(0))), \ldots\}$$

which is (isomorphic to) the set $\mathbb{N}$ of natural numbers. Similarly, the set of closed terms arising from the A-list constructors nil: $1 \to X$, cons: $A \times X \to X$ is the set $A^\star$ of finite sequences (of elements of A).

Although it is pleasant to know what an initial algebra looks like, in using initiality we do not need this knowledge. All we need to know is that there exists an initial algebra. Its defining property is sufficient to use it. There are abstract results, guaranteeing the existence of initial algebras for certain (continuous) functors, see e.g. [LS81, SP82], where initial algebras are constructed as suitable colimits, generalising the construction of least fixed points of continuous functions.

(2) The initiality format of induction has the important advantage that it generalises smoothly from natural numbers to other (algebraic) data types, like lists or trees. Once we know the signature containing the constructor operations of these data types, we know what the associated functor is and we can determine its initial algebra. This uniformity provided by initiality was first stressed by the 'ADT-group' [GTW78], and forms the basis for inductively defined types in many programming languages. For example, in the (functional) language ML, the user can introduce a new inductive type X via the notation

datatype $X = c_1$ of $\sigma_1(X) \mid \cdots \mid c_n$ of $\sigma_n(X)$.

The idea is that X is the carrier of the initial algebra associated with the constructors $c_1 \colon \sigma_1(X) \to X, \ldots, c_n \colon \sigma_n(X) \to X$. That is, with the functor $T(X) = \sigma_1(X) + \cdots + \sigma_n(X)$. The σ_i are existing types which may contain

X (positively).[6] The uniformity provided by the initial algebra format (and dually also by the final coalgebra format) is very useful if one wishes to automatically generate various rules associated with (co)inductively defined types (for example in programming languages like CHARITY [CS95] or in proof tools like PVS [ORR$^+$96], HOL/ISABELLE [GM93, Mel89, Pau90, Pau97], or COQ [PM93]).

Another advantage of the initial algebra format is that it is dual to the final coalgebra format, as we shall see in the next section. This forms the basis for the duality between induction and coinduction.

(3) We have indicated only in one example that uniqueness of maps out of an initial algebra corresponds to proof (as opposed to definition) by induction. To substantiate this claim further we show how the usual predicate formulation of induction for lists can be derived from the initial algebra formulation. This predicate formulation says that a predicate (or subset) $P \subseteq A^\star$ is equal to $A^\star$ in case nil $\in P$ and $\alpha \in P \Rightarrow \text{cons}(a, \alpha) \in P$, for all $a \in A$ and $\alpha \in A^\star$. Let us consider P as a set in its own right, with an explicit inclusion function $i : P \to A^\star$ (given by $i(x) = x$). The induction assumptions on P essentially say that P carries an algebra structure nil: $1 \to P$, cons: $A \times P \to P$, in such a way that the inclusion map $i : P \to A^\star$ is a map of algebras:

$$
\begin{array}{ccc}
1 + (A \times P) & \xrightarrow{\;id+(id\times i)\;} & 1 + (A \times A^\star) \\
{\scriptstyle [\text{nil,cons}]}\big\downarrow & & \cong\big\downarrow{\scriptstyle [\text{nil,cons}]} \\
P & \xrightarrow{\quad i \quad} & A^\star
\end{array}
$$

In other words: P is a subalgebra of $A^\star$. By initiality we get a function $j : A^\star \to P$ as on the left below. But then $i \circ j = id$, by uniqueness.

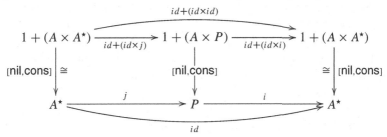

This means that $P = A^\star$, as we wished to derive.

---

[6] This definition scheme in ML contains various aspects which are not investigated here, e.g. it allows (a) $X = X(\vec{\alpha})$ to contain type variables $\vec{\alpha}$, (b) mutual dependencies between such definitions, (c) iteration of inductive definitions (so that, for example, the LIST operation which is obtained via this scheme can be used in the σ_i).

(4) The initiality property from Definition 2.5.3 allows us to define functions
$f: U \to V$ out of an initial algebra (with carrier) U. Often one wishes to
define functions $U \times D \to V$ involving an additional parameter ranging
over a set D. A typical example is the addition function plus: $\mathbb{N} \times \mathbb{N} \to \mathbb{N}$,
defined by induction on (say) its first argument, with the second argument
as parameter. One can handle such functions $U \times D \to V$ via Currying:
they correspond to functions $U \to V^D$. And the latter can be defined via the
initiality scheme. For example, we can define a Curryied addition function
plus: $\mathbb{N} \to \mathbb{N}^{\mathbb{N}}$ via initiality by putting an appropriate algebra structure
$1 + \mathbb{N}^{\mathbb{N}} \to \mathbb{N}^{\mathbb{N}}$ on $\mathbb{N}$ (see Example 2.5.4):

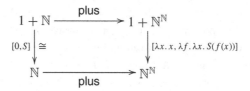

This says that

$$\text{plus}(0) = \lambda x.\, x \quad \text{and} \quad \text{plus}(n + 1) = \lambda x.\, S(\text{plus}(n)(x)).$$

Alternatively, one may formulate initiality 'with parameters',
see [Jac95], so that one can handle such functions $U \times D \to V$ directly.

2.6 Coalgebras and coinduction

In Section 2.4 we have seen that a 'co'-product $+$ behaves like a product
$\times$, except that the arrows point in opposite direction: one has coprojections
$X \to X + Y \leftarrow Y$ instead of projections $X \leftarrow X \times Y \to Y$, and cotupleing
instead of tupleing. One says that the coproduct $+$ is the dual of the product
$\times$, because the associated arrows are reversed. Similarly, a 'co'-algebra is the
dual of an algebra.

Definition 2.6.1 For a functor T, a *coalgebra* (or a *T-coalgebra*) is a pair
(U, c) consisting of a set U and a function $c: U \to T(U)$.

Like for algebras, we call the set U the *carrier* and the function c the *structure* or *operation* of the coalgebra (U, c). Because coalgebras often describe
dynamical systems (of some sort), the carrier set U is also called the *state
space*.

What, then, is the difference between an algebra $T(U) \to U$ and a coalgebra $U \to T(U)$? Essentially, it is the difference between construction and observation. An algebra consists of a carrier set U with a function $T(U) \to U$ going *into* this carrier U. It tells us how to construct elements in U. And a coalgebra consists of a carrier set U with a function $U \to T(U)$ in the opposite direction, going *out of* U. In this case we do not know how to form elements in U, but we only have operations acting on U, which may give us some information about U. In general, these coalgebraic operations do not tell us all there is to say about elements of U, so that we only have *limited access* to U. Coalgebras – like algebras – can be seen as models of a signature of operations – not of constructor operations, but of destructor/observer operations.

Consider for example the functor $T(X) = A \times X$, where A is a fixed set. A coalgebra $U \to T(U)$ consists of two functions $U \to A$ and $U \to U$, which we earlier called value: $U \to A$ and next: $U \to U$. With these operations we can do two things, given an element $u \in U$:

(1) produce an element in A, namely value(u);
(2) produce a next element in U, namely next(u).

Now we can repeat (1) and (2) and therefore form another element in A, namely value(next(u)). By proceeding in this way we can get for each element $u \in U$ an infinite sequence $(a_1, a_2, \ldots) \in A^{\mathbb{N}}$ of elements $a_n = \text{value}(\text{next}^{(n)}(u)) \in A$. This sequence of elements that u gives rise to is what we can *observe* about u. Two elements $u_1, u_2 \in U$ may well give rise to the same sequence of elements of A, without actually being equal as elements of U. In such a case one calls u_1 and u_2 observationally indistinguishable, or bisimilar.

Here is another example. Let the functor $T(X) = 1 + A \times X$ have a coalgebra pn: $U \to 1 + A \times U$, where 'pn' stands for 'possible next'. If we have an element $u \in U$, then we can see the following.

(1) Either pn(u) = $\kappa(*) \in 1 + A \times U$ is in the left component of $+$. If this happens, then our experiment stops, since there is no state (element of U) left with which to continue.
(2) Or pn(u) = $\kappa'(a, u) \in 1 + A \times U$ is in the right $+$-component. This gives us an element $a \in A$ and a next element $u' \in U$ of the carrier, with which we can proceed.

Repeating this we can observe for an element $u \in U$ either a finite sequence $(a_1, a_2, \ldots, a_n) \in A^{\star}$, or an infinite sequence $(a_1, a_2, \ldots) \in A^{\mathbb{N}}$. The observable outcomes are elements of the set $A^{\infty} = A^{\star} + A^{\mathbb{N}}$ of finite and infinite lists of a's.

These observations will turn out to be elements of the final coalgebra of the functors involved, see Example 2.6.3 and 2.6.5 below. But in order to formulate this notion of finality for coalgebras we first need to know what a 'homomorphism of coalgebras' is. It is, like in algebra, a function between the underlying sets which commutes with the operations. For example, let $T(X) = A \times X$ be the 'infinite list' functor as used above, with coalgebras $\langle h_1, t_1 \rangle \colon U_1 \to A \times U_1$ and $\langle h_2, t_2 \rangle \colon U_2 \to A \times U_2$. A homomorphism of coalgebras from the first to the second consists of a function $f \colon U_1 \to U_2$ between the carrier sets (state spaces) with $h_2 \circ f = h_1$ and $t_2 \circ f = f \circ t_1$ in:

$$
\begin{array}{ccc}
U_1 & \xrightarrow{\;f\;} & U_2 \\
\downarrow{\scriptstyle h_1} & & \downarrow{\scriptstyle h_2} \\
A & =\!=\!= & A
\end{array}
\quad \text{and} \quad
\begin{array}{ccc}
U_1 & \xrightarrow{\;f\;} & U_2 \\
\downarrow{\scriptstyle t_1} & & \downarrow{\scriptstyle t_2} \\
U_1 & \xrightarrow{\;f\;} & U_2
\end{array}
$$

These two diagrams can be combined into a single one:

$$
\begin{array}{ccc}
U_1 & \xrightarrow{\;f\;} & U_2 \\
\downarrow{\scriptstyle \langle h_1, t_1 \rangle} & & \downarrow{\scriptstyle \langle h_2, t_2 \rangle} \\
A \times U_1 & \xrightarrow{\;id \times f\;} & A \times U_2
\end{array}
$$

that is, into

$$
\begin{array}{ccc}
U_1 & \xrightarrow{\;f\;} & U_2 \\
\downarrow{\scriptstyle \langle h_1, t_1 \rangle} & & \downarrow{\scriptstyle \langle h_2, t_2 \rangle} \\
T(U_1) & \xrightarrow{\;T(f)\;} & T(U_2)
\end{array}
$$

Definition 2.6.2 Let T be a functor.

(i) A *homomorphism of coalgebras* (or, *map of coalgebras*, or *coalgebra map*) from a T-coalgebra $U_1 \xrightarrow{c_1} T(U_1)$ to another T-coalgebra $U_2 \xrightarrow{c_2} T(U_2)$ consists of a function $f \colon U_1 \to U_2$ between the carrier sets which commutes with the operations: $c_2 \circ f = T(f) \circ c_1$ as expressed by the following diagram:

$$
\begin{array}{ccc}
U_1 & \xrightarrow{\;f\;} & U_2 \\
\downarrow{\scriptstyle c_1} & & \downarrow{\scriptstyle c_2} \\
T(U_1) & \xrightarrow{\;T(f)\;} & T(U_2)
\end{array}
$$

(ii) A *final coalgebra* $d: Z \to T(Z)$ is a coalgebra such that for every coalgebra $c: U \to T(U)$ there is a unique map of coalgebras $(U, c) \to (Z, d)$.

Notice that where the initiality property for algebras allows us to define functions going *out of* an initial algebra, the finality property for coalgebras gives us means to define functions *into* a final coalgebra. Earlier we have emphasised that what is typical in a coalgebraic setting is that there are no operations for constructing elements of a state space (of a coalgebra), and that state spaces should therefore be seen as black boxes. However, if we know that a certain coalgebra is final, then we can actually form elements in its state space by this finality principle. The next example contains some illustrations. Besides a means for constructing elements, finality also allows us to define various operations on final coalgebras, as will be shown in a series of examples below. In fact, in this way one can put a certain algebraic structure on top of a coalgebra, see [Tur96] for a systematic study in the context of process algebras.

Now that we have seen the definitions of initiality (for algebras, see Definition 2.5.3) and finality (for coalgebras) we are in a position to see their similarities. At an informal level we can explain these similarities as follows. A typical initiality diagram may be drawn as:

$$
\begin{array}{ccc}
T(U) & \dashrightarrow & T(V) \\
{\scriptstyle \text{initial}\atop \text{algebra}} \Big\downarrow {\cong} & & \Big\downarrow {\text{base step}\atop {\text{plus}\atop \text{next step}}} \\
U & \underset{\text{'and-so-forth'}}{\dashrightarrow} & V
\end{array}
$$

The map 'and-so-forth' that is defined in this diagram applies the 'next step' operations repeatedly to the 'base step'. The pattern in a finality diagram is similar:

$$
\begin{array}{ccc}
V & \overset{\text{'and-so-forth'}}{\dashrightarrow} & U \\
{\text{observe}\atop {\text{plus}\atop \text{next step}}} \Big\downarrow & & \cong \Big\downarrow {\text{final}\atop \text{coalgebra}} \\
T(V) & \dashrightarrow & T(U)
\end{array}
$$

In this case the 'and-so-forth' map captures the observations that arise by repeatedly applying the 'next step' operation. This captures the observable behaviour.

The technique for defining a function $f: V \to U$ by finality is thus: describe the direct observations together with the single next steps of f as a coalgebra structure on V. The function f then arises by repetition. Hence a coinductive

definition of f does not determine f 'at once', but 'step-by-step'. In the next
section we shall describe proof techniques using bisimulations, which fully
exploit this step-by-step character of coinductive definitions.

But first we identify a simple coalgebra concretely, and show how we can
use finality.

Example 2.6.3 For a fixed set A, consider the functor $T(X) = A \times X$. We
claim that the final coalgebra of this functor is the set $A^{\mathbb{N}}$ of infinite lists of
elements from A, with coalgebra structure

$$\langle \text{head}, \text{tail} \rangle : A^{\mathbb{N}} \longrightarrow A \times A^{\mathbb{N}}$$

given by

$$\text{head}(\alpha) = \alpha(0) \quad \text{and} \quad \text{tail}(\alpha) = \lambda x. \, \alpha(x + 1).$$

Hence head takes the first element of an infinite sequence $(\alpha(0), \alpha(1), \alpha(2), \ldots)$
of elements of A, and tail takes the remaining list. We notice that the pair of
functions $\langle \text{head}, \text{tail} \rangle : A^{\mathbb{N}} \to A \times A^{\mathbb{N}}$ is an isomorphism.

We claim that for an arbitrary coalgebra $\langle \text{value}, \text{next} \rangle : U \to A \times U$ there is
a unique homomorphism of coalgebras $f : U \to A^{\mathbb{N}}$; it is given for $u \in U$ and
$n \in \mathbb{N}$ by

$$f(u)(n) = \text{value} \left(\text{next}^{(n)}(u) \right).$$

Then indeed, $\text{head} \circ f = \text{value}$ and $\text{tail} \circ f = f \circ \text{next}$, making f a map of
coalgebras. And f is unique in satisfying these two equations, as can be checked
easily.

Earlier in this section we saw that what we can observe about an element
$u \in U$ is an infinite list of elements of A arising as $\text{value}(u)$, $\text{value}(\text{next}(u))$,
$\text{value}(\text{next}(\text{next}(u)))$, ... Now we see that this observable behaviour of u is
precisely the outcome $f(u) \in A^{\mathbb{N}}$ at u of the unique map f to the final coalgebra.
Hence the elements of the final coalgebra give the observable behaviour. This
is typical for final coalgebras.

Once we know that $A^{\mathbb{N}}$ is a final coalgebra – or, more precisely, carries a final
coalgebra structure – we can use this finality to define functions into $A^{\mathbb{N}}$. Let
us start with a simple example, which involves defining the constant sequence
$\text{const}(a) = (a, a, a, \ldots) \in A^{\mathbb{N}}$ by coinduction (for some element $a \in A$). We
shall define this constant as a function $\text{const}(a) : 1 \to A^{\mathbb{N}}$, where $1 = \{*\}$
is a singleton set. Following the above explanation, we have to produce a
coalgebra structure $1 \to T(1) = A \times 1$ on 1, in such a way that $\text{const}(a)$ arises
by repetition. In this case the only thing we want to observe is the element
$a \in A$ itself, and so we simply define as coalgebra structure $1 \to A \times 1$ the

function $* \mapsto (a, *)$. Indeed, $\mathsf{const}(a)$ arises in the following finality diagram:

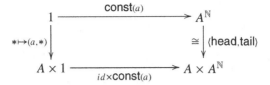

It expresses that $\mathsf{head}(\mathsf{const}(a)) = a$ and $\mathsf{tail}(\mathsf{const}(a)) = \mathsf{const}(a)$.

We consider another example, for the special case where $A = \mathbb{N}$. We now wish to define (coinductively) the function $\mathsf{from} \colon \mathbb{N} \to \mathbb{N}^{\mathbb{N}}$ which maps a natural number $n \in \mathbb{N}$ to the sequence $(n, n + 1, n + 2, n + 3, \ldots) \in \mathbb{N}^{\mathbb{N}}$. This involves defining a coalgebra structure $\mathbb{N} \to \mathbb{N} \times \mathbb{N}$ on the domain $\mathbb{N}$ of the function from that we are trying to define. The direct observation that we can make about a 'state' $n \in \mathbb{N}$ is n itself, and the next state is then $n + 1$ (in which we can directly observe $n + 1$). Repetition then leads to $\mathsf{from}(n)$. Thus we define the function from in the following diagram.

It is then determined by the equations $\mathsf{head}(\mathsf{from}(n)) = n$ and $\mathsf{tail}(\mathsf{from}(n)) = \mathsf{from}(n + 1)$.

We are now in a position to provide the formal background for the examples of coinductive definitions and proofs in Section 2.3. For instance, the function $\mathsf{merge} \colon A^{\mathbb{N}} \times A^{\mathbb{N}} \to A^{\mathbb{N}}$ which merges two infinite lists into a single one arises as the unique function to the final coalgebra $A^{\mathbb{N}}$ in:

$$
\begin{array}{ccc}
A^{\mathbb{N}} \times A^{\mathbb{N}} & \xrightarrow{\ \ \mathsf{merge}\ \ } & A^{\mathbb{N}} \\
{\scriptstyle \lambda(\alpha,\beta).\,(\mathsf{head}(\alpha),(\beta,\mathsf{tail}(\alpha)))} \downarrow & & \cong \downarrow {\scriptstyle \langle\mathsf{head},\mathsf{tail}\rangle} \\
A \times (A^{\mathbb{N}} \times A^{\mathbb{N}}) & \xrightarrow[\ id\times\mathsf{merge}\ ]{} & A \times A^{\mathbb{N}}
\end{array}
$$

Notice that the coalgebra structure on the left that we put on the domain $A^{\mathbb{N}} \times A^{\mathbb{N}}$ of merge corresponds to the defining 'coinduction' clauses for merge, as used in Section 2.3. It expresses the direct observation after a merge, together with the next state (about which we make a next direct observation).

It follows from the commutativity of the above diagram that

$$\mathsf{head}(\mathsf{merge}(\alpha, \beta)) = \mathsf{head}(\alpha) \quad \text{and} \quad \mathsf{tail}(\mathsf{merge}(\alpha, \beta)) = \mathsf{merge}(\beta, \mathsf{tail}(\alpha)).$$

The function even : $A^{\mathbb{N}} \to A^{\mathbb{N}}$ can similarly be defined coinductively, that is, by finality of $A^{\mathbb{N}}$, as follows:

$$
\begin{array}{ccc}
A^{\mathbb{N}} & \xrightarrow{\text{even}} & A^{\mathbb{N}} \\
{\scriptstyle \lambda\alpha.\,(\text{head}(\alpha),\text{tail}(\text{tail}(\alpha)))}\Big\downarrow & \cong & \Big\downarrow{\scriptstyle \langle\text{head},\text{tail}\rangle} \\
A \times A^{\mathbb{N}} & \xrightarrow[id\times\text{even}]{} & A \times A^{\mathbb{N}}
\end{array}
$$

The coalgebra structure on $A^{\mathbb{N}}$ on the left gives rise, by finality, to a unique coalgebra homomorphism, called even. By the commutatitivity of the diagram, it satisfies:

$$\text{head}(\text{even}(\alpha)) = \text{head}(\alpha) \quad \text{and} \quad \text{tail}(\text{even}(\alpha)) = \text{even}(\text{tail}(\text{tail}(\alpha))).$$

As before, we define

$$\text{odd}(\alpha) = \text{even}(\text{tail}(\alpha)).$$

Next we prove for all α in $A^{\mathbb{N}}$: merge(even(α), odd(α)) = α, by showing that merge $\circ$ $\langle$even, odd$\rangle$ is a homomorphism of coalgebras from $(A^{\mathbb{N}}, \langle\text{head}, \text{tail}\rangle)$ to $(A^{\mathbb{N}}, \langle\text{head}, \text{tail}\rangle)$. The required equality then follows by uniqueness, because the identity function $id: A^{\mathbb{N}} \to A^{\mathbb{N}}$ is (trivially) a homomorphism $(A^{\mathbb{N}}, \langle\text{head}, \text{tail}\rangle) \to (A^{\mathbb{N}}, \langle\text{head}, \text{tail}\rangle)$ as well. Thus, all we have to prove is that we have a homomorphism, i.e. that

$$\langle\text{head, tail}\rangle \circ (\text{merge}\circ\langle\text{even, odd}\rangle) = (id\times(\text{merge}\circ\langle\text{even, odd}\rangle))\circ\langle\text{head, tail}\rangle.$$

This follows from the following two computations.

$$
\begin{aligned}
\text{head}(\text{merge}(\text{even}(\alpha), \text{odd}(\alpha))) &= \text{head}(\text{even}(\alpha)) \\
&= \text{head}(\alpha).
\end{aligned}
$$

And:

$$
\begin{aligned}
\text{tail}(\text{merge}(\text{even}(\alpha), \text{odd}(\alpha))) &= \text{merge}(\text{odd}(\alpha), \text{tail}(\text{even}(\alpha))) \\
&= \text{merge}(\text{odd}(\alpha), \text{even}(\text{tail}(\text{tail}(\alpha)))) \\
&= \text{merge}(\text{even}(\text{tail}(\alpha)), \text{odd}(\text{tail}(\alpha))) \\
&= (\text{merge} \circ \langle\text{even, odd}\rangle)(\text{tail}(\alpha)).
\end{aligned}
$$

In Section 2.7, an alternative method for proving facts such as the one above, will be introduced, which is based on the notion of bisimulation.

Clearly, there are formal similarities between algebra maps and coalgebra maps. We leave it to the reader to check that coalgebra maps can be composed as functions, and that the identity function on the carrier of a coalgebra is a map of coalgebras. There is also the following result, which is dual – including its proof – to Lemma 2.5.5.

Lemma 2.6.4 (i) *Final coalgebras, if they exist, are uniquely determined (up to isomorphism).*

(ii) *A final coalgebra* $Z \to T(Z)$ *is a fixed point* $Z \overset{\cong}{\to} T(Z)$ *of the functor* T. □

Final coalgebras are generalisations of greatest fixed points of monotone functions. As for initial algebras, the existence of final coalgebras is more important than their actual (internal) structure. Their use is determined entirely by their finality property, and not by their structure. Often, the existence of a final coalgebra follows from general properties of the relevant functor (and of the underlying category), see e.g. [LS81, SP82, Adá03].

The unique existence of a map of coalgebras into a final coalgebra has two aspects: existence, which gives us a principle of definition by coinduction, and uniqueness, which gives us a principle of proof by coinduction. This will be further illustrated in a series of examples, which will occupy the remainder of this section.

Example 2.6.5 It is not hard to show that the final coalgebra of the functor $T(X) = 1 + (A \times X)$ has as carrier the set $A^\infty = A^\star + A^\mathbb{N}$ of finite and infinite lists of A's. The associated 'possible next' coalgebra structure

$$\text{pn}: A^\infty \longrightarrow 1 + A \times A^\infty \quad \text{is} \quad \alpha \mapsto \begin{cases} \kappa(*) & \text{if } \alpha = \langle \, \rangle \\ \kappa'(a, \alpha') & \text{if } \alpha = a \cdot \alpha' \end{cases}$$

is final: for an arbitrary coalgebra $g: U \to 1 + (A \times U)$ of the functor T there is a unique homomorphism of coalgebras $f: U \to A^\infty$. Earlier in this section we identified such lists in A^∞ as the observable behaviour for machines whose signature of operations is described by T.

We give some examples of coinductive definitions for such finite and infinite lists. First an easy one, describing an empty list nil: $1 \to A^\infty$ as the unique coalgebra homomorphisms in the following situation.

$$
\begin{array}{ccc}
1 & \xrightarrow{\quad \text{nil} \quad} & A^\infty \\
{\scriptstyle \kappa} \downarrow & & \cong \downarrow {\scriptstyle \text{pn}} \\
1 + (A \times 1) & \xrightarrow[id + (id \times \text{nil})]{} & 1 + (A \times A^\infty)
\end{array}
$$

This determines nil as $\text{pn}^{-1} \circ \kappa$. We define a prefix operation cons: $A \times A^\infty \to A^\infty$ as $\text{pn}^{-1} \circ \kappa'$.

We can coinductively define a list inclusion function list_incl: $A^\star \to A^\infty$ via the coalgebra structure $A^\star \to 1 + (A \times A^\star)$ given by

$$\alpha \mapsto \begin{cases} \kappa(*) & \text{if } \alpha = \text{nil} \\ \kappa'(a, \beta) & \text{if } \alpha = \text{cons}(a, \beta). \end{cases}$$

We leave it to the reader to (coinductively) define an infinite list inclusion $A^\mathbb{N} \to A^\infty$.

A next, more serious example, involves the concatenation function conc: $A^\infty \times A^\infty \to A^\infty$ which yields for two lists $x, y \in A^\infty$ a new list cons$(x, y) \in A^\infty$ which contains the elements of x followed by the elements of y. Coinductively one defines conc(x, y) by laying down what the possible observations are on this new list conc(x, y). Concretely, this means that we should define what pn(conc(x, y)) is. The intuition we have of concatenation tells us that the possible next pn(conc(x, y)) is the possible next pn(x) of x if x is not the empty list (i.e. if pn$(x) \neq \kappa(*) \in 1$), and the possible next pn(y) of y otherwise. This is captured in the coalgebra structure conc_struct: $A^\infty \times A^\infty \to 1 + (A \times (A^\infty \times A^\infty))$ given by:

$$(\alpha, \beta) \mapsto \begin{cases} \kappa(*) & \text{if } \text{pn}(\alpha) = \text{pn}(\beta) = \kappa(*) \\ \kappa'(a, (\alpha', \beta)) & \text{if } \text{pn}(\alpha) = \kappa'(a, \alpha') \\ \kappa'(b, (\alpha, \beta')) & \text{if } \text{pn}(\alpha) = \kappa(*) \text{ and } \text{pn}(\beta) = \kappa'(b, \beta'). \end{cases}$$

The concatenation function conc: $A^\infty \times A^\infty \to A^\infty$ that we wished to define arises as the unique coalgebra map resulting from conc_struct.

The interested reader may wish to prove (by uniqueness!) that:

$$\text{conc}(x, \text{nil}) = x = \text{conc}(\text{nil}, x)$$
$$\text{conc}(\text{conc}(x, y), z) = \text{conc}(x, \text{conc}(y, z)).$$

This makes A^∞ a monoid. It is clearly not commutative. One can also prove that conc(cons$(a, x), y)) = $ cons$(a, $conc$(x, y))$. The easiest way is to show that applying pn on both sides yields the same result. Then we are done, since pn is an isomorphism.

Example 2.6.6 Consider the functor $T(X) = 1 + X$ from Example 2.5.4. Remember that its initial algebra is given by the set $\mathbb{N} = \{0, 1, 2, \dots, \}$ of natural numbers with cotuple of zero and successor functions as algebra structure $[0, S]: 1 + \mathbb{N} \xrightarrow{\cong} \mathbb{N}$.

The final coalgebra $\overline{\mathbb{N}} \xrightarrow{\cong} 1 + \overline{\mathbb{N}}$ of T is the set

$$\overline{\mathbb{N}} = \{0, 1, 2, \dots, \} \cup \{\infty\}$$

of natural numbers augmented with an extra element ∞. The final coalgebra structure $\overline{\mathbb{N}} \to 1 + \overline{\mathbb{N}}$ is best called a predecessor pred because it sends

$$0 \mapsto \kappa(*), \qquad n + 1 \mapsto \kappa'(n), \qquad \infty \mapsto \kappa'(\infty)$$

where we have written the coprojections κ, κ' explicitly in order to emphasise the $+$-component to which $\mathsf{pred}(x) \in 1 + \overline{\mathbb{N}}$ belongs. This final coalgebra may be obtained by taking as the constant set A a singleton set 1 for the functor $X \mapsto 1 + (A \times X)$ in the previous example. And indeed, the set $1^\infty = 1^\star + 1^{\mathbb{N}}$ is isomorphic to $\overline{\mathbb{N}}$. The 'possible next' operation $\mathsf{pn}\colon 1^\infty \to 1 + (1 \times 1^\infty)$ is then indeed the predecessor.

The defining property of this final coalgebra $\mathsf{pred}\colon \overline{\mathbb{N}} \to 1 + \overline{\mathbb{N}}$ says that for every set U with a function $f\colon U \to 1 + U$ there is a unique function $g\colon U \to \overline{\mathbb{N}}$ in the following diagram.

$$
\begin{array}{ccc}
U & \dashrightarrow{\ \ g\ \ } & \overline{\mathbb{N}} \\
{\scriptstyle f}\downarrow & & \cong\downarrow{\scriptstyle \mathsf{pred}} \\
1 + U & \dashrightarrow[\ id+g\ ] & 1 + \overline{\mathbb{N}}
\end{array}
$$

This says that g is the unique function satisfying

$$\mathsf{pred}(g(x)) = \begin{cases} \kappa(*) & \text{if } f(x) = \kappa(*) \\ \kappa'(g(x')) & \text{if } f(x) = \kappa'(x'). \end{cases}$$

This function g gives us the behaviour that one can observe about systems with one button $X \to 1 + X$, as mentioned in the first (coalgebra) example in Section 2.2.

Consider now the function $f\colon \overline{\mathbb{N}} \times \overline{\mathbb{N}} \to 1 + (\overline{\mathbb{N}} \times \overline{\mathbb{N}})$ defined by

$$f(x, y) = \begin{cases} \kappa(*) & \text{if } \mathsf{pred}(x) = \mathsf{pred}(y) = \kappa(*) \\ \kappa'(\langle x', y\rangle) & \text{if } \mathsf{pred}(x) = \kappa'(x') \\ \kappa'(\langle x, y'\rangle) & \text{if } \mathsf{pred}(x) = \kappa(*),\ \mathsf{pred}(y) = \kappa'(y'). \end{cases}$$

This f puts a coalgebra structure on $\overline{\mathbb{N}} \times \overline{\mathbb{N}}$, for the functor $X \mapsto 1 + X$ that we are considering. Hence it gives rise to a unique coalgebra homomorphism $\oplus\colon \overline{\mathbb{N}} \times \overline{\mathbb{N}} \to \overline{\mathbb{N}}$ in the following situation.

$$
\begin{array}{ccc}
\overline{\mathbb{N}} \times \overline{\mathbb{N}} & \xrightarrow{\quad \oplus \quad} & \overline{\mathbb{N}} \\
{\scriptstyle f}\downarrow & & \cong\downarrow{\scriptstyle \mathsf{pred}} \\
1 + (\overline{\mathbb{N}} \times \overline{\mathbb{N}}) & \xrightarrow[\ id+\oplus\ ]{} & 1 + \overline{\mathbb{N}}
\end{array}
$$

Hence $\oplus$ is the unique function $\overline{\mathbb{N}} \times \overline{\mathbb{N}} \to \overline{\mathbb{N}}$ with

$$\mathsf{pred}(x \oplus y) = \begin{cases} \kappa(*) & \text{if } \mathsf{pred}(x) = \kappa(*) = \mathsf{pred}(y) \\ \kappa'(x \oplus y') & \text{if } \mathsf{pred}(x) = \kappa(*), \mathsf{pred}(y) = \kappa'(y') \\ \kappa'(x' \oplus y) & \text{if } \mathsf{pred}(x) = \kappa'(x'). \end{cases}$$

It is not hard to see that $n \oplus m = n + m$ for $n, m \in \mathbb{N}$ and $n \oplus \infty = \infty = \infty \oplus n$, so that $\oplus$ behaves like addition on the 'extended' natural numbers in $\overline{\mathbb{N}}$. One easily verifies that this addition function $\oplus \colon \overline{\mathbb{N}} \times \overline{\mathbb{N}} \to \overline{\mathbb{N}}$ is the special case (for $A = 1$) of the concatenation function $\mathsf{conc} \colon A^\infty \times A^\infty \to A^\infty$ that we introduced in the previous example. This special case distinguishes itself in an important aspect: it can be shown that concatenation (or addition) $\oplus \colon \overline{\mathbb{N}} \times \overline{\mathbb{N}} \to \overline{\mathbb{N}}$ on the extended natural numbers is commutative – e.g. by uniqueness, or by bisimulation (see [Rut00] for details) – whereas concatenation $\mathsf{conc} \colon A^\infty \times A^\infty \to A^\infty$ in general is not commutative. If A has more than two elements, then $\mathsf{conc}(x, y) \neq \mathsf{conc}(y, x)$, because they give rise to different observations, e.g. for both x, y singleton sequences containing different elements.

There exist also coalgebraic treatments of the *real* numbers, see for instance [PP02].

2.7 Proofs by coinduction and bisimulation

In this section, we shall give an alternative formulation for one of the earlier proofs by coinduction. The new proof does not directly exploit (the uniqueness aspect of) finality, but makes use of the notion of *bisimulation*. We also present one new example and then formulate the general case, allowing us to prove equalities on final coalgebras via bisimulations.

We recall from Example 2.6.3 that the final coalgebra of the functor $T(X) = A \times X$ is the set of infinite lists $A^{\mathbb{N}}$ of elements of A with coalgebra structure $\langle \mathsf{head}, \mathsf{tail} \rangle$. A *bisimulation* on this carrier $A^{\mathbb{N}}$ is a relation $\mathcal{R} \subseteq A^{\mathbb{N}} \times A^{\mathbb{N}}$ satisfying

$$(\alpha, \beta) \in \mathcal{R} \Rightarrow \begin{cases} \mathsf{head}(\alpha) = \mathsf{head}(\beta), & \text{and} \\ (\mathsf{tail}(\alpha), \mathsf{tail}(\beta)) \in \mathcal{R}. \end{cases}$$

Sometimes we shall also write $\mathcal{R}(\alpha, \beta)$ for $(\alpha, \beta) \in \mathcal{R}$.

Now $A^{\mathbb{N}}$ satisfies the following *coinductive proof principle*, or cpp for short: For all α and β in $A^{\mathbb{N}}$,

$$\text{if } (\alpha, \beta) \in \mathcal{R}, \text{ for some bisimulation } R \text{ on } A^{\mathbb{N}}, \text{ then } \alpha = \beta. \qquad \text{(cpp)}$$

Before we give a proof of the principle, which will be based on the finality of $A^{\mathbb{N}}$, we illustrate its use by proving, once again, for all α in $A^{\mathbb{N}}$,

$$\mathsf{merge}(\mathsf{even}(\alpha), \mathsf{odd}(\alpha)) = \alpha.$$

To this end, define the following relation on $A^{\mathbb{N}}$:

$$\mathcal{R} = \{(\mathsf{merge}(\mathsf{even}(\alpha), \mathsf{odd}(\alpha)), \alpha) \mid \alpha \in A^{\mathbb{N}}\}.$$

In order to prove the above equality it is, by the coinductive proof principle (cpp), sufficient to show that R is a bisimulation. First, for each pair $(\mathsf{merge}(\mathsf{even}(\alpha), \mathsf{odd}(\alpha)), \alpha) \in \mathcal{R}$ we have equal head's:

$$\mathsf{head}(\mathsf{merge}(\mathsf{even}(\alpha), \mathsf{odd}(\alpha))) = \mathsf{head}(\mathsf{even}(\alpha))$$
$$= \mathsf{head}(\alpha).$$

And secondly, if we have a pair $(\mathsf{merge}(\mathsf{even}(\alpha), \mathsf{odd}(\alpha)), \alpha)$ in $\mathcal{R}$, then applying tail on both sides yields a new pair in $\mathcal{R}$, since we can rewrite, using that $\mathsf{odd} = \mathsf{even} \circ \mathsf{tail}$,

$$\mathsf{tail}(\mathsf{merge}(\mathsf{even}(\alpha), \mathsf{odd}(\alpha))) = \mathsf{merge}(\mathsf{odd}(\alpha), \mathsf{tail}(\mathsf{even}(\alpha)))$$
$$= \mathsf{merge}(\mathsf{even}(\mathsf{tail}(\alpha)), \mathsf{even}(\mathsf{tail}(\mathsf{tail}(\alpha))))$$
$$= \mathsf{merge}(\mathsf{even}(\mathsf{tail}(\alpha)), \mathsf{odd}(\mathsf{tail}(\alpha))).$$

For a proof of the cpp, let $\mathcal{R}$ be any bisimulation on $A^{\mathbb{N}}$. If we consider $\mathcal{R}$ as a set (of pairs), then it can be supplied with an $A \times (-)$-coalgebra structure by defining a function

$$\gamma : \mathcal{R} \longrightarrow A \times \mathcal{R} \qquad (\alpha, \beta) \mapsto (\mathsf{head}(\alpha), (\mathsf{tail}(\alpha), \mathsf{tail}(\beta))).$$

Note that γ is well-defined since $(\mathsf{tail}(\alpha), \mathsf{tail}(\beta))$ is in $\mathcal{R}$, because $\mathcal{R}$ is a bisimulation. Now it is straightforward to show that the two projection functions

$$\pi_1 : \mathcal{R} \longrightarrow A^{\mathbb{N}} \quad \text{and} \quad \pi_2 : \mathcal{R} \longrightarrow A^{\mathbb{N}}$$

are homomorphisms of coalgebras from $(\mathcal{R}, \gamma)$ to $(A^{\mathbb{N}}, \langle \mathsf{head}, \mathsf{tail} \rangle)$. Therefore it follows from the finality (cf. Definition 2.6.2) of $A^{\mathbb{N}}$ that $\pi_1 = \pi_2$. That is, if $(\alpha, \beta) \in \mathcal{R}$ then $\alpha = \beta$.

The above definition of a bisimulation is a special instance of the following categorical definition of bisimulation, which was introduced in [AM89], and which applies to coalgebras of arbitrary functors T.

Definition 2.7.1 Let T be a functor. Take two T-coalgebras $(X, \alpha_X : X \to T(X))$ and $(Y, \alpha_Y : Y \to T(Y))$. A T-*bisimulation* between (X, α_X) and (Y, α_Y) is a relation $\mathcal{R} \subseteq X \times Y$ for which there exists a T-coalgebra structure $\gamma : \mathcal{R} \to T(\mathcal{R})$ such that the two projection functions $\pi_1 : \mathcal{R} \to X$ and

$\pi_2 \colon \mathcal{R} \to Y$ are homomorphisms of T-coalgebras:

$$
\begin{array}{ccccc}
X & \xleftarrow{\quad \pi_1 \quad} & \mathcal{R} & \xrightarrow{\quad \pi_2 \quad} & Y \\
{\scriptstyle \alpha_X} \big\downarrow & & {\scriptstyle \gamma} \big\downarrow & & \big\downarrow {\scriptstyle \alpha_Y} \\
T(X) & \xleftarrow[\quad T(\pi_1) \quad]{} & T(\mathcal{R}) & \xrightarrow[\quad T(\pi_2) \quad]{} & T(Y)
\end{array}
$$

We call a bisimulation between a coalgebra $(X,\ \alpha_X)$ and itself a bisimulation *on* X. And we use the following notation:

$$x \sim x' \iff \text{there exists a } T\text{-bisimulation } \mathcal{R} \text{ on } X \text{ with } (x, x') \in \mathcal{R}.$$

The general formulation of the coinduction proof principle is now as follows.

Theorem 2.7.2 *Let* $c \colon Z \xrightarrow{\ \cong\ } T(Z)$ *be the final T-coalgebra. For all z and z' in Z,*

$$\text{if } z \sim z' \text{ then } z = z'. \qquad\qquad (cpp)$$

As in the example above, the proof of this principle is immediate by finality: both the projections π_1 and π_2 are homomorphisms from $(\mathcal{R}, \gamma)$ to the final coalgebra (Z, c). By finality, $\pi_1 = \pi_2$, which proves the theorem.

This general version of the coinduction proof principle is surprisingly powerful, notwithstanding the fact that the proof of cpp is almost trivial. The reader is referred to [Rut00] for further examples of definitions and proofs by coinduction. In Section 2.8, we shall see how this coalgebraic notion of bisimulation coincides with the classical notion of Park and Milner for the case of processes.

There exist other formalisations of the notion of bisimulation: in [HJ98] a bisimulation is described as a coalgebra in a category of relations, for a suitably lifted functor (associated with the original functor T); in the context of (coalgebraic) modal logic the notion of behavioural equivalence if often used, see e.g. [CP07, Kli07]; in [JNW96], bisimulations occur as spans of so-called open maps; and in [Bar03, CHL03], stronger versions of bisimulation (and coinduction) are given called λ-bisimulations. But in a set-theoretic context, the above definition seems to be most convenient. Simulations, or 'bisimulations' in one direction only, are described in [HJ04].

The above categorical definition of bisimulation can be seen to be the formal (categorical) dual of the notion of *congruence* on algebras, which for T-algebras (U, a) and (V, b) can be defined as a relation $\mathcal{R} \subseteq U \times V$ for which there exists a T-algebra structure $c \colon T(\mathcal{R}) \to \mathcal{R}$ such that the two projection functions

$\pi_1 \colon \mathcal{R} \to U$ and $\pi_2 \colon \mathcal{R} \to V$ are homomorphisms of T-algebras:

$$
\begin{array}{ccc}
T(U) & \xleftarrow{\;T(\pi_1)\;} T(\mathcal{R}) \xrightarrow{\;T(\pi_2)\;} & T(V) \\
\scriptstyle a \downarrow & \scriptstyle c \downarrow & \downarrow \scriptstyle b \\
U & \xleftarrow{\;\pi_1\;} \mathcal{R} \xrightarrow{\;\pi_2\;} & V
\end{array}
$$

Using the above notions of congruence on algebras and bisimulation on coalgebras, the duality between induction and coinduction can be succinctly expressed as follows. For *initial algebras* (A, a), we have:

$$
\text{for every congruence relation } \mathcal{R} \subseteq A \times A, \quad \Delta_A \subseteq \mathcal{R}
$$

where $\Delta_A = \{(a, a) \mid a \in A\}$ is the diagonal on A. Dually, for *final coalgebras* (Z, z) we have the following:

$$
\text{for every bisimulation relation } \mathcal{R} \subseteq Z \times Z, \quad \mathcal{R} \subseteq \Delta_Z.
$$

One can show that the above property of initial algebras is precisely the familiar induction principle on algebras such as the natural numbers. (The above property of final coalgebras is trivially equivalent to the formulation of Theorem 2.7.2.) We refer the reader to [Rut00, Section 13] for further details.

2.8 Processes coalgebraically

In this section, we shall present labelled transition systems as coalgebras of a certain 'behaviour' functor B. We shall see that the corresponding coalgebraic notion of bisimulation coincides with the classical notion of Park and Milner. Finally, we shall introduce the final coalgebra for the functor B, the elements of which can be seen as (canonical representatives of) *processes*.

A (possibly non-deterministic) transition system $(X, A, \longrightarrow_X)$ consists of a set X of states, a set A of transition labels, and a transition relation $\longrightarrow_X \subseteq X \times A \times X$. As usual, we write $x \xrightarrow{a}_X x'$ for transitions $(x, a, x') \in \longrightarrow_X$.

Consider the functor B defined by

$$
B(X) = \mathcal{P}(A \times X) = \{V \mid V \subseteq A \times X\}
$$

A labeled transition system $(X, A, \longrightarrow_X)$ can be identified with a B-coalgebra $(X, \alpha_X \colon X \to B(X))$, by putting

$$
(a, x') \in \alpha_X(x) \quad \Longleftrightarrow \quad x \xrightarrow{a}_X x'.
$$

In other words, the class of all labelled transition systems coincides with the class of all B-coalgebras. Let $(X, A, \longrightarrow_X)$ and $(Y, A, \longrightarrow_Y)$ be two labelled transition systems with the same set A of labels. An interesting question is what a coalgebra homomorphism between these two transition systems (as coalgebras (X, α_X) and (Y, α_Y)) is, in terms of the transition structures $\longrightarrow_X$ and $\longrightarrow_Y$. Per definition, a B-homomorphism $f: (X, \alpha_X) \to (Y, \alpha_Y)$ is a function $f: X \to Y$ such that $B(f) \circ \alpha_X = \alpha_Y \circ f$, where the function $B(f)$, also denoted by $\mathcal{P}(A \times f)$, is defined by

$$B(f)(V) = \mathcal{P}(A \times f)(V) = \{\langle a, f(s)\rangle \mid \langle a, s\rangle \in V\}.$$

One can easily prove that the equality $B(f) \circ \alpha_X = \alpha_Y \circ f$ is equivalent to the following two conditions, for all $x \in X$:

(1) for all x' in X, if $x \xrightarrow{a}_X x'$ then $f(x) \xrightarrow{a}_Y f(x')$;
(2) for all y in Y, if $f(x) \xrightarrow{a}_Y y$ then there is an x' in X with $x \xrightarrow{a}_X x'$ and $f(x') = y$.

Thus a homomorphism is a function that preserves and reflects transitions. This notion is quite standard, but sometimes only preservation is required, see e.g. [JNW96].

There is the following well-known notion of bisimulation for transition systems [Mil89, Par81]: a bisimulation between transition systems X and Y (as above) is a relation $\mathcal{R} \subseteq X \times Y$ satisfying, for all $(x, y) \in \mathcal{R}$,

(i) for all x' in X, if $x \xrightarrow{a}_X x'$ then there is y' in Y with $y \xrightarrow{a}_Y y'$ and (x', y') $\in \mathcal{R}$;
(ii) for all y' in Y, if $y \xrightarrow{a}_Y y'$ then there is x' in X with $x \xrightarrow{a}_X x'$ and (x', y') $\in \mathcal{R}$.

For the relation between this notion of bisimulation and the notion of zig-zag relation from modal logic, see Chapter 1.

The coalgebraic notion of B-bisimulation (Definition 2.7.1) coincides with the above definition: If $\mathcal{R}$ is a B-bisimulation then conditions (i) and (ii) follow from the fact that both π_1 and π_2 are homomorphisms. Conversely, any relation $\mathcal{R}$ satisfying (i) and (ii) above can be seen to be a B-bisimulation by defining a coalgebra structure $\gamma : \mathcal{R} \to B(\mathcal{R})$ as follows:

$$\gamma(x, y) = \{ <a, (x', y') > \mid x \xrightarrow{a}_X x' \text{ and } y \xrightarrow{a}_Y y' \text{ and } (x', y') \in \mathcal{R} \}.$$

One then readily proves that π_1 and π_2 are homomorphisms.

A concrete example of a bisimulation relation between two transition systems X and Y is the following. Consider two systems X and Y:

$$X = \begin{pmatrix} x_0 \xrightarrow{\ b\ } x_1 \xrightarrow{\ b\ } \cdots \\ \quad a \Big\downarrow \qquad a \Big\downarrow \qquad \\ x_0' \qquad x_1' \qquad \end{pmatrix} \qquad Y = \begin{pmatrix} \overset{\curvearrowright}{y} \enspace b \\ a \Big\downarrow \\ y' \end{pmatrix}.$$

The relation

$$\{ (x_i, x_j) \mid i, j \geq 0 \} \ \cup \ \{ (x_i', x_j') \mid i, j \geq 0 \}$$

is then a bisimulation on X. And

$$\mathcal{R} = \{ (x_i, y) \mid i \geq 0 \} \ \cup \ \{ (x_i', y') \mid i \geq 0 \}$$

is a bisimulation between X and Y. The latter relation $\mathcal{R}$ is called a *functional* bisimulation because it is the graph

$$\{ (x, f(x)) \mid x \in X \}$$

of a homomorphism $f : X \to Y$ defined by $f(x_i) = y$ and $f(x_i') = y'$. Note that there exists no homomorphism in the reverse direction from Y to X.

For cardinality reasons, a final B-coalgebra cannot exist: by Lemma 2.6.4(ii), any final coalgebra is a fixed point: $X \cong \mathcal{P}(A \times X)$, and such a set does not exist because the cardinality of $\mathcal{P}(A \times X)$ is strictly greater than that of X (for non-empty sets of labels A). Therefore we restrict to so-called *finitely branching* transition systems, satisfying, for all states s,

$$\{ \langle a, s \rangle \mid s \xrightarrow{a}_X s' \} \text{ is finite.}$$

Such systems can be identified with coalgebras of the functor

$$B_f(X) = \mathcal{P}_f(A \times X) = \{ V \subseteq A \times X \mid V \text{ is finite} \}.$$

For this functor, a final coalgebra *does* exist. The proof, which is a bit technical, is due to Barr [Bar93] (see also [RT94, Rut00]), and is omitted here (cf. the discussion in Section 2.2).

In what follows, let (Π, π) be the final B_f-coalgebra, which is unique up to isomorphism. Borrowing the terminology of concurrency theory, we call the elements of Π *processes* and denote them by P, Q, R. As before, we shall denote transitions by

$$P \xrightarrow{a} Q \iff (a, Q) \in \pi(P).$$

Being a final coalgebra, (Π, π) satisfies the coinduction proof principle (Theorem 2.7.2): for all $P, Q \in \Pi$,

$$\text{if } P \sim Q \quad \text{then } P = Q.$$

The following theorem shows that we can view the elements of Π as canonical, minimal representatives of (finitely branching) labelled transition systems.

Theorem 2.8.1 *Let* (X, α_X) *be a* B_f-*coalgebra, that is, a finitely branching labelled transition system. By finality, there is a unique homomorphism* $f :$ $(X, \alpha_X) \to (\Pi, \pi)$. *It satisfies, for all* $x, x' \in X$:

$$x \sim x' \iff f(x) = f(x').$$

Proof The implication from left to right follows from the fact that homomorphisms are (functional) bisimulations and the coinduction proof principle. For the implication from right to left, note that

$$\mathcal{R} = \{(x, x') \in X \times X \mid f(x) = f(x')\}$$

is a bisimulation relation on X.   □

In conclusion of the present section, we define a number of operators on processes by coinduction, and then prove various of their properties by the coinduction proof principle.

As a first example, we define a non-deterministic merge operation on processes. To this end, we supply $\Pi \times \Pi$ with a B_f-coalgebra structure

$$\mu : \Pi \times \Pi \to B_f(\Pi \times \Pi)$$

defined by

$$\mu\langle P, Q \rangle = \{\langle a, \langle P', Q \rangle\rangle \mid P \overset{a}{\to} P'\} \cup \{\langle a, \langle P, Q' \rangle\rangle \mid Q \overset{a}{\to} Q'\}. \quad (2.5)$$

By finality of Π, there exists a unique B_f-homomorphism

$$\mathsf{merge} : \Pi \times \Pi \to \Pi.$$

We shall use the following standard notation:

$$P \mid Q \equiv \mathsf{merge}\langle P, Q \rangle.$$

It follows from the fact that merge is a homomorphism of transition systems, i.e. from

$$B_f(\mathsf{merge}) \circ \mu = \pi \circ \mathsf{merge}$$

that it satisfies precisely the following rules:

$$\frac{P \stackrel{a}{\to} P'}{P \mid Q \stackrel{a}{\to} P' \mid Q} \quad \text{and} \quad \frac{Q \stackrel{a}{\to} Q'}{P \mid Q \stackrel{a}{\to} P \mid Q'}. \tag{2.6}$$

The function $\mid$ satisfies a number of familiar properties. Let $\mathbf{0}$ be the *terminated* process: formally,

$$\mathbf{0} = \pi^{-1}(\emptyset)$$

for which no transitions exist. The following equalities

(1) $\mathbf{0} \mid P = P$;
(2) $P \mid Q = Q \mid P$;
(3) $(P \mid Q) \mid R = P \mid (Q \mid R)$,

are a consequence of (cpp) and the fact that the following relations are bisimulations on Π:

(a) $\{(\mathbf{0} \mid P, P) \mid P \in \Pi\}$;
(b) $\{(P \mid Q, Q \mid P) \mid P, Q \in \Pi\}$;
(c) $\{((P \mid Q) \mid R, P \mid (Q \mid R)) \mid P, Q, R \in \Pi\}$.

For instance, the first relation (a) is a bisimulation because we have transitions, for any P in Π:

$$\mathbf{0} \mid P \stackrel{a}{\to} \mathbf{0} \mid P' \quad \text{if and only if} \quad P \stackrel{a}{\to} P',$$

and $(\mathbf{0} \mid P', P')$ is again in the relation. For the second relation (b), consider a pair of processes $(P \mid Q, Q \mid P)$, and suppose that we have a transition step

$$P \mid Q \stackrel{a}{\to} R,$$

for some process R in Π. (The other case, where a first step of $Q \mid P$ is considered, is proved in exactly the same way.) It follows from the definition of merge that one of the following two situations applies: either there exists a transition $P \stackrel{a}{\to} P'$ and $R = P' \mid Q$, or there exists a transition $Q \stackrel{a}{\to} Q'$ and $R = P \mid Q'$. Let us consider the first situation, the second being similar. If $P \stackrel{a}{\to} P'$ then it follows again from the rules above that there exists also a transition

$$Q \mid P \stackrel{a}{\to} Q \mid P'.$$

But then we have mimicked the transition step of $P \mid Q$ by a transition step of $Q \mid P$, in such a way that the resulting processes are again in the relation:

$$(P' \mid Q, \; Q \mid P')$$

is again a pair in relation (b). This shows that also relation (b) is a bisimulation. For (c), the same kind of argument can be given.

Let us return for a moment to the coinductive definition of the merge operator above. There is a very close correspondence between the two transition rules (2.6) and the definition (2.5) of the coalgebra structure μ on $\Pi \times \Pi$. In fact, we could take the transition rules as a specification of the merge operator we were after; then use these rules to define μ as above; and finally define the merge operator by the homomorphism into Π, as we did above.

We illustrate this approach by the coinductive definition of a number of process operators at the same time, which together constitute a simple CCS-like process calculus. Let the set Exp of syntactic expressions (denoted by E, F, etc.) be given by

$$
\begin{aligned}
E ::= \;& \hat{0} \\
\mid \;& \hat{a} \quad \text{(for every } a \in A) \\
\mid \;& \hat{P} \quad \text{(for every } P \in \Pi) \\
\mid \;& E \hat{\upharpoonright} F \\
\mid \;& E \hat{+} F \\
\mid \;& E \hat{\,;\,} F.
\end{aligned}
$$

Here we use the symbol *hat* to indicate that we are dealing with syntactic entities. For instance, for every process $P \in \Pi$, the set Exp contains a syntactic expression $\hat{P}$. Thus we have mappings $A \to Exp$ and $\Pi \to Exp$.

Next we define a transition relation on Exp by the following axioms and rules:

$$\hat{a} \xrightarrow{a} \hat{0}$$

$$\hat{P} \xrightarrow{a} \hat{Q} \iff P \xrightarrow{a} Q \quad (\iff (a, Q) \in \pi(P))$$

$$\frac{E \xrightarrow{a} E'}{E \hat{+} F \xrightarrow{a} E'} \qquad \frac{F \xrightarrow{a} F'}{E \hat{+} F \xrightarrow{a} F'}$$

$$\frac{E \xrightarrow{a} E'}{E \hat{\upharpoonright} F \xrightarrow{a} E' \hat{\upharpoonright} F} \qquad \frac{F \xrightarrow{a} F'}{E \hat{\upharpoonright} F \xrightarrow{a} E \hat{\upharpoonright} F'}$$

$$\frac{E \xrightarrow{a} E'}{E \hat{\,;\,} F \xrightarrow{a} E' \hat{\,;\,} F} \qquad \frac{E \not\xrightarrow{} \text{ and } F \xrightarrow{a} F'}{E \hat{\,;\,} F \xrightarrow{a} F'}.$$

Having such a transition structure on Exp, we can define a B_f-coalgebra structure $\gamma : Exp \to B_f(Exp)$ by

$$\gamma(E) = \{\langle a, F \rangle \mid E \xrightarrow{a} F\}.$$

Note that by construction $\hat{\ } : \Pi \to Exp$ is now a coalgebra homomorphism.

By finality of Π, there exists a unique homomorphism $h : (Exp, \gamma) \to (\Pi, \pi)$ which assigns to each syntactic expression E a corresponding process $h(E) \in \Pi$. We can use it to define semantic operators on Π corresponding to the syntactic operators on Exp, as follows:

$$
\begin{array}{ccc}
\mathbf{0} & \stackrel{\text{def}}{=} & h(\hat{0}) \\
\mathbf{a} & \stackrel{\text{def}}{=} & h(\hat{a}) \\
P \mid Q & \stackrel{\text{def}}{=} & h(\hat{P} \,\hat{\mid}\, \hat{Q}) \\
P + Q & \stackrel{\text{def}}{=} & h(\hat{P} \,\hat{+}\, \hat{Q}) \\
P ; Q & \stackrel{\text{def}}{=} & h(\hat{P} \,\hat{;}\, \hat{Q}).
\end{array}
\tag{2.7}
$$

In this manner, we have obtained three operators on processes P and Q: the merge $P \mid Q$; the choice $P + Q$; and the sequential composition $P; Q$. (It is straightforward to check that the present definition of the merge coincides with the one given earlier.) The constant $\mathbf{0}$ is defined as the process that cannot make any transitions (since the transition relation on Exp does not specify any transitions for $\hat{0}$). As a consequence, $\mathbf{0}$ coincides with the terminated process (also denoted by $\mathbf{0}$) introduced earlier. The constant $\mathbf{a}$ denotes a process that can take a single a-step to $\mathbf{0}$ and then terminates. Furthermore it is worth noticing that the homomorphism h acts as the identity on processes; that is, $h(\hat{P}) = P$, which can be easily proved by (ccp) or directly by finality of Π. Also note that it is possible to add recursive process definitions to the above, see for instance [RT94]. This would allow us to use guarded equations such as $X = \hat{a} \,\hat{;}\, X \,\hat{+}\, \hat{b}$, which would define a process $P = h(X)$ with transitions $P \xrightarrow{a} P$ and $P \xrightarrow{b} \mathbf{0}$.

In the above, we have exploited the finality of the set Π of all processes to define constants and operators by coinduction. Essentially the same procedure can be followed to define operators on various other structures such as, for instance, formal languages and power series [Rut03] and binary trees [SR07].

A question that naturally arises is under which conditions the above type of definition scheme works, that is, when does it uniquely determine the operators one wants to define. As it turns out, this very much depends on the syntactic shape of the defining equations or, in terms of the transition relation defined on Exp above, on the shape of the axioms and rules used to specify the transition relation. There is in fact a close relationship between the various syntactic transition system specification *formats* studied in the literature (such as GSOS, tyft-tyxt, and the like), on the one hand, and well-formed coinductive definition schemes, on the other hand.

In conclusion of this section, let us indicate how the above construction of semantic operators out of operational specifications can be put into a general categorical perspective. First of all, we observe that the set Exp of expressions is the initial algebra of the functor

$$T(X) = 1 + A + \Pi + (X \times X) + (X \times X) + (X \times X)$$

where the constituents on the right correspond, respectively, to the constant symbol $\hat{0}$; the elements $\hat{a}$ with $a \in A$; the elements $\hat{P}$ with $P \in \Pi$; and the three operations of merge, choice, and sequential composition. Above we had already supplied the set Exp with a B_f-coalgebra structure (Exp, γ). Therefore Exp is a so-called *bialgebra*: a set which has both an algebra and a coalgebra structure. Similarly, the definition of the semantic operators above (2.7) supplies Π, which was defined as the final B_f-coalgebra, with a T-algebra structure, turning it thereby into a bialgebra as well. The relationship between the T-algebra and B_f-coalgebra structures on Exp and Π is provided by the fact that the mapping h above is *both* a homomorphism of B_f-coalgebras *and* a homomorphism of T-algebras. All of which can be pleasantly expressed by the following diagram:

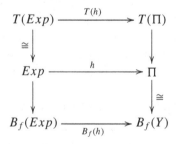

The interplay between algebra (syntactic operators) and coalgebra (their behaviour) has become an important topic of research within the coalgebra community. For further reading see for instance [RT94] and [TP97, Bar03, Jac06]. In these latter references, natural transformations called *distributive laws* are used to relate the syntax functor and the behaviour functor. Compositionality then comes for free. Other examples of the interplay between algebraic and coalgebraic structure include recent generalisations of Kleene's theorem and Kleene algebra to large families of coalgebras, including processes, Mealy machines, and weighted and probabilistic systems [BRS09, BBRS09].

2.9 Trace semantics, coalgebraically

Let $\longrightarrow \subseteq X \times A \times X$ be a transition system as in the previous section. As we have seen, it may be written as a coalgebra $(X, \alpha \colon X \to \mathcal{P}(A \times X))$. An execution is a sequence of consecutive transition steps:

$$x_0 \xrightarrow{a_0} x_1 \xrightarrow{a_1} x_2 \xrightarrow{a_2} \cdots$$

A trace of this transition system is then a sequence $\langle a_0, a_1, a_2, \ldots \rangle$ of actions occurring in such an execution.

This section describes a systematic way to capture such traces coalgebraically, following [HJ05, HJS07], which is general and generic. Here we concentrate on the powerset case. This involves both initial algebras and final coalgebras, in different 'universes'. The description involves a number of preparatory steps.

Finite executions and traces Our description applies to finite traces. In order to capture them we introduce an additional symbol $\checkmark$ for successful termination. We can do so by considering coalgebras of a slightly different functor, namely $\mathcal{P}(1 + A \times X)$ with additional singleton set $1 = \{\checkmark\}$. For a coalgebra $\alpha \colon X \to \mathcal{P}(1 + A \times X)$ we then write $x \xrightarrow{a} x'$ if $(a, x') \in \alpha(x)$ and $x \to \checkmark$ if $\checkmark \in \alpha(x)$.

We shall write $F(X) = 1 + A \times X$ for the functor inside the powerset. Hence we concentrate on $\mathcal{P}F$-coalgebras.

A finite execution is one that ends with $\checkmark$, as in $x_0 \xrightarrow{a_0} x_1 \xrightarrow{a_1} \cdots \xrightarrow{a_{n-1}} x_n \to \checkmark$. A trace is called finite if it comes from such a finite execution. We shall write $\mathrm{tr}(x)$ for the set of finite traces of executions that start in $x \in X$. This yields a function $\mathrm{tr} \colon X \to \mathcal{P}(A^\star)$ where $A^\star$ is the set of finite sequences of elements of A. Notice that $A^\star$ is the initial algebra of the functor F, see Example 2.5.6.

A category of relations A map of the form $X \to \mathcal{P}(Y)$ can be seen as a 'non-deterministic' function that yields a set of outcomes in Y for a single input element from X. It may be identified with a relation between X and Y, i.e. with a subset of the product $X \times Y$. We can understand such a function/relation as an arrow in a category *Rel* of sets and relations.

This category *Rel* has ordinary sets as objects. Morphism $X \to Y$ in *Rel* are ordinary functions $X \to \mathcal{P}(Y)$. They can be composed via 'relational' composition. For arrows $f \colon X \to Y$ and $g \colon Y \to Z$ in *Rel* we have to form $g \circ f \colon X \to Z$. As ordinary functions we define $g \circ f \colon X \to \mathcal{P}(Z)$ for $f \colon X \to \mathcal{P}(Y)$ and $g \colon Y \to \mathcal{P}(Z)$, by:

$$(g \circ f)(x) = \bigcup \{g(y) \mid y \in f(x)\}. \tag{2.8}$$

Notice that our notation is now (deliberately) ambiguous, depending on the category (or universe) in which we work. An arrow $X \to Y$ in *Set* is an ordinary function from X to Y, but an arrow $X \to Y$ in *Rel* is a 'non-deterministic' function $X \to \mathcal{P}(Y)$.

It is not hard to see that the singleton map $\{-\}\colon X \to \mathcal{P}(X)$ forms the identity map $X \to X$ on the object X in the category *Rel*. Explicitly, $\{-\} \circ f = f$ and $g \circ \{-\} = g$, for relational composition $\circ$.

There is an obvious functor $J\colon Set \to Rel$ that sends a set X to itself and a function $f\colon X \to Y$ to its graph relation $\{(x, f(x)) \mid x \in X\}$. This graph may be identified with the composite $X \xrightarrow{f} Y \xrightarrow{\{-\}} \mathcal{P}(Y)$.

Lifting the functor For the main result of this section we need to consider a $\mathcal{P}F$-coalgebra $(X, \alpha\colon X \to \mathcal{P}(F(X)))$ as an F-coalgebra $(X, \alpha\colon X \to F(X))$, by moving to the category *Rel*. Indeed, a map $X \to \mathcal{P}(F(X))$ is an arrow $X \to F(X)$ in *Rel*. In order to understand it as coalgebra we need to know that F is – or lifts to – a functor $\overline{F}\colon Rel \to Rel$. It is obvious how such lifting works on objects, namely $\overline{F}(X) = F(X)$, but how it works on morphisms in *Rel* requires some care.

For an arrow $X \to Y$ in *Rel* we need to construct a new map $FX \to FY$ in *Rel*. That is, a function $f\colon X \to \mathcal{P}(Y)$ yields a function $\overline{F}(f)\colon FX \to \mathcal{P}(F(Y))$, defined as follows.

$$
\begin{array}{ccc}
1 + A \times X & \xrightarrow{\;\;\overline{F}(f)\;\;} & \mathcal{P}(1 + A \times Y) \\
\checkmark & \longmapsto & \{\checkmark\} \\
(a, x) & \longmapsto & \{(a, y) \mid y \in f(x)\}.
\end{array}
$$

It is not hard to check that this 'lifting' of $F\colon Set \to Set$ to $\overline{F}\colon Rel \to Rel$ indeed preserves identities and composition – from *Rel*. It yields a commuting diagram:

$$
\begin{array}{ccc}
Rel & \xrightarrow{\;\;\overline{F}\;\;} & Rel \\
{\scriptstyle J}\big\uparrow & & \big\uparrow{\scriptstyle J} \\
Set & \xrightarrow{\;\;F\;\;} & Set
\end{array}
\qquad (2.9)
$$

The trace theorem The following result (from [HJ05]) combines initial algebras and final coalgebras for a description of trace semantics.

Theorem 2.9.1 *The initial F-algebra in Set yields a final $\overline{F}$-coalgebra in Rel.* $\square$

There are several ways to prove this result. A particularly snappy proof is presented in [HJS07, theorem 3.8]; it uses adjunctions and is therefore outside the scope of this chapter. Here we omit the proof and concentrate on the relevance of this result for trace semantics.

So we first spell out what is actually stated in the theorem. Recall from Example 2.5.6 that the initial algebra of the functor $F = 1 + A \times (-)$ is the set $A^\star$ of finite sequences of elements in A with operations [nil, cons]: $1 + A \times A^\star \xrightarrow{\cong} A^\star$. Since this initial algebra is an isomorphism, we can consider its inverse $A^\star \xrightarrow{\cong} F(A^\star)$, formally as an isomorphism in the category *Set*. By applying the functor $J: Set \to Rel$ from the diagram (2.9) this yields an isomorphism in *Rel*

$$A^\star = J(A^\star) \xrightarrow{\cong} J(F(A^\star)) = \overline{F}(J(A^\star)) = \overline{F}(A^\star),$$

which is an $\overline{F}$-coalgebra (recall that $\overline{F}$ is F and J the identity on objects/sets). The theorem claims that this map is the final $\overline{F}$-coalgebra in *Rel*.

In order to clarify this switch of categories we go a bit deeper into the details. Let's write $\beta = [\text{nil}, \text{cons}]^{-1}: A^\star \xrightarrow{\cong} 1 + A \times A^\star = F(A^\star)$ for the inverse of the initial algebra (in *Set*). It yields $J(\beta) = \{-\} \circ \beta: A^\star \to \mathcal{P}(F(A^\star))$. We claim that this β is an isomorphism $A^\star \to \overline{F}(A^\star)$, an isomorphism *in the category Rel!* This $J(\beta)$ may not look like an isomorphism, but we have to keep in mind that composition in *Rel*, as described in (2.8), is different from composition in *Set*. In general, for an isomorphism $f: Y \to X$ in *Set* we have in *Rel*:

$$\begin{aligned}
\left(J(f) \circ J(f^{-1}) \right)(x) &= \bigcup \left\{ J(f)(y) \mid y \in J(f^{-1})(x) \right\} && \text{by (2.8)} \\
&= \bigcup \left\{ \{f(y)\} \mid y \in \{f^{-1}(x)\} \right\} \\
&= \{f(f^{-1}(x))\} \\
&= \{x\} \\
&= id_X(x)
\end{aligned}$$

where the latter identity map id_X is the identity in *Rel*, given by the singleton map.

Assume now that we have a transition system $\alpha: X \to \mathcal{P}(1 + A \times X)$ as in the beginning of this section. We may now understand it as an $\overline{F}$-coalgebra $X \to \overline{F}(X)$. We shall do so and continue to work in the category *Rel*. The finality claimed in the theorem then yields a unique homomorphism in:

$$
\begin{array}{ccc}
X & \xrightarrow{\;\;\mathsf{tr}\;\;} & A^{\star} \\
\alpha \downarrow & & \downarrow \cong \\
\overline{F}(X) & \xrightarrow{\;\overline{F}(\mathsf{tr})\;} & \overline{F}(A^{\star})
\end{array}
$$

It is essential that this is a diagram in the category *Rel*. We shall unravel what commutation means, using composition as in (2.8). The composite $\overline{F}(\mathsf{tr}) \circ \alpha$ is the relation on $X \times (1 + A \times A^{\star})$ consisting of:

$$\{(x, \checkmark) \mid \checkmark \in \alpha(x)\} \;\cup\; \{(x, (a, \sigma)) \mid \exists x'.\, (a, x') \in \alpha(x) \wedge \sigma \in \mathsf{tr}(x')\}.$$

The other composition, $\cong \circ\, \mathsf{tr}$, yields the relation:

$$\{(x, \checkmark) \mid \mathsf{nil} \in \mathsf{tr}(x)\} \;\cup\; \{(x, (a, \sigma)) \mid \mathsf{cons}(a, \sigma) \in \mathsf{tr}(x)\}.$$

The equality of these sets yields the defining clauses for trace semantics, namely:

$$
\begin{aligned}
\mathsf{nil} \in \mathsf{tr}(x) &\iff x \to \checkmark \\
\mathsf{cons}(a, \sigma) \in \mathsf{tr}(x) &\iff \exists x'.\, x \xrightarrow{a} x' \wedge \sigma \in \mathsf{tr}(x'),
\end{aligned}
$$

where we have used the transition notation for the coalgebra α.

What we thus see is that the abstract idea of finality (for coalgebras) makes sense not only in the standard category/universe of sets and functions, but also in the world of sets and relations. This genericity can only be formulated and appreciated via the language of categories. It demonstrates clearly why the theory of coalgebras relies so heavily on category theory.

Theorem 2.9.1 allows for considerable generalisation. The crucial aspect of the powerset that is used is that it is a so-called monad, with the category *Rel* as its 'Kleisli' category. The result may be formulated more generally for suitable monads and functors F, see [HJS07]. It can then also be applied to probabilistic transition systems, and even to a combination of probabilistic and possibilistic (non-deterministic) systems (see [Jac08]).

2.10 Exercises

Exercise 2.10.1 Use initiality to define a function $sum : \mathbb{N}^{\star} \to \mathbb{N}$ such that $sum(\mathsf{nil}) = 0$ and

$$sum(a_1, \ldots, a_n) = a_1 + \cdots + a_n$$

for all $(a_1, \ldots, a_n) \in \mathbb{N}^{\star}$.

Exercise 2.10.2 Use initiality to define a function $L : \mathbb{N} \to \mathbb{N}^*$ such that

$$L(n) = (0, 1, 2, \ldots, n)$$

for all $n \geq 0$. Same question, now for $H : \mathbb{N} \to \mathbb{N}^*$ such that $H(0) = \langle \, \rangle$ and

$$H(n) = (0, 1, 2, \ldots, n - 1)$$

for all $n \geq 1$.

Exercise 2.10.3 A preorder $(P, \leq)$ can be viewed as a category. Objects are the elements of P and we have an arrow $p \to q$ iff $p \leq q$. An order-preserving *function* $f : P \to P$ can then be seen as a *functor* from the category P to itself. Show that least fixed points of f are precisely the initial algebras and that greatest fixed points correspond to final coalgebras.

Exercise 2.10.4 The set of (finite) binary trees with (node) labels in a given set A can be defined as the initial algebra BT_A of the functor

$$B(X) = 1 + (X \times A \times X).$$

Use initiality to define a function $size : BT_A \to \mathbb{N}$. Next use initiality to define two tree traversal functions of type $BT_A \to A^*$ that flatten a tree into a word consisting of its labels: one depth-first and one breadth-first.

Exercise 2.10.5 Let us call a relation $\mathcal{R} \subseteq \mathbb{N} \times \mathbb{N}$ a *congruence* if $(0, 0) \in \mathcal{R}$ and

$$\text{if} \quad (n, m) \in \mathcal{R} \quad \text{then} \quad (S(n), S(m)) \in \mathcal{R}$$

for all $(n, m) \in \mathbb{N} \times \mathbb{N}$.

(i) Show that any relation $\mathcal{R} \subseteq \mathbb{N} \times \mathbb{N}$ is a congruence iff there exists an algebra structure $\rho : 1 + \mathcal{R} \to \mathcal{R}$ such that the projections $\pi_1 : \mathcal{R} \to \mathbb{N}$ and $\pi_2 : \mathcal{R} \to \mathbb{N}$ are algebra homomorphisms.

(ii) Let $\Delta = \{(n, n) \mid n \in \mathbb{N}\}$. Use the initiality of $\mathbb{N}$ to show:

$$(*) \quad \text{if } \mathcal{R} \text{ is a congruence relation then} \quad \Delta \subseteq \mathcal{R}.$$

(iii) Show that $(*)$ is equivalent to the principle of mathematical induction, which says, for any predicate $P \subseteq \mathbb{N}$,

$$\text{if } P(0) \text{ and } \forall n \in \mathbb{N} : P(n) \Rightarrow P(n + 1), \quad \text{then } \forall n \in \mathbb{N} : P(n).$$

(iv) Note that the characterisation of congruence in (i) above is, in a precise sense, dual to the definition of T-bisimulation, for the functor $T(X) = 1 + X$.

Exercise 2.10.6 Use finality to define a function merge3 : $(A^{\mathbb{N}})^3 \to A^{\mathbb{N}}$ such that

$$\text{merge3}(\sigma, \tau, \rho) = (\sigma(0), \tau(0), \rho(0), \sigma(1), \tau(1), \rho(1), \ldots).$$

Next use merge3 to define the function $\text{merge}_{2,1}$ at the end of Section 2.3.

Exercise 2.10.7 Show that the singleton set $1 = \{*\}$ is (the carrier of) a final coalgebra for the functor $T(X) = X$. Show that it is also a final coalgebra for the functor $T(X) = X^A$, with A an arbitrary non-empty set.

Exercise 2.10.8 Is it possible to define the factorial function $F : \mathbb{N} \to \mathbb{N}$ given by $F(n) = n!$ by initiality? Hint: define by initiality a function $G : \mathbb{N} \to \mathbb{N} \times \mathbb{N}$ such that $\pi_1 \circ G = S$, the successor function, and $\pi_2 \circ G = F$.

Exercise 2.10.9 Let $2 = \{0, 1\}$ and let A be an arbitrary non-empty set. We consider $T(X) = 2 \times X^A$. We view a T-coalgebra $(o, n) : X \to 2 \times X^A$ as a deterministic automaton with transitions

$$x \xrightarrow{a} y \quad \Longleftrightarrow \quad n(x)(a) = y.$$

A state x is accepting (final) iff $o(x) = 1$. Consider the set

$$\mathcal{P}(A^*) = \{L \mid L \subseteq A^*\}$$

of languages over A. Define for $L \subseteq A^*$

$$o(L) = 1 \quad \Longleftrightarrow \quad \langle\,\rangle \in L$$
$$n(L)(a) = \{w \in A^* \mid \text{cons}(a, w) \in L\}.$$

Now show that $(\mathcal{P}(A^*), (o, n))$ is a final T-coalgebra. Hint: show that there is a unique homomorphism from any T-coalgebra $(o, n) : X \to 2 \times X^A$ into $(\mathcal{P}(A^*), (o, n))$ mapping any state $x \in X$ to the language that it accepts.

Exercise 2.10.10 Let $T(X) = 2 \times X^A$, as in Exercise 2.10.9, and consider a T-coalgebra $(o, n) : X \to 2 \times X^A$. Show that if x and x' in X are T-bisimilar then they are mapped by the final homomorphism to the same language. Conclude from this observation that T-bisimilarity is language equivalence.

Exercise 2.10.11 Let A be an arbitrary non-empty set. We view a $(-)^A$-coalgebra $n : X \to X^A$ as a deterministic automaton with transitions

$$x \xrightarrow{a} y \quad \Longleftrightarrow \quad n(x)(a) = y.$$

For $x \in X$ we define $x_\varepsilon = x$ and

$$x_{w \cdot a} = n(x_w)(a).$$

The set $A^\star$ carries a $(-)^A$-coalgebra structure $\gamma : A^\star \to (A^\star)^A$ given by

$$\gamma(w)(a) = w \cdot a.$$

Show that for any $(-)^A$-coalgebra $n : X \to X^A$ with initial state $x_o : 1 \to X$ there exists a unique $(-)^A$-coalgebra homomorphism $r : (A^\star, \gamma) \to (X, n)$ such that

$$r(w) = (x_0)_w.$$

(The function r could be called the *reachability* map.)

Exercise 2.10.12 Use finality to define, for any function $f : A \to A$, a function $iterate_f : A \to A^\mathbb{N}$ satisfying

$$iterate_f(a) = (a, f(a), f \circ f(a), \ldots).$$

Exercise 2.10.13 Show by the coinduction proof principle (cpp) that

$$\mathsf{even} \circ iterate_f = iterate_{f \circ f}$$

where even is defined in Equation (2.3) of Section 2.3.

Exercise 2.10.14 Prove by the coinduction proof principle (cpp) that

$$\mathsf{odd}(\mathsf{merge}(\sigma, \tau)) = \tau$$

for all $\sigma, \tau \in A^\mathbb{N}$. (See Section 2.3 for the definitions of odd and merge.)

Exercise 2.10.15 For a stream $\sigma \in A^\mathbb{N}$ we define

$$\sigma(0) \equiv \mathsf{head}(\sigma)$$
$$\sigma' \equiv \mathsf{tail}(\sigma)$$

and call these the *initial value* and the *stream derivative* of σ. Let $a \in A$ and consider the following *stream differential equation*:

$$\sigma(0) = a \qquad \sigma' = \sigma.$$

Compute the unique solution of this equation. For $a, b \in A$, compute the solution of the following system of equations:

$$\sigma(0) = a \qquad \sigma' = \tau$$
$$\tau(0) = b \qquad \tau' = \sigma.$$

Exercise 2.10.16 Which function $f : A^{\mathbb{N}} \to A^{\mathbb{N}}$ is the solution of the following (functional) stream differential equation?:

$$f(\sigma)(0) = \sigma(0)$$
$$f(\sigma)' = f(\sigma').$$

Exercise 2.10.17 The following system of stream differential equations (uniquely) defines two functions $\oplus, \otimes : \mathbb{N}^{\mathbb{N}} \times \mathbb{N}^{\mathbb{N}} \to \mathbb{N}^{\mathbb{N}}$:

$$(\sigma \oplus \tau)(0) = \sigma(0) + \tau(0) \qquad (\sigma \oplus \tau)' = \sigma' \oplus \tau'$$
$$(\sigma \otimes \tau)(0) = \sigma(0) \times \tau(0) \qquad (\sigma \otimes \tau)' = (\sigma' \otimes \tau) \oplus (\sigma \otimes \tau').$$

Show that, for all $n \geq 0$:

$$(\sigma \oplus \tau)(n) = \sigma(n) + \tau(n)$$
$$(\sigma \otimes \tau)(n) = \sum_{k=0}^{n} \binom{n}{k.} \times \sigma(k) \times \tau(n - k)$$

Exercise 2.10.18 Prove by the coinduction proof principle (cpp) that

$$(P + Q); R = (P; R) + (Q; R)$$

for all processes $P, Q, R \in \Pi$.

Bibliography

[Adá03]   J. Adámek. On final coalgebras of continuous functors. *Theoretical Computer Science*, **294**:3–29, 2003.

[AM75]   M.A. Arbib and E.G. Manes. *Arrows, Structures and Functors. The Categorical Imperative*. Academic Press, 1975.

[AM82]   M.A. Arbib and E.G. Manes. Parametrized data types do not need highly constrained parameters. *Information and Control*, **52**:139–158, 1982.

[AM89]   P. Aczel and N. Mendler. A final coalgebra theorem. In D.H. Pitt, A. Poigné, and D.E. Rydeheard, editors, *Category Theory and Computer Science*, number 389 in *Lecture Notes Computer Science*, pages 357–365. Springer, 1989.

[Awo06]   S. Awodey. *Category Theory*. Oxford University Press, 2006.

[Bar93]   M. Barr. Terminal coalgebras in well-founded set theory. *Theoretical Computer Science*, **114**(2):299–315, 1993. Corrigendum in *Theoretical Computer Science* **124**:189–192, 1994.

[Bar03]   F. Bartels. Generalised coinduction. *Mathematical Structures in Computer Science*, **13**(2):321–348, 2003.

[BBRS09] F. Bonchi, M.M. Bonsangue, J.J.M.M. Rutten, and A. Silva. Deriving syntax and axioms for quantitative regular behaviours. In *International Conference on Concurrency Theory (CONCUR 2009), Lecture Notes Computer Science*, Springer, 2009.

[BD94] R. Burstall and R. Diaconescu. Hiding and behaviour: an institutional approach. In A.W. Roscoe, editor, *A Classical Mind. Essays in Honour of C.A.R. Hoare*, pages 75–92. Prentice Hall, 1994.

[BM96] J. Barwise and L.S. Moss. *Vicious Circles: On the Mathematics of Nonwellfounded Phenomena*. CSLI Lecture Notes 60, Stanford, 1996.

[Bor94] F. Borceux. *Handbook of Categorical Algebra*, volume 50, 51 and 52 of *Encyclopedia of Mathematics*. Cambridge University Press, 1994.

[BRS09] M.M. Bonsangue, J.J.M.M. Rutten, and A. Silva. Algebras for Kripke polynomial coalgebras. In A. Pitts, editor, *Logic in Computer Science*. IEEE, Computer Science Press, 2009.

[BV96] J.W. de Bakker and E. Vink. *Control Flow Semantics*. MIT Press, 1996.

[BW90] M. Barr and Ch. Wells. *Category Theory for Computing Science*. Prentice Hall, 1990.

[CHL03] D. Cancila, F. Honsell and M. Lenisa. Generalized coiteration schemata. In H.P. Gumm, editor, *Coalgebraic Methods in Computer Science*, number **82**(1) in *Electronic Notes in Theoretical Computer Science*, Elsevier, 2003.

[Coh81] P.M. Cohn. *Universal Algebra*, volume 6 of *Mathematics and its Applications*. Reidel, 1981.

[CP07] C. Cîrstea and D. Pattinson. Modular proof systems for coalgebraic logics. *Theoretical Computer Science*, **388**:83–108, 2007.

[Cro93] R.L. Crole. *Categories for Types*. Cambridge Mathematical Textbooks. Cambridge University Press, 1993.

[CS95] J.R.B. Cockett and D. Spencer. Strong categorical datatypes II: A term logic for categorical programming. *Theoretical Computer Science*, **139**:69–113, 1995.

[EM85] H. Ehrig and B. Mahr. *Fundamentals of Algebraic Specification I: Equations and Initial Semantics*. Number 6 in EATCS Monographs. Springer, 1985.

[Fio96] M.P. Fiore. A coinduction principle for recursive data types based on bisimulation. *Information and Computation*, **127**(2):186–198, 1996.

[GD94] J.A. Goguen and R. Diaconescu. Towards an algebraic semantics for the object paradigm. In H. Ehrig and F. Orejas, editors, *Recent Trends in Data Type Specification*, number 785 in *Lecture Notes in Computer Science*, pages 1–29. Springer, 1994.

[GGM76] V. Giarrantana, F. Gimona, and U. Montanari. Observability concepts in abstract data specifications. In A. Mazurkiewicz, editor, *Mathematical Foundations of Computer Science*, number 45 in *Lecture Notes in Computer Science*, pages 576–587. Springer, 1976.

[GM82] J.A Goguen and J. Meseguer. Universal realization, persistent interconnection and implementation of abstract modules. In M. Nielsen and E.M. Schmidt, editors, *International Colloquium on Automata, Languages and Programming*, number 140 in *Lecture Notes in Computer Science*, pages 263–281. Springer, 1982.

[GM93] M.J.C. Gordon and T.F. Melham. *Introduction to HOL: A Theorem Proing Environment for Higher Order Logic.* Cambridge University Press, 1993.

[GM94] J.A. Goguen and G. Malcolm. Proof of correctness of object representations. In A.W. Roscoe, editor, *A Classical Mind. Essays in Honour of C.A.R. Hoare*, pages 119–142. Prentice Hall, 1994.

[GM96] J.A. Goguen and G. Malcolm. An extended abstract of a hidden agenda. In J. Meystel, A. Meystel, and R. Quintero, editors, *Proceedings of the Conference on Intelligent Systems: A Semiotic Perspective*, pages 159–167. *National Institute of Standards and Technology*, 1996.

[GTW78] J.A. Goguen, J. Thatcher, and E. Wagner. An initial algebra approach to the specification, correctness and implementation of abstract data types. In R. Yeh, editor, *Current Trends in Programming Methodoloy*, pages 80–149. Prentice Hall, 1978.

[Gum99] H.P. Gumm. Elements of the general theory of coalgebras. Notes of lectures given at *LUATCS'99: Logic, Universal Algebra, Theoretical Computer Science*, Johannesburg. Available as www.mathematik.uni-marburg.de/~gumm/Papers/ Luatcs.ps, 1999.

[HJ98] C. Hermida and B. Jacobs. Structural induction and coinduction in a fibrational setting. *Information and Computer*, **145**:107–152, 1998.

[HJ04] J. Hughes and B. Jacobs. Simulations in coalgebra. *Theoretical Computer Science*, **327**(1–2):71–108, 2004.

[HJ05] I. Hasuo and B. Jacobs. Context-free languages via coalgebraic trace semantics. In J.L. Fiadeiro, N. Harman, M. Roggenbach, and J. Rutten, editors, *Algebra and Coalgebra in Computer Science (CALCO'05)*, number 3629 in *Lecture Notes in Computer Science*, pages 213–231. Springer, 2005.

[HJS07] I. Hasuo, B. Jacobs, and A. Sokolova. Generic trace theory. *Logical Methods in Computer Science*, **3**(4:11), 2007.

[HL95] F. Honsell and M. Lenisa. Final semantics for untyped λ-calculus. In M. Dezani-Ciancaglini and G. Plotkin, editors, *Typed Lambda Calculi and Applications*, number 902 in *Lecture Notes in Computer Science*, pages 249–265. Springer, 1995.

[HP95] M. Hofmann and B.C. Pierce. A unifying type-theoretic framework for objects. *Journal of Functional Programming*, **5**(4):593–635, 1995.

[Jac95] B. Jacobs. Parameters and parametrization in specification using distributive categories. *Fundamental Informaticae*, **24**(3):209–250, 1995.

[Jac96a] B. Jacobs. Inheritance and cofree constructions. In P. Cointe, editor, *European Conference on Object-Oriented Programming*, number 1098 in *Lecture Notes in Computer Science*, pages 210–231. Springer, 1996.

[Jac96b] B. Jacobs. Objects and classes, co-algebraically. In B. Freitag, C.B. Jones, C. Lengauer, and H.-J. Schek, editors, *Object-Orientation with Parallelism and Persistence*, pages 83–103. Kluwer, 1996.

[Jac06] B. Jacobs. A bialgebraic review of deterministic automata, regular expressions and languages. In K. Futatsugi, J.-P. Jouannaud, and J. Meseguer, editors, *Algebra, Meaning and Computation: Essays Dedicated to Joseph*

A. *Goguen on the Occasion of His 65th Birthday*, number 4060 in *Lecture Notes in Computer Science*, pages 375–404. Springer, 2006.

[Jac08] B. Jacobs. Coalgebraic trace semantics for combined possibilistic and probabilistic systems. In J. Adámek and C. Kupke, editors, *Coalgebraic Methods in Computer Science*, volume **203**(5) of *Electronic Notes in Theoretical Computer Science*, pages 131–152. Elsevier, 2008.

[JNW96] A. Joyal, M. Nielsen, and G. Winskel. Bisimulation from open maps. *Information and Computation*, **127**(2):164–185, 1996.

[Kam83] S. Kamin. Final data types and their specification. *ACM Transactions on Programming Languages and Systems*, **5**(1):97–123, 1983.

[Kli07] B. Klin. Coalgebraic modal logic beyond sets. In M. Fiore, editor, *Mathematical Foundations of Programming Semantics*, number 173 in *Electronic Notes in Theoretical Computer Science*, Elsevier, Amsterdam, 2007.

[Kur01] A. Kurz. Specifying coalgebras with modal logic. *Theoretical Computer Science*, **260**(1–2):119–138, 2001.

[Kur06] A. Kurz. Coalgebras and their logics. *SIGACT News Logic Column*, **37**(2):57–77, 2006.

[Lan71] S. Mac Lane. *Categories for the Working Mathematician*. Springer, 1971.

[LS81] D.J. Lehmann and M.B. Smyth. Algebraic specification of data types: A synthetic approach. *Mathematical Systems Theory*, **14**:97–139, 1981.

[LS86] J. Lambek and P.J. Scott. *Introduction to Higher Order Categorical Logic*. Number 7 in Cambridge Studies in Advanced Mathematics. Cambridge University Press, 1986.

[MA86] E.G. Manes and M.A. Arbib. *Algebraic Appoaches to Program Semantics*. Texts and Monographs in Computer Science. Springer, 1986.

[Mal96] G. Malcolm. Behavioural equivalence, bisimulation and minimal realisation. In M. Haveraaen, O. Owe, and O.J. Dahl, editors, *Recent Trends in Data Type Specification*, number 1130 in *Lecture Notes in Computer Science*, pages 359–378. Springer, 1996.

[Man74] E.G. Manes. *Algebraic Theories*. Springer, 1974.

[Mel89] T.F. Melham. Automating recursive type definitions in higher order logic. In G. Birtwistle and P.A. Subrahmanyam, editors, *Current Trends in Hardware Verification and Automated Theorem Proving*, Lecture Notes in Computer Science, pages 341–386. Springer, 1989.

[Mil89] R. Milner. *A Calculus of Communicating Systems*. Lecture Notes in Computer Science, Springer, 1989.

[MT92] K. Meinke and J.V. Tucker. Universal algebra. In S. Abramsky, Dov M. Gabbai, and T.S.E. Maibaum, editors, *Handbook of Logic in Computer Science*, volume 1, pages 189–411. Oxford University Press, 1992.

[ORR+96] S. Owre, S. Rajan, J.M. Rushby, N. Shankar, and M. Srivas. PVS: Combining specification, proof checking, and model checking. In R. Alur and T.A. Henzinger, editors, *Computer Aided Verification*, number 1102 in *Lecture Notes in Computer Science*, pages 411–414. Springer, 1996.

[Par81] D.M.R. Park. Concurrency and automata on infinite sequences. In P. Deussen, editor, *Proceedings 5th GI Conference on Theoretical Computer Science*, number 104 in *Lecture Notes in Computer Science*, pages 15–32. Springer, 1981.

[Pau90] L.C. Paulson. Isabelle: The next 700 theorem provers. In P. Odifreddi, editor, *Logic and Computer Science*, pages 361–386. Academic Press, 1990. The APIC series, vol. 31.

[Pau97] L.C. Paulson. Mechanizing coinduction and corecursion in higher-order logic. *Journal of Logic and Computation*, 7:175–204, 1997.

[Pie91] B.C. Pierce. *Basic Category Theory for Computer Scientists*. MIT Press, 1991.

[Pit94] A.M. Pitts. A co-induction principle for recursively defined domains. *Theoretical Computer Science*, 124(2):195–219, 1994.

[Pit96] A.M. Pitts. Relational properties of domains. *Information and Computing*, 127(2):66–90, 1996.

[Plo81] G.D. Plotkin. A structural approach to operational semantics. Report DAIMI FN-19, Aarhus University, 1981.

[PM93] Ch. Paulin-Mohring. Inductive definitions in the system Coq. Rules and properties. In M. Bezem and J.F. Groote, editors, *Typed Lambda Calculi and Applications*, number 664 in *Lecture Notes in Computer Science*, pages 328–345. Springer, 1993.

[PP02] D. Pavlović and V. Pratt. The continuum as a final coalgebra. *Theoretical Computer Science*, 280 (1–2):105–122, 2002.

[Rei95] H. Reichel. An approach to object semantics based on terminal co-algebras. *Mathematical Structures in Computer Science*, 5:129–152, 1995.

[Rou96] W.C. Rounds. Feature logics. In J. van Benthem and A. ter Meulen, editors, *Handbook of Logic and Language*. Elsevier, 1996.

[RT94] J. Rutten and D. Turi. Initial algebra and final coalgebra semantics for concurrency. In J.W. de Bakker, W.P. de Roever, and G. Rozenberg, editors, *A Decade of Concurrency*, number 803 in *Lecture Notes in Computer Science*, pages 530–582. Springer, 1994.

[Rut00] J. Rutten. Universal coalgebra: a theory of systems. *Theoretical Computer Science*, 249:3–80, 2000.

[Rut03] J. Rutten. Behavioural differential equations: a coinductive calculus of streams, automata, and power series. *Theoretical Computer Science*, 308:1–53, 2003.

[SP82] M.B. Smyth and G.D. Plotkin. The category theoretic solution of recursive domain equations. *SIAM Journal of Computing*, 11:761–783, 1982.

[SR07] A. Silva and J. Rutten. Behavioural differential equations and coinduction for binary trees. In D. Leivant and R. de Queiroz, editors, *Logic, Language, Information and Computation, 14th International Workshop, WoLLIC 2007*, number 4576 in *Lecture Notes in Computer Science*, pages 322–336. Springer, 2007.

[TP97] D. Turi and G. Plotkin. Towards a mathematical operational semantics. In G. Winskel, editor, *Logic in Computer Science*, pages 280–291. IEEE, Computer Science Press, 1997.

[Tur96] D. Turi. *Functorial operational semantics and its denotational dual*. PhD thesis, Free University Amsterdam, 1996.

[Wal91] R.F.C. Walters. *Categories and Computer Science*. Carslaw Publications, Sydney, 1991. Also available as: Cambridge Computer Science Text 28, 1992.

[Wec92] W. Wechler. *Universal Algebra for Computer Scientists*. Number 25 in EATCS Monographs. Springer, Berlin, 1992.

[Wir90] M. Wirsing. Algebraic specification. In J. van Leeuwen, editor, *Handbook of Theoretical Computer Science*, volume B, pages 673–788. Elsevier/MIT Press, 1990.

3

The algorithmics of bisimilarity

LUCA ACETO, ANNA INGOLFSDOTTIR AND JIŘÍ SRBA

3.1 Introduction

A model for reactive computation, for example that of labelled transition systems [Kel76], or a process algebra (such as ACP [BW90], CCS [Mil89], CSP [Hoa85]) can be used to describe both implementations of processes and specifications of their expected behaviours. Process algebras and labelled transition systems therefore naturally support the so-called single-language approach to process theory, that is, the approach in which a single language is used to describe both actual processes and their specifications. An important ingredient of the theory of these languages and their associated semantic models is therefore a notion of behavioural equivalence or behavioural approximation between processes. One process description, say SYS, may describe an implementation, and another, say SPEC, may describe a specification of the expected behaviour. To say that SYS and SPEC are equivalent is taken to indicate that these two processes describe essentially the same behaviour, albeit possibly at different levels of abstraction or refinement. To say that, in some formal sense, SYS is an approximation of SPEC means roughly that every aspect of the behaviour of this process is allowed by the specification SPEC, and thus that nothing unexpected can happen in the behaviour of SYS. This approach to program verification is also sometimes called implementation verification or equivalence checking.

Designers using implementation verification to validate their (models of) reactive systems need only learn one language to describe both their systems and their specifications, and can benefit from the intrinsic compositionality of their descriptions, at least when they are using a process algebra for denoting the labelled transition systems in their models and an equivalence (or preorder) that is preserved by the operations in the algebra. Moreover, specifications presented as labelled transitions or as terms in a process algebra are rather detailed and typically describe both what a correct system should do and what behaviour it cannot afford. An implementation that conforms to such a detailed specification offers excellent correctness guarantees.

The single-language approach to the specification and verification of reactive systems underlies much of the work on process algebras, and several of the early classic textbooks on those languages, such as the above-mentioned ones, present verifications of non-trivial concurrent systems using equivalence or preorder checking. (See also the book [Bae90], which is entirely devoted to early applications of the process algebra ACP.) It became clear, however, rather early on in the development of verification techniques from the field of process algebra and in their application in the verification of case studies that tool support was necessary in the analysis of the behaviour of models of real-life computing systems. This realisation was, amongst others, a powerful incentive for the work on the development of software tools for computer-aided verification based on process-algebraic verification techniques and on the model of labelled transition systems underlying them. Examples of such tools are the Edinburgh Concurrency Workbench and its successors [CPS93, CS96], CADP [GLMS07] and mCRL2 [GKM+08].

In order to develop suitable tools for computer-aided verification and to understand their limitations, researchers needed to answer some of the most basic and fundamental questions that are naturally associated with the algorithmic problems underlying implementation verification.

- What equivalences or preorders over labelled transition systems are decidable, and over what classes of labelled transition systems?
- What equivalences or preorders are efficiently decidable over finite labelled transition systems or parallel compositions of such systems? And if so, by what algorithms?
- Are there equivalences that are (efficiently) decidable over classes of infinite labelled transition systems that can be 'finitely specified'?
- What is the computational complexity of checking decidable equivalences or preorders over 'interesting' classes of labelled transition systems? Can one come up with matching lower and upper bounds?

Apart from their usefulness in the development of the algorithmics of implementation verification, the questions above are of intrinsic and fundamental scientific interest within the field of concurrency theory and related fields of computer science. Indeed, the results that have been obtained over the years in an attempt to solve the algorithmic problems associated with equivalence and preorder checking over labelled transition systems and related models have put the theory of processes on a par with the classic theory of automata and formal languages (see, for instance, the textbooks [HU79, Sip06]) in terms of depth and elegance.

In this chapter, we shall address some of these questions and present classic results that have been achieved in the literature on concurrency theory since the 1980s. We shall mostly focus on (variations on) bisimilarity as the chosen notion of equivalence between (states in) labelled transition systems, but, where appropriate, we shall also hint at results that have been obtained for other equivalences and preorders in the literature. Our presentation will largely follow classical lines of exposition in the field of concurrency theory. However, in Sections 3.3.2–3.3.3, we shall present some well-known results in a new light, using the view of bisimilarity and other coinductively defined process semantics as games. We shall also highlight some general proof techniques based on tableaux techniques and on the so-called 'Defender's forcing technique' [JS08]. We feel that the use of these techniques makes the proofs of some results more transparent than the ones originally presented in the literature. Finally, where appropriate, we have elected to present proofs that allow us to introduce general and reusable proof techniques, even though they do not yield the best possible complexity bounds for some algorithmic problems. In such cases, we always give references to the papers offering the best-known complexity results.

Roadmap of the chapter The chapter is organised as follows. We begin by surveying the classical algorithms by Kanellakis and Smolka, and Paige and Tarjan, for computing bisimilarity over finite labelled transition systems in Section 3.2. There we also briefly mention the basic ideas underlying symbolic algorithms for bisimilarity checking based on reduced ordered binary decision diagrams. Section 3.3 is devoted to results on the computational complexity of bisimilarity, and related behavioural relations, over finite processes. In that section, we consider the complexity of the relevant decision problems when measured as a function of the 'size' of the input labelled transition system, as well as the one measured with respect to the length of the description of a parallel composition of labelled transition systems. In Section 3.4, we offer a glimpse of the plethora of remarkable decidability and complexity results that have been obtained for bisimilarity over classes of infinite-state processes. We conclude the chapter with a discussion of the main uses of bisimilarity checking in verification and tools (Section 3.5).

3.2 Classical algorithms for bisimilarity

In this section, we consider one of the most fundamental algorithmic problems associated with equivalence checking over labelled transition systems, namely the problem of deciding bisimilarity over finite labelled transition systems, that is, labelled transition systems with a finite set of states and finitely many transitions [San12, section 1.2]. It is well known that deciding language equivalence over this class of labelled transition systems is PSPACE-complete [HRS76]. (See also [SM73].) In sharp contrast with this negative result, efficient algorithms have been developed for deciding strong bisimilarity over finite labelled transition systems. Our main aim in this section is to present a brief exposition of two such classical algorithms that are due to Kanellakis and Smolka [KS83] (see also the journal version [KS90]) and to Paige and Tarjan [PT87]. Both these algorithms are essentially based on the characterisation of strong bisimilarity as a largest fixed point discussed in [San12, section 2.10.1], and Tarski's fixed point theorem [San12, theorem 2.3.21] plays an important role in establishing their correctness.

For the sake of readability, we recall here the classical notion of stratified bisimulation relations, which are also known as approximants to bisimilarity. We refer the interested reader to [San12, section 2.10.2] for more information.

Definition 3.2.1 A *labelled transition system* is a triple $(Pr, Act, \longrightarrow)$, where

- Pr is a set of *states*;
- Act is a set of *actions*; and
- $\longrightarrow \subseteq Pr \times Act \times Pr$ is a *transition relation*.

Definition 3.2.2 Given a labelled transition system $(Pr, Act, \longrightarrow)$, the *stratified bisimulation relations* [Mil80, HM85] $\sim_k \subseteq Pr \times Pr$ for $k \in \mathbb{N}$ are defined as follows:

- $E \sim_0 F$ for all $E, F \in Pr$;
- $E \sim_{k+1} F$ iff for each $a \in Act$: if $E \xrightarrow{a} E'$ then there is $F' \in Pr$ such that $F \xrightarrow{a} F'$ and $E' \sim_k F'$; and if $F \xrightarrow{a} F'$ then there is $E' \in Pr$ such that $E \xrightarrow{a} E'$ and $E' \sim_k F'$.

Given a labelled transition system $(Pr, Act, \longrightarrow)$, we define

$$\text{next}(E, a) = \{E' \in Pr \mid E \xrightarrow{a} E'\}$$

for $E \in Pr$ and $a \in Act$. We also define

$$\text{next}(E, *) = \bigcup_{a \in Act} \text{next}(E, a).$$

A labelled transition system is *image-finite* iff the set $\text{next}(E, a)$ is finite for every $E \in Pr$ and $a \in Act$.

The following lemma is a standard one.

Lemma 3.2.3 **([HM85])** *Assume that* $(\mathrm{Pr}, Act, \longrightarrow)$ *is an image-finite labelled transition system and let* $E, F \in \mathrm{Pr}$. *Then* $E \sim F$ *iff* $E \sim_k F$ *for all* $k \in \mathbb{N}$.

The characterisation of bisimilarity given in the above lemma immediately yields an algorithm skeleton for computing bisimilarity over any finite labelled transition system, namely:

Let $\sim_0$ be the universal relation over the set of states of the input labelled transition system. For each $i > 0$, compute the i-th approximant of bisimilarity $\sim_i$ until $\sim_i = \sim_{i-1}$.

If the input labelled transition system is finite, the computation of each approximant of bisimilarity can obviously be carried out effectively. Moreover, a very rough analysis indicates that the non-increasing sequence of approximants stabilises in $O(n^2)$ iterations, where n is the number of states in the labelled transition system. But how efficiently can the above algorithm skeleton be implemented? How can one best compute the i-th approximant of bisimilarity, for $i \geq 1$, from the previous one? And what is the complexity of optimal algorithms for the problem of computing bisimilarity over finite labelled transition systems?

The algorithms that we shall present in what follows indicate that, in sharp contrast with well-known results in formal language theory, the problem of deciding bisimilarity over finite labelled transition systems can be solved very efficiently. In Section 3.3.2, we shall discuss lower bounds on the complexity of checking bisimilarity over finite labelled transition systems. As confirmed by further results surveyed in later sections in this chapter, bisimilarity affords remarkable complexity and decidability properties that set it apart from other notions of equivalence and preorder over various classes of labelled transition systems.

3.2.1 Preliminaries

Let $(Pr, Act, \longrightarrow)$ be a finite labelled transition system. An equivalence relation over the set of states Pr can be represented as a partition of Pr, that is, as a set $\{B_0, \ldots, B_k\}$, $k \geq 0$, of non-empty subsets of Pr such that

- $B_i \cap B_j = \emptyset$, for all $0 \leq i < j \leq k$, and
- $Pr = B_0 \cup B_1 \cup \cdots \cup B_k$.

The sets B_i in a partition are usually called blocks. In what follows, we shall typically not distinguish between partitions and their associated equivalence relations.

Let π and π' be two partitions of Pr. We say that π' is a refinement of π if for each block $B' \in \pi'$ there exists some block $B \in \pi$ such that $B' \subseteq B$. Observe that if π' is a refinement of π, then the equivalence relation associated with π' is included in the one associated with π.

The algorithms for computing bisimilarity due to Kanellakis and Smolka, and Paige and Tarjan compute successive refinements of an initial partition π_{init} and converge to the largest strong bisimulation over the input finite labelled transition system. Algorithms that compute strong bisimilarity in this fashion are often called partition-refinement algorithms and reduce the problem of computing bisimilarity to that of solving the so-called *relational coarsest partitioning* problem [KS90, PT87]. In what follows, we shall present the main ideas underlying the above-mentioned algorithms. We refer the interested reader to the survey paper [CS01] for more information and for other algorithmic approaches to deciding bisimilarity over finite labelled transition systems.

3.2.2 The algorithm of Kanellakis and Smolka

Let $\pi = \{B_0, \ldots, B_k\}, k \geq 0$, be a partition of the set of states Pr. The algorithm due to Kanellakis and Smolka is based on the notion of splitter.

Definition 3.2.4 A splitter for a block $B_i \in \pi$ is a block $B_j \in \pi$ such that, for some action $a \in Act$, some states in B_i have a-labelled transitions whose target is a state in B_j and others do not.

Intuitively, thinking of blocks as representing approximations of equivalence classes of processes with respect to strong bisimilarity, the existence of a splitter B_j for a block B_i in the current partition indicates that we have a reason for distinguishing two groups of sets of states in B_i, namely those that afford an a-labelled transition leading to a state in B_j and those that do not. Therefore, B_i can be split by B_j with respect to action a into the two new blocks:

$$B_i^1 = \{s \mid s \in B_i \text{ and } s \xrightarrow{a} s', \text{ for some } s' \in B_j\} \quad \text{and}$$
$$B_i^2 = B_i \smallsetminus B_i^1.$$

This splitting results in the new partition

$$\pi' = \{B_0, \ldots, B_{i-1}, B_i^1, B_i^2, B_{i+1}, \ldots, B_k\},$$

which is a refinement of π. The basic idea underlying the algorithm of Kanellakis and Smolka is to iterate the splitting of some block B_i by some block B_j with respect to some action a until no further refinement of the current partition is possible. The resulting partition is often called the coarsest stable partition and coincides with strong bisimilarity over the input labelled transition system when the initial partition π_{init} is chosen to be $\{Pr\}$. (We shall define the notion of stable partition precisely in Section 3.2.3 since it plays an important role in the algorithm proposed by Paige and Tarjan. The definitions we present in this section suffice to obtain an understanding of the algorithm of Kanellakis and Smolka.)

Before presenting the details of the algorithm of Kanellakis and Smolka, we illustrate the intuition behind the algorithm by means of a couple of examples.

Example 3.2.5 Consider the labelled transition system depicted below.

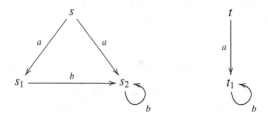

Since we are interested in computing bisimilarity, let the initial partition associated with this labelled transition system be $\{Pr\}$, where

$$Pr = \{s, s_1, s_2, t, t_1\}.$$

The block Pr is a splitter for itself. Indeed, some states in Pr afford a-labelled transitions while others do not. If we split Pr by Pr with respect to action a we obtain a new partition consisting of the blocks $\{s, t\}$ (the set of states that afford a-labelled transitions) and $\{s_1, s_2, t_1\}$ (the set of states that do not afford a-labelled transitions). Note that we would have obtained the same partition if we had done the splitting with respect to action b. You can now readily observe that neither of the blocks $\{s, t\}$ and $\{s_1, s_2, t_1\}$ can be split by the other with respect to any action. Indeed, states in each block are all bisimilar to one another, whereas states in different blocks are not.

Example 3.2.6   Consider now the following labelled transition system.

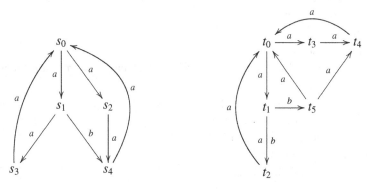

Let the initial partition associated with this labelled transition system be $\{Pr\}$, where

$$Pr = \{s_i, t_j \mid 0 \le i \le 4, 0 \le j \le 5\}.$$

The block Pr is a splitter for itself. Indeed, some states in Pr afford b-labelled transitions while others do not. If we split Pr by Pr with respect to action b we obtain a new partition consisting of the blocks

$$\{s_1, t_1\} \text{ and } \{s_i, t_j \mid 0 \le i \le 4, 0 \le j \le 5 \text{ with } i, j \ne 1\}.$$

Note now that the former block is a splitter for the latter with respect to action a. Indeed only states s_0 and t_0 in that block afford a-labelled transitions that lead to a state in the block $\{s_1, t_1\}$. The resulting splitting yields the partition

$$\{\{s_0, t_0\}, \{s_1, t_1\}, \{s_i, t_j \mid 2 \le i \le 4, 2 \le j \le 5\}\}.$$

The above partition can be refined further. Indeed, some states in the third block have a-labelled transitions leading to states in the first block, but others do not. Therefore the first block is a splitter for the third one with respect to action a. The resulting splitting yields the partition

$$\{\{s_0, t_0\}, \{s_1, t_1\}, \{s_3, s_4, t_2, t_4, t_5\}, \{s_2, t_3\}\}.$$

We continue by observing that the block $\{s_3, s_4, t_4, t_2, t_5\}$ is a splitter for itself with respect to action a. For example $t_5 \xrightarrow{a} t_4$, but the only a-labelled transition from s_4 is $s_4 \xrightarrow{a} s_0$. The resulting splitting yields the partition

$$\{\{s_0, t_0\}, \{s_1, t_1\}, \{t_5\}, \{s_3, s_4, t_2, t_4\}, \{s_2, t_3\}\}.$$

We encourage you to continue refining the above partition until you reach the coarsest stable partition. What is the resulting partition?

```
function split(B, a, π)
choose some state s ∈ B
B₁, B₂ := ∅
for each state t ∈ B do
    if s and t can reach the same set of blocks in π via a-labelled
    transitions
        then B₁ := B₁ ∪ {t}
        else B₂ := B₂ ∪ {t}
if B₂ is empty then return {B₁}
else return {B₁, B₂}
```

Fig. 3.1. The function split($B, a, π$).

```
π := {Pr}
changed := true
while changed do
    changed := false
    for each block B ∈ π do
        for each action a do
            sort the a-labelled transitions from states in B
            if split(B, a, π) = {B₁, B₂} ≠ {B}
            then refine π by replacing B with B₁ and B₂, and set
            changed to true
```

Fig. 3.2. The algorithm of Kanellakis and Smolka.

The pseudo-code for the algorithm of Kanellakis and Smolka is given in Figure 3.2. The algorithm uses the function split($B, a, π$) described in Figure 3.1, which, given a partition $π$, a block B in $π$ and an action a, splits B with respect to each block in $π$ and action a. For example, considering the labelled transition system in Example 3.2.6, the call

$$split(\{s_1, t_1\}, b, \{\{s_0, t_0\}, \{s_1, t_1\}, \{t_5\}, \{s_3, s_4, t_2, t_4\}, \{s_2, t_3\}\})$$

returns the pair ($\{s_1\}, \{t_1\}$) because the only block in the partition that can be reached from s_1 via a b-labelled transition is $\{s_3, s_4, t_2, t_4\}$, whereas t_1 can also reach the block $\{t_5\}$.

In order to decide efficiently whether the sets of blocks that can be reached from s and t are equal, the algorithm orders the transitions from each state lexicographically by their labels, and transitions with the same label are ordered by the block in the partition that contains the target state of the transition. Note that the algorithm in Figure 3.2 sorts the a-labelled transitions from states in a block B before calling split(B, a, π). This is necessary because a splitting of a block may change the ordering of transitions into that block. The lexicographic sorting of transitions can be done in $O(m + |Act|)$ time and space, and therefore in $O(m)$ time and space because the number of actions can be taken to be at most m, using a classical algorithm from [AHU74].

Theorem 3.2.7 (Kanellakis and Smolka) *When applied to a finite labelled transition system with n states and m transitions, the algorithm of Kanellakis and Smolka computes the partition corresponding to strong bisimilarity in time $O(nm)$.*

Proof We first argue that the algorithm of Kanellakis and Smolka is correct, that is, that when it reaches the coarsest stable partition π that partition is the one corresponding to strong bisimilarity over the input labelled transition system. To see this, let π_i, $i \geq 0$, denote the partition after the i-th iteration of the outermost loop in the algorithm in Figure 3.2. Below, we shall use π_i to denote also the equivalence relation induced by the partition π_i. Recall, furthermore, that $\sim_i$ denotes the i-th approximant to bisimilarity.

Observe, first of all, that

$$\sim \; \subseteq \; \sim_i \; \subseteq \; \pi_i$$

holds for each $i \geq 0$. This can be easily proved by induction on i. It follows that $\sim \; \subseteq \; \pi$.

Conversely, if π is a partition that cannot be refined further, then it is not hard to see that π is a post-fixed point of the function $F_\sim$ that was used in [San12, section 2.10.1] to characterise $\sim$ as a largest fixed point. Since $\sim$ is the largest post-fixed point of $F_\sim$, it follows that $\pi \; \subseteq \; \sim$. Therefore $\sim \; = \; \pi$.

As far as the complexity of the algorithm is concerned, note that the main loop of the algorithm is repeated at most $n - 1$ times. Indeed, the number of blocks in π must be between one and n, and this number increases at each iteration of the outermost loop of the algorithm that leads to a refinement of π. The calls to the function split take $O(m)$ time at each iteration of the main loop. Indeed, that function is called for each block and each action at most once, and in each call it considers each transition of every state in the block at most once. As we already remarked above, the sorting of transitions can be done in $O(m)$ time at each iteration of the main loop. Therefore we achieve the claimed $O(mn)$ complexity bound. □

Exercise 3.2.8 Fill in the details in the proof of correctness of the algorithm that we sketched above.

Remark 3.2.9 The algorithm of Kanellakis and Smolka also has $O(n + m)$ space complexity.

A natural question to ask at this point is whether the algorithm of Kanellakis and Smolka is optimal. As we shall see in the following section, the answer to this question is negative. Indeed, the time performance of a partition-refinement algorithm like the one we just discussed can be improved substantially by means of some clever use of data structures.

Remark 3.2.10 For the special case in which, for each action a and process s, the set

$$\{s' \mid s \xrightarrow{a} s'\}$$

has size at most a constant c, Kanellakis and Smolka presented in [KS83] (see also [KS90]) an $O(c^2 n \log n)$-time algorithm to decide strong bisimilarity. They also conjectured the existence of an $O(m \log n)$-time algorithm for the problem. This conjecture was confirmed by Paige and Tarjan by means of the algorithm we will present in the following section.

3.2.3 The algorithm of Paige and Tarjan

The algorithm of Paige and Tarjan is also based on the idea of partition refinement. However, by making use of more complex data structures, it significantly improves on the efficiency of the algorithm of Kanellakis and Smolka we discussed in the previous section. The low complexity of the algorithm of Paige and Tarjan is achieved by using information about previous splits to improve on the efficiency of future splits. In particular, each state can only appear in a number of splitters that is logarithmic in the number of states in the input labelled transition system.

In order to simplify the presentation of the algorithm, throughout this section we shall assume that the input finite labelled transition system is over a single action a. The extension of the algorithm to arbitrary finite labelled transition systems is only notationally more complex. (See also Exercise 3.3.12, which indicates that a single action is as general as any finite set of actions, also from the point of view of the complexity of algorithms.)

We begin our presentation of the algorithm of Paige and Tarjan by defining formally the notion of stable partition. In what follows, given a set of states S, we define:

$$\text{pre}(S) = \{s \mid s \xrightarrow{a} s' \text{ for some } s' \in S\}.$$

Definition 3.2.11 ((Coarsest) Stable partition)

- A set $B \subseteq Pr$ is stable with respect to a set $S \subseteq Pr$ if
  - either $B \subseteq \text{pre}(S)$
  - or $B \cap \text{pre}(S) = \emptyset$.
- A partition π is stable with respect to a set S if so is each block $B \in \pi$.
- A partition π is stable with respect to a partition π' if π is stable with respect to each block in π'.
- A partition π is stable if it is stable with respect to itself.

The coarsest stable refinement (of a partition π_{init}) is a stable partition that is refined by any other stable partition (that refines π_{init}).

Note that $B \subseteq Pr$ is stable with respect to a block $S \subseteq Pr$ if, and only if, S is not a splitter for B. (The notion of splitter was presented in Definition 3.2.4.)

Example 3.2.12 Consider the following labelled transition system.

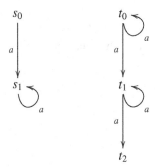

The block $\{s_i, t_i \mid 0 \le i \le 1\}$ is stable with respect to the set of states $\{s_i, t_j \mid 0 \le i \le 1, 0 \le j \le 2\}$. On the other hand, the block $\{s_i, t_j \mid 0 \le i \le 1, 0 \le j \le 2\}$ is not stable with respect to itself because

$$\text{pre}(\{s_i, t_j \mid 0 \le i \le 1, 0 \le j \le 2\}) = \{s_i, t_i \mid 0 \le i \le 1\}.$$

The coarsest stable partition over the above labelled transition system that refines $\{Pr\}$ is

$$\{\{s_0, s_1\}, \{t_0\}, \{t_1\}, \{t_2\}\}.$$

Note that this is the partition associated with $\sim$ over the above labelled transition system.

Exercise 3.2.13 Show that $\sim$ is the coarsest stable partition that refines $\{Pr\}$ over any finite labelled transition system with $Act = \{a\}$.

The basic idea behind the algorithm proposed by Paige and Tarjan is that, given a partition π of Pr, one can identify two different types of blocks B that act as splitters for π: simple and compound splitters.

Simple splitters are used to split blocks in π into two disjoint subsets as done in the algorithm of Kanellakis and Smolka. Below, we rephrase this notion using the definitions introduced above.

Definition 3.2.14 (Simple splitting) Let π be a partition and let B be a set of states in Pr. We write $\text{split}(B, \pi)$ for the refinement of π obtained as follows.

> For each block $B' \in \pi$ such that B' is not stable with respect to B, replace B' by the blocks
> $$B'_1 = B' \cap \text{pre}(B) \quad \text{and}$$
> $$B'_2 = B' \smallsetminus \text{pre}(B).$$

We call B a splitter for π when $\text{split}(B, \pi) \neq \pi$. In that case, we also say that π is refined with respect to B, and that $\text{split}(B, \pi)$ is the partition that results from that refinement.

For example, consider the labelled transition system in Example 3.2.12 and the partition $\{Pr\}$. As we already remarked, the block Pr is not stable with respect to itself. Moreover,

$$\text{split}(Pr, \{Pr\}) = \{\{s_0, s_1, t_0, t_1\}, \{t_2\}\}.$$

Therefore Pr is a splitter for $\{Pr\}$.

We observe the following useful properties of the function split and of the notion of stability.

Lemma 3.2.15

(1) Stability is preserved by refinement, that is, if π refines π' and π' is stable with respect to a set of states S, then so is π.

(2) Stability is preserved by union, that is, if π is stable with respect to sets S_1 and S_2, then π is also stable with respect to $S_1 \cup S_2$.

(3) Assume that $B \subseteq Pr$. Let π_1 and π_2 be two partitions of Pr such that π_1 refines π_2. Then $\text{split}(B, \pi_1)$ refines $\text{split}(B, \pi_2)$.

(4) Assume that $B, B' \subseteq Pr$. Let π be a partition of Pr. Then

$$\text{split}(B, \text{split}(B', \pi)) = \text{split}(B', \text{split}(B, \pi)),$$

that is, split is commutative.

Exercise 3.2.16 Prove the above lemma.

As a stepping stone towards introducing the algorithm of Paige and Tarjan, consider the following abstract version of the algorithm of Kanellakis and Smolka. The algorithm keeps a partition π that is initially the initial partition π_{init} and refines it until it reaches the coarsest stable partition that refines π_{init}. It repeats the following steps until π is stable:

(1) Find a set S that is a union of some of the blocks in π and is a splitter of π.
(2) Replace π by split(S, π).

This refinement algorithm works just as well if one restricts oneself to using only blocks of π as splitters. However, allowing the use of unions of blocks as splitters is one of the key ideas behind the algorithm of Paige and Tarjan.

In order to implement the algorithm efficiently, it is useful to reduce the problem to that of considering labelled transition systems without deadlocked states, i.e. to labelled transition systems in which each state has an outgoing transition. This can be done easily by preprocessing the initial partition π_{init} by splitting each block $B \in \pi_{\text{init}}$ into

$$B_1 = B \cap \text{pre}(Pr) \quad \text{and}$$
$$B_2 = B \setminus \text{pre}(Pr).$$

Note that the blocks B_2 generated in this way will never be split again by the refinement algorithm. Therefore we can run the refinement algorithm starting from the partition

$$\pi'_{\text{init}} = \{B_1 \mid B \in \pi_{\text{init}}\},$$

which is a partition of the set pre(Pr). The coarsest stable refinement of π'_{init} together with the blocks of the form B_2 for each $B \in \pi_{\text{init}}$ yield the coarsest stable refinement of π_{init}.

Exercise 3.2.17 Prove the claims we just made.

In order to achieve its time complexity, the Paige–Tarjan algorithm employs a very clever way of finding splitters. In addition to the current partition π, the algorithm maintains another partition X such that

• π is a refinement of X and
• π is stable with respect to X.

Initially, π is the initial partition π_{init} and $X = \{Pr\}$. The abstract version of the algorithm of Paige and Tarjan repeats the following steps until $\pi = X$:

(1) Find a block $S \in X \setminus \pi$.
(2) Find a block $B \in \pi$ such that $B \subseteq S$ and $\mid B \mid \leq \frac{|S|}{2}$.
(3) Replace S within X with the two sets B and $S \setminus B$.
(4) Replace π with split($S \setminus B$, split(B, π)).

The efficiency of the above algorithm relies on the heuristic for the choice of the block B at step 2 and on the use of what is usually called *three-way splitting* to implement step 4 efficiently. We now proceed to introduce the basic ideas behind the notion of three-way splitting.

Suppose that we have a partition π that is stable with respect to a set of states S that is a union of some of the blocks in π. Assume also that π is refined first with respect to a non-empty set $B \subset S$ and then with respect to $S \setminus B$. We have that:

- Refining π with respect to B splits a block $D \in \pi$ into two blocks $D_1 = D \cap \text{pre}(B)$ and $D_2 = D \setminus \text{pre}(B)$ if, and only if, D is not stable with respect to B.
- Refining further split(B, π) with respect to $S \setminus B$ splits the block D_1 into two blocks $D_{11} = D_1 \cap \text{pre}(S \setminus B)$ and $D_{12} = D_1 \setminus D_{11}$ if, and only if, D_1 is not stable with respect to $S \setminus B$.

A block S of the partition X is simple if it is also a block of π and is compound otherwise. Note that a compound block S contains at least two blocks of π. Such a block S can be partitioned into B and $S \setminus B$ in such a way that both the above-mentioned properties hold. The three-way splitting procedure outlined above gives the refinement of a partition with respect to a compound splitter.

Observe that refining split(B, π) with respect to $S \setminus B$ does *not* split the block D_2. This is because $D_2 \subseteq \text{pre}(S \setminus B)$. Indeed, since π is stable with respect to S, we have that either $D \subseteq \text{pre}(S)$ or $D \cap \text{pre}(S) = \emptyset$. If D is not stable with respect to B, it holds that

$$D \nsubseteq \text{pre}(B) \text{ and } D \cap \text{pre}(B) \neq \emptyset.$$

Therefore, $D \subseteq \text{pre}(S)$. Since $D_2 = D \setminus \text{pre}(B)$, we can immediately infer that $D_2 \subseteq \text{pre}(S \setminus B)$, as claimed. Moreover,

$$D_{12} = D_1 \setminus D_{11} = D \setminus \text{pre}(S \setminus B) = D_1 \cap (\text{pre}(B) \setminus \text{pre}(S \setminus B)).$$

The identity

$$D_{12} = D_1 \cap (\text{pre}(B) \setminus \text{pre}(S \setminus B))$$

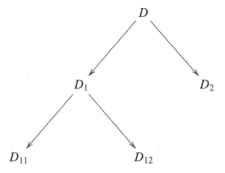

Fig. 3.3. Three-way splitting of a block. We use the following abbreviations:

$$D_1 = D \cap \mathrm{pre}(B)$$
$$D_2 = D \smallsetminus \mathrm{pre}(B)$$
$$D_{11} = D \cap \mathrm{pre}(B) \cap \mathrm{pre}(S \smallsetminus B) \quad \text{and}$$
$$D_{12} = D \smallsetminus \mathrm{pre}(S \smallsetminus B).$$

is the crucial observation underlying the implementation of the algorithm of Paige and Tarjan. We can visually depict the result of a three-way split of a block D as the binary tree depicted in Figure 3.3.

The time performance of the algorithm Paige and Tarjan relies on the following observations. First of all note that each state in the input labelled transition system is in at most $\log n + 1$ blocks B used as refining sets. This is because each refining set is at most half the size of the previous one. Moreover, as shown by Paige and Tarjan, a refinement step with respect to a block B can be implemented in time

$$O\left(\mid B \mid + \sum_{s \in B} \mid \mathrm{pre}(\{s\}) \mid\right)$$

by means of a careful use of data structures. An $O(m \log n)$ time bound for the algorithm follows.

In order to perform three-way splitting efficiently, namely in time proportional to the cardinality of the block B chosen at step 2 of the algorithm, the Paige–Tarjan algorithm uses an integer variable count(s, S) for each state s and each block S. Intuitively, count(s, S) records the number of states in S that can be reached from s via a transition.

Exercise 3.2.18 Use the variables count(s, S) to decide in constant time to which sub-block of D a state $s \in D$ belongs.

Apart from the count variables, the Paige–Tarjan algorithm uses additional data structures to achieve its efficiency. Blocks and states are represented by records. Each block of the partition π is stored as a doubly linked list containing its elements and has an associated integer variable recording its cardinality. Each block of X points to a doubly linked list containing the blocks in π included in it. Finally, each block of π points to the block of X that includes it. The implementation of the algorithm also uses a set C that contains the compound blocks of X. Initially, $C = \{Pr\}$ and π is the initial partition π_{init}.

An efficient implementation of the Paige–Tarjan algorithm repeats the steps given in Figure 3.4, taken from [PT87, page 981], until the set of compound blocks becomes empty.

Theorem 3.2.19 (Paige and Tarjan) *When applied to a finite labelled transition system with n states and m transitions using $\{Pr\}$ as the initial partition, the algorithm of Paige and Tarjan computes the partition corresponding to strong bisimilarity in time $O(m \log n)$.*

We refer interested readers to [CS01, PT87] for further details on the algorithm of Paige and Tarjan.

3.2.4 Computing bisimilarity, symbolically

The algorithms for computing bisimilarity we have presented above require that the input labelled transition system be fully constructed in advance. In practice, a labelled transition system describing a reactive system is typically specified as a suitable 'parallel composition' of some other labelled transition systems representing the behaviour of the system components. It is well known that the size of the resulting labelled transition system may grow exponentially with respect to the number of parallel components. This phenomenon is usually referred to as the state-explosion problem and is a major hindrance in the use of algorithms requiring the explicit construction of the input labelled transition system in the automatic verification of large reactive systems.

Amongst the approaches that have been proposed in order to deal with the state-explosion problem, we shall briefly present here the main ideas underlying a symbolic approach based on the use of reduced ordered binary decision diagrams (ROBDDs) [Bry86, Bry92] to represent finite labelled transition

(1) Remove a compound block S from C. Find the first two blocks in the list of blocks of π that are included in S and let B be the smallest, breaking ties arbitrarily.

(2) Replace S with $S \smallsetminus B$ and create a new simple block in X containing B as its only block of π. If S is still compound, put S back into C.

(3) Compute pre(B) and count(s, B). This is done as follows. Copy B into a temporary set B'. Compute pre(B) by scanning the edges with a target in B and adding the source of each such edge to pre(B) if it is not already contained in that set. During the count compute the count variables count(s, B).

(4) Replace π with split(B, π) as follows. For each block $D \in \pi$ such that $D \cap \text{pre}(B) \neq \emptyset$, split D into $D_1 = D \cap \text{pre}(B)$ and $D_2 = D \smallsetminus D_1$. This is done by scanning the elements of pre(B). For each $s \in \text{pre}(B)$, determine the block $D \in \pi$ containing it and create an associated block D' if one does not exist already. Move s from D to D'.

During the scanning, build a list of the blocks D that are split. After the scanning is done, process the list of split blocks as follows. For each such block with associated block D', mark D' as no longer being associated with D; eliminate the record for D if D is empty; if D is non-empty and the block of X containing D and D' has been made compound by the split, add this block to C.

(5) Compute pre(B) $\smallsetminus$ pre($S \smallsetminus B$). This is done by scanning the transitions whose target is in B'. For each such edge $s \xrightarrow{a} s'$, add s to pre(B) $\smallsetminus$ pre($S \smallsetminus B$) if s is not already in that set and count(s, B) = count(s, S).

(6) Replace π with split($S \smallsetminus B, \pi$) as done in step 4 above, but scanning pre(B) $\smallsetminus$ pre($S \smallsetminus B$) in lieu of pre(B).

(7) Update the count variables. This is done by scanning the transitions whose target is in B'. For each such transition $s \xrightarrow{a} s'$, decrement count(s, S). If this count becomes zero, delete the count record and make the transition point to count(s, B). When the scan is done, discard B'.

Fig. 3.4. The refinement steps of the Paige–Tarjan algorithm.

systems symbolically. The use of ROBDDs often permits a succinct representation of finite objects, and has led to breakthrough results in the automation of the solution to many combinatorial problems. The use of ROBDDs in the computation of bisimilarity over finite labelled transition systems has been proposed in [BS92].

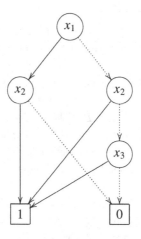

Fig. 3.5. Example of ROBDD where $x_1 < x_2 < x_3$.

We recall here that an ROBDD represents a boolean function as a rooted directed acyclic graph. The non-terminal nodes in the graph are labelled with input variables and the terminal nodes are labelled by boolean constants. Each non-terminal node has two outgoing edges, one per possible value of the boolean variable labelling it. In each path from the root of the graph to a terminal node, the variables respect a given total variable ordering. Finally, an ROBDD contains neither redundant tests nor duplicate nodes. The former requirement means that there is no non-terminal node in the graph whose two outgoing edges lead to the same node. The latter condition ensures that the sharing of nodes in an ROBDD is maximal, in that there are no two distinct nodes in the graph that are the roots of isomorphic sub-graphs. An example of ROBDD is given in Figure 3.5 where the solid edges leaving nodes labelled with variables represent the truth assignment true, while the dotted edges correspond to the thruth assignment false. We can see that if, e.g. x_1 is set to false, x_2 to false and x_3 to true, the whole boolean function evaluates to true as we reached the terminal node labelled with 1.

The crucial property of ROBDDs is their canonicity. This means that, for each boolean function with n arguments, there is exactly one ROBDD representing it with respect to the variable ordering $x_1 < x_2 < \cdots < x_n$, and therefore two ROBDDs representing the same function with respect to that ordering are isomorphic. For example, a boolean function is a tautology if, and only if, its associated ROBDD consists of a single node labelled with 1 (true) and it is satisfiable if, and only if, its associated ROBDD does not consist of a single node labelled with 0 (false).

Encoding a labelled transition system as an ROBDD The first step in using ROBBDs to compute bisimilarity over a finite labelled transition system is to encode the input labelled transition system. This is done as follows. The states in a finite labelled transition system with $n > 1$ states are represented by means of a function that associates with each state a distinct boolean vector of length $k = \lceil \log_2 n \rceil$. Each state s is therefore represented by a unique assignment of truth values to a vector of boolean variables $\vec{x} = (x_1, \dots, x_k)$. The set of actions labelling transitions is encoded in exactly the same way. Each action a is therefore represented by a unique assignment of truth values to a vector of boolean variables $\vec{y} = (y_1, \dots, y_\ell)$. The transition relation of the labelled transition system is represented by its characteristic function $\mathrm{Trans}(\vec{x}, \vec{y}, \vec{x}')$, which returns true exactly when $\vec{x}$, $\vec{y}$ and $\vec{x}'$ are the encodings of some state s, action a and state s', respectively, such that $s \xrightarrow{a} s'$. In the definition of the boolean formula describing the transition relation, the vector $\vec{x}' = (x_1', \dots, x_k')$ consists of distinct fresh variables, which are often called the target variables and are used to encode the targets of transitions.

Example 3.2.20 Consider, for instance, the labelled transition system over a single action depicted below. (We have omitted the label of the transitions and we shall not consider it in the encoding for the sake of simplicity.)

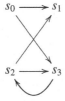

To encode the states in this labelled transition system, we use two boolean variables x_1 and x_2. Each state s_i, $i \in \{0, 1, 2, 3\}$, is represented by the binary representation of the number i. The boolean formula describing the transition relation is

$$(\overline{x_1} \wedge \overline{x_2} \wedge \overline{x_1'} \wedge x_2')$$
$$\vee$$
$$(\overline{x_1} \wedge \overline{x_2} \wedge x_1' \wedge x_2')$$
$$\vee$$
$$(x_1 \wedge \overline{x_2} \wedge x_1' \wedge x_2')$$
$$\vee$$
$$(x_1 \wedge \overline{x_2} \wedge \overline{x_1'} \wedge x_2')$$
$$\vee$$
$$(x_1 \wedge x_2 \wedge x_1' \wedge \overline{x_2'}).$$

For example, the transition from state s_2 to state s_3 is represented by the disjunct

$$x_1 \wedge \overline{x_2} \wedge x_1' \wedge x_2'$$

in the above formula. The first two conjuncts say that the source of the transition is the state whose encoding is the bit vector $(1, 0)$, namely s_2, and the last two say that the target is the state whose encoding is the bit vector $(1, 1)$, namely s_3.

The boolean formula $\text{Trans}(\vec{x}, \vec{y}, \vec{x'})$ can then be represented as an ROBDD choosing a suitable variable ordering. It is important to realise here that the size of the ROBDD for a boolean function depends crucially on the chosen variable ordering. Indeed, in the worst case, the size of an ROBDD is exponential in the number of variables. (See [Bry92] for a detailed, but very accessible, discussion of ROBDDs, their properties and their applications.) A useful property of the above-mentioned ROBDD representation of a labelled transition system is that the ROBDD describing the transition relation of a labelled transition system resulting from the application of the CCS operations of parallel composition, relabelling and restriction to a collection of component reactive systems (themselves represented as ROBDDs) is guaranteed to only grow linearly in the number of parallel components, provided an appropriate variable ordering is chosen, see [EFT93].

Remark 3.2.21 We remark that the above-stated linear upper bound applies to the size of the resulting ROBDD, but not necessarily to the intermediate ROBBDs that are constructed as stepping stones in the computation of the final result. However, in [EFT93], the authors claim that, in their practical experiments, the size of the intermediate ROBBDs never exceeded the size of the result ROBBD.

Symbolic computation of bisimilarity Like the aforementioned algorithms, the symbolic algorithm for computing bisimilarity is based upon the characterisation of bisimilarity as a largest fixed point given by Tarski's fixed-point theorem. In order to implement the iterative computation of the largest fixed point efficiently using ROBDDs, we need to rephrase the function $F_{\sim}$ in a way that is suitable for symbolic computation using ROBDD operations. The algorithm for the symbolic computation of bisimilarity is presented in Figure 3.6. In that algorithm, we assume that we are given two copies of the input labelled transition system with transition relations expressed by the boolean formulas $\text{Trans}(\vec{x}, \vec{y}, \vec{x'})$ and $\text{Trans}(\vec{z}, \vec{y}, \vec{z'})$. The algorithm computes the ROBDD representation of the boolean formula $\text{Bis}(\vec{x}, \vec{z})$ that encodes the characteristic function of the largest bisimulation over the input labelled transition system, that is, $\text{Bis}(s, s')$ returns true exactly when s and s' are bisimilar states in the labelled transition system.

---

(1) $\text{Bis}(\vec{x}, \vec{z}) := 1$
(2) `repeat`
   (a) $\text{Old}(\vec{x}, \vec{z}) := \text{Bis}(\vec{x}, \vec{z})$
   (b) $\text{Bis}(\vec{x}, \vec{z}) := \forall \vec{x}' \forall \vec{y}. \text{Trans}(\vec{x}, \vec{y}, \vec{x}') \Rightarrow (\exists \vec{z}'. \text{Trans}(\vec{z}, \vec{y}, \vec{z}') \wedge$
      $\text{Bis}(\vec{x}', \vec{z}')) \wedge \forall \vec{z}' \forall \vec{y}. \text{Trans}(\vec{z}, \vec{y}, \vec{z}') \Rightarrow (\exists \vec{x}'. \text{Trans}(\vec{x}, \vec{y}, \vec{x}') \wedge$
      $\text{Bis}(\vec{x}', \vec{z}'))$
(3) `until` $\text{Bis}(\vec{x}, \vec{z}) = \text{Old}(\vec{x}, \vec{z})$

Fig. 3.6. Algorithm for the symbolic computation of bisimilarity.

The algorithm in Figure 3.6 uses existential and universal quantification over boolean variables. These can be readily implemented in terms of the standard boolean operations. By way of example, if $f(x, y)$ is a boolean function then $\exists x. \ f(x, y)$ is a shorthand for $f(0, y) \vee f(1, y)$. We refer interested readers to [BS92, CS01] for further details on the efficient implementation of the ROBDD that encodes the right-hand side of the assignment at step 2 in the algorithm in Figure 3.6, as well as for a discussion of performance issues related to the appropriate choice of the variable ordering to be used in the computation.

3.2.5 Checking weak equivalences

The problem of checking observational equivalence (weak bisimilarity) over finite labelled transition systems can be reduced to that of checking strong bisimilarity using a technique called saturation. Intuitively, saturation amounts to

(1) first pre-computing the weak transition relation (see [San12, section 4.1]), and then
(2) constructing a new pair of finite processes whose original transitions are replaced with the weak transitions.

The question of whether two states are weakly bisimilar now amounts to checking strong bisimilarity over the saturated systems. Since the computation of the weak transition relation can be carried out in polynomial time, the problem of checking for weak bisimilarity can also be decided in polynomial time. The same holds true for the problem of checking observational congruence [Mil89]. (See [San12, section 4.4] for the definition of observational congruence, which is there called rooted weak bisimilarity.)

Efficient algorithms are also available for deciding a variation on the notion of weak bisimilarity called branching bisimilarity [GW96] over finite labelled transition systems (see [San12, section 4.9]). Notably, Groote and Vaandrager have developed in [GV90] an algorithm for checking branching bisimilarity that has time complexity $O(m \log m + mn)$ and space complexity $O(m + n)$.

3.3 The complexity of checking bisimilarity over finite processes

In the previous section, we saw that, unlike the classic notion of language equivalence, bisimilarity can be efficiently decided over finite labelled transition systems. In particular, the time complexity of the algorithm of Paige and Tarjan offers an upper bound on the time complexity of checking bisimilarity over finite labelled transition systems. This naturally raises the question of whether it is possible to provide lower bounds on the computational complexity of computing bisimilarity over such structures. Indeed, computer scientists often consider a decidable computational problem 'solved' when they possess matching lower and upper bounds on its computational complexity.

Our order of business in this section will be to survey some of the most notable results pertaining to lower bounds on the computational complexity of bisimilarity checking for several classes of finite labelled transition systems. We shall also present some rather general proof techniques that yield perspicuous proofs of the results we discuss in what follows.

Since the notion of bisimulation game plays an important role in our presentation of the complexity and decidability results discussed in the remainder of this chapter, we now proceed to introduce it briefly. (We refer the reader to [San12] and [AILS07] for more comprehensive discussions.)

3.3.1 Game characterisation of bisimulation-like relations

We shall use a standard game-theoretic characterisation of (bi)similarity, see, for instance, [Tho93, Sti95] and [San12, chapter 2]. A *bisimulation game* on a pair of processes (P_1, Q_1) is a two-player game between *Attacker* and *Defender*. The game is played in *rounds*. In each round the players change the *current pair of states* (P, Q) (initially $P = P_1$ and $Q = Q_1$) according to the following rules:

(1) Attacker chooses either P or Q, an action a and performs a move $P \xrightarrow{a} P'$ or $Q \xrightarrow{a} Q'$, depending on whether he chose P or Q.

(2) Defender responds by choosing the other process (either Q or P) and performs a move $Q \xrightarrow{a} Q'$ or $P \xrightarrow{a} P'$ under the same action a.

(3) The pair (P', Q') becomes the (new) current pair of states.

A *play* (of the bisimulation game) is a sequence of pairs of processes formed by the players according to the rules mentioned above. A play is finite iff one of the players gets stuck (cannot make a move); the player who gets stuck loses the play and the other player is the winner. If the play is infinite then Defender is the winner.

We use the following standard fact, see [Tho93, Sti95] and [San12, chapter 2].

Proposition 3.3.1 *It holds that $P \sim Q$ iff Defender has a winning strategy in the bisimulation game starting with the pair (P, Q), and $P \not\sim Q$ iff Attacker has a winning strategy in the corresponding game.*

The rules of the bisimulation game can be easily modified in order to capture other coinductively defined equivalences and preorders.

- In the *simulation preorder game*, Attacker is restricted to attack only from the (left-hand-side) process P. In the *simulation equivalence game*, Attacker can first choose a side (either P or Q) but after that he is not allowed to change the side any more.
- The *completed/ready simulation game* has the same rules as the simulation game but Defender is moreover losing in any configuration which breaks the extra condition imposed by the definition (i.e. P and Q should have the same set of initial actions in case of ready simulation, and their sets of initial actions should be both empty at the same time in case of completed simulation).
- In the *2-nested simulation preorder game*, Attacker starts playing from the left-hand-side process P and at most once during the play he is allowed to switch sides. (The soundness of this game follows from the characterisation provided in [AFI01].) In the *2-nested simulation equivalence game*, Attacker can initially choose any side but the sides can be changed at most once during the play.

3.3.2 Deciding bisimilarity over finite labelled transition systems is P-complete

The algorithmic results discussed in Section 3.2 indicate that strong, weak and branching bisimilarity can be decided over finite labelled transition systems more efficiently than language equivalence (and indeed than many other equivalences). This is good news for researchers and practitioners who develop and/or use software tools that implement various forms of bisimilarity checking. However, the size of the labelled transition systems on which the above-mentioned algorithms are run in practice is often huge. It is therefore natural to ask oneself whether one can devise efficient parallel algorithms for bisimilarity checking. Such algorithms might exploit the parallelism that is becoming increasingly available on our computers to speed up checking whether two processes are bisimilar or not. It would be very satisfying, as well as practically useful, if algorithms for checking bisimilarity could run on a highly parallel machine with a running time that is proportional to the logarithm of the size of the state space of the input labelled transition system using a feasible number of processors. But is an algorithm meeting the above desiderata likely to exist?

A most likely negative answer to the above question has been given by Balcázar, Gabarró and Santha, who showed in [BGS92] that deciding strong bisimilarity between finite labelled transition systems is P-complete; this means that it is one of the 'hardest problems' in the class P of problems solvable in deterministic polynomial time. P-complete problems are of interest because they appear to lack highly parallel solutions. So, showing that an algorithmic problem is P-complete is interpreted as strong evidence that the existence of an efficient parallel solution for it is unlikely. See, for instance, the book [GHR95] for much more information on P-completeness.

We shall now present the main ideas behind the hardness proof of the above mentioned result, which we reiterate below in the form of a theorem.

Theorem 3.3.2 (Balcázar, Gabarró and Santha 1992) *The bisimilarity checking problem between two states in a finite labelled transition system is P-complete.*

The theorem can be proved by offering a reduction from a problem that is already known to be P-complete to the problem of checking strong bisimilarity between a pair of finite-state processes P and Q. The reduction will be a so-called log-space reduction, which means that it is computable in deterministic logarithmic space.

Similarly as in the original proof by Balcázar, Gabarró and Santha, we will provide a reduction from the *monotone Circuit Value Problem* (mCVP), which is known to be P-complete (see, e.g. [Pap94]). However, the ideas in the reduction presented below are different from their original proof. For the purpose of this presentation we shall use the so-called *Defender's forcing technique*, which simplifies many of the constructions for hardness results. For a more detailed introduction to this technique consult [JS08].

A *monotone Boolean circuit* C is a finite directed acyclic graph in which the nodes are either of indegree zero (*input* nodes) or of indegree two and there is exactly one node of outdegree zero (the *output* node).

Each node in C that is not an input node is labelled with one of the symbols $\wedge$ and $\vee$, which stand for conjunction and disjunction, respectively.

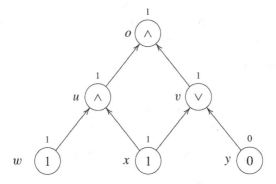

Fig. 3.7. An instance of mCVP together with assigned truth values.

An *input for the circuit* C is an assignment of the truth values 0 (false) or 1 (true) to all input nodes. Given an input, every node in the circuit can be uniquely assigned a truth value as follows:

- the value of an input node is given by the input assignment;
- the value of a node labelled with $\wedge$ or $\vee$ is the logical conjunction or disjunction of values of its two predecessors, respectively.

Given an input for the circuit, the *output value of the circuit* C is the value assigned to its output node.

The mCVP problem asks to decide, given a monotone Boolean circuit C and its input, whether its output value is true.

An example of a monotone Boolean circuit with an input assignment and computed values at each node is given in Figure 3.7.

Assume now a given monotone Boolean circuit C with the output node o and with a given input. We shall construct a finite labelled transition system and two of its processes P_o and Q_o such that if the output value of C is true then P_o and Q_o are strongly bisimilar, and if the output value is false then Q_o does not strongly simulate P_o. Such a construction will enable us to state a general claim about P-hardness for *all* relations between the simulation preorder and bisimilarity.

Remark 3.3.3 Indeed, we will be able to draw such a general conclusion for *any* (perhaps not even yet 'discovered') relation on processes R such that if $P \sim Q$ then $(P, Q) \in R$, and if Q does not simulate P then $(P, Q) \notin R$, because if the output value of C is true then $P \sim Q$ and hence $(P, Q) \in R$, and if the output value of C is false then Q does not simulate P and hence $(P, Q) \notin R$. Examples of such a relation R include, among others, simulation preorder/equivalence, completed simulation preorder/equivalence, ready simulation preorder/equivalence, 2-nested simulation preorder/equivalence and, of course, also bisimulation equivalence.

The processes of the constructed labelled transition system are

- P_{end},
- P_v and Q_v for every node v in C, and additionally,
- P_v', Q_v^ℓ and Q_v^r for every node v in C labelled with $\vee$.

The transition relation contains the following transitions:

- $P_v \xrightarrow{\ell} P_{v_1}$, $P_v \xrightarrow{r} P_{v_2}$, and $Q_v \xrightarrow{\ell} Q_{v_1}$, $Q_v \xrightarrow{r} Q_{v_2}$ for every node v in C labelled with $\wedge$ and with the predecessor nodes v_1 and v_2, and
- $P_v \xrightarrow{a} P_v'$, $P_v \xrightarrow{a} Q_v^\ell$, $P_v \xrightarrow{a} Q_v^r$, and
  $P_v' \xrightarrow{\ell} P_{v_1}$, $P_v' \xrightarrow{r} P_{v_2}$, and
  $Q_v \xrightarrow{a} Q_v^\ell$, $Q_v \xrightarrow{a} Q_v^r$, and
  $Q_v^\ell \xrightarrow{\ell} Q_{v_1}$, $Q_v^\ell \xrightarrow{r} P_{v_2}$, $Q_v^r \xrightarrow{r} Q_{v_2}$, $Q_v^r \xrightarrow{\ell} P_{v_1}$
  for every node v in C labelled with $\vee$ and with the predecessor nodes v_1 and v_2, and
- $P_v \xrightarrow{0} P_{end}$ for every input node v in C assigned the value false.

The reduction is clearly computable in log-space. An example of the construction, taking as the input circuit the one in Figure 3.7, is presented in Figure 3.8.

Exercise 3.3.4 Consider the transition system constructed in Figure 3.8. Argue that Defender has a winning strategy in the bisimulation game starting from (P_o, Q_o); in other words show that $P_o \sim Q_o$.   □

We will now show that

- if the output value of C is true then P_o and Q_o are strongly bisimilar, and
- if the output value of C is false then Q_o does not strongly simulate P_o.

As a conclusion, we will get that deciding *any* relation between the simulation preorder and strong bisimilarity on finite labelled transition systems is P-hard.

Let us consider a play in the bisimulation game between Attacker and Defender starting from the pair (P_o, Q_o). The idea is that, after finitely many rounds of a play, the players will eventually reach some input node. During each play, Attacker is trying to reach an input node P_v with assigned value false, as this is a winning configuration for Attacker. (Defender has no answer to the action 0 that Attacker can perform in the left-hand-side process.) On the other hand, Defender is trying to reach an input node with assigned value true, as Attacker loses in such a situation (no further actions are available).

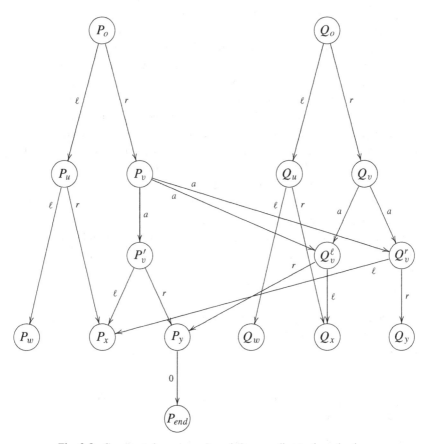

Fig. 3.8. Constructed processes P_o and Q_o according to the reduction.

The processes P_o and Q_o are constructed in such a way that in the current pair (P_v, Q_v), where v is labelled by $\wedge$, it is Attacker who chooses the next node and forces reaching the next pair (P_{v_i}, Q_{v_i}) for a chosen $i \in \{1, 2\}$ by playing either the action ℓ or r. If the current pair (P_v, Q_v) corresponds to a node v which is labelled by $\vee$, it should be Defender who decides the next pair of processes. This is achieved by using a particular instance of the so-called Defender's forcing technique [JS08]. Initially, Attacker has five possible moves under the action a from the pair (P_v, Q_v) where v is labelled by $\vee$. Clearly, the only possible attack is by playing $P_v \xrightarrow{a} P_v'$; all the remaining four moves can be matched by Defender in such a way that the play continues from a pair of identical processes (a clear winning position for Defender). Defender can now answer by playing either $Q_v \xrightarrow{a} Q_v^\ell$ or $Q_v \xrightarrow{a} Q_v^r$ and the players continue from the pair (P_v', Q_v^ℓ) or (P_v', Q_v^r), depending of Defender's choice. In the first case Attacker is forced to play the action ℓ and the players reach the pair (P_{v_1}, Q_{v_1}) (playing action r leads to an immediate loss for Attacker as Defender can again reach a pair of equal processes). Similarly, in the second case Attacker must play the action r and Defender forces the pair (P_{v_2}, Q_{v_2}).

To sum up, starting from the pair (P_o, Q_o), where o is the output node of the circuit, the players choose, step by step, one particular path in the circuit leading to an input node. From the current pair (P_v, Q_v), where v is labelled by $\wedge$, it is Attacker who chooses the next pair; if the node v is labelled by $\vee$ it is Defender who chooses (in two rounds) the next pair. Attacker wins if, and only if, the players reach a pair of processes that represent an input node with the assigned value false. Hence if the output value of C is true then Defender has a winning strategy in the strong bisimulation game. Note that if, on the other hand, Attacker has a winning strategy then it can be achieved by attacking only from the left-hand-side process (in this case, when the output value of C is false, there must be an input node set to false, because the circuit is monotone). Hence if the output value of C is false then Attacker has a winning strategy in the strong simulation game.

We have so argued for the following P-hardness theorem.

Theorem 3.3.5 *The equivalence checking problem between two processes in a finite-state, acyclic labelled transition system is P-hard for any relation between strong simulation preorder and strong bisimilarity.*

Exercise 3.3.6 Assume that the output of some given circuit C is true. Using the ideas of the proof presented above, generalise your solution to Exercise 3.3.4 in order to construct a bisimulation containing the pair (P_o, Q_o).

In fact, Sawa and Jančar proved in [SJ01] that the problem is P-hard for *all* relations between the trace preorder and bisimilarity. Their result is even more general, but the encoding is more involved.

Finally, note that in the reduction presented above we used four different actions. So the question is whether equivalence checking is P-hard even in case of a singleton action alphabet. Unfortunately, the answer is positive also in this case. For bisimilarity this result is a consequence of the original reduction provided by Balcázar, Gabarró and Santha [BGS92], which uses only a single action for the encoding of any alternating mCVP instance. In order to show that the problem is P-hard also for other behavioural equivalences and preorders, we shall now present a simple construction based on [Srb01], which provides a general log-space reduction of bisimilarity checking on labelled transition systems with several actions to bisimilarity checking over a one-letter action set.

Assume two given processes P and Q over an LTS T with the set of actions $\{a_1, a_2, \ldots, a_\ell\}$. We shall construct a modified LTS T' which contains all the processes of T together with some additional ones defined in the following way: for every transition $P_1 \xrightarrow{a_i} P_2$ in T we add into T'

- two transitions $P_1 \to P_{(P_1,a_i,P_2)}$ and $P_{(P_1,a_i,P_2)} \to P_2$ where $P_{(P_1,a_i,P_2)}$ is a newly added state, and
- a newly added path of length i from $P_{(P_1,a_i,P_2)}$.

Finally, for every process P in T we create in T' a newly added path of length $\ell + 1$ starting from P. As the LTS T' contains only one action, we omit its name from the transition relation. We shall call the newly added processes into T' *intermediate processes*. An example of the reduction is depicted in Figure 3.9.

Exercise 3.3.7 Consider the one-action LTS in Figure 3.9. Argue that Attacker has a winning strategy in the bisimulation game starting from the pair (P_1, P') where $P' = P_{(P_1,a_2,P_3)}$ and from the pair (P_1, P_2).

The reduction presented above can clearly be carried out in log-space. Moreover, we can observe the following property of the LTS T'.

Lemma 3.3.8 *Let P be a process of T and P' a newly added intermediate process in T'. Then $P \nsim P'$ in the LTS T'.*

Proof We describe Attacker's winning strategy from the pair (P, P'). In the first round Attacker plays the transition from P that starts the path of length $\ell + 1$ that was added to the LTS T'. Defender answers by a move from P'. Now if Defender ended again in some intermediate process, it must be in a branch starting from some $P_{(P_1,a_i,P_2)}$, but this configuration is winning for Attacker by not changing sides and by simply making the remaining ℓ moves along the path he chose initially. Defender cannot do as many moves and loses. If, on the other hand, Defender ended in some of the original processes in T, Attacker will change sides and play the sequence of $\ell + 1$ transitions available from this original processes. Again, Defender cannot match this sequence in the other process as the sequence of moves he has at his disposal is shorter by one. Hence Defender loses also in this case. □

Due to Lemma 3.3.8, we know that during any bisimulation game Defender is forced to play in T' in such a way that every current configuration consists either of two intermediate processes or of two processes from the original LTS T.

We can now observe that for any two processes P and Q in T we have $P \sim Q$ in T if, and only if, $P \sim Q$ in T'. Indeed, each move $P_1 \xrightarrow{a_i} P_2$ by the Attacker in the original LTS T is simulated by two moves $P_1 \to P_{(P_1,a_i,P_2)} \to P_2$ in the LTS T' and Defender can only answer by some corresponding two moves

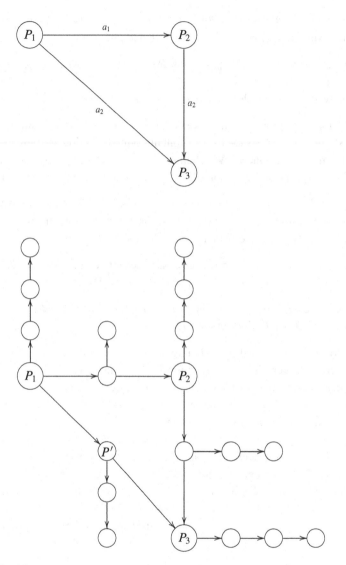

Fig. 3.9. Input LTS above and the one-action LTS below where $P' = P_{(P_1, a_2, P_3)}$.

such that in the intermediate state the length of the available path leading to a deadlock is the same as on the Attacker's side. Hence Defender has to use the sequence of two transitions that corresponds to the same action as played by Attacker. (Should Defender choose a different move, Attacker will easily win the game.) Similarly, if Defender has a winning strategy in the original LTS T, it can be easily extended to a winning strategy in T'.

Because the proposed reduction preserves acyclicity, we obtain the following theorem.

Theorem 3.3.9 *Strong bisimilarity checking over finite LTSs is log-space reducible to strong bisimilarity checking over finite LTSs over a one-letter action alphabet. Moreover, the reduction preserves acyclicity.*

By combining Theorem 3.3.5 and Theorem 3.3.9 we obtain the promised P-hardness result for finite labelled transition systems over a singleton action set.

Corollary 3.3.10 *The equivalence-checking problem between two processes in a finite, acyclic labelled transition system over a singleton action set is P-hard for any relation between the strong simulation preorder and strong bisimilarity.*

Remark 3.3.11 Note that the above presented reduction from LTS to a one-letter action alphabet LTS works even for infinite-state systems. The question is, though, what classes of infinite-state systems are closed under this construction and whether it is efficiently implementable. Indeed, as argued in [Srb01], this is true for may well-known classes of systems generated by, e.g. pushdown automata or Petri nets and the transformation is efficient and moreover preserves answers to μ-calculus model checking problems.

Exercise 3.3.12 Find a (small) modification of the reduction in the proof of Theorem 3.3.9 (see also the example in Figure 3.9), such that one can reach the following conclusion regarding the size of the constructed system over a one-letter action alphabet: if the original LTS has n states, m transitions and m' actions, then the constructed LTS has $O(n + m')$ states and $O(m)$ transitions. Since $m' \leq m$, this will imply that the constructed system has $O(n + m)$ states and $O(m)$ transitions.

It is well known that weak bisimilarity, observational congruence [Mil89], branching bisimilarity and rooted branching bisimilarity [GW96] coincide with strong bisimilarity over τ-free labelled transition systems. Since the actions used in constructing the labelled transition system from a monotone Boolean circuit as in the proof of Theorem 3.3.5 can be chosen to be different from τ, the proof of Theorem 3.3.5 also yields a log-space reduction of the monotone circuit value problem to that of deciding weak bisimilarity, observational congruence, branching bisimilarity and rooted branching bisimilarity over a finite, acyclic labelled transition system. We therefore have the following result.

Theorem 3.3.13 *The problem of deciding weak bisimilarity, observational congruence, branching bisimilarity and rooted branching bisimilarity between two states in a finite, acyclic labelled transition system is P-hard. This holds true even when the set of actions is a singleton.*

Readers who are familiar with [San12, section 2.10.2] will recall that, over image-finite labelled transition systems (and hence over finite labelled transition systems), strong bisimilarity coincides with the relation

$$\sim_\omega = \cap_{i \geq 0} \sim_i,$$

where $\sim_i$, $i \geq 0$, is the i-th approximant to bisimilarity. In their classic paper [HM85], Hennessy and Milner defined an alternative non-increasing (with respect to set inclusion) sequence $\simeq_i$, $i \geq 0$, of approximants to bisimilarity as follows:

- $P \simeq_0 Q$ always holds.
- $P \simeq_{i+1} Q$ iff for each sequence of actions w:

  (1) for each P' such that $P \xrightarrow{w} P'$, there is some Q' such that $Q \xrightarrow{w} Q'$ and $P' \simeq_i Q'$;
  (2) for each Q' such that $Q \xrightarrow{w} Q'$, there is some P' such that $P \xrightarrow{w} P'$ and $P' \simeq_i Q'$.

The relations $\simeq_i$, $i \geq 0$, are the so-called nested trace semantics [AFGI04]. For instance, $\simeq_1$ is trace equivalence and $\simeq_2$ is possible-futures equivalence [RB81]. Each of the $\simeq_i$, $i \geq 0$, is an equivalence relation and is preserved by the operators of CCS introduced in [San12, chapter 3].

Hennessy and Milner showed in [HM85] that, over image-finite labelled transition systems, strong bisimilarity also coincides with the relation

$$\simeq_\omega = \cap_{i \geq 0} \simeq_i.$$

In stark contrast to the P-completeness of bisimilarity checking over finite labelled transition systems, Kanellakis and Smolka proved in [KS90] the following result to the effect that computing the relations $\simeq_i$, $i \geq 1$, is much harder than computing bisimilarity.

Theorem 3.3.14 (Kanellakis and Smolka) *For each $i \geq 1$, the problem of deciding the equivalence $\simeq_i$ over finite labelled transition systems is PSPACE-complete.*

Proof Recall that $\simeq_1$ is just trace equivalence. Deciding trace equivalence over finite labelled transition systems is known to be PSPACE-complete. (See lemma 4.2 in [KS90], where this result is attributed to Chandra and Stockmeyer.) We are therefore left to prove the claim for $\simeq_i$, $i \geq 2$.

We begin by arguing that deciding the equivalence $\simeq_i$ is PSPACE-hard for each $i \geq 2$. To this end, we prove that $\simeq_1$ reduces (in polynomial time) to $\simeq_i$, for each $i \geq 2$. In order to show this claim, it suffices only to give a polynomial time reduction from $\simeq_i$ to $\simeq_{i+1}$, for each $i \geq 1$. In presenting the reduction from $\simeq_i$ to $\simeq_{i+1}$, we shall use the operators of action prefixing and choice from CCS that were introduced in [San12, section 3.1]. (Note that those operators can be viewed as operations over the class of finite labelled transition systems.)

The reduction works as follows. Let P and Q be two states in a finite labelled transition system. Define the processes P' and Q' thus:

$$P' = a.(P + Q) \text{ and}$$
$$Q' = a.P + a.Q,$$

where a is an arbitrary action in our labelled transition system. We claim that

$$P \simeq_i Q \text{ iff } P' \simeq_{i+1} Q'.$$

This can be shown as follows.

- If $P' \simeq_{i+1} Q'$ then the definition of $\simeq_i$ yields that $P \simeq_i P + Q \simeq_i Q$, from which $P \simeq_i Q$ follows by the transitivity of $\simeq_i$.
- Assume now that $P \simeq_i Q$ holds. We prove that $P' \simeq_{i+1} Q'$.

  We limit ourselves to showing that for each sequence of actions w and process P'' such that $P' \xrightarrow{w} P''$, there is some Q'' such that $Q' \xrightarrow{w} Q''$ and $P'' \simeq_i Q''$. We proceed by considering three cases, depending on whether w is empty, $w = a$ or w is of length at least two.

  - Suppose that w is empty. Then $P' = P''$ and $Q' = Q''$. Recall that $\simeq_i$ is a congruence with respect to action prefixing and choice. Therefore, since $P \simeq_i Q$ and choice is easily seen to be idempotent with respect to $\simeq_i$,

    $$P' = a.(P + Q) \simeq_i a.P \simeq_i a.P + a.P \simeq_i a.P + a.Q \simeq_i Q',$$

    and we are done.

  - Suppose that $w = a$. Then $P'' = P + Q$ and reasoning as in the previous case we infer that, for instance, $P'' \simeq_i P$. Since $Q' \xrightarrow{a} P$, we are done.

  - Suppose that w is of length at least two. In this case, it is easy to see that $Q' \xrightarrow{w} P''$ and the claim follows since $\simeq_i$ is reflexive.

Therefore $\simeq_i$ reduces to $\simeq_{i+1}$, for each $i \geq 1$, as claimed. It follows that $\simeq_1$ reduces (in polynomial time) to $\simeq_i$, for each $i \geq 2$, by applying the reduction given above $(i - 1)$ times.

Membership of each $\simeq_i$, $i \geq 2$, in PSPACE can be shown by reducing the problem of deciding $\simeq_i$ to the equivalence problem for non-deterministic finite automata (see, e.g. [Sip06]), which is a well-known PSPACE-complete problem [GJ79, SM73]. To this end, observe that, since we already know that $\simeq_1$ is in PSPACE, we can reason inductively as follows. Assume that

$\simeq_i$ is in PSPACE, for some $i \geq 1$. Using this assumption, we proceed to prove membership in PSPACE for $\simeq_{i+1}$. Let P and Q be two states in a finite labelled transition system. Let $\{B_1, \ldots, B_k\}$ be the partition of the set of states induced by the equivalence $\simeq_i$. (The partition can be computed using a polynomial amount of space since $\simeq_i$ is in PSPACE by our inductive assumption.)

Observe now that we can view our input finite labelled transition system as a non-deterministic finite automaton with either P or Q as start state and with any of the sets $B_1, \ldots, B_k$ as set of accept states. For each $\ell \in \{1, \ldots, k\}$, let $L_\ell(P)$ (respectively, $L_\ell(Q)$) denote the language accepted by the non-deterministic finite automaton that results by taking P (respectively, Q) as start state and B_ℓ as set of accept states. It is easy to see that

$$P \simeq_{i+1} Q \text{ iff } L_\ell(P) = L_\ell(Q), \text{ for each } \ell \in \{1, \ldots, k\}.$$

This yields membership in PSPACE for $\simeq_{i+1}$, which was to be shown. □

In the light of the above theorem, bisimilarity over finite labelled transition systems can be decided in polynomial time, but is the 'limit' of a non-increasing sequence of equivalences that are all PSPACE-complete. We shall meet analogues of this result in Section 3.4.

Remark 3.3.15 In the setting of equational axiomatisations of behavioural relations, the paper [AFGI04] presents hardness results for nested trace semantics that are akin to Theorem 3.3.14 and set them apart from bisimilarity. More precisely, in that reference, the authors show that, unlike bisimilarity, none of the relations $\simeq_i$, $i \geq 2$, affords a finite, ground-complete axiomatisation over basic CCS.

3.3.3 EXPTIME-completeness of equivalence checking on networks of finite processes

We have shown in Theorem 3.3.5 that the equivalence checking problem on finite, acyclic processes is P-hard for any relation between the simulation preorder and bisimilarity. In fact, the usually studied equivalences and preorders between the simulation preorder and bisimilarity, such as the completed, ready and 2-nested simulations preorders, are also decidable in deterministic polynomial time. (See [San12, chapter 6] or the encyclopaedic survey paper [Gla01] for the definition of those relations. An efficient algorithm for deciding the ready simulation preorder is described in [BP95].)

The aforementioned results are rather encouraging and bode well for the use of such relations in computer-aided implementation verification. However, one should realise that the complexity of the algorithms we have presented so far is measured with respect to the size of the input labelled transition system. These systems are called *flat systems*. However, in practice the studied LTS is often given indirectly, for example as a parallel composition of communicating finite-state agents. The semantics of such a composition is still given in terms of labelled transition systems; however, the resulting LTS is often of exponential size with respect to the size of the description of the system. The formalisms that provide such a succinct description of large labelled transition systems are called *non-flat systems*. In this section, we shall introduce one example of a non-flat system where a number of concurrent finite processes communicate via synchronisation on common actions and we shall study the complexity of bisimulation-like equivalence checking on such non-flat systems. As we shall see, the resulting decision problems become computationally hard in such a setting.

Let $(Pr_i, Act_i, \rightarrow_i)$ be a finite LTS for every i, $1 \leq i \leq n$. A *network of finite processes* is a parallel composition $P_1 \mid P_2 \mid \cdots \mid P_n$ where $P_i \in Pr_i$ for each $i \in \{1, \ldots, n\}$. The semantics of such a composition is given in terms of a flat LTS $(Pr, Act, \rightarrow)$ where

- $Pr = Pr_1 \times Pr_2 \times \cdots \times Pr_n$,
- $Act = Act_1 \cup Act_2 \cup \cdots \cup Act_n$, and
- $(Q_1, Q_2, \ldots, Q_n) \overset{a}{\rightarrow} (Q_1', Q_2', \ldots, Q_n')$ whenever $Q_i \overset{a}{\rightarrow}_i Q_i'$ if $a \in Act_i$, and $Q_i = Q_i'$ if $a \notin Act_i$.

The flattening of the network $P_1 \mid P_2 \mid \cdots \mid P_n$ is then the process $(P_1, P_2, \ldots, P_n)$ in the above-defined LTS and the equivalence checking problem on networks of finite processes is defined simply by using the standard notion on the underlying flattened systems.

It was shown by Rabinovich [Rab97] that equivalence checking for networks of finite processes with hiding of actions is PSPACE-hard for any relation between trace equivalence and bisimilarity. Rabinovich conjectured that the problem is EXPTIME-hard. Indeed, EXPTIME-hardness was already known for bisimilarity [JM96] and simulation equivalence [HKV97] and the conjecture was later partially confirmed by Laroussinie and Schnoebelen [LS00], who proved an EXPTIME-hardness result for all the relations between the simulation preorder and bisimilarity on networks of finite processes. In their proof, Laroussinie and Schnoebelen do not use any hiding of actions. Finally, Sawa [Saw03] settled Rabinovich's conjecture by showing that equivalence checking on networks of finite processes with hiding is EXPTIME-hard for all relations between the trace preorder and bisimilarity.

We shall now argue that many equivalence checking problems with respect to bisimulation-like equivalences/preorders are EXPTIME-complete on networks of finite processes (without hiding). Our exposition of the hardness result is based on the ideas from [LS00], though the construction is different in the technical details and the presentation is simplified by using the previously discussed Defender's forcing technique [JS08].

The EXPTIME-hardness proof is done by offering a polynomial-time reduction from the acceptance problem for alternating linear bounded automata (ALBA), a well-known EXPTIME-complete problem, see, e.g. [Sip06].

An ALBA is a tuple $M = (Q, Q_\exists, Q_\forall, \Sigma, \Gamma, \blacktriangleright, \blacktriangleleft, q_0, q_{acc}, q_{rej}, \delta)$ where

- $Q_\exists$ and $Q_\forall$ are finite, disjoint sets of existential, respectively universal, control states and $Q = Q_\exists \cup Q_\forall$,
- Σ is a finite input alphabet,
- $\Gamma \supseteq \Sigma$ is a finite tape alphabet,
- $\blacktriangleright, \blacktriangleleft \in \Gamma$ are the left and right end-markers,
- $q_0, q_{acc}, q_{rej} \in Q$ are the initial, accept and reject states, respectively, and
- $\delta : Q \setminus \{q_{acc}, q_{rej}\} \times \Gamma \to Q \times Q \times \Gamma \times \{-1, +1\}$ is a computation step function, such that whenever $\delta(p, x) = (q_1, q_2, y, d)$ then $x = \blacktriangleright$ iff $y = \blacktriangleright$ and if $x = \blacktriangleright$ then $d = +1$, and $x = \blacktriangleleft$ iff $y = \blacktriangleleft$ and if $x = \blacktriangleleft$ then $d = -1$.

We can, without loss of generality, assume that the input alphabet is binary, that is $\Sigma = \{a, b\}$ and that the tape alphabet only contains the symbols from the input alphabet and the end-markers, that is $\Gamma = \{a, b, \blacktriangleleft, \blacktriangleright\}$. We shall write $p \xrightarrow{x \to y, d} q_1, q_2$ whenever $\delta(p, x) = (q_1, q_2, y, d)$. The intuition is that if the machine M is in a state p and is reading the tape symbol x, it can replace x with y, move the tape head one position to the right (if $d = +1$) or to the left (if $d = -1$) and enter the control state q_1 or q_2 (depending on the type of the control state p the choice between q_1 and q_2 is either existential or universal).

A configuration of M is given by the current control state, the position of the tape head and the content of the tape; we write it as a triple from $Q \times \mathbb{N} \times (\{\blacktriangleright\} . \Gamma^* . \{\blacktriangleleft\})$. The head position on the left end-marker $\blacktriangleright$ is by definition 0. A *step of computation* is a relation between configurations, denoted by $\vdash$, that is defined using the function δ in the usual way. For example, for the transition $p \xrightarrow{a \to b, +1} q_1, q_2$ we get $(p, 1, \blacktriangleright aab\blacktriangleleft) \vdash (q_1, 2, \blacktriangleright bab\blacktriangleleft)$ and $(p, 1, \blacktriangleright aab\blacktriangleleft) \vdash (q_2, 2, \blacktriangleright bab\blacktriangleleft)$.

Given a word $w \in \Sigma^*$, the initial configuration of M is $(q_0, 1, \blacktriangleright w\blacktriangleleft)$. A configuration is called *accepting* if it is of the form $(q_{acc}, i, \blacktriangleright w'\blacktriangleleft)$, and it is called *rejecting* if it is of the form $(q_{rej}, i, \blacktriangleright w'\blacktriangleleft)$.

A *computation tree* on an input $w \in \Sigma^*$ is a labelled tree such that the root is labelled by the initial configuration, the leaves are the nodes labelled by accepting or rejecting configurations and every non-leaf node labelled by a configuration c with existential control state has exactly one child labelled with some c' such that $c \vdash c'$, and every non-leaf node labelled by a configuration c with universal control state has exactly two children labelled with c_1 and c_2 such that c_1 and c_2 are the two successor configurations of c, i.e. $c \vdash c_1$ and $c \vdash c_2$. Without loss of generality, we shall assume from now on that any computation tree is finite (see e.g. [Sip06, page 198]).

A computation tree on an input w is called *accepting* if its leaves are labelled only with accepting configurations. An ALBA M accepts a word $w \in \Sigma^*$, if there exists an accepting computation tree of M on w.

As already mentioned, the problem of deciding whether a given ALBA M accepts a given word $w \in \Sigma^*$ is EXPTIME-complete (see, e.g. [Sip06]).

Let M be a given ALBA with an input $w = w_1 w_2 \dots w_n \in \{a, b\}^*$. We shall construct (in polynomial time) two networks of finite processes

$$P = C(q_0, 1) \mid T_0^{\blacktriangleright} \mid T_1^{w_1} \mid T_2^{w_2} \mid \cdots \mid T_n^{w_n} \mid T_{n+1}^{\blacktriangleleft}$$

and

$$Q = D(q_0, 1) \mid T_0^{\blacktriangleright} \mid T_1^{w_1} \mid T_2^{w_2} \mid \cdots \mid T_n^{w_n} \mid T_{n+1}^{\blacktriangleleft}$$

such that

- if M accepts w then Defender has a winning strategy in the bisimulation game from (P, Q), and
- if M does not accept w then Attacker has a winning strategy in the simulation game from (P, Q).

Having shown these claims, we will be able to conclude that equivalence checking for *any* relation between the simulation preorder and bisimilarity on networks of finite processes is EXPTIME-hard. (This kind of general reasoning was explained in Remark 3.3.3.)

The intuition behind the construction is that in the processes

$$T_0^{\blacktriangleright}, T_1^{w_1}, T_2^{w_2}, \dots, T_n^{w_n}, T_{n+1}^{\blacktriangleleft}$$

we remember the actual content of the tape. Because the left and right end-markers cannot be rewritten, it is sufficient that the processes $T_0^{\blacktriangleright}$ and $T_{n+1}^{\blacktriangleleft}$ are one-state processes and because we assume that the rest of the tape consists only of the symbols a and b, the remaining processes $T_1^{w_1}, \dots, T_n^{w_n}$ will all contain exactly two states, remembering the current content of the particular tape cell. Additionally, the process P has the parallel component $C(p, i)$, which represents the current control state and the position of the tape head; similarly the same information is remembered in the process Q in the parallel component $D(p, i)$. In fact, the use of C or D is the only point where the processes P and

Q differ. The processes representing the tape cells will communicate with the process $C(p, i)$ or $D(p, i)$ using actions of the form (x, y, i), meaning that if the tape cell i contains the symbol x, it is going to remember the symbol y after the (hand-shake) communication takes place. Defining the processes $C(p, i)$ and $D(p, i)$ is rather straightforward. The only challenge is the implementation of the choice between the new control states q_1 and q_2. If p is a universal state then it will be Attacker who chooses one of them – implementation of this choice by the Attacker is easy. If p is an existential state, it will be Defender who chooses the next control state – this part of the construction will be implemented using the Defender's forcing technique, which was already used in the proof of Theorem 3.3.5 showing the P-hardness of the equivalence checking problem on flat processes. Finally, in the process $C(q_{rej}, i)$ Attacker will be able to perform a special action rej for which Defender will have no answer in the process $D(q_{rej}, i)$.

Formally, the reduction is computed as follows.

(1) Create a process $T_0^{\blacktriangleright}$ with the only transition $T_0^{\blacktriangleright} \xrightarrow{(\blacktriangleright, \blacktriangleright, 0)} T_0^{\blacktriangleright}$.

(2) Create a process $T_{n+1}^{\blacktriangleleft}$ with the only transition $T_{n+1}^{\blacktriangleleft} \xrightarrow{(\blacktriangleleft, \blacktriangleleft, n+1)} T_{n+1}^{\blacktriangleleft}$.

(3) For every i, $1 \le i \le n$, create two processes T_i^a and T_i^b with the transitions

- $T_i^a \xrightarrow{(a,b,i)} T_i^b$,
- $T_i^a \xrightarrow{(a,a,i)} T_i^a$,
- $T_i^b \xrightarrow{(b,a,i)} T_i^a$, and
- $T_i^b \xrightarrow{(b,b,i)} T_i^b$.

The following picture shows the processes constructed in parts (1)–(3).

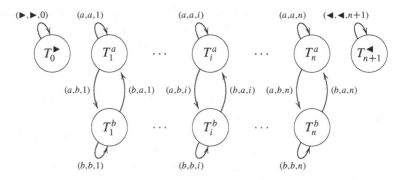

(4) For every i, $0 \le i \le n + 1$, and every transition $p \xrightarrow{x \to y, d} q_1, q_2$ in M such that $p \in Q_\forall$ create the processes $C(p, i)$, $C'(q_1, q_2, i + d, \forall)$, $C(q_1, i + d)$, $C(q_2, i + d)$ and $D(p, i)$, $D'(q_1, q_2, i + d, \forall)$, $D(q_1, i + d)$, $D(q_2, i + d)$ together with the transitions

- $C(p, i) \xrightarrow{(x,y,i)} C'(q_1, q_2, i + d, \forall)$,
- $C'(q_1, q_2, i + d, \forall) \xrightarrow{1} C(q_1, i + d)$,
- $C'(q_1, q_2, i + d, \forall) \xrightarrow{2} C(q_2, i + d)$, and
- $D(p, i) \xrightarrow{(x,y,i)} D'(q_1, q_2, i + d, \forall)$,
- $D'(q_1, q_2, i + d, \forall) \xrightarrow{1} D(q_1, i + d)$,
- $D'(q_1, q_2, i + d, \forall) \xrightarrow{2} D(q_2, i + d)$.

The two fragments of the leading processes in P and Q, pictured below for the rule $p \xrightarrow{x \to y, d} q_1, q_2$ with $p \in Q_\forall$, demonstrate the construction.

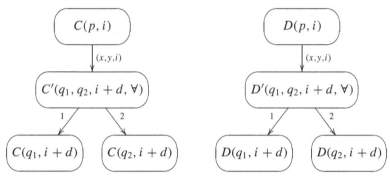

Consider a play in the bisimulation game starting from the pair of processes $C(p, i) \mid T$ and $D(p, i) \mid T$, where $T = T_0^{\blacktriangleright} \mid \cdots \mid T_i^x \mid \cdots \mid T_{n+1}^{\blacktriangleleft}$ is a parallel composition of the processes representing the tape content. Assume that there is a rule $p \xrightarrow{x \to y, d} q_1, q_2$. The only possible transition, a communication between $C(p, i)$, respectively $D(p, i)$, and T_i^x under the action (x, y, i), is uniquely determined in both of the processes $C(p, i) \mid T$ and $D(p, i) \mid T$. Hence, after one round of the bisimulation game, the players necessarily reach a pair of processes of the form $C'(q_1, q_2, i + d, \forall) \mid T'$ and $D'(q_1, q_2, i + d, \forall) \mid T'$ for some modified tape content T'. Now Attacker can play either the action 1 or 2 (without any communication) in order to select the next control state q_1 or q_2 of the ALBA M.

(5) For every i, $0 \le i \le n + 1$, and every transition $p \xrightarrow{x \to y, d} q_1, q_2$ in M such that $p \in Q_\exists$ create the processes $C(p, i)$, $C'(q_1, q_2, i + d, \exists)$, $C''(q_1, q_2, i + d)$, $C(q_1, i + d)$, $C(q_2, i + d)$ and $D(p, i)$, $D'(q_1, q_2, i + d, \exists)$, $D^1(q_1, q_2, i + d)$, $D^2(q_1, q_2, i + d)$, $D(q_1, i + d)$, $D(q_2, i + d)$ together with the transitions

- $C(p, i) \xrightarrow{(x,y,i)} C'(q_1, q_2, i + d, \exists)$,
- $C'(q_1, q_2, i + d, \exists) \xrightarrow{a} C''(q_1, q_2, i + d)$,
- $C'(q_1, q_2, i + d, \exists) \xrightarrow{a} D^1(q_1, q_2, i + d)$,
- $C'(q_1, q_2, i + d, \exists) \xrightarrow{a} D^2(q_1, q_2, i + d)$,

- $C''(q_1, q_2, i + d) \xrightarrow{1} C(q_1, i + d)$,
- $C''(q_1, q_2, i + d) \xrightarrow{2} C(q_2, i + d)$, and
- $D(p, i) \xrightarrow{(x,y,i)} D'(q_1, q_2, i + d, \exists)$,
- $D'(q_1, q_2, i + d, \exists) \xrightarrow{a} D^1(q_1, q_2, i + d)$,
- $D'(q_1, q_2, i + d, \exists) \xrightarrow{a} D^2(q_1, q_2, i + d)$,
- $D^1(q_1, q_2, i + d) \xrightarrow{1} D(q_1, i + d)$,
- $D^1(q_1, q_2, i + d) \xrightarrow{2} C(q_2, i + d)$,
- $D^2(q_1, q_2, i + d) \xrightarrow{2} D(q_2, i + d)$,
- $D^2(q_1, q_2, i + d) \xrightarrow{1} C(q_1, i + d)$.

The added transitions for the rule $p \xrightarrow{x \to y, d} q_1, q_2$ where $p \in Q_\exists$ are depicted below.

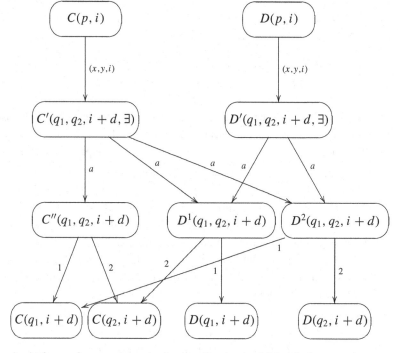

As before, after one round of any play in the bisimulation game starting from $C(p, i) \mid T$ and $D(p, i) \mid T$ (where T is the parallel composition of processes representing the tape content) the players necessarily end in a pair consisting of processes of the form $C'(q_1, q_2, i + d, \exists) \mid T'$ and $D'(q_1, q_2, i + d, \exists) \mid T'$. Attacker is now forced to play the action a (no communication) in the left-hand-side process and enter the state $C''(q_1, q_2, i + d) \mid T'$ – any other attack gives Defender the possibility to enter the same state chosen by Attacker and leads therefore to a losing line of play for Attacker. Defender answers either by entering the state $D^1(q_1, q_2, i + d) \mid T'$ or $D^2(q_1, q_2, i + d) \mid T'$. From the pair consisting of the processes $C''(q_1, q_2, i + d) \mid T'$ and $D^1(q_1, q_2, i + d) \mid T'$, Attacker clearly has to play the action 1 (no communication) in order to avoid reaching a pair of equal processes after Defender's answer to his move. Similarly, from the pair consisting of the processes $C''(q_1, q_2, i + d) \mid T'$ and $D^2(q_1, q_2, i + d) \mid T'$, Attacker has to play the action 2. That means that the play will continue either from the pair consisting of $C(q_1, i + d) \mid T'$ and $D(q_1, i + d) \mid T'$, or from the one consisting of $C(q_2, i + d) \mid T'$ and $D(q_2, i + d) \mid T'$. Note that it was Defender who selected the next control state of the ALBA in this case.

(6) Finally, for every i, $0 \leq i \leq n + 1$, add $C(q_{rej}, i) \xrightarrow{rej} C(q_{rej}, i)$.

This ensures that if during some play the players reach a rejecting configuration, Attacker wins by performing the action rej in the left-hand-side process to which Defender has no answer in the right-hand-side process.

To sum up, the players can force each other to faithfully simulate a computation of a given ALBA M on a word w. Attacker is selecting the successor configuration if the present control state is universal, Defender does the selection if the present control state is existential. Recall that we assumed that the computation tree of M on w does not have any infinite branches. We can therefore conclude that if M accepts w then Defender can force any play to reach a pair of processes representing an accepting leaf in the computation tree when it is Attacker's turn to play next. This is clearly a winning position for Defender as no continuation of the play is possible in either of the processes. On the other hand, if M does not accept w, Attacker can force any play to reach a pair of processes representing a rejecting leaf in the computation tree when it is his turn to play the action rej, and Defender loses. In this case, Attacker is moreover able to implement the winning strategy by playing exclusively in the left-hand-side process. Therefore we can state the following generic hardness result.

Theorem 3.3.16 *The equivalence checking problem between two networks of finite processes is EXPTIME-hard for any relation between the strong simulation preorder and strong bisimilarity.*

Notice now that because essentially all bisimulation-like equivalences and preorders studied in the literature are decidable in polynomial time on flat systems, we get an immediate EXPTIME-algorithm for these equivalence checking problems on non-flat systems, simply by flattening the networks of finite processes (causing an exponential increase in size) and running the polynomial time algorithms on the flattened system. Hence we obtain the following corollary.

Corollary 3.3.17 *The problems of checking the simulation preorder and equivalence, completed simulation preorder and equivalence, ready simulation preorder and equivalence, 2-nested simulation preorder and equivalence, and bisimilarity on networks of finite processes are EXPTIME-complete.*

3.4 Decidability results for bisimilarity over infinite-state systems

We shall now consider the questions of decidability/undecidability of bisimilarity on so-called *infinite-state systems*, i.e. labelled transition systems with infinitely many reachable states. For example, these systems naturally arise when one models *infinite data domains*, such as counters, integer variables, stacks and queues, or *unbounded control structures*, like recursive procedure calls, dynamic process creation and mobility, and in *parameterised reasoning* involving an arbitrary number of identical processes.

Of course, an infinite-state system cannot be passed as an input to an algorithm as it is. We need to find a suitable *finite representation* of such a system in order to ask decidability questions. For the purpose of this chapter, we shall consider the concept of process rewrite systems as it provides a finite description of many well-studied formalisms like pushdown automata or Petri nets. After introducing process rewrite systems, we shall focus on two selected results. First, we shall argue that bisimilarity is decidable over the class of Basic Parallel Processes (BPP), which form the so-called communication-free subclass of Petri nets. The result will be proved using the *tableau technique*, which is applicable also in many other cases. Second, we will demonstrate that bisimilarity is undecidable over the whole class of Petri nets. Finally we give an overview of the current state of the art in the area.

3.4.1 Process rewrite systems

We start by introducing several well-studied classes of infinite-state processes by means of process rewrite systems (PRS). Process rewrite systems are an elegant and universal approach defined, in the form presented in this chapter, by Mayr [May00]. Mayr's definition unifies and extends some previously introduced formalisms for infinite-state systems (see, e.g. the overview articles [BCMS01, BE97, Mol96]).

Let $Const$ be a set of *process constants*. The classes of process expressions called 1 (process constants plus the empty process), $\mathcal{P}$ (parallel process expressions), $\mathcal{S}$ (sequential process expressions), and $\mathcal{G}$ (general process expressions) are defined by the following abstract syntax

$$
\begin{array}{ll}
1: & E ::= \epsilon \mid X \\
\mathcal{P}: & E ::= \epsilon \mid X \mid E \mid E \\
\mathcal{S}: & E ::= \epsilon \mid X \mid E.E \\
\mathcal{G}: & E ::= \epsilon \mid X \mid E \mid E \mid E.E
\end{array}
$$

where 'ϵ' is the *empty process*, X ranges over $Const$, the operator '.' stands for sequential composition and '|' stands for parallel composition. Obviously, $1 \subset \mathcal{S}$, $1 \subset \mathcal{P}$, $\mathcal{S} \subset \mathcal{G}$ and $\mathcal{P} \subset \mathcal{G}$. The classes $\mathcal{S}$ and $\mathcal{P}$ are incomparable and $\mathcal{S} \cap \mathcal{P} = 1$.

We do not distinguish between process expressions related by a *structural congruence*, which is the smallest congruence over process expressions such that the following laws hold:

- '.' is associative,
- '|' is associative and commutative, and
- 'ϵ' is a unit for both '.' and '|'.

Definition 3.4.1 Let $\alpha, \beta \in \{1, \mathcal{S}, \mathcal{P}, \mathcal{G}\}$ be classes of process expressions such that $\alpha \subseteq \beta$ and let Act be a set of *actions*. An (α, β)-PRS [May00] is a finite set

$$
\Delta \subseteq (\alpha \smallsetminus \{\epsilon\}) \times Act \times \beta
$$

of *rewrite rules*, written $E \xrightarrow{a} F$ for $(E, a, F) \in \Delta$. By $Const(\Delta)$ we denote the set of process constants that appear in Δ and by $Act(\Delta)$ the set of actions that appear in Δ.

An (α, β)-PRS determines a labelled transition system whose *states* are process expressions from the class β (modulo the structural congruence), Act is the set of *labels*, and the *transition relation* is the least relation satisfying the following SOS rules (recall that '|' is commutative).

$$
\frac{(E \xrightarrow{a} E') \in \Delta}{E \xrightarrow{a} E'} \qquad \frac{E \xrightarrow{a} E'}{E.F \xrightarrow{a} E'.F} \qquad \frac{E \xrightarrow{a} E'}{E \mid F \xrightarrow{a} E' \mid F}.
$$

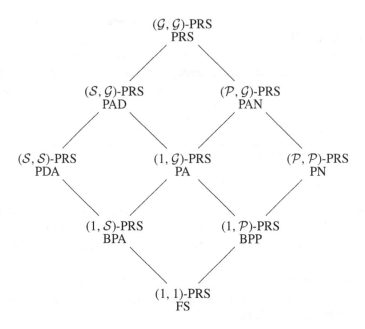

Fig. 3.10. Hierarchy of process rewrite systems.

Many classes of infinite-state systems studied so far – e.g. basic process algebra (BPA), basic parallel processes (BPP), pushdown automata (PDA), Petri nets (PN) and process algebra (PA) – are contained in the hierarchy of process rewrite systems presented in Figure 3.10. This hierarchy is strict with respect to strong bisimilarity and we refer the reader to [May00] for further discussions.

We shall now take a closer look at the classes forming the PRS hierarchy.

Finite-state processes Finite-state processes (FS) – or equivalently $(1, 1)$-PRS – generate a class of transition systems with finitely many reachable states. Here rules are of the form

$$X \xrightarrow{a} Y \quad \text{or} \quad X \xrightarrow{a} \epsilon$$

where $X, Y \in \mathcal{C}onst(\Delta)$ and $a \in \mathcal{A}ct(\Delta)$.

Basic process algebra Basic process algebra (BPA) – or equivalently $(1, \mathcal{S})$-PRS – represents the class of processes introduced by Bergstra and Klop in, for instance, [BK85]. BPA is a model of purely sequential process behaviour such that a process constant can be replaced by a finite sequence of symbols via prefix rewriting. For example the rewrite rules

$$X \xrightarrow{a} X.Y \quad \text{and} \quad X \xrightarrow{b} \epsilon \quad \text{and} \quad Y \xrightarrow{c} X$$

allow us to perform the sequence of transitions

$$X \xrightarrow{a} X.Y \xrightarrow{a} X.Y.Y \xrightarrow{b} Y.Y \xrightarrow{c} X.Y \xrightarrow{a} X.Y.Y \xrightarrow{a} X.Y.Y.Y$$

where the sequential composition of the process constants behaves like a stack with the top on the left-hand side. This class also corresponds to the transition systems associated with context-free grammars in Greibach normal form, in which only left-most derivations are allowed.

Basic parallel processes Basic parallel processes (BPP) – or equivalently $(1, \mathcal{P})$-PRS – are a fragment of CCS [Mil89] without restriction, relabelling and communication. It is a parallel analogue of BPA where any occurrence of a process constant inside a parallel composition can be replaced by a number of process constants put in parallel. For example, the rewrite rules

$$X \xrightarrow{a} X \mid Y \mid Y \quad \text{and} \quad Y \xrightarrow{b} \epsilon$$

allow us to derive the following sequence of transitions:

$$X \xrightarrow{a} X \mid Y \mid Y \xrightarrow{b} X \mid Y \xrightarrow{a} X \mid Y \mid Y \mid Y \xrightarrow{b} X \mid Y \mid Y \xrightarrow{a} X \mid Y \mid Y \mid Y \mid Y.$$

The class BPP was first studied by Christensen [Chr93], and it is equivalent to the communication-free subclass of Petri nets (each transition has exactly one input place). The classes BPA and BPP are also called *simple process algebras*.

Pushdown processes Pushdown processes (PDA) – or equivalently $(\mathcal{S}, \mathcal{S})$-PRS – represent the class of processes introduced via sequential prefix rewriting with unrestricted rules. Caucal [Cau92] showed that an arbitrary unrestricted $(\mathcal{S}, \mathcal{S})$-PRS can be transformed into a PDA system (where rewrite rules are of the form $pX \xrightarrow{a} q\gamma$ such that p and q are control states, X is a stack symbol and γ is a sequence of stack symbols) in such a way that their generated transition systems are isomorphic. Hence $(\mathcal{S}, \mathcal{S})$-PRS and PDA are equivalent formalisms.

PA-processes PA-processes (PA for process algebra) – or equivalently $(1, \mathcal{G})$-PRS – represent the class of processes originally introduced by Bergstra and Klop in [BK84]. This formalism combines the parallel and sequential operator but allows for neither communication nor global-state control.

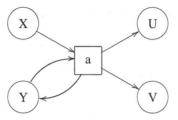

Fig. 3.11. A Petri net fragment corresponding to the rule $X \mid Y \xrightarrow{a} U \mid V \mid Y$

Petri nets Petri nets (PN) – or equivalently $(\mathcal{P}, \mathcal{P})$-PRS – represent the class of processes that correspond to the standard and well-studied notion of labelled place/transition (P/T) nets as originally proposed by Petri [Pet62]. In fact, $(\mathcal{P}, \mathcal{P})$-PRS capture exactly the class of Petri nets with multiple arcs (see, e.g. [Pet81]). The correspondence between $(\mathcal{P}, \mathcal{P})$-PRS and Petri nets is straightforward: process constants are names of places in the Petri net, any expression from $\mathcal{P}$ appearing during a computation is represented as a marking where the number of occurrences of a process constant gives the number of tokens in the place named after the process constant, and every rule gives rise to a labelled transition in the net as depicted in the example in Figure 3.11.

PAD, PAN and PRS processes The systems PAD, PAN and PRS correspond to $(\mathcal{S}, \mathcal{G})$-PRS, $(\mathcal{P}, \mathcal{G})$-PRS and $(\mathcal{G}, \mathcal{G})$-PRS, respectively. These classes complete the hierarchy of process rewrite systems and were introduced by Mayr; see [May00]. The PAD class is the smallest common generalisation of PA and PDA [May98] and PAN is a combination of the models PA and PN [May97a]. The most general class PRS subsumes all the previously mentioned classes. It is worth mentioning that even the class $(\mathcal{G}, \mathcal{G})$-PRS is not Turing powerful since, e.g. the reachability problem (i.e. whether from a given process expression we can in finitely many steps reach another given process expression) remains decidable [May00]. In fact, reachability remains decidable even in the recently introduced generalisation of PRS called *weakly extended process rewrite systems* [KŘS05], where a finite control-unit with a monotonic behaviour provides an extra control over the process behaviours.

Further motivation for studying the classes from the PRS hierarchy can be found in [Esp02] and the classes from the PRS hierarchy also have a direct link with interprocedural control-flow analysis of programs [EK99].

Bisimilarity-checking problem The problem we shall now study is whether we can decide the following:

> Given two processes from some class in the PRS hierarchy, are the two processes bisimilar or not?

First, we shall argue that this problem is decidable for the BPP class and then we prove its undecidability for Petri nets.

3.4.2 Deciding bisimilarity on BPP using a tableau technique

Our aim is now to show decidability of bisimilarity on BPP. Christensen, Hirshfeld and Moller first proved this positive result in [Chr93, CHM93], using the so-called *tableau technique*. The presentation of the decidability result in this section is based on their proof.

We shall now introduce our running example. Without loss of generality we assume that in what follows any BPP system Δ uses the process constants $\mathcal{C}\mathrm{onst}(\Delta) = \{X_1, \ldots, X_n\}$ for some n.

Example 3.4.2 Assume a BPP system Δ with the following rules.

$$
\begin{aligned}
X_1 &\xrightarrow{a} X_1 \mid X_2 \\
X_2 &\xrightarrow{b} X_3 \\
X_3 &\xrightarrow{b} \epsilon \\
X_4 &\xrightarrow{a} X_4 \mid X_3 \mid X_3.
\end{aligned}
$$

We encourage the reader to draw initial fragments of labelled transition systems generated by the processes X_1 and X_4 and to establish that $X_1 \sim X_4$. $\square$

We mention the standard fact that any BPP process E over Δ can be viewed as a Parikh vector $\phi(E) = (k_1, k_2, \ldots, k_n) \in \mathbb{N}^n$, where $\mathcal{C}\mathrm{onst}(\Delta) = \{X_1, X_2, \ldots, X_n\}$ and k_i is the number of occurrences of X_i in E. Hence the Parikh vector simply counts the number of occurrences of the different process constants in a given expression. Clearly, two BPP processes E and F are structurally congruent if and only if $\phi(E) = \phi(F)$.

Example 3.4.3 The rules from Example 3.4.2 can be viewed as rules over Parikh vectors in the following way.

$$
\begin{aligned}
(1, 0, 0, 0) &\xrightarrow{a} (1, 1, 0, 0) \\
(0, 1, 0, 0) &\xrightarrow{b} (0, 0, 1, 0) \\
(0, 0, 1, 0) &\xrightarrow{b} (0, 0, 0, 0) \\
(0, 0, 0, 1) &\xrightarrow{a} (0, 0, 2, 1).
\end{aligned}
$$

A sequence of transitions

$$
X_1 \xrightarrow{a} X_1 \mid X_2 \xrightarrow{a} X_1 \mid X_2 \mid X_2 \xrightarrow{b} X_1 \mid X_2 \mid X_3 \xrightarrow{b} X_1 \mid X_2
$$

then has a straightforward analogue over Parikh vectors, namely

$$(1, 0, 0, 0) \xrightarrow{a} (1, 1, 0, 0) \xrightarrow{a} (1, 2, 0, 0) \xrightarrow{b} (1, 1, 1, 0) \xrightarrow{b} (1, 1, 0, 0).$$

□

Definition 3.4.4 Let $\alpha = (\alpha_1, \ldots, \alpha_n) \in \mathbb{N}^n$ and $\beta = (\beta_1, \ldots, \beta_n) \in \mathbb{N}^n$.

- By $\alpha + \beta$ we denote a component-wise addition defined by $\alpha + \beta = (\alpha_1 + \beta_1, \ldots, \alpha_n + \beta_n) \in \mathbb{N}^n$.
- We define a lexicographical ordering $<_\ell$ such that $\alpha <_\ell \beta$ iff there is some $k, 0 \leq k \leq n$, such that $\alpha_k < \beta_k$ and $\alpha_i = \beta_i$ for all $i, 1 \leq i < k$.
- We define a component-wise ordering $\leq_c$ such that $\alpha \leq_c \beta$ iff $\alpha_i \leq \beta_i$ for every $i, 1 \leq i \leq n$, i.e. iff there is $\alpha' \in \mathbb{N}^n$ such that $\beta = \alpha + \alpha'$. We write $\alpha <_c \beta$ iff $\alpha \leq_c \beta$ and $\alpha \neq \beta$.

Observe that $<_\ell$ is a well-founded ordering – that is, there is no infinite sequence $\alpha_1, \alpha_2, \ldots$ such that $\alpha_1 >_\ell \alpha_2 >_\ell \ldots$ – and note that $\alpha \neq \beta$ implies that either $\alpha <_\ell \beta$ or $\beta <_\ell \alpha$. The following fact is known as Dickson's lemma.

Lemma 3.4.5 ([Dic13]) *Every infinite sequence from $\mathbb{N}^n$ has an infinite non-decreasing subsequence with respect to $\leq_c$.*

Before we describe the construction of a tableau proving bisimilarity of BPP processes, we introduce some simple facts about stratified bisimulation relations introduced in Definition 3.2.2 that will be used in the proof of soundness.

We note, first of all, that labelled transition systems generated by BPP processes are clearly image-finite.

An important property of labelled transition systems generated by BPP processes is that the stratified bisimulation relations $\sim_k$ are congruences. This fact will be essential in the soundness proof of the tableau construction.

Lemma 3.4.6 *Let E, F and G be BPP processes over Δ. If $E \sim_k F$ then $(E \mid G) \sim_k (F \mid G)$ for any $k \in \mathbb{N}$.*

Exercise 3.4.7 Prove Lemma 3.4.6.

By Lemma 3.2.3 and Lemma 3.4.6 we can conclude that bisimilarity on BPP is a congruence.

Lemma 3.4.8 *Let E, F and G be BPP processes over Δ. If $E \sim F$ then $(E \mid G) \sim (F \mid G)$.*

We can now proceed with the description of the tableau technique in order to demonstrate decidability of bisimilarity on BPP. Let E and F be BPP processes over the set of rules Δ. Recall that by $\phi(E)$ and $\phi(F)$ we denote the corresponding Parikh vectors over $\mathbb{N}^n$.

A *tableau* for E and F is a maximal proof tree rooted with $(\phi(E), \phi(F))$ and built according to the following rules. Let $(\alpha, \beta) \in \mathbb{N}^{2n}$ be a node in the tree. A node (α, β) is either *terminal (leaf)* or *non-terminal*. The following nodes are terminal:

- (α, α) is a *successful leaf* for any $\alpha \in \mathbb{N}^n$,
- (α, β) is a *successful leaf* if $\mathsf{next}(\alpha, *) \cup \mathsf{next}(\beta, *) = \emptyset$,
- (α, β) is an *unsuccessful leaf* if for some $a \in Act(\Delta)$ it is the case that $\mathsf{next}(\alpha, a) \cup \mathsf{next}(\beta, a) \neq \emptyset$, and either $\mathsf{next}(\alpha, a) = \emptyset$ or $\mathsf{next}(\beta, a) = \emptyset$.

We say that a node is an *ancestor* of (α, β) if it is on the path from the root to (α, β) and at least one application of the rule EXPAND (defined later) separates them. If (α, β) is not a leaf then we reduce it using the following RED rules as long as possible.

$$\mathrm{RED}_L \quad \frac{(\alpha, \beta)}{(\gamma + \omega, \beta)} \qquad \begin{array}{l} \text{if there is an ancestor } (\gamma, \delta) \text{ or } (\delta, \gamma) \text{ of } (\alpha, \beta) \text{ such} \\ \text{that } \gamma <_\ell \delta \text{ and } \alpha = \delta + \omega \text{ for some } \omega \in \mathbb{N}^n \end{array}$$

$$\mathrm{RED}_R \quad \frac{(\alpha, \beta)}{(\alpha, \gamma + \omega)} \qquad \begin{array}{l} \text{if there is an ancestor } (\gamma, \delta) \text{ or } (\delta, \gamma) \text{ of } (\alpha, \beta) \text{ such} \\ \text{that } \gamma <_\ell \delta \text{ and } \beta = \delta + \omega \text{ for some } \omega \in \mathbb{N}^n \,. \end{array}$$

If no reduction RED is applicable and the resulting node is not a leaf, we apply the rule EXPAND for a set of relations S_a, $a \in Act(\Delta)$, where $S_a \subseteq \mathsf{next}(\alpha, a) \times \mathsf{next}(\beta, a)$ such that

- for each $\alpha' \in \mathsf{next}(\alpha, a)$, there is some $\beta' \in \mathsf{next}(\beta, a)$ such that $(\alpha', \beta') \in S_a$, and
- for each $\beta' \in \mathsf{next}(\beta, a)$, there is some $\alpha' \in \mathsf{next}(\alpha, a)$ such that $(\alpha', \beta') \in S_a$.

Note that there are several possible relations S_a that might satisfy the condition above:

$$\mathrm{EXPAND} \quad \frac{(\alpha, \beta)}{\{(\alpha', \beta') \mid a \in Act(\Delta) \wedge (\alpha', \beta') \in S_a\}}.$$

The set notation used in the rule EXPAND means that each element (α', β') in the conclusion of the rule becomes a new child in the proof tree. Now, we start again applying the RED rules to every such child (which is not a leaf) as long as possible. Note that reduction rules are applicable to a node iff the node is not terminal (leaf).

We call a tableau for (E, F) *successful* if it is maximal (no further rules are applicable) and all its leaves are successful.

Example 3.4.9 A successful tableau for X_1 and X_4 of the BPP system Δ from Example 3.4.2 is given below.

$$\cfrac{\cfrac{\cfrac{(1,0,0,0),(0,0,0,1)}{(1,1,0,0),(0,0,2,1)}\ \text{EXPAND}}{(0,1,0,1),(0,0,2,1)}\ \text{RED}_L}{\cfrac{(0,1,2,1),(0,0,4,1)}{(0,0,4,1),(0,0,4,1)}\ \text{RED}_L \qquad \cfrac{}{(0,0,1,1),(0,0,1,1)}}\ \text{EXPAND}$$

Note that for the first application of the rule EXPAND there was only one choice of how to pair the successor processes (due to the fact that X_1 and X_2 have unique a-successors). Then the rule RED_L is applicable because

$$\underbrace{(0,0,0,1)}_{\gamma} <_\ell \underbrace{(1,0,0,0)}_{\delta}\,,$$

$$\underbrace{(1,1,0,0)}_{\alpha} = \underbrace{(1,0,0,0)}_{\delta} + \underbrace{(0,1,0,0)}_{\omega} \text{ and}$$

$$(0,1,0,1) = \underbrace{(0,0,0,1)}_{\gamma} + \underbrace{(0,1,0,0)}_{\omega}\,.$$

Now no more RED_L nor RED_R are applicable, so we can apply the rule EXPAND. Again, there is a unique a-successor in both processes (left child) and a unique b-successor in both processes (right child). The right child is by definition a successful leaf. By one more applications of the RED_L rule on the left child where $\underbrace{(0,0,2,1)}_{\gamma} <_\ell \underbrace{(0,1,0,1)}_{\delta}$ and where $\omega = (0,0,2,0)$, we complete the tableau as the created child is a successful leaf. $\qquad\square$

Lemma 3.4.10 *Any tableau for BPP processes E and F is finite and there are only finitely many tableaux.*

Proof We first show that any tableau for E and F is finite. To this end, observe, first of all, that any tableau for E and F is finitely branching because $Act(\Delta)$ is a finite set and for a given $a \in Act(\Delta)$ any relation S_a is finite and there are finitely many such relations. Should the tableau be infinite, there must be an infinite branch, which, gives an infinite sequence of vectors from $\mathbb{N}^{2n}$. Since the rules RED can be used only finitely many times in a sequence (they decrease the $<_\ell$ order, which is well founded), there must be an infinite subsequence of vectors on which the rule EXPAND was applied. Using Dickson's Lemma 3.4.5, this sequence must contain an infinite non-decreasing subsequence $(\alpha_1, \beta_1) \leq_c$

$(\alpha_2, \beta_2) \leq_c \ldots$ However, the rule EXPAND cannot be applied on (α_2, β_2) since one of the RED rules is applicable. This is a contradiction.

Since there are only finitely many relations S_a for any $a \in Act(\Delta)$ available in the EXPAND rule and there are finitely many possibilities for an application of the RED rule, there are always finitely many possibilities for extending an already existing partial tableau. Suppose that there were infinitely many tableaux starting from $(\phi(E), \phi(F))$. Then there must be a tableau with an infinite branch, which contradicts that every tableau is finite. $\qquad \square$

Lemma 3.4.11 (Completeness) *Let E and F be two BPP processes over Δ. If $E \sim F$ then there is a successful tableau for E and F.*

Proof We construct inductively a tableau with root $(\phi(E), \phi(F))$ such that every node (α, β) in the tableau satisfies $\alpha \sim \beta$. Hence this tableau cannot contain any unsuccessful leaf and it must be finite because of Lemma 3.4.10. Suppose that (α, β) is already a node in the tableau such that $\alpha \sim \beta$ and consider the rule RED_L applied on (α, β). We may assume, without loss of generality, that (γ, δ) is an ancestor of (α, β). By induction, $\gamma \sim \delta$, which means by Lemma 3.4.8 that $(\gamma + \omega) \sim (\delta + \omega) = \alpha \sim \beta$. Hence $(\gamma + \omega) \sim \beta$. Similarly for RED_R. From the definition of bisimilarity it follows that the rule EXPAND is also forward sound, i.e. if $\alpha \sim \beta$ then we can choose for every $a \in Act(\Delta)$ a relation S_a such that $(\alpha', \beta') \in S_a$ implies that $\alpha' \sim \beta'$. $\qquad \square$

Lemma 3.4.12 (Soundness) *Let E and F be two BPP processes over Δ. If there is a successful tableau for E and F then $E \sim F$.*

Proof For the sake of contradiction assume that there is a successful tableau for E and F and $E \not\sim F$. We show that we can construct a path from the root $(\phi(E), \phi(F))$ to some leaf, such that for any pair (α, β) on this path $\alpha \not\sim \beta$.

If $E \not\sim F$ then using Lemma 3.2.3 there is a minimal k such that $E \not\sim_k F$. Notice that if $\alpha \not\sim_k \beta$ such that k is minimal and we apply the rule EXPAND, then at least one of its children (α', β') satisfies $\alpha' \not\sim_{k-1} \beta'$. We choose such a child to extend our path from the root.

If we apply RED_L on (α, β) where $\alpha \not\sim_k \beta$ and k is minimal, then the corresponding ancestor (γ, δ) is separated by at least one application of EXPAND and so $\gamma \sim_k \delta$. This implies that $(\gamma + \omega) \not\sim_k \beta$, otherwise using Lemma 3.4.6 we get that $\alpha = (\delta + \omega) \sim_k (\gamma + \omega) \sim_k \beta$, which is a contradiction with $\alpha \not\sim_k \beta$. The same is true for RED_R. Thus there must be a path from the root to some leaf such that for any pair (α, β) on this path $\alpha \not\sim \beta$. This is a contradiction with the fact that the path contains a successful leaf. $\qquad \square$

We can now conclude that it is decidable whether $E \sim F$ for given BPP processes E and F. Indeed, $E \sim F$ iff there is a successful tableau for E and F (Lemma 3.4.11 and Lemma 3.4.12). Moreover, there are only finitely many tableaux and all of them are finite. We can therefore state the following theorem.

Theorem 3.4.13 ([CHM93]) *It is decidable whether $E \sim F$ for any two given BPP processes E and F.*

Remark 3.4.14 As mentioned above, one can in principle view BPP processes as elements over the free commutative monoid $(\mathbb{N}^n, +, (0, \ldots, 0))$. Because bisimilarity is a congruence over this monoid (Lemma 3.4.8), we can apply a classical result to the effect that every congruence on a finitely generated commutative semigroup is finitely generated [Red65], in order to derive the positive decidability result. For further references on this topic see [Hir94a, BCMS01, Jan08].

Unfortunately, the complexity of the above-presented tableau-based proof for decidability of bisimilarity on BPP is unknown – no primitive recursive upper bound was given. Only recently, Jančar proved the containment of the problem in PSPACE [Jan03] using a different technique based on the so-called dd-functions. Together with the previously known PSPACE-hardness result from [Srb03], PSPACE-completeness of the problem was finally shown.

Even though the tableau technique did not provide the best complexity upper bound in this case, it demonstrates a useful proof strategy that is applicable also to several other classes of systems. A successful tableau can be viewed as a compact (finite) representation of Defender's winning strategy (which is in general infinite). What is, in principle, happening during the tableau construction is that we repeatedly use the rule EXPAND in order to simulate possible attacks on the pair of processes present in the tableau. Defender's strategy corresponds to the selection of appropriate sets S_a for every available action a. Because for infinite state systems a construction of such a tableau using only the EXPAND rule might not terminate, we need a way to ensure termination. How to do this depends on the particular infinite-state system in question. In case of BPP, the guarantee of termination is based on the fact that bisimilarity is a congruence, and we can therefore ensure that any constructed tableau is finite by means of the application of the rules RED_L and RED_R. We can call this approach *simplification* of the sub-goals.

In fact, the assumptions in the proof of soundness and completeness of the tableau technique are quite general, which allows us to extend the technique to cover several other variants/extensions of BPP processes like, e.g. lossy BPP, BPP with interrupt and discrete timed-arc BPP nets [Srb02].

The tableau technique has been frequently used in the literature. Here we limit ourselves to mentioning a few references relevant to the classes in the PRS hierarchy. Hüttel and Stirling designed tableau rules in order to show that bisimilarity is decidable on normed BPA [HS98]. (Normed means that all process constants in the BPA system can be reduced to the empty process ϵ in finitely many transitions.) In that reference, the authors use a similar congruence property in order to simplify the sub-goals in the tableau. A tableau technique proved useful also for the decidability of *weak* bisimilarity on a subclass of BPP processes [Sti01].

Considerably more involved applications of the tableau technique can be found in the proofs of decidability of bisimilarity for normed PA-processes [HJ99], normed pushdown systems [Sti98] as well as for general pushdown system [Sti00].

Other uses of the tableau technique include model checking problems for various temporal logics [BEM96, Cle90, LP85, SW91] and some other problems, such as those addressed in [May97b, Sti03].

As already mentioned for the class BPP, tableau techniques do not always provide the most efficient algorithms from the computational complexity point of view. There have been other techniques developed for proving decidability of bisimilarity, most notably the techniques based on *finite bisimulation bases*. In some instances these techniques provide polynomial time algorithms for bisimilarity on infinite-state systems. For a regularly updated list of references consult [Srb04]. Readers interested in an intuitive explanation of such techniques are directed to some recent overview articles [KJ06, Jan08].

3.4.3 Undecidability of bisimilarity on Petri nets

In this section we shall demonstrate a negative result for bisimilarity checking on infinite-state labelled transition systems generated by Petri nets. The presentation of the result is to a large extent based on [JS08], slightly simplifying the original proof by Jančar [Jan95]. The proof is done by reduction from the halting problem for 2-counter Minsky machines.

A *(Minsky) 2-counter machine (MCM)* M, with *non-negative* counters c_1 and c_2, is a sequence of (labelled) instructions:

$$1 : instr_1; \ 2 : instr_2; \ \ldots \ n : instr_n$$

where $instr_n = $ HALT and each $instr_i$, for $i \in \{1, 2, \ldots, n-1\}$, is of the following two types (assuming $j, k \in \{1, 2, \ldots, n\}, r \in \{1, 2\}$):

Type (1) $c_r := c_r + 1$; goto j
Type (2) if $c_r = 0$ then goto j else ($c_r := c_r - 1$; goto k).

The instructions of type (1) are called *increment instructions*, the instructions of type (2) are *zero-test (and decrement) instructions*.

The *computation* of M on the input $(i_1, i_2) \in \mathbb{N} \times \mathbb{N}$ is the sequence of configurations (i, n_1, n_2), starting with $(1, i_1, i_2)$, where $i \in \{1, 2, \ldots, n\}$ is the label of the instruction to be performed, and $n_1, n_2 \in \mathbb{N}$ are the (current) counter values; the sequence is determined by the instructions in the obvious way. The computation is either finite, i.e. halting by reaching the instruction $n :$ HALT, or infinite.

We define *inf-MCM* as the problem to decide whether the computation of a given 2-counter MCM on $(0, 0)$ is infinite, and we recall the following well-known fact.

Proposition 3.4.15 [Min67] *Problem inf-MCM is undecidable.*

Given a 2-counter machine M with n instructions, we construct a $(\mathcal{P}, \mathcal{P})$-PRS system (a Petri net) with $Const = \{q_1, q_2, \ldots, q_n, q_1', q_2', \ldots, q_n', C_1, C_2\}$ in which $q_1 \sim q_1'$ iff the computation of M on $(0, 0)$ is infinite. We use the pair of process constants q_i, q_i' for (the label of) the i-th instruction, $i \in \{1, 2, \ldots, n\}$, and the constants C_1, C_2 for unary representations of the values of the counters c_1, c_2. We define the following rules corresponding to (all) instructions of M (where action a can be read as 'addition', i.e. increment, d as 'decrement', z as 'zero', and h as 'halt').

'$i : c_r := c_r + 1$; goto j':

$$q_i \xrightarrow{a} q_j \mid C_r \qquad\qquad q_i' \xrightarrow{a} q_j' \mid C_r$$

'$i :$ if $c_r = 0$ then goto j else $(c_r := c_r - 1$; goto $k)$':

$$
\begin{array}{ll}
q_i \mid C_r \xrightarrow{d} q_k & q_i' \mid C_r \xrightarrow{d} q_k' \\
q_i \xrightarrow{z} q_j & q_i' \xrightarrow{z} q_j' \\
q_i \mid C_r \xrightarrow{z} q_j' \mid C_r & q_i' \mid C_r \xrightarrow{z} q_j \mid C_r
\end{array}
$$

'$n :$ HALT':

$$q_n \xrightarrow{h} \epsilon$$

Let (i, n_1, n_2) be a configuration of M. It will be represented by the pair of processes

$$q_i \mid C_1^{n_1} \mid C_2^{n_2} \quad \text{and} \quad q_i' \mid C_1^{n_1} \mid C_2^{n_2}$$

where $C_r^{n_r}$ for $r \in \{1, 2\}$ is a parallel composition of n_r process constants C_r. If the current instruction is increment, it is clear that, no matter how Attacker and Defender play, in one round they reach a pair of processes that represent the successor configuration (one occurrence of C_r is added on both sides). If the current instruction is zero-test and decrement and Attacker plays the action d, Defender can only mimic the move under d in the other process and both players remove one occurrence of C_r on both sides, again reaching a configuration representing the successor configuration of M. The same happens if the counter c_r is empty and Attacker plays using the rule $q_i \xrightarrow{z} q_j$ or $q_i' \xrightarrow{z} q_j'$. Defender's only choice is to play using the rule $q_i' \xrightarrow{z} q_j'$ or $q_i \xrightarrow{z} q_j$ in the other process and the players faithfully simulate the computation of the machine M. The only situation where Attacker can 'cheat' is when the counter c_r is not empty and Attacker plays the action z according to one of the four available rules (two on the left-hand side and two on the right-hand side). Nevertheless, Defender can in this case answer on the other side under the action z is such a way that the players reach a pair of syntactically equal processes, a clear win for Defender.

The rules for the zero-test and decrement instruction provide another example of the use of *Defender's forcing technique* [JS08] as it was already explained in the proofs of Theorem 3.3.5 and Theorem 3.3.16.

To sum up we note that if M halts on $(0, 0)$ then Attacker can force the correct simulation of M in both components of the starting pair q_1 and q_1' and finally win by playing $q_n \xrightarrow{h} \epsilon$ (because there is no such rule for q_n'). If the computation of M on $(0, 0)$ is infinite then Defender forces Attacker to perform the correct simulation of the infinite computation and Defender wins the game.

This implies the following undecidability result.

Theorem 3.4.16 ([Jan95]) *Bisimilarity on Petri nets is undecidable.*

Remark 3.4.17 We remind the reader of the fact that the simulation of a 2-counter Minsky machine by a Petri net, as outlined above, provides only a so-called *weak simulation*. This means that the Petri net can mimic any behaviour of the Minsky machine, but also displays some additional 'cheating' behaviours. Indeed, the Petri net might decide to use the action z (for zero) even if the counter is not empty. This means, for instance, that the reachability problem for Petri nets is still decidable (as mentioned before even for the whole class of PRS, a superclass of Petri nets), but bisimilarity has the extra power to filter out such incorrect behaviours and hence bisimilarity checking is undecidable.

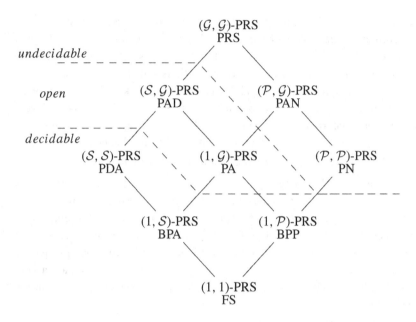

Fig. 3.12. (Un)decidability results for strong bisimilarity.

3.4.4 Overview of results

An overview of the state of the art for strong bisimilarity checking over the classes of processes from the PRS hierarchy is provided in Figure 3.12. As shown in Theorem 3.4.16, bisimilarity is undecidable for PN and the two classes above it. It is on the other hand decidable for PDA [Sen98, Sti00] and hence also for BPA (direct proofs are also available in [CHS95, BCS95]), and for BPP (Theorem 3.4.13). It is remarkable that most other behavioural equivalences apart from bisimilarity are undecidable already for BPA and BPP. Bar-Hillel, Perles, and Shamir [BHPS61] showed that the equivalence problem for languages generated by context-free grammars is undecidable. In fact, all the equivalences in van Glabbeek's spectrum [Gla01] (apart from bisimilarity) are undecidable for BPA [HT95, GH94]. For the case of BPP, Hirshfeld [Hir94b] showed that once again language equivalence is undecidable and as before none of the equivalences from van Glabbeek's spectrum coarser than bisimilarity are decidable [Hüt94]. Finally, we note that decidability of bisimilarity remains an open problem for PAD and PA, though for normed PA processes a positive decidability result already exists [HJ99].

For the case of weak bisimilarity, we know that it is not only undecidable but even highly undecidable (complete for the class Σ_1^1 on the first level of the analytical hierarchy) for PDA, PA and PN [JS08]. The problem still remains open for BPA and BPP.

For further references the reader may consult [Srb04], where an on-line and updated list of results is available (including also results for strong/weak regularity checking problems). Some recent overview articles [BCMS01, MSS04, KJ06, Jan08] provide further introduction to the area of equivalence checking over infinite-state systems.

3.5 The use of bisimilarity checking in verification and tools

As we stated in Section 3.1, a model of computation like that of labelled transition systems can be used to describe both implementations of processes and specifications of their expected behaviours. A notion of behavioural equivalence or preorder over labelled transition systems can therefore be used as the formal yardstick to establish the correctness of a proposed implementation with respect to a specification, when both are represented as objects in that model. Furthermore, from a foundational viewpoint, in the single-language approach to process theory, the informal notion of 'process' is formally characterised as an equivalence class of labelled transition systems with respect to some chosen behavioural relation.

In the light of the importance of behavioural relations in the single-language approach to process theory and of the lack of consensus on what constitutes a 'reasonable' notion of observable behaviour for reactive systems, it is perhaps not overly surprising that the literature on concurrency theory offers a large variety of behavioural semantics over labelled transition systems. (See the encyclopaedic survey paper [Gla01] and the conference article [Gla93] for the definition of a large number of those relations. Chapter 5 and chapter 6 in [San12] provide a smaller representative sample.) However, as the results we surveyed in the previous sections indicate, various notions of bisimilarity stand out amongst the plethora of available behavioural semantics because of their pleasing mathematical properties and the remarkable algorithmic, complexity and decidability results that are available for them. Those algorithmic results make notions of bisimilarity the prime candidates for implementation in software tools for computer-aided verification based on the single-language approach to process theory, such as CADP [GLMS07], the Edinburgh Concurrency Workbench and its further incarnations [CPS93, CS96], and mCRL2 [GKM$^+$08] to name but a few. After about two decades from the first development of such tools and of their use in computer-aided verification, it is natural to try to assess the actual applications of bisimilarity checking in the practice of verification. This is our aim in the present section. Let us state at the outset that we cannot possibly hope to give a comprehensive account of the available software tools and of their applications here. What we shall try to do instead is to highlight some of the most common uses of bisimilarity checking in the practice of (computer-aided) verification and sometimes how, and whether, they are used in applications of the representative tools we have mentioned above. Apart from the references we present below, our presentation is also based on personal communications with Rance Cleaveland, Hubert Garavel and Jan Friso Groote.

3.5.1 Some uses of bisimilarity checking

Variations on the notion of bisimilarity play several roles in verification. In the remainder of this section, in order to focus our discussion, we shall only consider those that, to our mind, are the most common and/or remarkable ones.

Bisimilarity as a correctness criterion As mentioned above, bisimilarity can be used as the notion of behavioural relation for establishing formally that implementations are correct with respect to specifications expressed as labelled transition systems. In the light of the results we discussed in previous sections, the choice of bisimilarity as a formal yardstick for proving correctness is algorithmically attractive.

However, notions of bisimilarity are amongst the finest semantics in van Glabbeek's lattice of behavioural semantics over labelled transition systems. This begs the questions of whether bisimulation-like behavioural equivalences are coarse enough in practice and whether such an approach to verification is widely applicable. Answers to those questions vary from researcher to researcher and we are not aware of systematic studies on the applicability of bisimilarity in verification. However, the experts we consulted tended to agree that weak and branching bisimilarity [GW96, Mil89] are, in general, adequate in applications and are far more efficient than other alternatives, both in manual and in computer-aided correctness proofs. By way of example, Rance Cleaveland, one of the chief architects behind the development and the applications of the Concurrency Workbench of the New Century [CS96], wrote to us [Cle09]:

> I personally have not found bisimulation to be unnecessarily restrictive when comparing a specification LTS to an implementation LTS, but this is because in almost all the cases I have worked with, the specification is deterministic.

Hubert Garavel, the chief architect of CADP [GLMS07], supported this view and wrote [Gar09]:

> In practice, you can do a lot by using strong bisimulation, branching bisimulation, and safety equivalence together (with their preorders). I do not remember a case where a more exotic equivalence would have been mandatory.

(Safety equivalence was introduced in [BFG$^+$91] in order to provide a topological characterisation of safety properties in branching-time semantics. Two processes are related by the safety preorder iff whenever the left-hand-side process performs a sequence of τ actions followed by a visible action a then the right-hand-side can also perform a sequence of τ actions followed by a in such a way that the resulting processes are again related by the safety preorder. It turns out that, mirroring the situation in linear-time semantics [AL91, MP89], safety properties are exactly the closed sets in the topology induced by this preorder.) There are a few notorious examples of implementations and specifications that are not bisimulation equivalent, such as Bloom's two-writer register [Blo88], which can be proved correct in trace semantics. However, such examples are rare [Gro09].

There are also some interesting variations on using bisimilarity as a direct verification technique. The INRIA-Sophia Antipolis team of Robert de Simone and others proposed the notion of 'observation criteria' [BRdSV89]. The basic idea behind this notion is

(1) to define contexts (that is, open systems with which the implementation labelled transition system is expected to interact) describing 'usage scenarios',
(2) to put the system being verified in these contexts, and
(3) then use bisimilarity to compare the composite system to a labelled transition system representing an expected result.

One example of successful application of this approach is provided by [RC04], where Ray and Cleaveland used this idea to good effect in verifying a medical-device model. (In that paper, the verification method is called 'unit verification'.) A closely related analysis technique is presented in [Vaa90], together with some applications. All these approaches may be seen as special instances of the notion of context-dependent bisimilarity developed in [Lar86] and are based on the idea to combat the state-explosion problem by focusing on fragments of system behaviour; the context is responsible for identifying the relevant fragments. An early example of a compositional protocol verification using context-dependent bisimilarity may be found in [LM92].

According to Jan Friso Groote [Gro09], when using the verification tool mCRL2 [GKM$^+$08], a very common approach is currently to minimise a state space with respect to weak or branching bisimilarity and to inspect the resulting labelled transition system using a visualisation tool (in their setting, the tool ltsgraph from the mCRL2 tool set). (If the graphs are not too large, reducing them further using weak trace equivalence often simplifies the picture even more and is satisfactory when the interesting properties are trace properties.) Bisimilarity is the key technology for this approach, which is also supported and adopted by CADP [GLMS07] when the state space of the (minimised) model is small enough that one can draw it and verify it visually.

The debate on which notion of behavioural relation is the most 'reasonable' (in some sense) and the most suitable in verification (see also the discussion in [San12, section 5.14]) has been going on at least since the publication of Milner's first book on the *Calculus of Communicating Systems* [Mil80]. (See, for instance, the postings related to this issue that appeared in a very interesting debate that raged on the Concurrency mailing list in the late 1980s and early 1990s [Con90].) We feel that this chapter is not the most appropriate setting for a thorough discussion of the relative merits of linear and branching time semantics in verification, as this would lead us astray from the main gist of this contribution. We refer our readers to, for example, the articles [Gla94, NV07] for further interesting discussions of this issue and more pointers to the literature. In the former reference, van Glabbeek presents arguments for performing verifications using behavioural relations that, like various forms of bisimilarity, preserve the 'internal structure' of processes. The advantage of this approach is that verifications using such equivalences apply to any coarser behavioural relation based on testing scenarios. In the latter reference, Nain and Vardi argue instead that branching-time-based behavioural equivalences are not suitable for use in verification because they distinguish processes that cannot be told apart by any reasonable notion of observation. (See also the article [BIM95].)

We hope that we have provided enough information to our readers so that they can draw their own conclusions on this long-standing debate.

Bisimilarity as a tool for checking other behavioural relations Algorithms for computing bisimilarity over finite labelled transition systems can be used to compute other behavioural relations. See, for instance, the paper [CH93] for an early example of this application of bisimilarity. In that reference, Cleaveland and Hennessy showed how to compute the testing semantics from [DNH84] by using algorithms for bisimilarity checking. The resulting algorithms have been implemented in the Edinburgh Concurrency Workbench and its further incarnations [CPS93, CS96].

Moreover, minimisation with respect to bisimilarity can be used to improve on the efficiency of computing other behavioural relations. Indeed, since bisimilarity is a finer relation than the others in van Glabbeek's lattice, one can minimise systems before comparing them with respect to the chosen behavioural semantics.

In the specific case of the classic simulation preorder (see [San12, exercise 1.4.17] or [Gla01] for a definition of this relation), there has been some interesting work on combining the computation of the simulation preorder with bisimulation minimisation. The main idea behind this line of work is to intertwine the computation of simulation with minimisation, so that one can terminate early whenever the constraints of the simulation preorder are violated – see, for instance, the paper [TC01], which reports experimental data indicating that this approach yields a substantial improvement upon the best-known algorithm for computing the simulation preorder, even when the systems are minimised with respect to bisimulation equivalence before applying the simulation algorithm. It is interesting to note that, even though the simulation preorder looks deceptively similar to bisimilarity, recasting the simulation problem as a coarsest partition problem, which is the basic idea underlying the algorithms we discussed in Section 3.2, does not appear to be at all easy. See, for instance, the paper [GP08] for a detailed discussion of this issue in relation to earlier proposals.

Bisimulation minimisation as a preprocessing step Minimising a finite labelled transition system modulo bisimilarity can be used to reduce the size of a system description before applying model checking [CGP00]. The use of bisimilarity in this context is particularly attractive because, as essentially shown in [HM85], bisimilarity provides an abstraction technique that preserves the truth and falsehood of any formula expressed in the μ-calculus [Koz83], and hence all CTL* [Dam94], CTL [CE81, McM93], and LTL [Pnu77] properties. Moreover, as we saw in Section 3.2.4, bisimilarity can be computed symbolically and automatically over finite labelled transition systems.

Despite the aforementioned mathematically pleasing properties of minimisation with respect to bisimilarity, which make it a promising preprocessing step before applying model checking, and the increasing use of model checking formulas in the modal μ-calculus with data, state-space reduction is not used in verifications using mCRL2 [Gro09]. Instead, mCRL2 reduces the model checking problem to that of finding a solution to a Parameterised Boolean Equation System [GW05]. As Jan Friso Groote wrote to us [Gro09]:

> Bisimulation reduction is not of much (practical) relevance here.

This conclusion is supported by the work by Fisler and Vardi reported in [FV98, FV02]. In [FV98], the authors provided experimental evidence showing that the use of bisimulation minimisation as a preprocessing step to model checking does reduce the resource requirements of model checking. However, the work presented in that reference also indicates that the cost of bisimulation minimisation often exceeds that of model checking significantly. In [FV02], Fisler and Vardi provide experimental and analytical comparisons between symbolic model checking for invariance properties and three novel ROBBD-based algorithms that combine bisimulation minimisation and model checking based on the original algorithms given in [BFH91, LY92, PT87]. Their results indicate that the integrated algorithms are less efficient than model checking and strongly suggest that performing bisimulation minimisation does not lead to improvements over the direct use of model checking.

Bisimilarity in compositional verification In the context of compositional verification approaches, bisimilarity can be used to minimise components before each composition. This is the so-called minimise-then-compose heuristic, which can also be used as a means to combat the state-explosion problem in the generation of the labelled transition system for a composite system from those for its components.

Such an approach is used substantially in verifications using the tools CADP and FDR [For00], but is never used in applications of mCRL2 [Gro09]. According to Jan Friso Groote [Gro09], the benefits offered by bisimilarity do not differ very much from those provided by other equivalences in van Glabbeek's spectrum in this respect, but its algorithmic efficiency makes it more applicable than other behavioural semantics.

Bisimilarity as a tool to handle infinite-state systems Minimisation of a system with respect to bisimilarity can sometimes be used to collapse infinite labelled transition systems to finite ones. A system that is bisimilar to a finite one is often called a *regular* process. Regularity checking has been studied substantially over the classes of infinite-state systems from the PRS hierarchy, see, e.g. [Srb04] for an overview of results in that area.

The existence of a finite quotient of a hybrid or real-time system with respect to bisimilarity is the key theoretical step behind tool support for the verification of such systems [AILS07, AD94, AHLP00]. In the case of hybrid and timed automata, bisimilarity, while not explicitly present in the implementation of the algorithms embodied in tools such as HyTech [HHWT97], Kronos [BDM+98] and Uppaal [BDL+06], serves as a mathematical enabler of model checking and as theoretical background for providing correctness and termination arguments for the implemented algorithms.

The same phenomenon holds true for probabilistic and stochastic systems; see, for instance, [GH02, Hil96, LS91]. In the setting of stochastic processes, notions of Markovian bisimilarity [Hil96] play a key role since they are consistent with the notion of lumping over continuous-time Markov chains [Buc94]. This means that, whenever two processes are Markovian bisimilar, they are guaranteed to possess the same performance characteristics.

3.5.2 Concluding remarks

Overall, apart from its very satisfying mathematical properties and its strong connections with logics and games, bisimilarity is computationally superior to the other behavioural semantics that have been considered in the literature on concurrency theory. Its algorithmic, complexity and decidability properties that have been surveyed in this chapter are, to our mind, truly remarkable. As far as its suitability for and actual uses in verification are concerned, we hope that we have been able to provide our readers with enough information to draw their own conclusions. We feel confident that the debate on the merits of bisimilarity and related notions will continue for some time amongst concurrency theorists and members of the computer-aided-verification community. Perhaps, this is a sign of the fact that, despite divergences of opinions, the notion of bisimilarity is considered important, or at least interesting, by researchers in the aforementioned communities and that it has become part of our cultural heritage. Why would it be worth discussing otherwise?

Acknowledgements We thank Rance Cleaveland, Hubert Garavel and Jan Friso Groote for their contributions to the development of Section 3.5. Without their expert and thought-provoking opinions that section would have been much less informative and rather uninteresting, if not plain boring. We are also indebted to Arnar Birgisson for his detailed reading of, and his comments on, parts of the chapter. Luca Aceto and Anna Ingolfsdottir were partly supported by the projects 'The Equational Logic of Parallel Processes' (nr. 060013021) and 'New Developments in Operational Semantics' (nr. 080039021) of The Icelandic Research Fund. Jiří Srba acknowledges partial support from the Ministry of Education of the Czech Republic, grant no. MSM0021622419. The chapter was revised while Luca Aceto held an Abel Extraordinary Chair at Universidad Complutense de Madrid, Spain, supported by the NILS Mobility Project.

Bibliography

[AD94] R. Alur and D.L. Dill. A theory of timed automata. *Theoretical Computer Science*, **126**(2):183–235, 1994. Fundamental Study.

[AFGI04] L. Aceto, W. Fokkink, R. van Glabbeek, and A. Ingolfsdottir. Nested semantics over finite trees are equationally hard. *Information and Computation*, **191**(2):203–232, 2004.

[AFI01] L. Aceto, W. Fokkink, and A. Ingolfsdottir. 2-nested simulation is not finitely equationally axiomatizable. In *Proceedings of the 18th International Symposium on Theoretical Aspects of Computer Science, STACS 2001 (Dresden)*, volume 2010 of *Lecture Notes in Computer Science*, pages 39–50. Springer-Verlag, 2001.

[AHLP00] R. Alur, T.A. Henzinger, G. Lafferriere, and G.J. Pappas. Discrete abstractions of hybrid systems. In *Proceedings of the IEEE*, **88**: 971–984, 2000.

[AHU74] A.V. Aho, J.E. Hopcroft, and J.D. Ullman. *The Design and Analysis of Computer Algorithms*. Addison-Wesley, 1974.

[AILS07] L. Aceto, A. Ingolfsdottir, K.G. Larsen, and J. Srba. *Reactive Systems: Modelling, Specification and Verification*. Cambridge University Press, 2007.

[AL91] M. Abadi and L. Lamport. The existence of refinement mappings. *Theoretical Computer Science*, **82**(2):253–284, 1991.

[Bae90] J. Baeten, editor. *Applications of Process Algebra*. Cambridge Tracts in Theoretical Computer Science 17. Cambridge University Press, 1990.

[BCMS01] O. Burkart, D. Caucal, F. Moller, and B. Steffen. Verification on infinite structures. In J. Bergstra, A. Ponse, and S. Smolka, editors, *Handbook of Process Algebra*, chapter 9, pages 545–623. Elsevier Science, 2001.

[BCS95] O. Burkart, D. Caucal, and B. Steffen. An elementary decision procedure for arbitrary context-free processes. In *Proceedings of the 20th International Symposium on Mathematical Foundations of Computer Science (MFCS'95)*, volume 969 of *LNCS*, pages 423–433. Springer-Verlag, 1995.

[BDL⁺06] G. Behrmann, A. David, K.G. Larsen, J. Håkansson, P. Pettersson, W. Yi, and M. Hendriks. UPPAAL 4.0. In *Third International Conference on the Quantitative Evaluation of Systems (QEST 2006), 11–14 September 2006, Riverside, California, USA*, pages 125–126. IEEE Computer Society, 2006.

[BDM⁺98] M. Bozga, C. Daws, O. Maler, A. Olivero, S. Tripakis, and S. Yovine. Kronos: A model-checking tool for real-time systems. In A.J. Hu and M.Y. Vardi, editors, *Computer Aided Verification, 10th International Conference, CAV '98, Vancouver, BC, Canada, June 28–July 2, 1998, Proceedings*, volume 1427 of *Lecture Notes in Computer Science*, pages 546–550. Springer-Verlag, 1998.

[BE97] O. Burkart and J. Esparza. More infinite results. *Bulletin of the European Association for Theoretical Computer Science*, **62**:138–159, June 1997. Columns: Concurrency.

[BEM96] J.C. Bradfield, J. Esparza, and A. Mader. An effective tableau system for the linear time μ-calculus. In *Proceedings of the 23rd International Colloquium on Automata, Languages and Programming (ICALP'96)*, volume 1099 of *LNCS*, pages 98–109. Springer-Verlag, 1996.

[BFG⁺91] A. Bouajjani, J.-C. Fernandez, S. Graf, C. Rodriguez, and J. Sifakis. Safety for branching time semantics. In J. Leach Albert, B. Monien, and M. Rodríguez, editors, *Proceedings 18th ICALP*, Madrid, volume 510 of *Lecture Notes in Computer Science*, pages 76–92. Springer-Verlag, 1991.

[BFH91] A. Bouajjani, J.-C. Fernandez, and N. Halbwachs. Minimal model generation. In E.M. Clarke and R.P. Kurshan, editors, *Proceedings of the 2nd International Conference on Computer-Aided Verification*, New

Brunswick, NJ, USA June 1990, volume 531 of *Lecture Notes in Computer Science*, pages 197–203. Springer-Verlag, 1991.

[BGS92] J. Balcazar, J. Gabarro, and M. Santha. Deciding bisimilarity is P-complete. *Formal Aspects of Computing*, 4:638–648, 1992.

[BHPS61] Y. Bar-Hillel, M. Perles, and E. Shamir. On formal properties of simple phrase structure grammars. *Zeitschrift für Phonetik, Sprachwissenschaft, und Kommunikationsforschung*, 14:143–177, 1961.

[BIM95] B. Bloom, S. Istrail, and A. Meyer. Bisimulation can't be traced. *Journal of the ACM*, 42(1):232–268, 1995.

[BK84] J. Bergstra and J.W. Klop. Process algebra for synchronous communication. *Information and Control*, 60(1/3):109–137, 1984.

[BK85] J.A. Bergstra and J.W. Klop. Algebra of communicating processes with abstraction. *Theoretical Computer Science*, 37:77–121, 1985.

[Blo88] B. Bloom. Constructing two-writer registers. *IEEE Transactions on Computers*, 37(12):1506–1514, 1988.

[BP95] B. Bloom and R. Paige. Transformational design and implementation of a new efficient solution to the ready simulation problem. *Science of Computer Programming*, 24(3):189–220, 1995.

[BPS01] J. Bergstra, A. Ponse, and S.A. Smolka, editors. *Handbook of Process Algebra*. Elsevier, 2001.

[BRdSV89] G. Boudol, V. Roy, R. de Simone, and D. Vergamini. Process calculi, from theory to practice: Verification tools. In J. Sifakis, editor, *Automatic Verification Methods for Finite State Systems*, volume 407 of *Lecture Notes in Computer Science*, pages 1–10. Springer-Verlag, 1989.

[Bry86] R.E. Bryant. Graph-based algorithms for boolean function manipulation. *IEEE Transactions on Computers*, C-35(6):677–691, 1986.

[Bry92] R.E. Bryant. Symbolic boolean manipulation with ordered binary-decision diagrams. *ACM Computing Surveys*, 24(3):293–318, 1992.

[BS92] A. Bouali and R. de Simone. Symbolic bisimulation minimisation. In *Proceedings of CAV'92*, volume 663 of *Lecture Notes in Computer Science*, pages 96–108. Springer-Verlag, 1992.

[Buc94] P. Buchholz. Exact and ordinary lumpability in finite Markov chains. *Journal of Applied Probability*, 31(1):59–75, 1994.

[BW90] J. Baeten and P. Weijland. *Process Algebra*. Cambridge Tracts in Theoretical Computer Science 18. Cambridge University Press, 1990.

[Cau92] D. Caucal. On the regular structure of prefix rewriting. *Theoretical Computer Science*, 106(1):61–86, 1992.

[CE81] E.M. Clarke and E.A. Emerson. Design and synthesis of synchronization skeletons using branching-time temporal logic. In D. Kozen, editor, *Proceedings of the Workshop on Logic of Programs,* Yorktown Heights, volume 131 of *Lecture Notes in Computer Science*, pages 52–71. Springer-Verlag, 1981.

[CGP00] E.M. Clarke, O. Grumberg, and D.A. Peled. *Model Checking*. MIT Press, 2000.

[CH93] R. Cleaveland and M. Hennessy. Testing equivalence as a bisimulation equivalence. *Formal Aspects of Computing*, 5(1):1–20, 1993.

[CHM93] S. Christensen, Y. Hirshfeld, and F. Moller. Bisimulation is decidable for basic parallel processes. In *Proceedings of the 4th International Conference on Concurrency Theory (CONCUR'93)*, volume 715 of *LNCS*, pages 143–157. Springer-Verlag, 1993.

[Chr93] S. Christensen. *Decidability and decomposition in process algebras*. PhD thesis, The University of Edinburgh, 1993.

[CHS95] S. Christensen, H. Hüttel, and C. Stirling. A polynomial algorithm for deciding bisimilarity of normed context-free processes. *Information and Computation*, 12(2):143–148, 1995.

[Cle09] R. Cleaveland. Personal communication, January 2009.

[Cle90] R. Cleaveland. Tableau-based model checking in the propositional mu-calculus. *Acta Informatica*, 27(8):725–747, 1990.

[Con90] Concurrency mailing list archive, 1988–1990. Available online at http://homepages.cwi.nl/~bertl/concurrency/.

[CPS93] R. Cleaveland, J. Parrow, and B. Steffen. The concurrency workbench: A semantics-based verification tool for finite state systems. *ACM Transactions on Programming Languages and Systems*, 15(1):36–72, 1993.

[CS96] R. Cleaveland and S. Sims. The NCSU Concurrency Workbench. In R. Alur and T.A. Henzinger, editors, *Proceedings of the 8th International Conference on Computer Aided Verification*, New Brunswick, NJ, USA, July/August 1996, volume 1102 of *Lecture Notes in Computer Science*, pages 394–397. Springer-Verlag, 1996.

[CS01] R. Cleaveland and O. Sokolsky. Equivalence and preorder checking for finite-state systems. In Bergstra *et al.* [BPS01], chapter 6, pages 391–424.

[Dam94] M. Dam. CTL* and ECTL* as fragments of the modal μ-calculus. *Theoretical Computer Science*, 126:77–96, 1994.

[Dic13] L.E. Dickson. Finiteness of the odd perfect and primitive abundant numbers with distinct factors. *American Journal of Mathematics*, 35:413–422, 1913.

[DNH84] R. De Nicola and M. Hennessy. Testing equivalences for processes. *Theoretical Computer Science*, 34:83–133, 1984.

[EFT93] R. Enders, T. Filkorn, and D. Taubner. Generating BDDs for symbolic model checking in CCS. *Distributed Computing*, 6(3):155–164, 1993.

[EK99] J. Esparza and J. Knoop. An automata-theoretic approach to interprocedural data-flow analysis. In *Proceedings of the 2nd International Conference on Foundations of Software Science and Computation Structures (FOSSACS'99)*, volume 1578 of *LNCS*, pages 14–30. Springer-Verlag, 1999.

[Esp02] J. Esparza. Grammars as processes. In W. Brauer, H. Ehrig, J. Karhumäki, and A. Salomaa, editors, *Formal and Natural Computing*, volume 2300 of *LNCS*, pages 277–297. Springer-Verlag, 2002.

[For00] Formal Systems (Europe) Ltd. *Failures-Divergence Refinement – FRD2 User Manual*, 2000.

[FV98] K. Fisler and M.Y. Vardi. Bisimulation minimization in an automata-theoretic verification framework. In G. Gopalakrishnan and P.J. Windley, editors, *Formal Methods in Computer-Aided Design, 2nd International Conference, FMCAD '98, Palo Alto, California, USA, November 4–6,*

1998, Proceedings, volume 1522 of *Lecture Notes in Computer Science*, pages 115–132. Springer-Verlag, 1998.

[FV02]   K. Fisler and M.Y. Vardi. Bisimulation minimization and symbolic model checking. *Formal Methods in System Design*, **21**(1):39–78, 2002.

[Gar09]   H. Garavel. Personal communication, January 2009.

[GH94]   J.F. Groote and H. Hüttel. Undecidable equivalences for basic process algebra. *Information and Computation*, **115**(2):353–371, 1994.

[GH02]   H. Garavel and H. Hermanns. On combining functional verification and performance evaluation using CADP. In L.-H. Eriksson and P.A. Lindsay, editors, *FME 2002: Formal Methods – Getting IT Right, International Symposium of Formal Methods Europe, Copenhagen, Denmark, July 22–24, 2002, Proceedings*, volume 2391 of *Lecture Notes in Computer Science*, pages 410–429. Springer-Verlag, 2002.

[GHR95]   R. Greenlaw, H. James Hoover, and W.R. Ruzzo. *Limits to Parallel Computation: P-Completeness Theory*. Oxford University Press, 1995.

[GJ79]   M.R. Garey and D.S. Johnson. *Computers and Intractability*. W. H. Freeman, 1979. A guide to the theory of NP-completeness, A Series of Books in the Mathematical Sciences.

[GKM+08]   J.F. Groote, J. Keiren, A. Mathijssen, B. Ploeger, C. Stappers, C. Tankink, Y. Usenko, M. van Weerdenburg, W. Wesselink, T. Willemse, and J. van der Wulp. The mCRL2 toolset. In *Proceedings International Workshop on Advanced Software Development Tools and Techniques (WASDeTT 2008)*, 2008.

[Gla93]   R. van Glabbeek. The linear time–branching time spectrum II: the semantics of sequential processes with silent moves. In E. Best, editor, *Proceedings CONCUR 93*, Hildesheim, Germany, volume 715 of *Lecture Notes in Computer Science*, pages 66–81. Springer-Verlag, 1993.

[Gla94]   R. van Glabbeek. What is branching time semantics and why to use it? *Bulletin of the EATCS*, **53**:191–198, 1994.

[Gla01]   R. van Glabbeek. The linear time–branching time spectrum. I. The semantics of concrete, sequential processes. In Bergstra *et al.* [BPS01], pages 3–99.

[GLMS07]   H. Garavel, F. Lang, R. Mateescu, and W. Serwe. CADP 2006: A toolbox for the construction and analysis of distributed processes. In W. Damm and H. Hermanns, editors, *Proceedings of the 19th International Conference on Computer Aided Verification CAV'2007 (Berlin, Germany)*, volume 4590 of *Lecture Notes in Computer Science*. Springer-Verlag, 2007.

[GP08]   R. van Glabbeek and B. Ploeger. Correcting a space-efficient simulation algorithm. In A. Gupta and S. Malik, editors, *Computer Aided Verification, 20th International Conference, CAV 2008, Princeton, NJ, USA, July 7–14, 2008, Proceedings*, volume 5123 of *Lecture Notes in Computer Science*, pages 517–529. Springer-Verlag, 2008.

[Gro09]   J.F. Groote. Personal communication, January 2009.

[GV90]   J.F. Groote and F. Vaandrager. An efficient algorithm for branching bisimulation and stuttering equivalence. In M. Paterson, editor, *Proceedings 17th ICALP*, Warwick, volume 443 of *Lecture Notes in Computer Science*, pages 626–638. Springer-Verlag, July 1990.

[GW96] R. van Glabbeek and W.P. Weijland. Branching time and abstraction in bisimulation semantics. *Journal of the ACM*, **43**(3):555–600, 1996.

[GW05] J.F. Groote and T.A.C. Willemse. Parameterised boolean equation systems. *Theoretical Computer Science*, **343**(3):332–369, 2005.

[HHWT97] T.A. Henzinger, P.-H. Ho, and H. Wong-Toi. HYTECH: A model checker for hybrid systems. In O. Grumberg, editor, *Computer Aided Verification, 9th International Conference, CAV '97, Haifa, Israel, June 22-25, 1997, Proceedings*, volume 1254 of *Lecture Notes in Computer Science*, pages 460–463. Springer-Verlag, 1997.

[Hil96] J. Hillston. *A Compositional Approach to Performance Modelling*. Cambridge University Press, 1996.

[Hir94a] Y. Hirshfeld. Congruences in commutative semigroups. Technical report ECS-LFCS-94-291, Department of Computer Science, University of Edinburgh, 1994.

[Hir94b] Y. Hirshfeld. Petri nets and the equivalence problem. In *Proceedings of the 7th Workshop on Computer Science Logic (CSL'93)*, volume 832 of *Lecture Notes in Computer Science*, pages 165–174. Springer-Verlag, 1994.

[HJ99] Y. Hirshfeld and M. Jerrum. Bisimulation equivalence is decidable for normed process algebra. In *Proceedings of 26th International Colloquium on Automata, Languages and Programming (ICALP'99)*, volume 1644 of *LNCS*, pages 412–421. Springer-Verlag, 1999.

[HKV97] D. Harel, O. Kupferman, and M.Y. Vardi. On the complexity of verifying concurrent transition systems. In *Proceedings of the 8th International Conference on Concurrency Theory (CONCUR'07)*, volume 1243 of *LNCS*, pages 258–272. Springer-Verlag, 1997.

[HM85] M. Hennessy and R. Milner. Algebraic laws for nondeterminism and concurrency. *Journal of the ACM*, **32**(1):137–161, 1985.

[Hoa85] C.A.R. Hoare. *Communicating Sequential Processes*. Prentice-Hall, 1985.

[HRS76] H.B. Hunt, D.J. Rosenkrantz, and T.G. Szymanski. On the equivalence, containment, and covering problems for the regular and context-free languages. *Journal of Computer and System Sciences*, **12**:222–268, 1976.

[HS98] H. Hüttel and C. Stirling. Actions speak louder than words: Proving bisimilarity for context-free processes. *Journal of Logic and Computation*, **8**(4):485–509, 1998.

[HT95] D.T. Huynh and L. Tian. On deciding readiness and failure equivalences for processes in Σ_2^P. *Information and Computation*, **117**(2):193–205, 1995.

[HU79] J.E. Hopcroft and J.D. Ullman. *Introduction to Automata Theory, Languages and Computation*. Addison-Wesley, 1979.

[Hüt94] H. Hüttel. Undecidable equivalences for basic parallel processes. In *Proceedings of the 2nd International Symposium on Theoretical Aspects of Computer Software (TACS'94)*, volume 789 of *LNCS*, pages 454–464. Springer-Verlag, 1994.

[Jan95] P. Jančar. Undecidability of bisimilarity for Petri nets and some related problems. *Theoretical Computer Science*, **148**(2):281–301, 1995.

[Jan03] P. Jančar. Strong bisimilarity on basic parallel processes is PSPACE-complete. In *Proceedings of the 18th Annual IEEE Symposium on Logic* in Computer Science (LICS'03), pages 218–227. IEEE Computer Society Press, 2003.

[Jan08] P. Jančar. Selected ideas used for decidability and undecidability of bisimilarity. In *Proceedings of the 12th International Conference on Developments in Language Theory (DLT'08)*, volume 5257 of *LNCS*, pages 56–71. Springer-Verlag, 2008.

[JM96] L. Jategaonkar and A.R. Meyer. Deciding true concurrency equivalences on safe, finite nets. *Theoretical Computer Science*, 154(1):107–143, 1996.

[JS08] P. Jančar and J. Srba. Undecidability of bisimilarity by defender's forcing. *Journal of the ACM*, 55(1):1–26, 2008.

[Kel76] R.M. Keller. Formal verification of parallel programs. *Communications of the ACM*, 19(7):371–384, 1976.

[KJ06] A. Kučera and P. Jančar. Equivalence-checking on infinite-state systems: Techniques and results. *Theory and Practice of Logic Programming*, 6(3):227–264, 2006.

[Koz83] D.Kozen. Results on the propositional mu-calculus. *Theoretical Computer Science*, 27:333–354, 1983.

[KŘS05] M. Křetínský, V. Řehák, and J. Strejček. Reachability of Hennessy–Milner properties for weakly extended PRS. In *Proceedings of the 25th Conference on Foundations of Software Technology and Theoretical Computer Science (FSTTCS'05)*, volume 3821 of *LNCS*, pages 213–224. Springer-Verlag, 2005.

[KS83] P.C. Kanellakis and S.A. Smolka. CCS expressions, finite state processes, and three problems of equivalence. In *Proceedings of the 2nd Annual ACM SIGACT-SIGOPS Symposium on Principles of Distributed Computing (PODC'83)*, pages 228–240. ACM, 1983.

[KS90] P.C. Kanellakis and S.A. Smolka. CCS expressions, finite state processes, and three problems of equivalence. *Information and Computation*, 86(1):43–68, May 1990.

[Lar86] K.G. Larsen. *Context-dependent bisimulation between processes*. PhD thesis, Department of Computer Science, University of Edinburgh, 1986.

[LM92] K.G. Larsen and R. Milner. A compositional protocol verification using relativized bisimulation. *Information and Computation*, 99(1):80–108, 1992.

[LP85] O. Lichtenstein and A. Pnueli. Checking that finite state concurrent programs satisfy their linear specification. In *Conference Record of the 12th Annual ACM Symposium on Principles of Programming Languages*, pages 97–107, New Orleans, Louisiana, January 1985.

[LS91] K.G. Larsen and A. Skou. Bisimulation through probabilistic testing. *Information and Computation*, 94(1):1–28, 1991.

[LS00] F. Laroussinie and Ph. Schnoebelen. The state explosion problem from trace to bisimulation equivalence. In *Proceedings of the 3rd International Conference on Foundations of Software Science and Computation Structures (FOSSACS'00)*, volume 1784 of *LNCS*, pages 192–207. Springer-Verlag, 2000.

[LY92] D. Lee and M. Yannakakis. Online minimization of transition systems (extended abstract). In *Proceedings of the 24th Annual ACM Symposium* on the Theory of Computing, pages 264–274, Victoria, British Columbia, Canada, 4–6 May 1992.

[May97a] R. Mayr. Combining petri nets and PA-processes. In *Proceedings of the 3rd International Symposium on Theoretical Aspects of Computer Software (TACS'97)*, volume 1281 of *LNCS*, pages 547–561. Springer-Verlag, 1997.

[May97b] R. Mayr. Tableau methods for PA-processes. In *Proceedings of International Conference on Automated Reasoning with Analytic Tableaux and Related Methods (TABLEAUX'97)*, volume 1227 of *LNCS*, pages 276–290. Springer-Verlag, 1997.

[May98] R. Mayr. *Decidability and complexity of model checking problems for infinite-state systems*. PhD thesis, TU-München, 1998.

[May00] R. Mayr. Process rewrite systems. *Information and Computation*, 156(1):264–286, 2000.

[McM93] K. McMillan. *Symbolic Model Checking*. Kluwer Academic, 1993.

[Mil80] R. Milner. *A Calculus of Communicating Systems*, volume 92 of *Lecture Notes in Computer Science*. Springer-Verlag, 1980.

[Mil89] R. Milner. *Communication and Concurrency*. Prentice-Hall, 1989.

[Min67] M.L. Minsky. *Computation: Finite and Infinite Machines*. Prentice-Hall, 1967.

[Mol96] F. Moller. Infinite results. In *Proceedings of the 7th International Conference on Concurrency Theory (CONCUR'96)*, volume 1119 of *Lecture Notes in Computer Science*, pages 195–216. Springer-Verlag, 1996.

[MP89] Z. Manna and A. Pnueli. The anchored version of the temporal framework. In J.W. de Bakker, W.P. de Roever, and G. Rozenberg, editors, *REX School/Workshop on Linear Time, Branching Time and Partial Order in Logics and Models for Concurrency*, Noordwijkerhout, The Netherlands, May/June 1988, volume 354 of *Lecture Notes in Computer Science*, pages 201–284. Springer-Verlag, 1989.

[MSS04] F. Moller, S. Smolka, and J. Srba. On the computational complexity of bisimulation, redux. *Information and Computation*, 192(2):129–143, 2004.

[NV07] S. Nain and M.Y. Vardi. Branching vs. linear time: Semantical perspective. In K.S. Namjoshi, T. Yoneda, T. Higashino, and Y. Okamura, editors, *Automated Technology for Verification and Analysis, 5th International Symposium, ATVA 2007, Tokyo, Japan, October 22–25, 2007, Proceedings*, volume 4762 of *Lecture Notes in Computer Science*, pages 19–34. Springer-Verlag, 2007.

[Pap94] Ch.H. Papadimitriou. *Computational Complexity*. Addison-Wesley, 1994.

[Pet62] C.A. Petri. *Kommunikation mit Automaten*. PhD thesis, Darmstadt, 1962.

[Pet81] J.L. Peterson. *Petri Net Theory and the Modelling of Systems*. Prentice-Hall, 1981.

[Pnu77] A. Pnueli. The temporal logic of programs. In *Proceedings 18th Annual Symposium on Foundations of Computer Science*, pages 46–57. IEEE, 1977.

[PT87] R. Paige and R.E. Tarjan. Three partition refinement algorithms. *SIAM Journal on Computing*, 16(6):973–989, 1987.

[Rab97] A.M. Rabinovich. Complexity of equivalence problems for concurrent systems of finite agents. *Information and Computation*, **139**(2):111–129, 1997.

[RB81] W.C. Rounds and S.D. Brookes. Possible futures, acceptances, refusals and communicating processes. In *22nd Annual Symposium on Foundations of Computer Science, Nashville, Tennessee*, pages 140–149, New York, 1981. IEEE.

[RC04] A. Ray and R. Cleaveland. Unit verification: the CARA experience. *Software Tools for Technology Transfer*, **5**(4):351–369, 2004.

[Red65] L. Redei. *The Theory of Finitely Generated Commutative Semigroups*. Oxford University Press, 1965.

[San12] D. Sangiorgi. *An Introduction to Bisimulation and Coinduction*. Cambridge University Press, 2012.

[Saw03] Z. Sawa. Equivalence checking of non-flat systems is EXPTIME-hard. In *Proceedings of the 14th International Conference on Concurrency Theorem (CONCUR'03)*, volume 2761 of *LNCS*, pages 233–248. Springer-Verlag, 2003.

[Sen98] G. Senizergues. Decidability of bisimulation equivalence for equational graphs of finite out-degree. In *Proceedings of the 39th Annual IEEE Symposium on Foundations of Computer Science*, pages 120–129. IEEE, 1998.

[Sip06] M. Sipser. *Introduction to the Theory of Computation*. Course Technology, 2006.

[SJ01] Z. Sawa and P. Jančar. P-hardness of equivalence testing on finite-state processes. In *Proceedings of the 28th Annual Conference on Current Trends in Theory and Practice of Informatics (SOFSEM'01)*, volume 2234 of *LNCS*, pages 326–345. Springer-Verlag, 2001.

[SM73] L.J. Stockmeyer and A.R. Meyer. Word problems requiring exponential time. In *Proceedings 5th ACM Symposium on Theory of Computing, Austin, Texas*, pages 1–9, 1973.

[Srb01] J. Srba. On the power of labels in transition systems. In *Proceedings of the 12th International Conference on Concurrency Theory (CONCUR'01)*, volume 2154 of *LNCS*, pages 277–291. Springer-Verlag, 2001.

[Srb02] J. Srba. Note on the tableau technique for commutative transition systems. In *Proceedings of the 5th International Conference on Foundations of Software Science and Computation Structures (FOSSACS'02)*, volume 2303 of *LNCS*, pages 387–401. Springer-Verlag, 2002.

[Srb03] J. Srba. Strong bisimilarity of simple process algebras: Complexity lower bounds. *Acta Informatica*, **39**:469–499, 2003.

[Srb04] J. Srba. *Roadmap of Infinite Results, volume 2: Formal Models and Semantics*. World Scientific, 2004. An updated version can be downloaded from the author's home-page.

[Sti95] C. Stirling. Local model checking games. In *Proceedings of the 6th International Conference on Concurrency Theory (CONCUR'95)*, volume 962 of *LNCS*, pages 1–11. Springer-Verlag, 1995.

[Sti98] C. Stirling. Decidability of bisimulation equivalence for normed pushdown processes. *Theoretical Computer Science*, **195**(2):113–131, 1998.

[Sti00] C. Stirling. Decidability of bisimulation equivalence for pushdown processes. Available from the author's homepage, 2000.

[Sti01] C. Stirling. Decidability of weak bisimilarity for a subset of basic parallel processes. In *Proceedings of the 4th International Conference on Foundations of Software Science and Computation Structures (FOSSACS'01)*, volume 2030 of *LNCS*, pages 379–393. Springer-Verlag, 2001.

[Sti03] C. Stirling. Bisimulation and language equivalence. In *Logic for Concurrency and Synchronisation*, volume 18 of *Trends Log. Stud. Log. Libr.*, pages 269–284. Kluwer, 2003.

[SW91] C. Stirling and D. Walker. Local model checking in the modal mu-calculus. *Theoretical Computer Science*, **89**(1):161–177, 1991.

[TC01] L. Tan and R. Cleaveland. Simulation revisited. In T. Margaria and W. Yi, editors, *Tools and Algorithms for the Construction and Analysis of Systems, 7th International Conference, TACAS 2001 Held as Part of the Joint European Conferences on Theory and Practice of Software, ETAPS 2001 Genova, Italy, April 2–6, 2001, Proceedings*, volume 2031 of *Lecture Notes in Computer Science*, pages 480–495. Springer-Verlag, 2001.

[Tho93] W. Thomas. On the Ehrenfeucht–Fraïssé game in theoretical computer science (extended abstract). In *Proceedings of the 4th International Joint Conference CAAP/FASE, Theory and Practice of Software Development (TAPSOFT'93)*, volume 668 of *LNCS*, pages 559–568. Springer-Verlag, 1993.

[Vaa90] F. Vaandrager. Some observations on redundancy in a context. In Baeten [Bae90], pages 237–260.

4

Bisimulation and logic

COLIN STIRLING

4.1 Introduction

Bisimulation is a rich concept which appears in various areas of theoretical computer science as this book testifies. Besides its origin by Park [Pa81] as a small refinement of the behavioural equivalence originally defined by Hennessy and Milner between basic concurrent processes [HM80, HM85], it was independently, and earlier, defined and developed in the context of the model theory of modal logic (under the names of *p-relations* and *zigzag relations*) by Van Benthem [vB84] to give an exact account of which subfamily of first-order logic is definable in modal logic. Interestingly, to make their definition of process equivalence more palatable, Hennessy and Milner introduced a modal logic to characterise it. For more details of the history of bisimulation see Chapter 1.

A labelled transition system (LTS) is a triple $(Pr, Act, \rightarrow)$, see [San12], where Pr is a non-empty set of states or processes, Act is a set of labels and $\rightarrow \subseteq \wp(Pr \times Act \times Pr)$ is the transition relation. As usual, we write $P \xrightarrow{a} Q$ when $(P, a, Q) \in \rightarrow$. A transition $P \xrightarrow{a} Q$ indicates that P can perform action a and become Q. In logical presentations, there is often extra structure in a transition system, a labelling of states with atomic propositions (or colours): let $Prop$ be a set of propositions with elements p, q. Formally, this extra component is a *valuation*, a function $V : Prop \rightarrow \wp(Pr)$ that maps each $p \in Prop$ to a set $V(p) \subseteq Pr$ (those states coloured p). An LTS with a valuation is often called a *Kripke model*.[1]

We recall the important definition of bisimulation and bisimilarity, see [San12].

---

[1] Traditionally, a Kripke model has unlabelled transitions of the form $P \rightarrow Q$ representing that state Q is *accessible* to P.

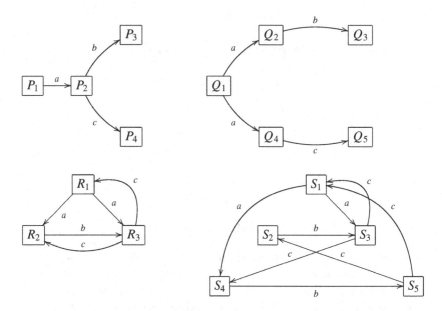

Fig. 4.1. Examples of bisimilar and non-bisimilar processes.

Definition 4.1.1 A binary relation $\mathcal{R}$ on states of an LTS is a *bisimulation* if whenever $P_1 \mathcal{R} P_2$ and $a \in A$,

(1) for all P_1' with $P_1 \xrightarrow{a} P_1'$, there is P_2' such that $P_2 \xrightarrow{a} P_2'$ and $P_1' \mathcal{R} P_2'$;
(2) for all P_2' with $P_2 \xrightarrow{a} P_2'$, there is P_1' such that $P_1 \xrightarrow{a} P_1'$ and $P_1' \mathcal{R} P_2'$.

P_1 is *bisimilar* to P_2, $P_1 \sim P_2$, if there is a bisimulation $\mathcal{R}$ with $P_1 \mathcal{R} P_2$. □

In the case of an enriched LTS with valuation V there is an extra clause in the definition of a bisimulation that it preserves colours:

(0) for all $p \in Prop$, $P_1 \in V(p)$ iff $P_2 \in V(p)$.

Definition 4.1.1 assumes that a bisimulation relation is between states of a single LTS. Occasionally, we also allow bisimulations between states of *different* LTSs (a minor relaxation because the disjoint union of two LTSs is an LTS).

Example 4.1.2 In Figure 4.1, $R_1 \sim S_1$ because the following relation $\mathcal{R}$ is a bisimulation $\{(R_1, S_1), (R_2, S_2), (R_2, S_4), (R_3, S_3), (R_3, S_5)\}$. For instance, take the pair $(R_3, S_3) \in \mathcal{R}$; we need to show it obeys the hereditary conditions of Definition 4.1.1. $R_3 \xrightarrow{c} R_1$ and $R_3 \xrightarrow{c} R_2$; however, $S_3 \xrightarrow{c} S_1$ and $(R_1, S_1) \in \mathcal{R}$; also, $S_3 \xrightarrow{c} S_4$ and $(R_2, S_4) \in \mathcal{R}$. If this transition system were enriched with $V(p) = \{R_2, S_4\}$ then R_1 and S_1 would no longer be bisimilar. Furthermore,

$P_1 \not\sim Q_1$ because P_2 can engage in both b and c transitions whereas Q_2 and Q_4 cannot. □

In the remainder of this chapter, we shall describe key relationships between logics and bisimulation. In Section 4.2, we examine the Hennessy–Milner modal characterisation of bisimilarity. In Section 4.3 we prove van Benthem's expressiveness result that modal logic corresponds to the fragment of first-order logic that is bisimulation invariant. These results are then extended in Sections 4.4 and 4.5 to modal mu-calculus, that is, modal logic with fixed points, and to the bisimulation invariant fragment of monadic second-order logic.

4.2 Modal logic and bisimilarity

Let M be the following modal logic where a ranges over *Act*.

$$\phi ::= \mathtt{tt} \mid \neg\phi \mid \phi_1 \vee \phi_2 \mid \langle a \rangle \phi.$$

A formula is either the 'true' formula $\mathtt{tt}$, the negation of a formula, $\neg\phi$, a disjunction of two formulas, $\phi_1 \vee \phi_2$, or a *modal* formula, $\langle a \rangle \phi$, 'diamond a ϕ'. M is often called Hennessy–Milner logic as it was introduced by Hennessy and Milner to clarify process equivalence [HM80, HM85]. Unlike a standard presentation of modal logic at that time, such as [Ch80], it is *multi-modal*, involving families of modal operators, one for each element of *Act*, and it avoids atomic propositions. The inductive stipulation below defines when a state $P \in Pr$ of a LTS L has a modal property ϕ, written $P \models_L \phi$; however we drop the index L.

$$
\begin{aligned}
&P \models \mathtt{tt} \\
&P \models \neg\phi && \text{iff} && P \not\models \phi \\
&P \models \phi_1 \vee \phi_2 && \text{iff} && P \models \phi_1 \text{ or } P \models \phi_2 \\
&P \models \langle a \rangle \phi && \text{iff} && P' \models \phi \text{ for some } P' \text{ with } P \xrightarrow{a} P'.
\end{aligned}
$$

The critical clause here is the interpretation of $\langle a \rangle$ as 'after some a-transition'; for instance, $Q_1 \models \langle a \rangle \langle b \rangle \mathtt{tt}$, where Q_1 is in Figure 4.1, because $Q_1 \xrightarrow{a} Q_2$ and $Q_2 \models \langle b \rangle \mathtt{tt}$. In the context of full propositional modal logic over an enriched LTS with a valuation V one adds propositions $p \in Prop$, with semantic clause

$$P \models p \text{ iff } P \in V(p).$$

Other connectives are introduced as follows: 'false', $\mathtt{ff} = \neg\mathtt{tt}$, conjunction, $\phi_1 \wedge \phi_2 = \neg(\neg\phi_1 \vee \neg\phi_2)$, implication, $\phi_1 \rightarrow \phi_2 = \neg\phi_1 \vee \phi_2$ and the dual modal operator 'box a', $[a]\phi = \neg\langle a\rangle\neg\phi$. Derived semantic clauses for these defined connectives are as follows.

$$P \not\models \mathtt{ff}$$
$$P \models \phi_1 \wedge \phi_2 \quad \text{iff} \quad P \models \phi_1 \text{ and } P \models \phi_2$$
$$P \models \phi_1 \rightarrow \phi_2 \quad \text{iff} \quad \text{if } P \models \phi_1 \text{ then } P \models \phi_2$$
$$P \models [a]\phi \quad \text{iff} \quad P' \models \phi \text{ for every } P' \text{ with } P \xrightarrow{a} P'.$$

So, $[a]$ means 'after every a-transition'; for example $P_1 \models [a]\langle b\rangle\mathtt{tt}$ whereas $Q_1 \not\models [a]\langle b\rangle\mathtt{tt}$, where these are in Figure 4.1, because $Q_1 \xrightarrow{a} Q_4$ and $Q_4 \not\models \langle b\rangle\mathtt{tt}$.

Exercise 4.2.1 Show the following using the inductive definition of the satisfaction relation $\models$ where the processes are depicted in Figure 4.1.

(1) $S_2 \models [a](\langle b\rangle\mathtt{tt} \wedge \langle c\rangle\mathtt{tt})$
(2) $S_1 \not\models [a](\langle b\rangle\mathtt{tt} \wedge \langle c\rangle\mathtt{tt})$
(3) $S_2 \models [b][c](\langle a\rangle\mathtt{tt} \vee \langle c\rangle\mathtt{tt})$
(4) $S_1 \models [b][c](\langle a\rangle\mathtt{tt} \vee \langle c\rangle\mathtt{tt})$.   □

A natural notion of equivalence between states of an LTS is induced by the modal logic (with or without atomic propositions).

Definition 4.2.2 P and P' have the same modal properties, written $P \equiv_M P'$, if $\{\phi \in M \mid P \models \phi\} = \{\phi \in M \mid P' \models \phi\}$.   □

Bisimilar states have the same modal properties.

Theorem 4.2.3 *If $P \sim P'$ then $P \equiv_M P'$.*

Proof By structural induction on $\phi \in M$ we show for any P, P' if $P \sim P'$ then $P \models \phi$ iff $P' \models \phi$. The base case is when ϕ is $\mathtt{tt}$ which is clear (as is the case $p \in Prop$ when considering an enriched LTS). For the inductive step, there are three cases when $\phi = \neg\phi_1$, $\phi = \phi_1 \vee \phi_2$ and $\phi = \langle a\rangle\phi_1$, assuming the property holds for ϕ_1 and for ϕ_2. We just consider the last of these three and leave the other two as an exercise for the reader. Assume $P \models \langle a\rangle\phi_1$. So, $P \xrightarrow{a} P_1$ and $P_1 \models \phi_1$ for some P_1. However, $P \sim P'$ and so $P' \xrightarrow{a} P_1'$ for some P_1' such that $P_1 \sim P_1'$. By the induction hypothesis, if $Q \sim Q'$ then $Q \models \phi_1$ iff $Q' \models \phi_1$. Therefore, $P_1' \models \phi_1$ because $P_1 \models \phi_1$ and so $P' \models \langle a\rangle\phi_1$, as required. A symmetric argument applies if $P' \models \langle a\rangle\phi$.   □

The converse is true in the circumstance that the LTS is *image-finite*: that is, when the set $\{P' \mid P \xrightarrow{a} P'\}$ is finite for each $P \in Pr$ and $a \in Act$, see [San12].

Theorem 4.2.4 *If the LTS is image-finite and $P \equiv_M P'$ then $P \sim P'$.*

Proof By showing that the binary relation $\equiv_M$ is a bisimulation. Assume $P \equiv_M P'$. If the LTS is enriched then, clearly, $P \models p$ iff $P' \models p$ for any $p \in Prop$. Assume $P \xrightarrow{a} P_1$. We need to show that $P' \xrightarrow{a} P_i'$ such that $P_1 \equiv_M P_i'$. Since $P \models \langle a \rangle \mathtt{tt}$ also $P' \models \langle a \rangle \mathtt{tt}$ and, so, the set $\{P_i' \mid P' \xrightarrow{a} P_i'\}$ is non-empty. As the LTS is image-finite, this set is finite, say $\{P_1', \ldots, P_n'\}$. If $P_1 \not\equiv_M P_i'$ for each $i : 1 \leq i \leq n$ then there are formulas $\phi_1, \ldots, \phi_n$ of M where $P_1 \not\models \phi_i$ and $P_i' \models \phi_i$ and so $P_1 \not\models \phi'$ and $P_i' \models \phi'$ for each i when $\phi' = \phi_1 \vee \ldots \vee \phi_n$. But this contradicts $P \equiv_M P'$ as $P \not\models [a]\phi'$ and $P' \models [a]\phi'$. So, for some P_i', $1 \leq i \leq n$, $P_1 \equiv_M P_i'$. The proof for the case $P' \xrightarrow{a} P_1'$ is symmetric. □

Theorems 4.2.3 and 4.2.4 together are known as the *Hennessy–Milner theorem*, the modal characterisation of bisimilarity. Modal formulas can, therefore, be witnesses for inequivalent (image-finite) processes; an example is that $\langle a \rangle [b] \mathtt{ff}$ distinguishes Q_1 and P_1 of Figure 4.1.

Exercise 4.2.5 Sets of formulas of M can be stratified according to their modal depth. The *modal depth* of $\phi \in M$, $\mathrm{md}(\phi)$, is defined inductively: $\mathrm{md}(\mathtt{tt}) = 0$; $\mathrm{md}(\neg\phi) = \mathrm{md}(\phi)$; $\mathrm{md}(\phi_1 \vee \phi_2) = \max\{\mathrm{md}(\phi_1), \mathrm{md}(\phi_2)\}$; $\mathrm{md}(\langle a \rangle \phi) = \mathrm{md}(\phi) + 1$. Let $\equiv_M^n$ mean having the same modal properties with modal depth at most n and recall the stratified bisimilar relations $\sim_n$ defined in [San12]. What Hennessy and Milner showed is $P \sim_n P'$ iff $P \equiv_M^n P'$.

(1) Prove by induction on n, $P \sim_n P'$ iff $P \equiv_M^n P'$.
(2) Therefore, show that the restriction to image-finite LTSs in Theorem 4.2.4 is essential.
(3) Assume an LTS where Act is finite and which need not be image-finite. Show that for each $P \in Pr$ and for each $n \geq 0$, there is a formula ϕ of modal depth n such that $P' \models \phi$ iff $P' \sim_n P$. (Hint: if Act is finite then for each $n \geq 0$ there are only finitely many inequivalent formulas of model depth n.) □

Exercise 4.2.6 Let M^∞ be modal logic M with arbitrary countable disjunction (and, therefore, conjunction because of negation). If Φ is a countable set of formulas then $\bigvee \Phi$ is a formula whose semantics is: $P \models \bigvee \Phi$ iff $P \models \phi$ for some $\phi \in \Phi$. Prove that if Pr is a countable set then $P \sim Q$ iff $P \equiv_{M^\infty} Q$. □

Next, we identify when a process has the Hennessy–Milner property [BRV01].

Definition 4.2.7 $P \in Pr$ has the *Hennessy–Milner property* iff if $P' \equiv_M P$ then $P' \sim P$. □

Exercise 4.2.8 *Pr* is *modally saturated* if for each $a \in Act$, $P \in Pr$ and $\Phi \subseteq M$ if for each finite set $\Phi' \subseteq \Phi$ there is a $Q \in \{Q \mid P \xrightarrow{a} Q\}$ and $Q \models \phi$ for all $\phi \in \Phi'$ then there is a $Q \in \{Q \mid P \xrightarrow{a} Q\}$ such that $Q \models \phi$ for all $\phi \in \Phi$. Show that if *Pr* is modally saturated then each $P \in Pr$ has the Hennessy–Milner property. (See, for instance, [BRV01] for the notion of modal saturation and how to build LTSs with this feature using ultrafilter extensions.) □

A formula ϕ is *characteristic* for process P (with respect to bisimilarity) provided that $P \models \phi$ and if $P' \models \phi$ then $P' \sim P$. An LTS is *acyclic* if its transition graph does not contain cycles; that is, if $P \in Pr$ and $P \xrightarrow{a} P'$ and $P' \xrightarrow{a_1} P_1 \xrightarrow{a_2} \ldots \xrightarrow{a_n} P_n$ for $n \geq 0$ then $P \neq P_n$.

Proposition 4.2.9 *Assume an acyclic LTS* $(Pr, Act, \rightarrow)$ *where Pr, Act and Prop are finite. If* $P \in Pr$ *then there is a formula* $\phi \in M$ *that is characteristic for* P.

Proof Assume an acyclic LTS with finite sets *Pr*, *Act* and *Prop*. For each $P \in Pr$ we define a propositional formula PROP(P) and for each $a \in Act$ a modal formula MOD(a, P). Then FORM(P) = PROP(P) $\wedge \bigwedge\{$MOD(a, P) $\mid a \in Act\}$ is the characteristic formula for P.

$$\text{PROP}(P) = \bigwedge\{p \in Prop \mid P \models p\} \wedge \bigwedge\{\neg p \in Prop \mid P \not\models p\}$$
$$\text{MOD}(a, P) = \bigwedge\{\langle a \rangle \text{FORM}(P') \mid P \xrightarrow{a} P'\} \wedge [a] \bigvee\{\text{FORM}(P') \mid P \xrightarrow{a} P'\}$$

where as usual $\bigwedge \emptyset = \mathtt{tt}$ and $\bigvee \emptyset = \mathtt{ff}$. We need to show that FORM(P) is indeed well-defined and a modal formula; and that it is characteristic for P. The first depends on the fact that the LTS is acyclic and that the sets *Pr*, *Act* and *Prop* are finite; why? The proof that FORM(P) is characteristic for P is also left as an exercise for the reader. □

Example 4.2.10 The LTS in Figure 4.2 is acyclic with $Pr = \{P_1, \ldots, P_4\}$, $Act = \{a, b\}$ and $Prop = \emptyset$. Now,

$$\text{FORM}(P_2) = \text{FORM}(P_4) = [a]\mathtt{ff} \wedge [b]\mathtt{ff}$$
$$\text{FORM}(P_3) = \langle a \rangle \text{FORM}(P_4) \wedge [a]\text{FORM}(P_4) \wedge [b[\mathtt{ff}$$
$$\text{FORM}(P_1) = \langle a \rangle \text{FORM}(P_2) \wedge \langle a \rangle \text{FORM}(P_3) \wedge$$
$$[a](\text{FORM}(P_2) \vee \text{FORM}(P_3)) \wedge [b]\mathtt{ff} .$$

Here, we construct the formulas starting from the nodes P_2 and P_4 that have no outgoing transitions; then we construct the formula for P_3; and then finally for P_1. □

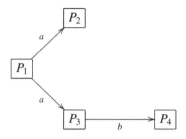

Fig. 4.2. The transition graph for Example 4.2.10.

Exercise 4.2.11 Give an example of a finite-state P such that no formula of M is characteristic for P. □

Exercise 4.2.12 Recall that trace equivalence equates two states P and Q if they can perform the same *finite sequences* of transitions, see [San12].

(1) Show that Proposition 4.2.9 also holds for trace equivalence. That is, assume an acyclic LTS where Pr and Act are finite and $Prop$ is empty. Prove that if $P \in Pr$ then there is formula $\phi \in M$ that is characteristic for P with respect to trace equivalence.
(2) Construct the characteristic formula for P_1 and Q_1 of Figure 4.1. □

4.3 Bisimulation invariance

An alternative semantics of modal logic emphasises *properties*. Relative to a LTS and valuation V, let $\|\phi\| = \{P \mid P \models \phi\}$: we can think of $\|\phi\|$ as the property expressed by ϕ on the LTS. In the case of the LTS in Figure 4.2, $\|\langle a\rangle\text{tt} \vee \langle b\rangle\text{tt}\| = \{P_1, P_3\}$.

Exercise 4.3.1 Define $\|\phi\|$ on a LTS directly by induction on ϕ (without appealing to the satisfaction relation $\models$). □

Another way of understanding Theorem 4.2.3 is that properties of states of an LTS expressed by modal formulas are *bisimulation invariant*: if $P \in \|\phi\|$ and $P \sim P'$ then $P' \in \|\phi\|$. There are many kinds of properties that are not bisimulation invariant. Examples include counting of successor transitions, 'has three a-transitions', or invocations of finiteness such as 'is finite-state' or behavioural cyclicity, 'has a sequence of transitions that is eventually cyclic': each of these properties distinguishes P_1 and Q_1 in Figure 4.3 even though

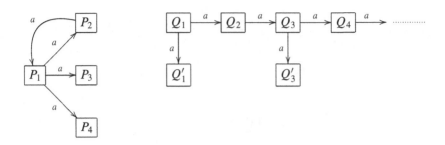

Fig. 4.3. More transition graphs

$P_1 \sim Q_1$. The definition of invariance is neither restricted to *monadic* properties nor to a particular logic within which properties of LTSs are expressed.

Definition 4.3.2 Assume Pr^n is $(Pr \times \ldots \times Pr)$ n-times, $n \geq 1$.

(1) An n-ary property, $n \geq 1$, of a LTS is a set $\Gamma \subseteq Pr^n$.
(2) Property $\Gamma \subseteq Pr^n$ is *bisimulation invariant* if whenever $(P_1, \ldots, P_n) \in \Gamma$ and $P_i \sim P_i'$ for each $i : 1 \leq i \leq n$, then also $(P_1', \ldots, P_n') \in \Gamma$.   □

Exercise 4.3.3

(1) Prove that the property $\{(P, Q) \mid P, Q$ are trace equivalent$\}$ is bisimulation invariant. More generally, show that if $\equiv$ is a behavioural equivalence between processes such that $P \sim Q$ implies $P \equiv Q$, then $\equiv$ is bisimulation invariant.
(2) A property $\Gamma \subseteq Pr^n$ is *safe for bisimulation* if whenever $(P_1, \ldots, P_n) \in \Gamma$ and $P_1 \sim P_1'$ then $(P_1', \ldots, P_n') \in \Gamma$ for some $P_2', \ldots, P_n'$ (a notion due to van Benthem [vB98]). Show that the general transition relations $\xrightarrow{w}$, $w \in Act^*$ (defined in [San12]) are safe for bisimulation.
(3) Show that if Γ is bisimulation invariant then it is safe for bisimulation.

    □

Another logic within which to express properties of a LTS is first-order logic, FOL. It has a countable family of variables *Var* typically represented as x, y, z and a binary relation E_a for each $a \in Act$ (and a monadic predicate p for each $p \in Prop$ when the LTS is enriched). Formulas of FOL have the following form:

$$\phi ::= p(x) \mid x E_a y \mid x = y \mid \neg\phi \mid \phi_1 \vee \phi_2 \mid \exists x.\phi.$$

To interpret formulas with free variables we need a valuation $\sigma : Var \to Pr$ that associates a state with each variable. Also, we use a standard 'updating' notation: $\sigma\{P_1/x_1, \ldots, P_n/x_n\}$ is the valuation that is the same as σ except that its value for x_i is P_i, $1 \leq i \leq n$ (where each x_i is distinct). We inductively define when the FOL formula ϕ is true on an LTS L with respect to a valuation σ as $\sigma \models_L \phi$, where again we drop the index L:

$$
\begin{array}{ll}
\sigma \models p(x) & \text{iff} \quad \sigma(x) \in V(p) \\
\sigma \models x E_a y & \text{iff} \quad \sigma(x) \xrightarrow{a} \sigma(y) \\
\sigma \models x = y & \text{iff} \quad \sigma(x) = \sigma(y) \\
\sigma \models \neg\phi & \text{iff} \quad \sigma \not\models \phi \\
\sigma \models \phi_1 \vee \phi_2 & \text{iff} \quad \sigma \models \phi_1 \text{ or } \sigma \models \phi_2 \\
\sigma \models \exists x.\phi & \text{iff} \quad \sigma\{P/x\} \models \phi \text{ for some } P \in Pr.
\end{array}
$$

The universal quantifier, the dual of $\exists x$, is introduced as $\forall x.\phi = \neg\exists x.\neg\phi$. Its derived semantic clause is: $\sigma \models \forall x.\phi$ iff $\sigma\{P/x\} \models \phi$ for all $P \in Pr$.

Example 4.3.4 Assume $\sigma(x_1) = P_1$ and $\sigma(x_2) = Q_1$ of Figure 4.3. Then the following pair hold:

(1) $\sigma \models \exists x.\exists y.\exists z.(x_1 E_a x \wedge x_1 E_a y \wedge x_1 E_a z \wedge x \neq y \wedge x \neq z \wedge y \neq z)$
(2) $\sigma \models \forall y.\forall z.(x_2 E_a y \wedge y E_a z \rightarrow z \neq x_2)$. $\qquad\square$

There is a recognised translation of modal formulas into first-order formulas, for instance, see [BRV01].

Definition 4.3.5 The FOL translation of modal formula ϕ relative to variable x is $T_x(\phi)$ which is defined inductively:

$$
\begin{array}{ll}
T_x(p) & = p(x) \\
T_x(\text{tt}) & = x = x \\
T_x(\neg\phi) & = \neg\, T_x(\phi) \\
T_x(\phi_1 \vee \phi_2) & = T_x(\phi_1) \vee T_x(\phi_2) \\
T_x(\langle a \rangle \phi) & = \exists y.\, x E_a y \wedge T_y(\phi).
\end{array}
$$

$\qquad\square$

Exercise 4.3.6

(1) For each of the following formulas ϕ, present its FOL translation $T_x(\phi)$.
    (a) $[a]\langle b \rangle \text{tt}$
    (b) $\langle a \rangle p \rightarrow [a]\langle a \rangle p$
    (c) $[a]([a]p \rightarrow p) \rightarrow [a]p$.
(2) FOL^2 is first-order logic when *Var* is restricted to two variables $\{x, y\}$ which can be reused in formulas. Show that modal formulas can be translated into FOL^2. $\qquad\square$

The translation of modal formulas into FOL, Definition 4.3.5, is clearly correct as it imitates the semantics.

Proposition 4.3.7 $P \models \phi$ *iff* $\sigma\{P/x\} \models T_x(\phi)$.

Proof By structural induction on $\phi \in M$. For the base cases, first $P \models p$ iff $P \in V(p)$ iff $\sigma\{P/x\} \models p(x)$ iff $\sigma\{P/x\} \models T_x(p)$. Similarly, for the other base case, $P \models \mathtt{tt}$ iff $\sigma\{P/x\} \models x = x$ iff $\sigma\{P/x\} \models T_x(\mathtt{tt})$. For the inductive step we only examine the interesting case when $\phi = \langle a \rangle \phi_1$. $P \models \phi$ iff $P' \models \phi_1$ for some P' where $P \xrightarrow{a} P'$ iff $\sigma\{P'/z\} \models T_z(\phi_1)$ for some P' where $P \xrightarrow{a} P'$, by the induction hypothesis, iff $\sigma\{P/x\} \models \exists z. \, x E_a z \wedge T_z(\phi_1)$ iff $\sigma\{P/x\} \models T_x(\phi)$.   □

A FOL formula with free variables is bisimulation invariant if the property it expresses is bisimulation invariant.

Definition 4.3.8   Formula $\phi \in$ FOL whose free variables belong to $\{x_1, \ldots, x_n\}$ is bisimulation invariant if $\{(P_1, \ldots, P_n) \mid \sigma\{P_1/x_1, \ldots, P_n/x_n\} \models \phi\}$ is bisimulation invariant.   □

Corollary 4.3.9   *Any first-order formula* $T_x(\phi)$ *is bisimulation invariant.*   □

Not all first-order formulas are bisimulation invariant. The two formulas in Example 4.3.4 are cases; the first says that 'x_1 has at least three different a-transitions'. Van Benthem introduced the notion of bisimulation (as a p-relation and a zig-zag relation) to identify which formulas $\phi(x) \in$ FOL with one free variable are equivalent to modal formulas [vB96].

Definition 4.3.10   A FOL formula $\phi(x)$ is equivalent to modal $\phi' \in M$ provided that for any LTS and for any state P, $\sigma\{P/x\} \models \phi$ iff $P \models \phi'$.   □

Van Benthem proved Proposition 4.3.12: a FOL formula $\phi(x)$ is equivalent to a modal formula iff it is bisimulation invariant. The proof utilises some model theory. Some notation first: if Φ is a set of first-order formulas then $\Phi \models \psi$ provided that for any LTS and valuation σ, if for all $\phi \in \Phi, \sigma \models \phi$ then $\sigma \models \psi$. The *compactness theorem* for first-order logic states that if $\Phi \models \psi$ then there is a *finite* set $\Phi' \subseteq \Phi$ such that $\Phi' \models \psi$. Next we state a further property of first-order logic that will also be used.

Fact 4.3.11   If Φ is a set of first-order formulas all of whose free variables belong to $\{x_1, \ldots, x_n\}$ and $\sigma\{P_1/x_1, \ldots, P_n/x_n\} \models \phi$ for all $\phi \in \Phi$, then there is a LTS and processes $P'_1, \ldots, P'_n \in Pr$ such that $\sigma\{P'_1/x_1, \ldots, P'_n/x_n\} \models \phi$ for all $\phi \in \Phi$ and each P'_i has the Hennessy–Milner property (Definition 4.2.7).   □

Proposition 4.3.12 *A FOL formula $\phi(x)$ is equivalent to a modal formula iff $\phi(x)$ is bisimulation invariant.*

Proof If $\phi(x)$ is equivalent to a modal formula ϕ' then $\{P \mid \sigma\{P/x\} \models \phi\}$ $= \|\phi'\|$ which is bisimulation invariant. For the converse property, assume that $\phi(x)$ is bisimulation invariant. Consider the following family $\Phi =$ $\{T_x(\psi) \mid \psi \in M$ and $\{\phi(x)\} \models T_x(\psi)\}$. We prove $\Phi \models \phi(x)$ and, therefore, by the compactness theorem, $\phi(x)$ is equivalent to a modal formula ψ' such that $T_x(\psi') \in \Phi$. Assume $\sigma\{P/x\} \models \psi$ for all $\psi \in \Phi$. We need to show that $\sigma\{P/x\} \models \phi$. We choose a P with the Hennessy–Milner property by Fact 4.3.11. Let $\Psi = \{T_x(\psi) \mid P \models \psi\}$. First, $\Phi \subseteq \Psi$. Next we show that $\Psi \cup \{\phi\}$ is satisfiable. For suppose otherwise, $\Psi \models \neg\phi$ and so by the compactness theorem there is a finite subset $\Psi' = \{T_x(\psi_1), \ldots, T_x(\psi_k)\} \subseteq \Psi$ such that $\Psi' \models \neg\phi$. But then $\phi \models T_x(\psi')$ where ψ' is the modal formula $\neg\psi_1 \vee \ldots \vee \neg\psi_k$ and so $T_x(\psi') \in \Phi$ which contradicts that $\Phi \subseteq \Psi$. Therefore, for some Q, $\sigma\{Q/x\} \models \psi$ for all $\psi \in \Psi$ and $\sigma\{Q/x\} \models \phi$. However, $Q \sim P$ and because ϕ is bisimulation invariant, $\sigma\{P/x\} \models \phi$ as required. $\square$

Exercise 4.3.13 Prove that a FOL formula $\phi(x_1, \ldots, x_n)$ is bisimulation invariant iff it is equivalent to a boolean combination of formulas of the following form $T_{x_1}(\psi_{11}), \ldots, T_{x_1}(\psi_{1k_1}), \ldots, T_{x_n}(\psi_{n1}), \ldots, T_{x_n}(\psi_{nk_n})$ for some $k_1, \ldots, k_n \geq 0$. $\square$

An alternative proof of Proposition 4.3.12 appeals to *tree* (or forest) models. A LTS is a forest if it is acyclic and the 'target' of each transition is unique; if $P \xrightarrow{a} Q$ and $R \xrightarrow{b} Q$ then $P = R$ and $a = b$. The transition graph that is rooted at Q_1 in Figure 4.3 is a tree (a forest with a single tree).

Given a LTS there is a way of unfolding $P \in Pr$ and all its reachable processes into a tree rooted at P which is called *unravelling*.

Definition 4.3.14 Assume a LTS $L = (Pr, Act, \rightarrow)$ with $P_0 \in Pr$. The k-unravelling of P_0, for $k \geq 0$, is the following LTS, $L_k = (Pr_k, Act, \rightarrow_k)$ where

(1) $Pr_k = \{P_0 a_1 k_1 P_1 \ldots a_n k_n P_n \mid n \geq 0, 0 \leq k_i \leq k, P_0 \xrightarrow{a_1} P_1 \ldots \xrightarrow{a_n} P_n\}$;
(2) if $P \xrightarrow{a} P'$ and P is the final state in $\pi \in Pr_k$ then $\pi \rightarrow_k \pi a k' P'$ for each $0 \leq k' \leq k$;
(3) if V is the valuation for L then V_k is the valuation for L_k where $V_k(p) = \{\pi \in Pr_k \mid P$ is final in π and $P \in V(p)\}$.

The ω-unravelling of P_0, the LTS L_ω, permits all indices $k \geq 0$: so, Pr_ω includes all sequences $P_0 a_1 k_1 P_1 \ldots a_n k_n P_n$ such that $P_0 \xrightarrow{a_1} P_1 \ldots \xrightarrow{a_n} P_n$ and each $k_i \geq 0$. $\square$

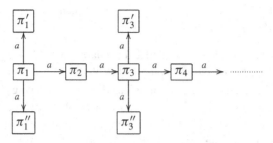

Fig. 4.4. Unravelled LTS.

Example 4.3.15 The 0-unravelling of P_1 of Figure 4.3 is presented in Figure 4.4 where $\pi_1 = P_1$, $\pi_{2(i+1)} = \pi_{2i+1}a0P_2$, $\pi_{2i+1} = \pi_{2i}a0P_1$ $\pi'_{2i+1} = \pi_{2i+1}a0P_3$ and $\pi''_{2i+1} = \pi_{2i+1}a0P_4$. The reader is invited to describe the 2-unravelling and the ω-unravelling of P_1. □

Proposition 4.3.16 *For any LTS and $k : 0 \leq k \leq \omega$, if $P \in Pr$ and $\pi \in Pr_k$ and the final state in π is P, then $P \sim \pi$.*

Proof Clearly, the binary relation $\mathcal{R} \subseteq Pr \times Pr_k$ containing all pairs (P, π) when the final state of π is P is a bisimulation because first, $P \in V(p)$ iff $\pi \in V_k(p)$ and second, $P \xrightarrow{a} P'$ iff $\pi \xrightarrow{a}_k \pi ak'P'$ for $k' \leq k$. □

Exercise 4.3.17 Let R_1 and S_1 be the processes depicted in Figure 4.1.

(1) Define the 0-unravellings of R_1 and S_1.
(2) Define the ω-unravelling of R_1 and S_1 and show that they are isomorphic.
(3) Assume L is a LTS containing P and Q and $P \sim Q$. Show that the ω-unravellings of P and Q are isomorphic.
(4) Reprove Proposition 4.3.12 using ω-unravelled LTSs. □

4.4 Modal mu-calculus

Modal logic M of Section 4.2 is not very expressive. For instance, temporal properties of states of a LTS, such as liveness, 'this desirable property will eventually hold', and safety, 'this defective property never holds', are not expressible in M. (Prove this; hint, use Exercise 4.2.5.) Such properties have been found to be very useful when analysing the behaviour of concurrent systems. Modal mu-calculus, μM, modal logic with fixpoints, introduced by Kozen [Ko83], has the required extra expressive power.

The setting for μM is the complete lattice generated by the *powerset* construction $\wp(Pr)$ where the ordering is $\subseteq$, join is union and meet is intersection, $\emptyset$ is the bottom element and Pr is the top element, see [San12].

Exercise 4.4.1 Consider a LTS and recall the definitions of monotone and continuous function f on the powerset $\wp(Pr)$: f is monotone provided that if $S \subseteq S'$ then $f(S) \subseteq f(S')$; f is continuous just in case if $S_1, \ldots, S_n, \ldots$ is an increasing sequence of subsets of Pr (that is, if $i \leq j$ then $S_i \subseteq S_j \subseteq Pr$), then $f(\bigcup_i S_i) = \bigcup_i f(S_i)$; see [San12].

(1) Define the semantic functions $\|\langle a \rangle\|$ and $\|[a]\|$ on $\wp(Pr)$ such that for any $\phi \in M$, $\|\langle a \rangle\|\|\phi\| = \|\langle a \rangle \phi\|$ and $\|[a]\|\|\phi\| = \|[a]\phi\|$.
(2) Show that these functions $\|\langle a \rangle\|$ and $\|[a]\|$ are monotone.
(3) Prove that $\|\langle a \rangle\|$ is continuous iff the LTS is image-finite with respect to the label a; that is, if for each $P \in Pr$, the set $\{P' \mid P \xrightarrow{a} P'\}$ is finite. $\qquad\square$

The new constructs of μM over and above those of M are

$$\phi ::= X \mid \ldots \mid \mu X. \phi$$

where X ranges over a family of propositional variables. The semantics for a formula ϕ of μM is the set $\|\phi\|_V \subseteq Pr$ where V is a valuation that not only maps elements of *Prop* but also propositional variables to $\wp(Pr)$. As usual we employ updating notation: $\|\phi\|_{V\{S/X\}}$ uses valuation V' like V except that $V'(X) = S$.

Exercise 4.4.2 Assume that ϕ is a formula of M when extended with propositional variables. Prove that if all free occurrences of X in ϕ are within the scope of an even number of negations and V is a valuation then the function $f : \wp(Pr) \to \wp(Pr)$ such that $f(S) = \|\phi\|_{V\{S/X\}}$ is monotone. Therefore, show the following (see [San12])

(1) the least fixed point **lfp**(f) exists and is the intersection of all pre-fixed points, $\bigcap \{S \mid f(S) \subseteq S\}$;
(2) the greatest fixed point **gfp**(f) exists and is the union of post-fixed points, $\bigcup \{S \mid S \subseteq f(S)\}$. $\qquad\square$

In the case of $\mu X. \phi$ there is, therefore, the restriction that all free occurrences of X in ϕ are within the scope of an even number of negations (to guarantee monotonicity). This formula expresses the least fixed point **lfp** of the semantic function induced by ϕ. Its dual, $\nu X. \phi$, expresses the greatest fixed point **gfp** and is a derived construct in μM: $\nu X. \phi = \neg \mu X. \neg \phi \{\neg X/X\}$. Here are the semantics for μM formulas.

$$\|p\|_V = V(p)$$

$$\|Z\|_V = V(Z)$$

$$\|\neg\phi\|_V = Pr - \|\phi\|_V$$

$$\|\phi_1 \vee \phi_2\|_V = \|\phi_1\|_V \cup \|\phi_2\|_V$$

$$\|\langle a\rangle\phi\|_V = \{P \in Pr \mid \text{for some } Q. \ P \xrightarrow{a} Q \text{ and } Q \in \|\phi\|_V\}$$

$$\|\mu Z.\phi\|_V = \bigcap\{S \subseteq Pr \mid \|\phi\|_{V\{S/Z\}} \subseteq S\}.$$

Exercise 4.4.3 Extend the first part of Exercise 4.4.2 by proving that if all free occurrences of X in $\phi \in \mu M$ are within the scope of an even number of negations and V is a valuation then the function f on $\wp(Pr)$ such that $f(S) = \|\phi\|_{V\{S/X\}}$ for $S \subseteq Pr$ is monotone. □

Derived semantic clauses for other connectives are below:

$$\|\phi_1 \wedge \phi_2\|_V = \|\phi_1\|_V \cap \|\phi_2\|_V$$

$$\|[a]\phi\|_V = \{P \in Pr \mid \text{for all } Q. \ \text{if } P \xrightarrow{a} Q \text{ then } Q \in \|\phi\|_V\}$$

$$\|\nu Z.\phi\|_V = \bigcup\{S \subseteq Pr \mid S \subseteq \|\phi\|_{V\{S/Z\}}\}.$$

P satisfies the μM formula ϕ relative to valuation V, $P \models_V \phi$, iff $P \in \|\phi\|_V$; as usual we omit V wherever possible.

The standard theory of fixpoints tells us, see [San12], that if f is a monotone function on a lattice, we can construct $\mathbf{lfp}(f)$ by applying f repeatedly on the least element of the lattice to form an increasing chain, whose limit is the least fixed point. Similarly, $\mathbf{gfp}(f)$ is constructed by applying f repeatedly on the largest element to form a decreasing chain, whose limit is the greatest fixed point. The stages of these iterations $\mu^\alpha X.\phi$ and $\nu^\alpha X.\phi$ can be defined as M^∞ formulas, see Exercise 4.2.6, inductively as follows

$$\begin{aligned}
\mu^0 X.\phi &= \texttt{ff} & \nu^0 X.\phi &= \texttt{tt} \\
\mu^{\beta+1} X.\phi &= \phi\{\mu^\beta X.\phi/X\} & \nu^{\beta+1} X.\phi &= \phi\{\nu^\beta X.\phi/X\} \\
\mu^\lambda X.\phi &= \bigvee_{\beta<\lambda} \mu^\beta X.\phi & \nu^\lambda X.\phi &= \bigwedge_{\beta<\lambda} \nu^\beta X.\phi.
\end{aligned}$$

So for a minimal fixpoint formula $\mu X.\phi$, if P satisfies the fixpoint, it satisfies some iterate, say the $(\beta+1)$th so that $P \models \mu^{\beta+1} X.\phi$. Now if we *unfold* this formula once, we get $P \models \phi\{\mu^\beta X.\phi/X\}$. Therefore, the fact that P satisfies the fixpoint depends, via ϕ, on the fact that other states in Pr satisfy the fixpoint *at smaller iterates than P does*. So if one follows a chain of dependencies, the chain terminates. Therefore, μ means 'finite looping', which, with a little refinement, is sufficient to understand the logic μM. On the other hand, for a maximal fixpoint $\nu X . \phi$, there is no such decreasing chain: $P \models \nu X . \phi$ iff $P \models \nu^\beta X . \phi$ for every iterate β iff $P \models \phi\{\nu^\beta X . \phi / X\}$ for every iterate β iff $P \models \phi\{\nu X . \phi / X\}$, and so we may loop for ever.

Example 4.4.4 Assume P_1 is the process in Figure 4.3, which can repeatedly do an a transition. P_1 fails to have the property $\mu X . [a]X$ (which expresses that there cannot be an infinite sequence of a transitions). Consider its iterates, $\mu^1 X . [a]X = [a]\mathrm{ff}$, so P_3 and P_4 have this property; $\mu^3 X . [a]X$ is $[a][a][a]\mathrm{ff}$ and $\mu^\omega X . [a]X$ is $\bigvee_{n \geq 0}[a]^n \mathrm{ff}$ where $[a]^0 \mathrm{ff} = \mathrm{ff}$ and $[a]^{i+1} \mathrm{ff} = [a][a]^i \mathrm{ff}$. Consequently, $P_1 \models \nu X . \langle a \rangle X$. Iterates of this formula include $\nu^\omega X . \langle a \rangle X = \bigwedge_{n \geq 0}\langle a \rangle^n \mathrm{tt}$ where $\langle a \rangle^i$ is $\langle a \rangle$ i-times. $\square$

Exercise 4.4.5 What properties are expressed by the following formulas?

(1) $\mu X . p \vee [a]X$
(2) $\mu X . q \vee (p \wedge \langle a \rangle X)$
(3) $\nu X . \neg p \wedge [a]X$
(4) $\mu X . \nu Y . (p \wedge [a]X) \vee (\neg p \wedge [a]Y)$. $\square$

Definition 4.2.2 of $\equiv_M$, 'having the same modal properties', is extended to μM; so, $P \equiv_{\mu M} P'$ means P and P' have the same μM properties, as expressed by *closed* formulas of μM (that is, formulas without free variables). Bisimilar states have the same μM properties.

Theorem 4.4.6 *If $P \sim P'$ then $P \equiv_{\mu M} P'$.*

Proof The proof of this uses Exercise 4.2.6 that M^∞ characterises bisimilarity and the observation above that closed formulas of μM can be translated into M^∞. $\square$

Theorem 4.4.7 *If the LTS is image-finite and $P \equiv_{\mu M} P'$ then $P \sim P'$.*

Proof Because μM contains M this follows directly from Theorem 4.2.4. $\square$

Is image-finiteness still necessary in Theorem 4.4.7? In Exercise 4.2.5 the relationship between stratified bisimilarity, $\sim_n$, and formulas of M with modal depth n is explored. It is possible $P \not\sim Q$ but $P \sim_n Q$ for all $n \geq 0$ and so, $P \equiv_M Q$. For instance, let P be $\sum_{i \geq 0} P_i$ and $Q = P + R$ where $P_{j+1} \xrightarrow{a} P_j$, P_0 has no a transitions and $R \xrightarrow{a} R$. Unlike P, Q has an infinite sequence of a transitions: so, $P \not\equiv_{\mu M} Q$ (because $P \models \mu X . [a]X$). So, a more sophisticated example is needed for the presence of image-finiteness.

Example 4.4.8 The following example is from [BS07]. It uses a key property of μM, 'the finite model property': if $P \models \phi$ then there is a finite LTS and a P' within it with $P' \models \phi$. Let $\phi_1, \phi_2, \ldots$ be an enumeration of all closed μM formulas over the finite label set $\{a, b\}$ that are true at some state of some LTS. Let Pr_i, with initial state P_i, be a finite LTS such that $P_i \models \phi_i$, with all Pr_i disjoint. Let Pr_0 be constructed by taking an initial state P_0 and making $P_0 \xrightarrow{a} P_i$ for all $i > 0$. Similarly, let Pr'_0 be constructed from initial state P'_0 with transitions $P'_0 \xrightarrow{a} P_i$ for all $i > 0$ and $P'_0 \xrightarrow{a} P'_0$. Clearly, $P'_0 \not\sim P_0$ because in Pr'_0 it is possible to defer indefinitely the choice of which Pr_i to enter. On the other hand, suppose that ψ is a closed μM formula, and w.l.o.g. assume the topmost operator is a modality. If the modality is $[b]$, ψ is true of both P_0 and P'_0; if it is $\langle b \rangle$, ψ is false of both; if ψ is $\langle a \rangle \psi'$, then ψ is false at both P_0 and P'_0 iff ψ' is unsatisfiable, and true at both otherwise; if ψ is $[a]\psi'$, then ψ is true at both P_0 and P'_0 iff ψ' is valid, and false at both otherwise. Consequently, $P_0 \equiv_{\mu M} P'_0$. $\qquad\qquad\square$

Definition 4.2.7 can be extended to μM formulas: $P \in Pr$ has the extended Hennessy–Milner property provided that if $P \equiv_{\mu M} P'$ then $P' \sim P$. Little is known about this property except that, if P has the Hennessy–Milner property then it also has the extended Hennessy–Milner property.

Exercise 4.4.9 In Exercise 4.2.8 a modally saturated LTS was defined. This notion does not readily extend to μM formulas. A set of μM formulas is *unsatisfiable* if there is not a LTS and a process P belonging to it such that P satisfies every formula in the set. Show that there is an unsatisfiable set $\Phi \subseteq \mu M$ such that every finite subset $\Phi' \subseteq \Phi$ is satisfiable. Show that this is equivalent to showing that μM fails the compactness theorem. $\qquad\square$

Another indication that μM is more expressive than M is that it contains characteristic formulas with respect to bisimilarity for finite-state processes. So, the restriction to *acyclic* LTSs in Proposition 4.2.9 can be relaxed.

Proposition 4.4.10 *Assume* $(Pr, Act, \to)$ *where* Pr, Act *and* $Prop$ *are finite. If* $P \in Pr$ *then there is a formula* $\phi \in \mu M$ *that is characteristic for* P.

Proof Let $(Pr, Act, \to)$ be a LTS with finite sets Act, $Prop$ and Pr. Assume we want to define a characteristic formula for $P \in Pr$. Let $P_1, \ldots, P_n$ be the distinct elements of Pr with $P = P_1$ and let $X_1, \ldots, X_n$ be distinct propositional variables. We define a 'modal equation' $X_i = \phi_i(X_1, \ldots, X_n)$ for each

i which captures the behaviour of P_i.

$$
\begin{aligned}
X_i &= \text{PROP}(P_i) \wedge \bigwedge\{\text{MOD}'(a, P) \mid a \in Act\} \text{ where} \\
\text{PROP}(P_i) &= \bigwedge\{p \in Prop \mid P \models p\} \wedge \bigwedge\{\neg p \in Prop \mid P \not\models p\} \\
\text{MOD}'(a, P_i) &= \bigwedge\{\langle a\rangle X_j \mid P_i \xrightarrow{a} P_j\} \wedge [a]\bigvee\{X_j \mid P_i \xrightarrow{a} P_j\}
\end{aligned}
$$

where as usual $\bigwedge \emptyset = \mathtt{tt}$ and $\bigvee \emptyset = \mathtt{ff}$. We now define the characteristic formula for P_1 as ψ_1 where

$$\psi_n = \nu X_n.\phi_n(X_1, \ldots, X_n)$$
$$\vdots \qquad \vdots$$
$$\psi_j = \nu X_j.\phi_j(X_1, \ldots, X_j, \psi_{j+1}, \ldots, \psi_n)$$
$$\vdots \qquad \vdots$$
$$\psi_1 = \nu X_1.\phi_1(X_1, \psi_2, \ldots, \psi_n).$$

The proof that ψ_1 is characteristic for P is left as an exercise for the reader. □

Example 4.4.11 Let R_1, R_2 and R_3 be the processes in Figure 4.1 and assume $Prop = \emptyset$. The modal equations are as follows.

$$X_1 = \phi_1(X_1, X_2, X_3) = (\langle a\rangle X_2 \wedge \langle a\rangle X_3) \wedge [a](X_2 \vee X_3) \wedge [b]\mathtt{ff} \wedge [c]\mathtt{ff}$$
$$X_2 = \phi_2(X_1, X_2, X_3) = [a]\mathtt{ff} \wedge \langle b\rangle X_3 \wedge [b]X_3 \wedge [c]\mathtt{ff}$$
$$X_3 = \phi_3(X_1, X_2, X_3) = [a]\mathtt{ff} \wedge [b]\mathtt{ff} \wedge \langle c\rangle X_1 \wedge \langle c\rangle X_2 \wedge [c](X_1 \vee X_2).$$

So, ψ_3 is $\nu X_3.\phi_3(X_1, X_2, X_3)$, and ψ_2 is $\nu X_2.\phi_2(X_1, X_2, \psi_3)$ and ψ_1 is the following formula

$$\nu X_1.(\langle a\rangle\psi_2 \wedge \langle a\rangle\psi_3) \wedge [a](\psi_2 \vee \psi_3) \wedge [b]\mathtt{ff} \wedge [c]\mathtt{ff}.$$

The reader can check that $S_1 \models \psi_1$ where S_1 is also in Figure 4.1. □

Exercise 4.4.12 Provide a characteristic formula for P_1 of Figure 4.3 and show that Q_1 in the same figure satisfies it. □

The proof of Proposition 4.4.10 shows that a characteristic formula for a finite state process only uses greatest fixpoints. Furthermore, there is a more succinct representation if simultaneous fixpoints are allowed.[2] One application of characteristic formulas is the reduction of equivalence checking (whether two given processes are equivalent) to model checking (whether a given process has a given property). This is especially useful in the case when only one of

---

[2] Instead of defining ψ_i iteratively in the proof of Proposition 4.4.10, they are defined at the same time in a vectorial form.

the two given processes is finite state, see [KJ06] for a survey of known results which also covers weak bisimilarity and preorder checking.

A simple corollary of Theorem 4.4.6 is that μM has the tree model property. If a μM formula has a model, it has a model that is a tree. Just 0-unravel, see Definition 4.3.14, the original model, thereby preserving bisimulation. This can be strengthened to the *bounded branching degree* tree model property (just cut off all the branches that are not actually required by some diamond subformula; this leaves at most (number of diamond subformulas) branches at each node).

Clearly we cannot translate μM into FOL because of the fixpoints. (See Exercise 4.4.9.) However, it can be translated into monadic second-order logic.

4.5 Monadic second-order logic and bisimulation invariance

MSO, monadic second-order logic of LTSs, extends FOL in Section 4.3 by allowing quantification over subsets of Pr. The new constructs over and above those of FOL are

$$\phi ::= X(x) \mid \ldots \mid \exists X.\phi$$

where X ranges over a family of monadic predicate variables, and $\exists X.\phi$ quantifies over such predicates. To interpret formulas with free predicate and individual variables we extend a valuation σ to include a mapping from predicate variables to sets of states. We inductively define when MSO formula ϕ is true on an LTS L with respect to a valuation σ as $\sigma \models_L \phi$, where again we drop the index L. The new clauses are as follows.

$$\sigma \models X(x) \text{ iff } \sigma(x) \in \sigma(X)$$
$$\sigma \models \exists X.\phi \text{ iff } \sigma\{S/X\} \models \phi \text{ for some } S \subseteq Pr.$$

The universal monadic quantifier, the dual of $\exists X$, is $\forall X.\phi = \neg\exists X.\neg\phi$. Its derived semantic clause is: $\sigma \models \forall X.\phi$ iff $\sigma\{S/X\} \models \phi$ for all $S \subseteq Pr$.

Example 4.5.1 Given a LTS with $Act = \{a\}$ the property that it is three colourable is expressible in MSO as follows

$$\exists X.\exists Y.\exists Z.\,\forall x.\,\phi(x, X, Y, Z) \wedge \forall y.\,\forall z.\,\psi(y, z, X, Y, Z)$$

where $\phi(x, X, Y, Z)$ expresses x has a unique colour X, Y or Z

$$(X(x) \wedge \neg Y(x) \wedge \neg Z(x)) \vee (\neg X(x) \wedge Y(x) \wedge \neg Z(x))$$
$$\vee (\neg X(x) \wedge \neg Y(x) \wedge Z(x))$$

and $\psi(y, z, X, Y, Z)$ confirms that if there is an a transition from y to z then they are not coloured the same

$$y E_a z \rightarrow \neg(X(y) \wedge X(z)) \wedge \neg(Y(y) \wedge Y(z)) \wedge \neg(Z(y) \wedge Z(z)).$$

$\square$

There is a translation of μM formulas into MSO that extends Definition 4.3.5.

Definition 4.5.2 The MSO translation of μM formulas ϕ relative to variable x is $T_x^+(\phi)$ which is defined inductively.

$$\begin{aligned}
T_x^+(p) &= p(x) \\
T_x^+(X) &= X(x) \\
T_x^+(\text{tt}) &= x = x \\
T_x^+(\neg\phi) &= \neg T_x^+(\phi) \\
T_x^+(\phi_1 \vee \phi_2) &= T_x^+(\phi_1) \vee T_x^+(\phi_2) \\
T_x^+(\langle a \rangle \phi) &= \exists y. x E_a y \wedge T_y^+(\phi) \\
T_x^+(\mu X. \phi) &= \forall X. (\forall y. (T_y^+(\phi) \rightarrow X(y))) \rightarrow X(x).
\end{aligned}$$

$\square$

The translation of a least fixpoint formula uses quantification and implication to capture that x belongs to every pre-fixed point.

Exercise 4.5.3 For each of the following formulas ϕ, present its MSO translation $T_x^+(\phi)$.

(1) $\mu X. p \vee [a]X$
(2) $\mu X. q \vee (p \wedge \langle a \rangle X)$
(3) $\nu X. \neg p \wedge [a]X$
(4) $\mu X. \nu Y. (p \wedge [a]X) \vee (\neg p \wedge [a]Y)$.

$\square$

The translation of μM formulas into MSO, Definition 4.5.2, is correct.

Proposition 4.5.4 *If for each variable Z, $V(Z) = \sigma(Z)$ then $P \models_V \phi$ iff $\sigma\{P/x\} \models T_x^+(\phi)$.*

Proof By structural induction on $\phi \in M$. The proofs for the modal and boolean cases follow Proposition 4.3.7. There are just the two new cases. $P \models_V X$ iff $P \in V(X)$ iff $P \in \sigma(X)$ iff $\sigma\{P/x\}(x) \in \sigma\{P/x\}(X)$ iff $\sigma\{P/x\} \models T_x^+(X)$. $P \models_V \mu X. \phi$ iff for all S, if $\|\phi\|_{V\{S/X\}} \subseteq S$ then $P \in S$ iff for all S, if $\forall y, y \models_{V\{S/X\}} \phi$ implies $y \in S$ then $P \in S$ iff for all S, if $\forall y, \sigma\{S/X\} \models T_y^+(\phi)$ by the induction hypothesis where σ obeys that for all Z, $\sigma(Z) = V(Z)$ iff $\sigma\{P/x\} \models \forall X.\,(\forall y.\,(T_y^+(\phi) \to X(y))) \to X(x)$ iff $\sigma\{P/x\} \models T_x^+(\mu X.\,\phi)$. $\square$

A corollary of Theorem 4.4.6 is that if ϕ is a closed μM formula then the MSO formula $\psi(x) = T_x^+(\phi)$ with one free variable is bisimulation invariant. As with FOL there are formulas of MSO which are not bisimulation invariant. Therefore, it is natural to ask the question whether van Benthem's theorem, Proposition 4.3.12, can be extended to MSO formulas. The following result was shown by Janin and Walukiewicz [JW96].

Proposition 4.5.5 *A MSO formula $\phi(x)$ is equivalent to a closed μM formula iff $\phi(x)$ is bisimulation invariant.*

However, its proof utilises automata (and games) which we shall provide a flavour of.

The aim is now to think of a *different* characterisation of logics on LTSs using automata or games which operate *locally* on the LTS (compare [San12]). A particular logical formula of MSO or μM can only mention finitely many different elements of *Prop* and finitely many different elements of *Act*; therefore, we assume now that these sets are finite in any given LTS. They will constitute finite *alphabets* for automata; let $\Sigma_1 = Act$ and $\Sigma_2 = \wp Prop$, where $\wp$ is the powerset construct.

Let us begin with the notion of an automaton familiar from introductory computer science courses.

Definition 4.5.6 An automaton $A = (S, \Sigma, \delta, s_0, F)$ consists of a finite set of states S, a finite alphabet Σ, a transition function δ, an initial state $s_0 \in S$ and an acceptance condition F.

Traditionally, A does not operate on LTSs but on words, recognising a language, a subset of Σ^*. Assuming A is non-deterministic, its transition function δ : $S \times \Sigma \to \wp S$. Given a word $w = a_1 \ldots a_n \in \Sigma^*$, a *run* of A on w is a sequence of states $s_0 \ldots s_n$ that traverses w, so $s_{i+1} \in \delta(s_i, a_{i+1})$ for each $i : 0 \le i < n$. The run is *accepting* if the sequence $s_0 \ldots s_n$ obeys F: classically, $F \subseteq S$ is the subset of accepting states and $s_0 \ldots s_n$ is accepting if the last state $s_n \in F$. There may be many different runs of A on w, some accepting the others rejecting, or no runs at all. The language *recognised* by A is the set of words for which there is at least one accepting run.

Example 4.5.7 Let $A = (\{s_0, s_1\}, \{a\}, \delta, s_0, \{s_0\})$ with $\delta(s_0, a) = \{s_1\}$ and $\delta(s_1, a) = \{s_0\}$. The language accepted by A is the set $\{a^{2n} \mid n \ge 0\}$ of even length words. $\square$

A simple extension is recognition of infinite length words. A run of A on $w = a_1 \ldots a_i \ldots$ is an infinite sequence of states $\pi = s_0 \ldots s_i \ldots$ that travels over w, so $s_{i+1} \in \delta(s_i, a_{i+1})$, for all $i \geq 0$; it is accepting if it obeys the condition F. Let $inf(\pi) \subseteq S$ contain exactly the states that occur infinitely often in π. Classically, $F \subseteq Q$ and π is accepting if $inf(\pi) \cap F \neq \emptyset$ which is the Büchi acceptance condition.

Büchi automata are an alternative notation for characterising infinite paths of a LTS. There are different choices according to the alphabet Σ. If $\Sigma = \Sigma_1$ and $\pi = P_0 \xrightarrow{a_1} P_1 \xrightarrow{a_2} \ldots$ is an infinite sequence of transitions, then $\pi \models A$ if the automaton accepts the word $a_1 a_2 \ldots$; alternatively, $\Sigma = \Sigma_2$ and $\pi \models A$ if it accepts $Prop(P_0) Prop(P_1) \ldots$ where $Prop(P)$ is the subset of $Prop$ that is true at P.

Exercise 4.5.8 Let $Prop = \{p\}$, $S = \{s, t\}$, $\delta(s, \{p\}) = \{t\}$, $\delta(s, \emptyset) = \{s\}$, $\delta(t, \{p\}) = \{t\}$ and $\delta(t, \emptyset) = \{t\}$, $s_0 = s$ and $F = \{t\}$. What property of an infinite run of a LTS does this Büchi automaton express? □

When each formula of a logic is equivalent to an automaton, satisfiability checking reduces to the *non-emptiness* problem for those automata: whether an automaton accepts *some* word (path or whatever). This may have algorithmic benefits in reducing an apparently complex satisfiability question into simple graph-theoretic procedures: a Büchi automaton, for instance, is non-empty if there is a path $s_0 \to^* s \in F$ and a cycle $s \to^* s$ (equivalent to an eventually cyclic model). Indeed the introduction of Büchi and Rabin automata was for showing decidability of monadic second-order theories by reducing them to automata, see the tutorial text [GTW02] for details.

The idea of recognising bounded branching *trees* extends the definition of A to accept n-branching infinite trees. With a word automaton, a state s' belonged to $\delta(s, a)$; now it is tuples $(s'_1, \ldots, s'_n)$ that belong to $\delta(s, a)$. A tree automaton traverses the tree, descending from a node to all n-child nodes, so the automaton splits itself into n copies, and proceeds independently. A run of the automaton is then an n-branching infinite tree labelled with states of the automaton. A run is accepting if *every* path through this tree satisfies the acceptance condition F. In the case of Rabin acceptance $F = \{(G_1, R_1), \ldots, (G_k, R_k)\}$ where each $G_i, R_i \subseteq S$ and π obeys F if there is a j such that $inf(\pi) \cap G_j \neq \emptyset$ and $inf(\pi) \cap R_j = \emptyset$. A variant definition is *parity* acceptance where F maps each state s of the automaton to a *priority* $F(s) \in \mathbb{N}$. We say that a path satisfies F if the least priority seen infinitely often is even. It is not hard to see that a parity condition is a special case of a Rabin condition; it is also true, though somewhat trickier, that a Rabin automaton can be translated to an equivalent parity automaton. Such automata can recognise bounded branching unravellings of LTSs.

Exercise 4.5.9 Tree automata characterise rooted n-branching infinite tree LTS models for μM formulas. Such a model $L \models A$ if A accepts the behaviour tree that replaces each state $P \in Pr$ with $Prop(P)$. Let $Prop = \{p\}$, $S = \{s, t\}$, $\delta(s, \{p\}) = \{(s, s)\}$, $\delta(s, \emptyset) = \{(t, t)\}$, $\delta(t, \{p\}) = \{(s, s)\}$ and $\delta(t, \emptyset) = \{(t, t)\}$ and $s_0 = s$. This automaton A has parity acceptance condition $F(s) = 1$ and $F(t) = 2$. What μM formula is equivalent to A over infinite binary-tree models? (Hint: what fixpoints are 'coded' by states s and t?) $\square$

There is a slight mismatch between (the unravellings of) LTSs and bounded branching trees because of the fixed branching degree and the explicit indexed successors; for instance, see the unravelled LTS of Figure 4.4. What is wanted is an automaton that can directly recognise a LTS and which preserves the virtue of a simple *local* definition of a transition function. We shall define a variant of alternating parity automata which is due to Walukiewicz (also see [KVW00]).

The range of a transition function of an automaton A will be a *local formula*. For a word automaton, if $\delta(s, a) = \{s_1, \ldots, s_m\}$ then it is the formula $s_1 \vee \ldots \vee s_m$. For an n-branching tree automaton if $\delta(s, a) = \{(s_1^1, \ldots, s_n^1), \ldots, (s_1^m, \ldots, s_n^m)\}$ then it is $((1, s_1^1) \wedge \ldots \wedge (n, s_n^1)) \vee \ldots \vee ((1, s_1^m) \wedge \ldots \wedge (n, s_n^m))$: here the element (i, s') means create an i-th child with label s'. A word or tree is accepted if there exists an accepting run for that word or tree; hence, the disjuncts. However, for a tree, every path through it must be accepting; hence the conjuncts. In *alternating* word automata, the transition function is given as an arbitrary boolean expression over states: for instance, $\delta(s, a) = s_1 \wedge (s_2 \vee s_3)$. In alternating tree automata it is a boolean expression over directions and states: for instance, $((1, s_1) \wedge (1, s_2)) \vee (2, s_3)$. Now the definition of a run becomes a tree in which successor transitions obey the boolean formula. In particular, even for an alternating automaton on words, a run is a tree, and not just a word. The acceptance criterion is as before, that every path of the run must be accepting. An alternating automaton is just a two-player game too where one player $\forall$ is responsible for $\wedge$ choices and the other player $\exists$ for $\vee$ choices.

The transition function for an automaton A that recognises LTSs has the form $\delta : S \times \Sigma_2 \rightarrow \Phi(\Sigma_1, S)$ where $\Phi(X, Y)$ is a set of formulas over X and Y. One idea is that this formula could be a simple modal formula. For instance, if s is the current automaton state at $P \in Pr$ and $\delta(s, Prop(P)) = \langle a \rangle s_1 \wedge [c] s_2$ and $P \xrightarrow{a} P_1$, $P \xrightarrow{b} P_2$, $P \xrightarrow{c} Q_i$, for all $i \geq 0$ then the automaton moves to P_1 with state s_1 and to each Q_i with state s_2. As with tree automata, a run of A on a LTS is a labelled tree of arbitrary degree. Such 'modal' automata when the acceptance condition for infinite branches is the parity condition have the same expressive power as μM.

However, to prove Proposition 4.5.5 Janin and Walukiewicz use FOL formulas. The idea for atomic predicates is to replace pairs (i, s) of a tree automaton with elements of $U = \{(a, s) \mid a \in \Sigma_1 \text{ and } s \in S\}$. Now, for each $s \in S$ and $W \subseteq Prop$, $\delta(s, W)$ is a formula of the form

$$(*) \exists x_1 \ldots \exists x_k . (u_1(x_1) \wedge \ldots \wedge u_k(x_k)) \wedge \forall x . (u_1(x) \vee \ldots \vee u_k(x))$$

where each $u_i \in U$. An example is $\phi = \exists x_1 . \exists x_2 . (a, s)(x_1) \wedge (b, s')(x_2) \wedge \forall x . (a, s)(x) \vee (b, s')(x)$. If t labels the state P of the LTS and $W = Prop(P)$ and $\delta(t, W) = \phi$ and $P \xrightarrow{a} P_i$, $P \xrightarrow{b} Q_j$, $i, j > 0$, then the automaton at the next step would spawn a copy at each P_i with state s and each Q_j with state s'. Notice that such a formula is quite similar to the components $\bigwedge MOD'(a, P)$ of a characteristic formula described in Proposition 4.4.10. Every μM formula is equivalent to such an automaton; the different kinds of fixpoint are catered for in the parity acceptance condition.

Let $dis(x_1, \ldots, x_n)$ be the FOL formula $\bigwedge_{1 \leq i < j \leq n} x_i \neq x_j$. There is a very similar characterisation of MSO formulas over trees where now each $\delta(s, W)$ has the form

$$(**) \exists x_1 \ldots \exists x_k . (D \wedge u_1(x_1) \wedge \ldots \wedge u_k(x_k)) \wedge \forall x . D' \rightarrow (u_1(x) \vee \ldots \vee u_k(x))$$

where $D = dis(x_1, \ldots, x_k)$ and $D' = dis(x, x_1, \ldots, x_k)$.

Now the result follows: if $\phi(x)$ is an MSO formula that is bisimulation invariant then it is true on any n-unravelled model and so $(*)$ and $(**)$ will be equivalent for $n \geq k$.

Bibliography

[vB84] J. van Benthem. Correspondence theory. In *Handbook of Philosophical Logic*, Vol. II, D. Gabbay and F. Guenthner, editors, pages 167–248, Reidel, 1984.

[vB96] J. van Benthem. *Exploring Logical Dynamics*. CSLI Publications, 1996.

[vB98] J. van Benthem. Program constructions that are safe for bisimulation, *Studia Logica*, **60**:311–330, 1998.

[BRV01] P. Blackburn, M. de Rijke and Y. Venema. *Modal Logic*, Cambridge University Press, 2001.

[BS07] J. Bradfield and C. Stirling, Modal mu-calculi. In *Handbook of Modal Logic*, P. Blackburn, J. van Benthem and F. Wolter, editior pages 721–756, Elsevier, 2007.

[Ch80] B. Chellas, *Modal Logic: An Introduction*. Cambridge University Press, 1980.

[GTW02] E. Grädel, W. Thomas and T. Wilke (editors), *Automata, Logics, and Infinite Games, Lecture Notes in Computer Science*, **2500**, 2002.

[HM80] M. Hennessy and R. Milner, On observing nondeterminism and concurrency, *Lecture Notes in Computer Science*, **85**:295–309, 1980.

[HM85] M. Hennessy and R. Milner. Algebraic laws for nondeterminism and concurrency. *Journal of Association of Computer Machinery*, **32**:137–162, 1985.

[JW96] D. Janin and I. Walukiewicz, On the expressive completeness of the propositional mu-calculus with respect to monadic second order logic. *Lecture Notes in Computer Science*, **1119**:263–277, 1996.

[Ko83] D. Kozen, Results on the propositional mu-calculus. *Theoretical Computer Science*, **27**:333–354, 1983.

[KJ06] A. Kučera and P. Jančar, Equivalence-checking on infinite-state systems: techniques and results. *Theory and Practice of Logic Programming*, **6**(3):227–264, 2006.

[KVW00] O. Kupferman, M. Vardi and P. Wolper, An automata-theoretic approach to branching-time model checking. *Journal of Association of Computer Machinery*, **42**(2):312–360, 2000.

[Pa81] D. Park. Concurrency and automata on infinite sequences. *Lecture Notes in Computer Science*, **154**:561–572 1981.

[San12] D. Sangiorgi. *An Introduction to Bisimulation and Coinduction*. Cambridge University Press, 2012.

5

Howe's method for higher-order languages

ANDREW PITTS

5.1 Introduction

A fundamental requirement for any notion of equality between programs is that it be a *congruence*, in other words an equivalence relation that is compatible with the various syntactical constructs of the programming language. Being an equivalence relation, in particular being transitive, allows one to use a familiar technique of equational reasoning, namely the deduction of an equality $P \simeq P'$ via a chain of intermediate equalities, $P \simeq P_1 \simeq \cdots \simeq P_n \simeq P'$. Being compatible enables the use of an even more characteristic technique of equational reasoning, substitution of equals for equals, whereby an equality between compound phrases, $C[P] \simeq C[P']$, is deduced from an equality between sub-phrases, $P \simeq P'$. If one regards the meaning of a program to be its $\simeq$-equivalence class, then compatibility says that this semantics is *compositional* – the meaning of a compound phrase is a function of the meanings of its constituent sub-phrases.

This book is concerned with coinductively defined notions of program equality based on the notion of bisimulation. For these, the property of being an equivalence relation is easy to establish, whereas the property of compatibility can sometimes be difficult to prove and indeed in some cases is false.[1] This is particularly the case for languages involving *higher-order* features, that is, ones permitting functions and processes to be data that can be manipulated by functions and processes. For example, the language might feature parameterised programs $P(x)$ where the parameter x can be instantiated not with simple data (booleans, numbers, names, finite trees, . . .), but with other programs Q. In

---

[1] The classic example is the failure of weak bisimilarity to be preserved by summation in Milner's CCS [Mil89, section 5.3].

this case, although it is usually easy to see that a bisimilarity $\simeq$ satisfies

$$\forall Q.\ P(x) \simeq P'(x) \ \Rightarrow \ P(Q) \simeq P'(Q),$$

for compatibility of $\simeq$ we have to establish the stronger property

$$\forall Q, Q'.\ P(x) \simeq P'(x) \ \wedge \ Q \simeq Q' \ \Rightarrow \ P(Q) \simeq P'(Q').$$

This is often hard to prove directly from the definition of $\simeq$.

In this chapter we present a method for establishing such congruence properties of coinductively defined program equalities, due originally to Howe [How89]. It is one that has proved to be particularly effective in the presence of higher-order functions. Howe's method was originally developed partly to give a direct proof that Abramsky's notion of *applicative bisimilarity* is a congruence for his 'lazy' λ-calculus [Abr90]. The latter consists of the terms of the untyped λ-calculus equipped with a non-strict, or call-by-name evaluation strategy.[2] Abramsky's original proof of congruence is via a denotational semantics of the language,[3] whereas Howe's method provides a more direct route to this purely syntactic result, just making use of the language's operational semantics. Such syntactical methods can often be very brittle: small changes to the language's syntax or operational semantics may break the method. This has proved not to be the case for Howe's method; essentially the same technique has been applied, first by Howe and then by others, to quite a variety of higher-order languages, both typed and untyped, featuring both sequential functions and concurrent processes, and with a variety of different operational semantics. Although far from being a universal panacea for proofs of congruence, Howe's method certainly deserves the space we give it in this book.

Chapter outline Howe's definitive account of his method [How96] uses a general framework that can be specialised to a number of different functional languages and evaluation strategies. Here we prefer to explain the method by giving some concrete examples of it in action. To see the wood from the trees, the examples are as syntactically simple as possible. In fact we use applicative similarity and bisimilarity for the untyped λ-calculus with a call-by-value evaluation strategy as the running example; these notions are explained in Sections 5.2 and 5.3. Then in Section 5.4 we see how far we can get with

---

[2] The terminology 'lazy' is now more commonly used as a synonym for a call-by-need evaluation strategy (as used by the Haskell functional programming language, for example) rather than for the call-by-name strategy.

[3] It is a corollary of his 'domain theory in logical form' [Abr91]; see [Pit97a] for an alternative denotational proof making use of logical relations.

a proof of the congruence property for applicative similarity directly from its coinductive definition. This motivates the use of Howe's 'precongruence candidate' construction, which is explained in Section 5.5 and used to prove that applicative similarity for the call-by-value λ-calculus is a precongruence and hence that applicative bisimilarity is a congruence.

Section 5.6 explains an important consequence of this congruence result, namely that applicative bisimilarity for this language coincides with a Morris-style [Mor69] contextual equivalence, in which terms of the language are identified if they behave the same in all contexts (with respect to some fixed notion of observation). The coincidence of these two notions of program equality depends upon the deterministic nature of evaluation in call-by-value λ-calculus. So in Section 5.7 we consider what happens if we add a non-deterministic feature; we use 'erratic' binary choice as our example. As Howe observed, in such a non-deterministic setting his precongruence candidate construction can still be used to prove congruence results for bisimilarities, via a finesse involving transitive closure.

In Section 5.8 we illustrate a perhaps less well-known application of Howe's method, namely to proving 'context lemmas' [Mil77] for contextual equivalences. In general, such lemmas tell us that two terms behave the same in all contexts, that is, are contextually equivalent iff they behave the same in some restricted collection of contexts. Context lemmas are a useful way of establishing certain basic properties of contextual equivalence – for example, that terms with the same reduction behaviour are contextually equivalent. We consider the restriction to contexts that are 'Uses of Closed Instantiations' and the associated 'CIU-equivalence' of Mason and Talcott [MT91]. Specifically, we use Howe's method to show that for call-by-value λ-calculus with erratic choice, and for the observational scenario based on 'may-terminate', CIU-equivalence is a congruence and (hence) coincides with contextual equivalence. This result is representative of the way Howe's method can be used to establish context lemmas for contextual equivalences.

Section 5.9 briefly considers the call-by-name version of all these results. Section 5.10 summarises what is involved in Howe's method and then in Section 5.11 we outline some other applications of it that occur in the literature and assess its limitations.

Table 5.1 gives the notation we use for the various types of preorder and equivalence considered in this chapter.

Prerequisites The reader is assumed to have some familiarity with the basic notions of λ-calculus and its use in programming language semantics; see [Pie02, chapter 5], for example. The first few paragraphs of the next section summarise what we need of this material.

Table 5.1. *Preorders and equivalences used in this chapter.*

		call-by-value	call-by-name
applicative	similarity	$\precsim_v$	$\precsim_n$
	bisimilarity	$\simeq_v$	$\simeq_n$
contextual	preorder	$\leq_v$	$\leq_n$
	equivalence	$=_v$	$=_n$
CIU	preorder	$\leq_v^{ciu}$	$\leq_n^{ciu}$
	equivalence	$=_v^{ciu}$	$=_n^{ciu}$

5.2 Call-by-value λ-calculus

We take the set Λ of λ-*terms* and the subset $V \subseteq \Lambda$ of λ-*values* to be given by the following grammar

$$e \in \Lambda ::= v \mid e\,e$$
$$v \in V ::= x \mid \lambda x.e \tag{5.1}$$

where x ranges over a fixed, countably infinite set *Var* of *variables*. An occurrence of a variable x in a λ-term e is a *free occurrence* if it is not within the scope of any λx. The *substitution* of e for all free occurrences of x in e' is denoted $e'\{e/x\}$; more generally a simultaneous substitution is written $e'\{e_1, \ldots, e_n/x_1, \ldots, x_n\}$. As usual when making a substitution $e'\{e/x\}$, we do not want free occurrences in e of a variable x' to become bound by occurrences of $\lambda x'$ in e'; in other words, substitution should be 'capture-avoiding'. To achieve this we identify the syntax trees generated by the above grammar up to α-*equivalence* of λ-bound variables: thus the elements of Λ and V are really α-equivalence classes of abstract syntax trees, but we refer to a class by naming one of its representatives. For example if x, y, z are distinct variables, then $\lambda y.\,x$ and $\lambda z.\,x$ are equal λ-terms (being α-equivalent) and $(\lambda y.\,x)\{y/x\}$ is $\lambda z.\,y$, not $\lambda y.\,y$.

The finite set of variables occurring free in $e \in \Lambda$ is denoted $\mathsf{fv}(e)$. If $\overline{x} \in \wp_{fin}(Var)$ is a finite set of variables, we write

$$\Lambda(\overline{x}) \stackrel{\text{def}}{=} \{e \in \Lambda \mid \mathsf{fv}(e) \subseteq \overline{x}\}$$
$$V(\overline{x}) \stackrel{\text{def}}{=} \{v \in V \mid \mathsf{fv}(v) \subseteq \overline{x}\} \tag{5.2}$$

for the subsets of λ-terms and λ-values whose free variables are all in $\overline{x}$. Thus $\Lambda(\emptyset)$ is the subset of *closed* λ-terms and $V(\emptyset)$ is the set of closed λ-abstractions.

Call-by-value evaluation of closed λ-terms is the binary relation $\Downarrow_v \subseteq \Lambda(\emptyset) \times V(\emptyset)$ inductively defined by the following two rules.

$$\frac{}{v \Downarrow_v v} \qquad \text{(Val)}$$

$$\frac{e_1 \Downarrow_v \lambda x.\, e \qquad e_2 \Downarrow_v v \qquad e\{v/x\} \Downarrow_v v'}{e_1\, e_2 \Downarrow_v v'}. \qquad \text{(Cbv)}$$

Exercise 5.2.1 Consider the closed λ-values

$$one \overset{\text{def}}{=} \lambda x.\, \lambda y.\, x\, y$$

$$two \overset{\text{def}}{=} \lambda x.\, \lambda y.\, x\, (x\, y)$$

$$succ \overset{\text{def}}{=} \lambda n.\, \lambda x.\, \lambda y.\, x\, (n\, x\, y).$$

(These are the first two 'Church numerals' and the successor function for Church numerals; see [Pie02, sect. 5.2], for example.) For all $u, v, w \in V(\emptyset)$, show that $succ\, one\, u\, v \Downarrow_v w$ if and only if $two\, u\, v \Downarrow_v w$. Is it the case that $succ\, one \Downarrow_v two$ holds?

Exercise 5.2.2 Prove that evaluation is *deterministic*, that is, satisfies

$$e \Downarrow_v v_1 \,\wedge\, e \Downarrow_v v_2 \,\Rightarrow\, v_1 = v_2. \qquad (5.3)$$

Show that it is also partial, in the sense that for some closed λ-term $e \in \Lambda(\emptyset)$ there is no v for which $e \Downarrow_v v$ holds. [Hint: consider $e = (\lambda x.\, x\, x)(\lambda x.\, x\, x)$, for example.]

Call-by-value evaluation is sometimes called *strict evaluation*, in contrast with non-strict, or *call-by-name* evaluation. We will consider the latter in Section 5.9.

5.3 Applicative (bi)similarity for call-by-value λ-calculus

We wish to define an equivalence relation $\simeq\, \subseteq \Lambda(\emptyset) \times \Lambda(\emptyset)$ that equates two closed λ-terms $e_1, e_2 \in \Lambda(\emptyset)$ if they have the same behaviour with respect to call-by-value evaluation. But what does 'behaviour' mean in this case? It is too simplistic to require that e_1 and e_2 both evaluate to the same λ-value (or both diverge); for example we might hope that the λ-term $succ\, one$ from Exercise 5.2.1 is behaviourally equivalent to the λ-value *two* even though it does not evaluate to it under call-by-value evaluation. To motivate the kind of behavioural equivalence we are going to consider, recall that a λ-abstraction $\lambda x.\, e$ is a notation for a *function*; and indeed via the operation of substitution it determines a function on closed λ-values, mapping $v \in V(\emptyset)$ to $e\{v/x\} \in \Lambda(\emptyset)$. So if $e_1 \simeq e_2$ and $e_i \Downarrow_v \lambda x_i. e'_i$ (for $i = 1, 2$), it seems reasonable to require that $\lambda x_1. e'_1$ and $\lambda x_2. e'_2$ determine the same functions $V(\emptyset) \to \Lambda(\emptyset)$ modulo $\simeq$, in the sense that $e'_1\{v/x_1\} \simeq e'_2\{v/x_2\}$ should hold for all $v \in V(\emptyset)$. This property of an equivalence relation $\simeq$ is not yet a definition of it, because of the circularity it involves. We can break that circularity by taking the *greatest*[4] relation with this property, in other words by making a coinductive definition.

Definition 5.3.1 (Applicative simulation)   A relation $S \subseteq \Lambda(\emptyset) \times \Lambda(\emptyset)$ is a *(call-by-value) applicative simulation* if for all $e_1, e_2 \in \Lambda(\emptyset)$, $e_1 \, S \, e_2$ implies

$$e_1 \Downarrow_v \lambda x. e'_1 \;\Rightarrow\; \exists e'_2.\; e_2 \Downarrow_v \lambda x. e'_2 \,\wedge\, \forall v \in V(\emptyset).\; e'_1\{v/x\} \, S \, e'_2\{v/x\}.$$

$$\text{(v-Sim)}$$

It is an *applicative bisimulation* if both S and its reciprocal $S^{op} = \{(e, e') \mid e' \, S \, e\}$ are applicative simulations. Note that the union of a family of applicative (bi)simulations is another such. So there is a largest applicative simulation, which we call *applicative similarity* and write as $\lesssim_v$; and there is a largest applicative bisimulation, which we call *applicative bisimilarity* and write as $\simeq_v$.

Example 5.3.2 It follows from Exercise 5.2.1 that

$$\{(succ\,one, two)\} \cup \{(e, e) \mid e \in \Lambda(\emptyset)\}$$

is an applicative bisimulation. Hence *succ one* and *two* are applicatively bisimilar, *succ one* $\simeq_v$ *two*.

Definition 5.3.1 (and Theorem 5.6.5 below) extends smoothly to many applied λ-calculi. For example, it provides a useful tool for proving equivalences between pure functional programs involving algebraic data types; see [Gor95] and [Pit97b, section 3].

Applicative similarity is by definition the greatest post-fixed point for the monotone endofunction $F : \wp(\Lambda(\emptyset) \times \Lambda(\emptyset)) \to \wp(\Lambda(\emptyset) \times \Lambda(\emptyset))$ that maps S to

$$F(S) \overset{\text{def}}{=} \{(e_1, e_2) \mid \forall x, e'_1.\; e_1 \Downarrow_v \lambda x. e'_1 \;\Rightarrow\; \exists e'_2.\; e_2 \Downarrow_v \lambda x. e'_2 \,\wedge$$
$$\forall v.\; e'_1\{v/x\} \, S \, e'_2\{v/x\}\}.$$

---

[4] Taking the *least* such relation does not lead anywhere interesting, since that least relation is empty.

By the Knaster–Tarski fixed-point theorem [San12, theorem 2.3.21], it is also the greatest fixed point $\mathsf{gfp}(F)$ and hence we have:

$$e_1 \lesssim_v e_2$$
$$\Leftrightarrow \forall x, e_1'. e_1 \Downarrow_v \lambda x. e_1' \Rightarrow \exists e_2'. e_2 \Downarrow_v \lambda x. e_2' \wedge \forall v. e_1'\{v/x\} \lesssim_v e_2'\{v/x\}. \tag{5.4}$$

Similarly, applicative bisimulation satisfies:

$$e_1 \simeq_v e_2$$
$$\Leftrightarrow \forall x, e_1'. e_1 \Downarrow_v \lambda x. e_1' \Rightarrow \exists e_2'. e_2 \Downarrow_v \lambda x. e_2' \wedge \forall v. e_1'\{v/x\} \simeq_v e_2'\{v/x\}$$
$$\wedge \forall x, e_2'. e_2 \Downarrow_v \lambda x. e_2' \Rightarrow \exists e_1'. e_1 \Downarrow_v \lambda x. e_1' \wedge \forall v. e_1'\{v/x\} \simeq_v e_2'\{v/x\}. \tag{5.5}$$

Exercise 5.3.3 Show that the identity relation $\{(e, e) \mid e \in \Lambda(\emptyset)\}$ is an applicative bisimulation. Show that if $\mathcal{S}_1$ and $\mathcal{S}_2$ are applicative (bi)simulations, then so is their composition $\mathcal{S}_1 \circ \mathcal{S}_2 = \{(e_1, e_3) \mid \exists e_2. e_1 \mathcal{S}_1 e_2 \wedge e_2 \mathcal{S}_2 e_3\}$. Deduce that $\lesssim_v$ is a preorder (reflexive and transitive relation) and that $\simeq_v$ is an equivalence relation (reflexive, symmetric and transitive relation).

Because evaluation is deterministic (Exercise 5.2.2), applicative bisimulation is the equivalence relation generated by the preorder $\lesssim_v$:

Proposition 5.3.4 *For all* $e_1, e_2 \in \Lambda(\emptyset)$, $e_1 \simeq_v e_2$ *holds iff* $e_1 \lesssim_v e_2$ *and* $e_2 \lesssim_v e_1$.

Proof Since $\simeq_v$ and $\simeq_v^{op}$ are both applicative bisimulations, and hence both applicative simulations, they are contained in the greatest one, $\lesssim_v$. Thus $e_1 \simeq_v e_2$ implies $e_1 \lesssim_v e_2$ and $e_2 \lesssim_v e_1$.

Conversely, since $\lesssim_v$ satisfies property (v-Sim) and $\Downarrow_v$ satisfies (5.3), it follows that $\lesssim_v \cap \lesssim_v^{op}$ is an applicative bisimulation and hence is contained in $\simeq_v$. Thus $e_1 \lesssim_v e_2$ and $e_2 \lesssim_v e_1$ together imply $e_1 \simeq_v e_2$. □

Exercise 5.3.5 Show that

$$(\forall v \in V(\emptyset). \; e_1 \Downarrow_v v \Rightarrow e_2 \Downarrow_v v) \Rightarrow e_1 \lesssim_v e_2. \tag{5.6}$$

[Hint: show that the union of $\{(e_1, e_2) \mid \forall v. \; e_1 \Downarrow_v v \Rightarrow e_2 \Downarrow_v v\}$ with the identity relation is an applicative simulation.]

Deduce that β_v-equivalence is contained in applicative bisimilarity, that is, $(\lambda x. e)v \simeq_v e\{v/x\}$.

Exercise 5.3.6 Show by example that η-equivalence is not contained in applicative bisimilarity, in other words that $e \simeq_v \lambda x. e\, x$ (where $x \notin \mathsf{fv}(e)$) does not always hold. What happens if e is a λ-value?

Exercise 5.3.7 Show that $\lambda x. e_1 \lesssim_v \lambda x. e_2$ holds iff $e_1\{v/x\} \lesssim_v e_2\{v/x\}$ holds for all $v \in V(\emptyset)$.

5.4 Congruence

We noted in Exercise 5.3.3 that applicative bisimilarity is an equivalence relation. To qualify as a reasonable notion of semantic equality for λ-terms, $\simeq_v$ should not only be an equivalence relation, but also be a congruence; in other words it should also respect the way λ-terms are constructed. There are two such constructions: formation of application terms ($e_1, e_2 \mapsto e_1 e_2$) and formation of λ-abstractions ($x, e \mapsto \lambda x. e$). The second is a variable-binding operation and to make sense of the statement that it respects applicative bisimilarity we first have to extend $\simeq_v$ to a binary relation between all λ-terms, open as well as closed. To do this we will regard the free variables in a λ-term as implicitly λ-bound and use the property of $\lesssim_v$ noted in Exercise 5.3.7.

Definition 5.4.1 (Open extension of applicative (bi)similarity) Given a finite set of variables $\overline{x} = \{x_1, \ldots, x_n\} \in \wp_{\text{fin}}(Var)$ and λ-terms $e, e' \in \Lambda(\overline{x})$, we write

$$\overline{x} \vdash e \lesssim_v e' \tag{5.7}$$

if $e\{v_1, \ldots, v_n/x_1, \ldots, x_n\} \lesssim_v e'\{v_1, \ldots, v_n/x_1, \ldots, x_n\}$ holds for all $v_1, \ldots, v_n \in V(\emptyset)$. Similarly

$$\overline{x} \vdash e \simeq_v e' \tag{5.8}$$

means $e\{v_1, \ldots, v_n/x_1, \ldots, x_n\} \simeq_v e'\{v_1, \ldots, v_n/x_1, \ldots, x_n\}$ holds for all $v_1, \ldots, v_n \in V(\emptyset)$.

Definition 5.4.2 (λ-term relations) The relations (5.7) and (5.8) are examples of what we call a λ-*term relation*, by which we mean a set $\mathcal{R}$ of triples $(\overline{x}, e, e')$ where $\overline{x} \in \wp_{\text{fin}}(Var)$ and $e, e' \in \Lambda(\overline{x})$. We will use mixfix notation and write $\overline{x} \vdash e \,\mathcal{R}\, e'$ to indicate that $(\overline{x}, e, e') \in \mathcal{R}$. We call a λ-term relation $\mathcal{R}$ *symmetric* if

$$\forall \overline{x} \in \wp_{\text{fin}}(Var). \, \forall e, e' \in \Lambda(\overline{x}). \, \overline{x} \vdash e \,\mathcal{R}\, e' \implies \overline{x} \vdash e' \,\mathcal{R}\, e, \tag{Sym}$$

transitive if

$$\forall \overline{x} \in \wp_{\text{fin}}(Var). \, \forall e, e', e'' \in \Lambda(\overline{x}).$$
$$\overline{x} \vdash e \,\mathcal{R}\, e' \wedge \overline{x} \vdash e' \,\mathcal{R}\, e'' \implies \overline{x} \vdash e \,\mathcal{R}\, e'' \tag{Tra}$$

and *compatible* if

$$\forall \overline{x} \in \wp_{\text{fin}}(Var). \; x \in \overline{x} \;\Rightarrow\; \overline{x} \vdash x \; \mathcal{R} \; x \qquad\qquad (\text{Com1})$$

$$\forall \overline{x} \in \wp_{\text{fin}}(Var). \; \forall x \in Var - \overline{x}. \; \forall e, e' \in \Lambda(\overline{x} \cup \{x\}).$$
$$\overline{x} \cup \{x\} \vdash e \; \mathcal{R} \; e' \;\Rightarrow\; \overline{x} \vdash \lambda x . e \; \mathcal{R} \; \lambda x . e' \qquad (\text{Com2})$$

$$\forall \overline{x} \in \wp_{\text{fin}}(Var). \; \forall e_1, e_1', e_2, e_2' \in \Lambda(\overline{x}).$$
$$\overline{x} \vdash e_1 \; \mathcal{R} \; e_1' \;\wedge\; \overline{x} \vdash e_2 \; \mathcal{R} \; e_2' \;\Rightarrow\; \overline{x} \vdash e_1 e_2 \; \mathcal{R} \; e_1' e_2'. \qquad (\text{Com3})$$

Property (Com1) is a special case of *reflexivity*:

$$\forall \overline{x} \in \wp_{\text{fin}}(Var). \; \forall e \in \Lambda(\overline{x}). \; \overline{x} \vdash e \; \mathcal{R} \; e. \qquad\qquad (\text{Ref})$$

Indeed, it is not hard to see that a compatible λ-term relation has to be reflexive. We say that $\mathcal{R}$ is a *precongruence* if it has the properties (Tra), (Com1), (Com2) and (Com3); and we call it a *congruence* if it also satisfies property (Sym).

Exercise 5.4.3 Prove that every compatible λ-term relation is reflexive. Deduce that property (Com3) implies

$$\forall \overline{x} \in \wp_{\text{fin}}(Var). \; \forall e_1, e_1', e_2 \in \Lambda(\overline{x}). \; \overline{x} \vdash e_1 \; \mathcal{R} \; e_1' \;\Rightarrow\; \overline{x} \vdash e_1 e_2 \; \mathcal{R} \; e_1' e_2$$
$$(\text{Com3L})$$

$$\forall \overline{x} \in \wp_{\text{fin}}(Var). \; \forall e_1, e_1', e_2 \in \Lambda(\overline{x}). \; \overline{x} \vdash e_2 \; \mathcal{R} \; e_2' \;\Rightarrow\; \overline{x} \vdash e_1 e_2 \; \mathcal{R} \; e_1 e_2'.$$
$$(\text{Com3R})$$

Show that if $\mathcal{R}$ is transitive, then (Com3L) and (Com3R) together imply (Com3).

Remark 5.4.4 (Motivating Howe's method) We will eventually prove that the open extension of applicative similarity is a precongruence relation (Theorem 5.5.5). It is illuminating to see how far we can get with a direct proof of this before we have to introduce the machinery of Howe's method. Combining Exercise 5.3.3 with the way the open extension is defined from the relation on closed λ-terms in Definition 5.4.1, it follows that properties (Tra), (Ref), and hence also (Com1), hold when $\mathcal{R}$ is $\precsim_v$. In the same way, the property in Exercise 5.3.7 implies (Com2). So to complete the proof that $\precsim_v$ is a precongruence, we just have to prove that it has property (Com3); and for this it is sufficient to prove the special case when $\overline{x} = \emptyset$, that is, to prove

$$\forall e_1, e_1', e_2, e_2' \in \Lambda(\emptyset). \; e_1 \precsim_v e_1' \;\wedge\; e_2 \precsim_v e_2' \;\Rightarrow\; e_1 e_2 \precsim_v e_1' e_2'. \qquad (*)$$

Since we know that $\precsim_v$ is a preorder, proving $(*)$ is equivalent to proving the following two special cases (cf. Exercise 5.4.3).

$$\forall e_1, e_1' \in \Lambda(\emptyset). \; e_1 \precsim_v e_1' \;\Rightarrow\; \forall e_2 \in \Lambda(\emptyset). \; e_1 e_2 \precsim_v e_1' e_2 \qquad (*_1)$$

$$\forall e_2, e_2' \in \Lambda(\emptyset). \; e_2 \precsim_v e_2' \;\Rightarrow\; \forall e_1 \in \Lambda(\emptyset). \; e_1 e_2 \precsim_v e_1 e_2'. \qquad (*_2)$$

Given the coinductive definition of $\lesssim_v$ (Definition 5.3.1), an obvious strategy for proving these properties is to show that

$$\mathcal{S}_1 \stackrel{\text{def}}{=} \{(e_1\,e_2, e_1'\,e_2) \mid e_1 \lesssim_v e_1' \wedge e_2 \in \Lambda(\emptyset)\}$$

$$\mathcal{S}_2 \stackrel{\text{def}}{=} \{(e_1\,e_2, e_1\,e_2') \mid e_1 \in \Lambda(\emptyset) \wedge e_2 \lesssim_v e_2'\}$$

are contained in applicative simulations; for then $\mathcal{S}_i$ is contained in the largest such, $\lesssim_v$, which gives $(*_i)$. We leave the proof of this for $\mathcal{S}_1$ as a straightforward exercise (Exercise 5.4.5). Proving $(*_2)$ by the same method as in that exercise is not so easy. Let us see why. It would suffice to show that

$$e_2 \lesssim_v e_2' \tag{5.9}$$

$$e_1\,e_2 \Downarrow_v \lambda x.\,e \tag{5.10}$$

implies

$$\exists e'.\ e_1\,e_2' \Downarrow_v \lambda x.\,e' \ \wedge \ \forall v \in V(\emptyset).\ e\{v/x\} \lesssim_v e'\{v/x\}. \tag{†}$$

The syntax-directed nature of the rules (Val) and (Cbv) inductively defining $\Downarrow_v$ mean that (5.10) holds because for some e_3 and e_4 we have

$$e_1 \Downarrow_v \lambda x.\,e_3 \tag{5.11}$$

$$e_2 \Downarrow_v \lambda x.\,e_4 \tag{5.12}$$

$$e_3\{\lambda x.\,e_4/x\} \Downarrow_v \lambda x.\,e. \tag{5.13}$$

Then since $\lesssim_v$ is an applicative simulation, from (5.9) and (5.12) we conclude that there is some e_4' with

$$e_2' \Downarrow_v \lambda x.\,e_4' \tag{5.14}$$

and $\forall v.\ e_4\{v/x\} \lesssim_v e_4'\{v/x\}$, which by Exercise 5.3.7 implies

$$\lambda x.\,e_4 \lesssim_v \lambda x.\,e_4'. \tag{5.15}$$

So to prove (†) we just have to show that

$$\exists e'.\ e_3\{\lambda x.\,e_4'/x\} \Downarrow_v \lambda x.\,e' \ \wedge \ \forall v.\ e\{v/x\} \lesssim_v e'\{v/x\}. \tag{††}$$

In view of (5.13) and the fact that $\lesssim_v$ is an applicative simulation, to prove (††) we just need to show that $e_3\{\lambda x.\,e_4/x\} \lesssim_v e_3\{\lambda x.\,e_4'/x\}$. This would follow from (5.15) if we knew that applicative similarity has the following substitution property:

$$\forall \overline{x} \in \wp_{\text{fin}}(Var).\, \forall x \in Var - \overline{x}.\, \forall e \in \Lambda(\overline{x} \cup \{x\}).\, \forall v, v' \in V(\overline{x}).$$

$$\overline{x} \vdash v \lesssim_v v' \ \Rightarrow \ \overline{x} \vdash e\{v/x\} \lesssim_v e\{v'/x\}. \tag{5.16}$$

Unfortunately the property $(*_2)$ that we are trying to prove is very similar to this property (consider taking e to be $e_1\,x$) and we are stuck. To get unstuck, in the next section we use Howe's method of constructing a relation $(\lesssim_v)^H$ out of $\lesssim_v$ that has property (5.16) by construction and which can be proved equal to $\lesssim_v$ via an induction over evaluation $\Downarrow_v$ (the key Lemma 5.5.4).

Exercise 5.4.5 Prove property $(*_1)$ by showing that

$$\{(e_1\,e_2, e_1'\,e_2) \mid e_1 \lesssim_v e_1' \,\wedge\, e_2 \in \Lambda(\emptyset)\} \cup \lesssim_v$$

is an applicative simulation.

5.5 Howe's construction

Given a λ-term relation $\mathcal{R}$, the λ-term relation $\mathcal{R}^H$ is inductively defined from $\mathcal{R}$ by the following rules. It is an instance of what Howe calls the 'precongruence candidate' [How96, sect. 3].

$$\frac{\bar{x} \vdash x\ \mathcal{R}\ e}{\bar{x} \vdash x\ \mathcal{R}^H\ e} \tag{How1}$$

$$\frac{\bar{x} \cup \{x\} \vdash e_1\ \mathcal{R}^H\ e_1' \qquad \bar{x} \vdash \lambda x.e_1'\ \mathcal{R}\ e_2 \qquad x \notin \bar{x}}{\bar{x} \vdash \lambda x.e_1\ \mathcal{R}^H\ e_2} \tag{How2}$$

$$\frac{\bar{x} \vdash e_1\ \mathcal{R}^H\ e_1' \qquad \bar{x} \vdash e_2\ \mathcal{R}^H\ e_2' \qquad \bar{x} \vdash e_1'\,e_2'\ \mathcal{R}\ e_3}{\bar{x} \vdash e_1\,e_2\ \mathcal{R}^H\ e_3}. \tag{How3}$$

We will need the following general properties of $(\_)^H$ whose proof we leave as an exercise.

Lemma 5.5.1

(i) *If $\mathcal{R}$ is reflexive, then $\mathcal{R}^H$ is compatible.*
(ii) *If $\mathcal{R}$ is transitive, then $\bar{x} \vdash e_1\ \mathcal{R}^H\ e_2$ and $\bar{x} \vdash e_2\ \mathcal{R}\ e_3$ imply $\bar{x} \vdash e_1\ \mathcal{R}^H\ e_3$.*
(iii) *If $\mathcal{R}$ is reflexive and transitive, then $\bar{x} \vdash e_1\ \mathcal{R}\ e_2$ implies $\bar{x} \vdash e_1\ \mathcal{R}^H\ e_2$.*

$\square$

Definition 5.5.2 (Substitutivity and closure under substitution)
A λ-term relation $\mathcal{R}$ is called *(value) substitutive* if for all $\bar{x} \in \wp_{\mathrm{fin}}(Var)$, $x \in Var - \bar{x}$, $e, e' \in \Lambda(\bar{x} \cup \{x\})$ and $v, v' \in V(\bar{x})$

$$\bar{x} \cup \{x\} \vdash e\ \mathcal{R}\ e' \,\wedge\, \bar{x} \vdash v\ \mathcal{R}\ v' \;\Rightarrow\; \bar{x} \vdash e\{v/x\}\ \mathcal{R}\ e'\{v'/x\}. \tag{Sub}$$

Note that if $\mathcal{R}$ is also reflexive, then this implies

$$\overline{x} \cup \{x\} \vdash e \, \mathcal{R} \, e' \wedge v \in V(\overline{x}) \Rightarrow \overline{x} \vdash e\{v/x\} \, \mathcal{R} \, e'\{v/x\}. \qquad \text{(Cus)}$$

We say that $\mathcal{R}$ is *closed under value-substitution* if it satisfies (Cus).

Note that because of the way the open extension of applicative similarity and bisimilarity are defined (Definition 5.4.1), evidently they are closed under value-substitution. It is less clear that they are substitutive; this will follow from the coincidence of $\lesssim_v$ with $(\lesssim_v)^H$ that we prove below, because of the following result.

Lemma 5.5.3 *If $\mathcal{R}$ is reflexive, transitive and closed under value-substitution, then $\mathcal{R}^H$ is substitutive and hence also closed under value-substitution.*

Proof Property (Sub) for $\mathcal{R}^H$ follows from property (Cus) for $\mathcal{R}$ by induction on the derivation of $\overline{x} \cup \{x\} \vdash e \, \mathcal{R}^H \, e'$ from the rules (How1)–(How3), using Lemma 5.5.1(iii) in case e is a variable. $\qquad \square$

Specialising Lemmas 5.5.1 and 5.5.3 to the case $\mathcal{R} = \lesssim_v$, we now give the key property needed to show that $(\lesssim_v)^H$ is in fact equal to $\lesssim_v$.

Lemma 5.5.4 (Key lemma, version 1) *If $e_1 \Downarrow_v \lambda x.\,e$ and $\emptyset \vdash e_1 \, (\lesssim_v)^H \, e_2$, then $e_2 \Downarrow_v \lambda x.\,e'$ holds for some e' satisfying $\{x\} \vdash e \, (\lesssim_v)^H \, e'$.*

Proof We show that

$$\mathcal{E} \stackrel{\text{def}}{=} \{(e_1, \lambda x.\,e) \mid \forall e_2.\; \emptyset \vdash e_1 \, (\lesssim_v)^H \, e_2$$
$$\Rightarrow \exists e'.\; e_2 \Downarrow_v \lambda x.\,e' \wedge \{x\} \vdash e \, (\lesssim_v)^H \, e'\}$$

is closed under the two rules (Val) and (Cbv) inductively defining $\Downarrow_v$.

Closure under (Val): When $e_1 = \lambda x.\,e$, for any e_2 if $\emptyset \vdash \lambda x.\,e \, (\lesssim_v)^H \, e_2$ holds, it must have been deduced by an application of rule (How2) to

$$\{x\} \vdash e \, (\lesssim_v)^H \, e_1' \qquad (5.17)$$
$$\lambda x.\,e_1' \lesssim_v e_2 \qquad (5.18)$$

for some e_1'. Since $\lesssim_v$ is an applicative simulation, from (5.18) it follows that $e_2 \Downarrow_v \lambda x.\,e'$ holds for some e' with

$$\{x\} \vdash e_1' \lesssim_v e'. \qquad (5.19)$$

Applying Lemma 5.5.1(ii) to (5.17) and (5.19) gives $\{x\} \vdash e \, (\lesssim_v)^H \, e'$. So we do indeed have $(\lambda x.\,e, \lambda x.\,e) \in \mathcal{E}$.

Closure under (Cbv): Suppose

$$(e_1, \lambda x.\,e_2),\, (e_1', \lambda x.\,e_2'),\, (e_2\{\lambda x.\,e_2'/x\}, \lambda x.\,e_3) \in \mathcal{E}.$$

We have to show that $(e_1 e_1', \lambda x. e_3) \in \mathcal{E}$. For any e, if $\emptyset \vdash e_1 e_1' \ (\precsim_v)^H \ e$ holds it must have been deduced by an application of rule (How3) to

$$\emptyset \vdash e_1 \ (\precsim_v)^H \ e_4 \tag{5.20}$$

$$\emptyset \vdash e_1' \ (\precsim_v)^H \ e_4' \tag{5.21}$$

$$e_4 e_4' \precsim_v e \tag{5.22}$$

for some e_4, e_4'. Since $(e_1, \lambda x. e_2), (e_1', \lambda x. e_2') \in \mathcal{E}$, it follows from (5.20) and (5.21) that

$$e_4 \Downarrow_v \lambda x. e_5 \tag{5.23}$$

$$\{x\} \vdash e_2 \ (\precsim_v)^H \ e_5 \tag{5.24}$$

$$e_4' \Downarrow_v \lambda x. e_5' \tag{5.25}$$

$$\{x\} \vdash e_2' \ (\precsim_v)^H \ e_5'$$

hold for some e_5, e_5', and hence also that

$$\emptyset \vdash \lambda x. e_2' \ (\precsim_v)^H \ \lambda x. e_5'. \tag{5.26}$$

Now we can apply the substitutivity property of $(\precsim_v)^H$ (Lemma 5.5.3) to (5.24) and (5.26) to get $\emptyset \vdash e_2\{\lambda x. e_2'/x\} \ (\precsim_v)^H \ e_5\{\lambda x. e_5'/x\}$. From this and the fact that $(e_2\{\lambda x. e_2'/x\}, \lambda x. e_3) \in \mathcal{E}$, it follows that for some e_6 it is the case that

$$e_5\{\lambda x. e_5'/x\} \Downarrow_v \lambda x. e_6 \tag{5.27}$$

$$\{x\} \vdash e_3 \ (\precsim_v)^H \ e_6. \tag{5.28}$$

Applying rule (Cbv) to (5.23), (5.25) and (5.27), we have that $e_4 e_4' \Downarrow_v \lambda x. e_6$. Then since $\precsim_v$ is an applicative simulation, from this and (5.22) we get that $e \Downarrow_v \lambda x. e'$ holds for some e' with

$$\{x\} \vdash e_6 \precsim_v e' \tag{5.29}$$

and hence also with $\{x\} \vdash e_3 \ (\precsim_v)^H \ e'$ (by Lemma 5.5.1(ii) on (5.28) and (5.29)). Therefore we do indeed have $(e_1 e_1', \lambda x. e_3) \in \mathcal{E}$. $\qquad\square$

Theorem 5.5.5 (Applicative bisimilarity is a congruence) *The open extension of applicative similarity is a precongruence relation and hence the open extension of applicative bisimilarity is a congruence relation.*

Proof By Lemma 5.5.3, $(\precsim_v)^H$ is closed under value-substitution:

$$\{x\} \vdash e \ (\precsim_v)^H \ e' \ \Rightarrow \ \forall v \in V(\emptyset). \ e\{v/x\} \ (\precsim_v)^H \ e'\{v/x\}.$$

Therefore the key Lemma 5.5.4 implies that $(\precsim_v)^H$ restricted to closed λ-terms is an applicative simulation. So it is contained in the largest one, $\precsim_v$:

$$\emptyset \vdash e_1 \ (\precsim_v)^H \ e_2 \ \Rightarrow \ e_1 \precsim_v e_2.$$

Using closure of $(\precsim_v)^H$ under value-substitution once again, this lifts to open terms:

$$\overline{x} \vdash e_1 \ (\precsim_v)^H \ e_2 \ \Rightarrow \ \overline{x} \vdash e_1 \precsim_v e_2.$$

In view of Lemma 5.5.1(iii), this means that the λ-term relations $(\precsim_v)^H$ and $\precsim_v$ are equal. Since $(\precsim_v)^H$ is compatible by Lemma 5.5.1(i) and since we already know that $\precsim_v$ is transitive, it follows that $\precsim_v = (\precsim_v)^H$ is a precongruence relation.   □

5.6 Contextual equivalence

One of the important consequences of Theorem 5.5.5 is that applicative bisimilarity coincides with the standard notion of *contextual equivalence* for the call-by-value λ-calculus. A λ-term *context* C is a syntax tree with a unique[5] 'hole' $[\cdot]$

$$C \in Con ::= [\cdot] \ \Big| \ \lambda x. C \ \Big| \ C\, e \ \Big| \ e\, C \tag{5.30}$$

and $C[e]$ denotes the λ-term that results from filling the hole with a λ-term e:

$$\begin{aligned} [\cdot][e] &= e \\ (\lambda x. C)[e] &= \lambda x. C[e] \\ (C\, e')[e] &= C[e]\, e' \\ (e'\, C)[e] &= e'\, C[e]. \end{aligned} \tag{5.31}$$

We also write $C[C']$ for the context resulting from replacing the occurrence of $[\cdot]$ in the syntax tree C by the tree C'.

Remark 5.6.1 (Contexts considered too concrete) Note that (5.31) is a 'capturing' form of substitution – free variables in e may become bound in $C[e]$; for example, $(\lambda x. -)[x] = \lambda x. x$. This means that it does not make sense to identify contexts up to renaming of λ-bound variables, as we do with λ-terms. For example, if x and x' are distinct variables, then $C_1 = \lambda x. [\cdot]$ and $C_2 = \lambda x'. [\cdot]$

---

[5] In the literature one also finds treatments that use contexts with finitely many (including zero) occurrences of the hole. While it does not affect the associated notion of contextual equivalence, the restriction to 'linear' contexts that we use here makes for some technical simplifications.

are distinct contexts that give different results when their hole is filled with x: $C_1[x] = \lambda x. x \neq \lambda x'. x = C_2[x]$. The concreteness of the above notion of 'context' forces us to take care with the actual names of bound variables. This might not seem so bad for the λ-calculus, because it is syntactically so simple. However it becomes increasingly irksome if one is producing fully formalised and machine-checked proofs, or if one is dealing with more complicated programming languages with more complex forms of binding. Several different remedies have been proposed for this problem of overly concrete representations of contexts. We explain one of them in Remark 5.6.7, but postpone discussing it until we have given a more-or-less classical development of contextual equivalence based on the above, rather too concrete notion of context.

Continuing the 'hygiene' of keeping track of free variables through use of the sets $\Lambda(\overline{x})$ indexed by sets $\overline{x}$ of variables, and following [CH07, fig. 7], let us inductively define subsets $Con(\overline{x}; \overline{x}')$ of contexts by the rules:

$$\frac{}{[\cdot] \in Con(\overline{x}; \overline{x})} \qquad (\text{Con1})$$

$$\frac{C \in Con(\overline{x}; \overline{x}' \cup \{x\}) \qquad x \notin \overline{x}'}{\lambda x. C \in Con(\overline{x}; \overline{x}')} \qquad (\text{Con2})$$

$$\frac{C \in Con(\overline{x}; \overline{x}') \qquad e \in \Lambda(\overline{x}')}{C e \in Con(\overline{x}; \overline{x}')} \qquad (\text{Con3})$$

$$\frac{e \in \Lambda(\overline{x}') \qquad C \in Con(\overline{x}; \overline{x}')}{e C \in Con(\overline{x}; \overline{x}')} \qquad (\text{Con4})$$

For example, if $x \notin \overline{x}$ then $\lambda x. [\cdot] \in Con(\overline{x} \cup \{x\}; \overline{x})$. The role in the above definition of the double indexing over both $\overline{x}$ and $\overline{x}'$ becomes clearer once one notes the following properties, (5.32) and (5.33). They are easily proved, the first by induction on the derivation of $C \in Con(\overline{x}; \overline{x}')$ from the rules (Con1)–(Con4), the second by induction on the derivation of $C' \in Con(\overline{x}'; \overline{x}'')$.

$$e \in \Lambda(\overline{x}) \wedge C \in Con(\overline{x}; \overline{x}') \implies C[e] \in \Lambda(\overline{x}') \qquad (5.32)$$
$$C \in Con(\overline{x}; \overline{x}') \wedge C' \in Con(\overline{x}'; \overline{x}'') \implies C'[C] \in Con(\overline{x}; \overline{x}''). \qquad (5.33)$$

In particular, the elements of $Con(\overline{x}; \emptyset)$ are *closing contexts* for λ-terms with free variables in $\overline{x}$: if $e \in \Lambda(\overline{x})$ and $C \in Con(\overline{x}; \emptyset)$, then $C[e] \in \Lambda(\emptyset)$ is a closed λ-term, which we can consider evaluating.

Definition 5.6.2 (Contextual equivalence) The *contextual preorder* with respect to call-by-value evaluation is the λ-term relation given by

$$\overline{x} \vdash e_1 \leq_v e_2 \quad \overset{\text{def}}{=} \quad \forall C \in Con(\overline{x}; \emptyset). \ C[e_1] \Downarrow_v \implies C[e_2] \Downarrow_v$$

where in general we write $e \Downarrow_v$ to mean that $e \Downarrow_v v$ holds for some v. The λ-term relation of *contextual equivalence*, $\overline{x} \vdash e_1 =_v e_2$, holds iff $\overline{x} \vdash e_1 \leq_v e_2$ and $\overline{x} \vdash e_2 \leq_v e_1$.

Exercise 5.6.3   Show that $\leq_v$ is a precongruence relation (Definition 5.4.2). [Hint: for property (Com2), given $C \in Con(\overline{x}; \emptyset)$ consider $C[\lambda x . [\cdot]] \in Con(\overline{x} \cup \{x\}; \emptyset)$; for property (Com3), given $C \in Con(\overline{x}; \emptyset)$ consider $C[e_1 [\cdot]]$ and $C[[\cdot] e_2']$ and use Exercise 5.4.3.]

Lemma 5.6.4   *If $\overline{x} \vdash e_1 \lesssim_v e_2$ and $C \in Con(\overline{x}; \overline{x}')$, then $\overline{x}' \vdash C[e_1] \lesssim_v C[e_2]$.*

Proof By induction on the derivation of $C \in Con(\overline{x}; \overline{x}')$ from the rules (Con1)–(Con4), using Theorem 5.5.5. $\square$

Theorem 5.6.5 (Applicative bisimilarity is contextual equivalence)
For all $\overline{x} \in \wp_{\mathrm{fin}}(Var)$ and $e_1, e_2 \in \Lambda(\overline{x})$, $\overline{x} \vdash e_1 \lesssim_v e_2$ iff $\overline{x} \vdash e_1 \leq_v e_2$ (and hence $\overline{x} \vdash e_1 \simeq_v e_2$ iff $\overline{x} \vdash e_1 =_v e_2$).

Proof We first prove

$$\overline{x} \vdash e_1 \lesssim_v e_2 \;\Rightarrow\; \overline{x} \vdash e_1 \leq_v e_2. \tag{5.34}$$

If $\overline{x} \vdash e_1 \lesssim_v e_2$, then for any $C \in Con(\overline{x}; \emptyset)$ by Lemma 5.6.4 we have $C[e_1] \lesssim_v C[e_2]$. Since $\lesssim_v$ is an applicative bisimulation, this means in particular that $C[e_1] \Downarrow_v$ implies $C[e_2] \Downarrow_v$. So by definition, $\overline{x} \vdash e_1 \leq_v e_2$.

To prove the converse of (5.34), first note that it suffices to show that $=_v$ restricted to closed λ-terms is an applicative simulation and hence contained in $\lesssim_v$. For then, if we have $\overline{x} \vdash e_1 \leq_v e_2$, by repeated use of the congruence property (Com2) (which we know holds of $=_v$ from Exercise 5.6.3), we get $\emptyset \vdash \lambda \overline{x} . e_1 =_v \lambda \overline{x} . e_2$ and hence $\lambda \overline{x} . e_1 \lesssim_v \lambda \overline{x} . e_2$; but then we can use Exercise 5.3.7 to deduce that $\overline{x} \vdash e_1 \lesssim_v e_2$.

So we just have to show that $\{(e_1, e_2) \mid \emptyset \vdash e_1 \leq_v e_2\}$ has the applicative simulation property. If $\emptyset \vdash e_1 \leq_v e_2$ and $e_1 \Downarrow_v \lambda x . e_1'$, then $C[e_1] \Downarrow_v$ with $C = [\cdot]$, so $C[e_2] \Downarrow_v$, that is, $e_2 \Downarrow_v \lambda x . e_2'$ for some e_2'. From Exercise 5.3.5 we thus have $e_i \simeq_v \lambda x . e_i'$ and hence by (5.34) that

$$\emptyset \vdash \lambda x . e_1' =_v e_1 \leq_v e_2 =_v \lambda x . e_2'.$$

So $\emptyset \vdash \lambda x . e_1' \leq_v \lambda x . e_2'$ and hence for any $v \in V(\emptyset)$ we can use the congruence property of $\leq_v$ (Exercise 5.6.3) to deduce that $\emptyset \vdash (\lambda x . e_1') v \leq_v (\lambda x . e_2') v$. From Exercise 5.3.5 and (5.34), we have $\emptyset \vdash (\lambda x . e_i') v =_v e_i' \{v/x\}$ and therefore $\emptyset \vdash e_1' \{v/x\} \leq_v e_2' \{v/x\}$. Thus $\{(e_1, e_2) \mid \emptyset \vdash e_1 \leq_v e_2\}$ does indeed have property (v-Sim). $\square$

As a corollary of the coincidence of contextual equivalence with applicative bisimulation, we have the following extensionality properties of λ-terms modulo $=_v$.

Corollary 5.6.6 (Extensionality) *Given variables* $\overline{x} = \{x_1, \ldots, x_n\}$ *and* λ-*terms* $e, e' \in \Lambda(\overline{x})$, *then* $\overline{x} \vdash e =_v e'$ *iff* $\emptyset \vdash \lambda\overline{x}.\ e =_v \lambda\overline{x}.\ e'$ *iff*

$$\forall v_1 \ldots, v_n \in V(\emptyset).\ \emptyset \vdash e\{v_1, \ldots, v_n/x_1, \ldots, x_n\} =_v e\{v_1, \ldots, v_n/x_1, \ldots, x_n\}.$$

Proof Just note that these properties hold of $\simeq_v$ (by definition of the open extension in Definition 5.4.1 and using Exercise 5.3.7); so we can apply Theorem 5.6.5. $\square$

Remark 5.6.7 ('Context free' contextual equivalence) We noted in Remark 5.6.1 that the notion of context is unpleasantly concrete – it prevents one from working uniformly at the level of α-equivalence classes of syntax trees. In fact one can dispense with contexts entirely and work instead with a coinductive characterisation of the contextual preorder and equivalence phrased in terms of λ-term relations. (This is an instance of the 'relational' approach to contextual equivalence first proposed by Gordon [Gor98] and Lassen [Las98a, Las98b].) The contextual preorder turns out to be the largest λ-term relation $\mathcal{R}$ that is both compatible (Definition 5.4.2) and *adequate* (for call-by-value evaluation), which by definition means

$$\forall e.\, e' \in \Lambda(\emptyset).\ \emptyset \vdash e\ \mathcal{R}\ e' \ \Rightarrow\ (e{\Downarrow_v} \ \Rightarrow\ e'{\Downarrow_v}). \qquad \text{(v-Adeq)}$$

To see this, let $\mathbb{C}\mathbb{A}$ be the collection of all compatible and adequate λ-term relations and let

$$\leq^{ca}_v \overset{\text{def}}{=} \bigcup \mathbb{C}\mathbb{A}. \qquad (5.35)$$

We first want to show that $\leq^{ca}_v \in \mathbb{C}\mathbb{A}$ and hence that $\leq^{ca}_v$ is the largest compatible and adequate λ-term relation. Note that the identity relation $\{(\overline{x}, e, e) \mid e \in \Lambda(\overline{x})\}$ is in $\mathbb{C}\mathbb{A}$; so $\leq^{ca}_v$ is reflexive and hence in particular satisfies compatibility property (Com1). It is clear that properties (Com2) and (v-Adeq) are closed under taking unions of relations, so that $\leq^{ca}_v$ has these properties; but the same is not true for property (Com3). However, if $\mathcal{R}_1, \mathcal{R}_2 \in \mathbb{C}\mathbb{A}$ then it is easy to see that the composition $\mathcal{R}_1 \circ \mathcal{R}_2$ is also in $\mathbb{C}\mathbb{A}$; hence $\leq^{ca}_v \circ \leq^{ca}_v \subseteq \leq^{ca}_v$, that is, $\leq^{ca}_v$ is transitive. So by Exercise 5.4.3, for (Com3) it is enough to show that $\leq^{ca}_v$ satisfies (Com3L) and (Com3R); and this is straightforward, since unlike (Com3) these properties clearly are closed under taking unions of relations.

So the largest compatible and adequate λ-term relation not only exists, but is reflexive and transitive.

To see that $\leq_v^{ca}$ coincides with the contextual preorder, first note that it is immediate from its definition that $\leq_v$ is adequate; and we noted in Exercise 5.6.3 that it is a precongruence. So $\leq_v \in \mathbb{CA}$ and hence $\leq_v \subseteq \leq_v^{ca}$. Since $\leq_v^{ca}$ is a precongruence we can prove

$$\overline{x} \vdash e_1 \leq_v^{ca} e_2 \,\wedge\, C \in Con(\overline{x}; \overline{x}') \;\Rightarrow\; \overline{x}' \vdash C[e_1] \leq_v^{ca} C[e_2]$$

in the same way that Lemma 5.6.4 was proved. Thus

$$\overline{x} \vdash e_1 \leq_v^{ca} e_2$$
$$\Rightarrow\; \forall C \in Con(\overline{x}; \emptyset).\; \emptyset \vdash C[e_1] \leq_v^{ca} C[e_2]$$
$$\Rightarrow\; \forall C \in Con(\overline{x}; \emptyset).\; C[e_1]\Downarrow_v \;\Rightarrow\; C[e_2]\Downarrow_v \quad \text{since } \leq_v^{ca} \text{ is adequate}$$
$$\Rightarrow\; \overline{x} \vdash e_1 \leq_v e_2.$$

So altogether we have that $\leq_v^{ca}$ is equal to $\leq_v$.

Exercise 5.6.8 Show that $=_v$ is the largest λ-term relation that is both compatible and *bi-adequate*:

$$\forall e.e' \in \Lambda(\emptyset).\; \emptyset \vdash e \,\mathcal{R}\, e' \;\Rightarrow\; (e\Downarrow_v \Leftrightarrow e'\Downarrow_v). \qquad \text{(Bi-adeq)}$$

Exercise 5.6.9 Adapt the proof of Theorem 5.6.5 to give a direct proof (that is, a proof making no use of $\leq_v$) of the fact that $\lesssim_v$ coincides with the relation $\leq_v^{ca}$ defined in (5.35).

5.7 The transitive closure trick

We noted in Proposition 5.3.4 that because the evaluation relation $\Downarrow_v$ is deterministic, applicative bisimilarity is the symmetrisation of applicative similarity: $\simeq_v \,=\, \lesssim_v \cap \lesssim_v^{op}$. We used this observation in Section 5.5 to deduce that $\simeq_v$ is a congruence by using Howe's method to show that $\lesssim_v$ is a precongruence. What happens if we add features to the λ-calculus that cause $\simeq_v$ to be different from $\lesssim_v \cap \lesssim_v^{op}$? Can one apply Howe's method directly to $\simeq_v$ to deduce that it is a congruence in that case? Note that Howe's 'precongruence candidate' construction $(\_)^H$ has an asymmetric nature: $\mathcal{R}^H$ is obtained from $\mathcal{R}$ by inductively closing under the compatibility properties (Com1)–(Com3) at the same time composing with $\mathcal{R}$ *on the right*. (This is needed to get the proof of the key Lemma 5.5.4 to go through.) So if we apply $(\_)^H$ to $\simeq_v$ we do not get a symmetric relation, therefore it cannot coincide with $\simeq_v$ and hence in particular we cannot hope to transfer the congruence properties of $(\simeq_v)^H$ to $\simeq_v$ in quite the same way that we did for applicative similarity. However, as Howe observed [How96, lemma 3.3], the transitive closure of $(\simeq_v)^H$ is a symmetric relation and this fact is sufficient to deduce congruence of $\simeq_v$ via $(\simeq_v)^H$. We will illustrate this refinement of the method by adding an 'erratic' *choice operator* ($\oplus$) to the call-by-value λ-calculus, which does indeed cause $\simeq_v$ to be different from $\lesssim_v \cap \lesssim_v^{op}$ (see Exercise 5.7.1).

Let the set $\Lambda^\oplus$ of $\lambda^\oplus$-*terms* and the subset $V^\oplus \subseteq \Lambda^\oplus$ of $\lambda^\oplus$-*values* consist of λ-terms and λ-values (modulo α-equivalence) extended with a binary operation $\oplus$:

$$e \in \Lambda^\oplus ::= v \mid e\,e \mid e \oplus e,$$
$$v \in V^\oplus ::= x \mid \lambda x.\,e.$$

(5.36)

We write $\Lambda^\oplus(\overline{x})$ (respectively, $V^\oplus(\overline{x})$) for the subset of $\lambda^\oplus$-terms (respectively, $\lambda^\oplus$-values) whose free variables are in the finite set $\overline{x}$ of variables. A $\lambda^\oplus$-*term relation* $\mathcal{R}$ is a family of binary relations $\overline{x} \vdash (\_) \mathcal{R} (\_)$ on $\Lambda^\oplus(\overline{x})$, as $\overline{x}$ ranges over $\wp_{\text{fin}}(Var)$ (cf. Definition 5.4.2). $\mathcal{R}$ is a *congruence* if it has the properties (Sym), (Tra), (Com1)–(Com3) and an additional compatibility property for the new term constructor:

$$\forall \overline{x} \in \wp_{\text{fin}}(Var).\, \forall e_1, e'_1, e_2, e'_2 \in \Lambda(\overline{x}).$$
$$\overline{x} \vdash e_1 \mathcal{R} e'_1 \wedge \overline{x} \vdash e_2 \mathcal{R} e'_2 \Rightarrow \overline{x} \vdash e_1 \oplus e_2 \mathcal{R} e'_1 \oplus e'_2. \quad \text{(Com4)}$$

(As before, satisfaction of (Com1)–(Com4) implies that $\mathcal{R}$ is reflexive; so a congruence is in particular an equivalence relation.)

We extend call-by-value evaluation to a relation $\Downarrow_v \subseteq \Lambda^\oplus(\emptyset) \times \Lambda^\oplus(\emptyset)$ by adding to (Val) and (Cbv) the two rules

$$\frac{e_i \Downarrow_v v}{e_1 \oplus e_2 \Downarrow_v v} \quad (i = 1, 2). \quad \text{(Ch)}$$

The definitions of call-by-value applicative similarity ($\lesssim_v$) and bisimilarity ($\simeq_v$) on closed $\lambda^\oplus$-terms are as in Definition 5.3.1 except that $\Lambda(\emptyset)$ is replaced by the extended set $\Lambda^\oplus(\emptyset)$; and these relations are extended to $\lambda^\oplus$-term relations as in Definition 5.4.1, using closed $\lambda^\oplus$-value-substitutions.

Exercise 5.7.1 Defining

$$v_1 \stackrel{\text{def}}{=} \lambda x.\, x$$
$$v_2 \stackrel{\text{def}}{=} \lambda y.\, ((\lambda x.\, x\, x)\,(\lambda x.\, x\, x))$$
$$v \stackrel{\text{def}}{=} \lambda z.\, (v_1 \oplus v_2)$$
$$e \stackrel{\text{def}}{=} v \oplus (\lambda z.\, v_1) \oplus (\lambda z.\, v_2),$$

show that $v \lesssim_v e \lesssim_v v$, but that $v \not\simeq_v e$. (Compare this with the examples in [San12, chapter 5], such as Exercise 5.8.11, showing the difference between trace equivalence and bisimilarity for labelled transition systems; recall that testing equivalence implies trace equivalence.)

We wish to prove that call-by-value applicative bisimilarity is a congruence for $\lambda^\oplus$-terms. We can still do so using Howe's precongruence candidate construction $(\_)^H$, which in this setting sends a $\lambda^\oplus$-term relation $\mathcal{R}$ to the $\lambda^\oplus$-term relation $\mathcal{R}^H$ inductively defined by the rules (How1)–(How3) from Section 5.5 together with an extra rule for the new binary operation, $\oplus$:

$$\frac{\bar{x} \vdash e_1 \; \mathcal{R}^H \; e_1' \qquad \bar{x} \vdash e_2 \; \mathcal{R}^H \; e_2' \qquad \bar{x} \vdash e_1' \oplus e_2' \; \mathcal{R} \; e_3}{\bar{x} \vdash e_1 \oplus e_2 \; \mathcal{R}^H \; e_3}. \qquad \text{(How4)}$$

The rule follows the same pattern as for the existing λ-calculus constructs and does not disturb the validity of the general properties of $(\_)^H$ given in Lemmas 5.5.1 and 5.5.3. More delicate is the analogue of the key Lemma 5.5.4, since it depends not only upon the syntactical form of $e \oplus e'$, but also upon its operational semantics, as defined by the rules (Ch).

Lemma 5.7.2 (Key lemma, version 2) *For all $e_1, \lambda x.e, e_2 \in \Lambda^\oplus(\emptyset)$*

$$e_1 \Downarrow_v \lambda x.e \;\wedge\; \emptyset \vdash e_1 \; (\simeq_v)^H \; e_2$$
$$\Rightarrow \exists e' \in \Lambda^\oplus.\; e_2 \Downarrow_v \lambda x.e' \;\wedge\; \{x\} \vdash e \; (\simeq_v)^H \; e'. \quad (5.37)$$

Proof This can be proved by showing that

$$\mathcal{E} \stackrel{\text{def}}{=} \{(e_1, \lambda x.e) \mid \forall e_2.\; \emptyset \vdash e_1 \; (\simeq_v)^H \; e_2$$
$$\Rightarrow \exists e'.\; e_2 \Downarrow_v \lambda x.e' \;\wedge\; \{x\} \vdash e \; (\simeq_v)^H \; e'\}$$

is closed under the rules (Val), (Cbv) and (Ch) inductively defining $\Downarrow_v$ for $\lambda^\oplus$-terms. The proof of closure under (Val) and (Cbv) is exactly as in the proof of Lemma 5.5.4. We give the proof of closure under the $i = 1$ case of (Ch), the argument for the other case being symmetric.

So suppose $(e_1, \lambda x.e) \in \mathcal{E}$. We have to show for any $e_1' \in \Lambda^\oplus(\emptyset)$ that $(e_1 \oplus e_1', \lambda x.e) \in \mathcal{E}$. For any e_2, if $\emptyset \vdash e_1 \oplus e_1' \; (\simeq_v)^H \; e_2$ holds it must have been deduced by an application of rule (How4) to

$$\emptyset \vdash e_1 \; (\simeq_v)^H \; e_3 \qquad\qquad (5.38)$$
$$\emptyset \vdash e_1' \; (\simeq_v)^H \; e_3' \qquad\qquad (5.39)$$
$$e_3 \oplus e_3' \simeq_v e_2 \qquad\qquad (5.40)$$

for some e_3, e_3'. Since $(e_1, \lambda x. e) \in \mathcal{E}$, it follows from (5.38) that for some e'' it is the case that

$$e_3 \Downarrow_v \lambda x. e'' \tag{5.41}$$

$$\overline{x} \vdash e \ (\simeq_v)^H \ e''. \tag{5.42}$$

Applying (Ch) to (5.41), we get $e_3 \oplus e_3' \Downarrow_v \lambda x. e''$. Since $\simeq_v$ is an applicative bisimulation, it follows from this and (5.40) that

$$e_2 \Downarrow_v \lambda x. e' \tag{5.43}$$

$$\overline{x} \vdash e'' \simeq_v e'. \tag{5.44}$$

Applying Lemma 5.5.1(ii) to (5.42) and (5.44), we get $\overline{x} \vdash e \ (\simeq_v)^H \ e'$. Therefore we do indeed have $(e_1 \oplus e_1', \lambda x. e) \in \mathcal{E}$. $\square$

The lemma implies that $(\simeq_v)^H$ is an applicative simulation; but to get the applicative *bi*simulation property we have to move to its transitive closure.

Definition 5.7.3 (Transitive closure) The *transitive closure* of a $\lambda^\oplus$-term relation $\mathcal{R}$, is the $\lambda^\oplus$-term relation $\mathcal{R}^+$ inductively defined by the rules

$$\frac{\overline{x} \vdash e \ \mathcal{R} \ e'}{\overline{x} \vdash e \ \mathcal{R}^+ \ e'} \qquad \frac{\overline{x} \vdash e \ \mathcal{R}^+ \ e' \qquad \overline{x} \vdash e' \ \mathcal{R}^+ \ e''}{\overline{x} \vdash e \ \mathcal{R}^+ \ e''}. \tag{TC}$$

Exercise 5.7.4 Show that if $\mathcal{R}$ is compatible, then so is $\mathcal{R}^+$. Show that if $\mathcal{R}$ is closed under value-substitution, then so is $\mathcal{R}^+$.

Lemma 5.7.5 *If a $\lambda^\oplus$-term relation $\mathcal{R}$ is an equivalence relation, then so is $(\mathcal{R}^H)^+$.*

Proof Being a transitive closure, $(\mathcal{R}^H)^+$ is of course transitive; and since $\mathcal{R}$ is reflexive, by Lemma 5.5.1(i) $\mathcal{R}^H$ is reflexive and hence so is $(\mathcal{R}^H)^+$. So the real issue is the symmetry property. To prove $\overline{x} \vdash e \ (\mathcal{R}^H)^+ \ e' \Rightarrow \overline{x} \vdash e' \ (\mathcal{R}^H)^+ \ e$, it suffices to prove

$$\overline{x} \vdash e \ \mathcal{R}^H \ e' \Rightarrow \overline{x} \vdash e' \ (\mathcal{R}^H)^+ \ e \tag{5.45}$$

and then argue by induction on the derivation of $\overline{x} \vdash e \ (\mathcal{R}^H)^+ \ e'$ from the rules (TC). To prove (5.45), one argues by induction on the derivation of $\overline{x} \vdash e \ \mathcal{R}^H \ e'$ from the rules (How1)–(How4), using Lemma 5.5.1(iii). In addition to that lemma, for closure under (How2)–(How4) one has to use the fact that $(\mathcal{R}^H)^+$ satisfies (Com2)–(Com4) respectively, which follows from Lemma 5.5.1(i) and Exercise 5.7.4. $\square$

Theorem 5.7.6 *Call-by-value applicative bisimilarity is a congruence relation for $\lambda^\oplus$-terms.*

Proof We show that $\simeq_v$ is equal to $((\simeq_v)^H)^+$. The former is an equivalence relation and the latter is a compatible $\lambda^\oplus$-term relation by Lemma 5.5.1(i) and Exercise 5.7.4; so altogether $\simeq_v = ((\simeq_v)^H)^+$ is a congruence relation.

We have $\simeq_v \subseteq (\simeq_v)^H \subseteq ((\simeq_v)^H)^+$ by Lemma 5.5.1(iii) and by definition of $(\_)^+$. For the reverse inclusion, since $((\simeq_v)^H)^+$ is closed under value-substitution (Lemma 5.5.3 and Exercise 5.7.4), it suffices to show that its restriction to closed $\lambda^\oplus$-terms is a call-by-value applicative bisimulation. From Lemma 5.7.2 we get

$$e_1 \Downarrow_v \lambda x.e \wedge \emptyset \vdash e_1 (\simeq_v)^H e_2$$
$$\Rightarrow \exists e' \in \Lambda^\oplus.\ e_2 \Downarrow_v \lambda x.e' \wedge \forall e'' \in \Lambda^\oplus(\emptyset).\ \emptyset \vdash e\{e''/x\} ((\simeq_v)^H)^+ e'\{e''/x\}$$

(using the fact that $((\simeq_v)^H)^+$ is closed under value-substitution and contains $\simeq_v{}^H$). Therefore

$$e_1 \Downarrow_v \lambda x.e \wedge \emptyset \vdash e_1 ((\simeq_v)^H)^+ e_2$$
$$\Rightarrow \exists e' \in \Lambda^\oplus.\ e_2 \Downarrow_v \lambda x.e' \wedge \forall e'' \in \Lambda^\oplus(\emptyset).\ \emptyset \vdash e\{e''/x\} ((\simeq_v)^H)^+ e'\{e''/x\}.$$

So $\emptyset \vdash (\_) ((\simeq_v)^H)^+ (\_)$ is an applicative simulation; and since by Lemma 5.7.5 it is a symmetric relation, it is in fact an applicative bisimulation, as required.

$\square$

5.8 CIU-equivalence

Howe's method has been applied most often in the literature to prove congruence properties of various kinds of bisimilarity. It is less well known that it also provides a useful method for proving congruence of 'CIU' equivalences. This form of equivalence was introduced by Mason and Talcott in their work on contextual equivalence of impure functional programs [MT91, MT92], but is prefigured by Milner's context lemma for contextual equivalence for the pure functional language PCF [Mil77]. In both cases the form of program equivalence of primary concern is the kind studied in Section 5.6, namely contextual equivalence. The quantification over all contexts that occurs in its definition (recall Definition 5.6.2) makes it hard to prove either specific instances of, or general properties of contextual equivalence. Therefore one seeks alternative characterisations of contextual equivalence that make such tasks easier. One approach is to prove a 'context lemma' to the effect that quantification over all contexts can be replaced by quantification over a restricted class of contexts without affecting the associated contextual equivalence. As we now explain, the coincidence of CIU-equivalence with contextual equivalence is exactly such a result.

We take the acronym 'CIU' to stand for a permutation of '*U*ses of *C*losed *I*nstantiations': the 'closed instantiations' part refers to the fact that CIU-equivalence is first defined on closed terms and then extended to open ones via closing substitutions (just as for applicative bisimulation in Definition 5.4.1); the 'uses' part refers to the fact that closed terms are identified when they have the same evaluation behaviour in any context that 'uses' its hole, that is, in any Felleisen-style *evaluation context* [FH92]. Thus CIU-equivalence is a form of contextual equivalence in which restrictions are placed upon the kind of contexts in which operational behaviour of program phrases is observed. The restrictions make it easier to establish some properties of CIU-equivalence compared with contextual equivalence itself, for which there are no restrictions upon the contexts. Once one has proved that CIU-equivalence is a congruence, it is straightforward to see that it actually coincides with contextual equivalence. Therefore the notion of CIU-equivalence is really a means of establishing properties of contextual equivalence, namely the ones that stem from the reduction properties of terms, such as those in Exercise 5.8.5.

We illustrate these ideas in this section by defining CIU-equivalence for call-by-value λ-calculus with erratic choice ($\oplus$), using Howe's method to prove that it is a congruence and hence that it coincides with contextual equivalence.

We will adopt the more abstract, relational approach to contextual equivalence outlined in Remark 5.6.7: the contextual preorder $\leq_v$ for the call-by-value $\lambda^{\oplus}$-calculus is the largest $\lambda^{\oplus}$-term relation that is both compatible (that is, satisfies (Com1)–(Com4)) and adequate (that is, satisfies (v-Adeq)). At the same time, rather than using Felleisen's notion of 'evaluation context', which in this case would be

$$E ::= [\cdot] \mid E\,e \mid v\,E,$$

we will use an 'inside out' representation of such contexts as a stack of basic *evaluation frames* (which in this case are $[\cdot]e$ and $v[\cdot]$). Such a representation of evaluation contexts yields a convenient, structurally inductive characterisation of the 'may evaluate to some value in call-by-value' property used in the definition of contextual equivalence (Lemma 5.8.3); see [Pit02, section 4] for a more detailed explanation of this point.

Definition 5.8.1 (Frame stacks) The set $Stk^{\oplus}$ of call-by-value *frame stacks* is given by

$$s \in Stk^{\oplus} ::= \mathtt{nil} \mid [\cdot]e :: s \mid v[\cdot] :: s. \qquad (5.46)$$

As for terms and values, we write $Stk^{\oplus}(\overline{x})$ for the subset of frame stacks whose free variables are in the finite set $\overline{x}$. Given $s \in Stk^{\oplus}(\overline{x})$ and $e \in \Lambda^{\oplus}(\overline{x})$, we get a term $E_s[e] \in \Lambda^{\oplus}(\overline{x})$, defined by:

$$\begin{cases} E_{\mathtt{nil}}[e] & \overset{\text{def}}{=} e \\ E_{[\cdot]e'::s}[e] & \overset{\text{def}}{=} E_s[e\,e'] \\ E_{v[\cdot]::s}[e] & \overset{\text{def}}{=} E_s[v\,e]. \end{cases} \tag{5.47}$$

Definition 5.8.2 (Transition and may-termination) The binary relation of call-by-value *transition* between pairs $(s\,,\,e)$ of frame stacks and closed $\lambda^{\oplus}$-terms

$$(s\,,\,e) \to_{\mathrm{v}} (s'\,,\,e')$$

is defined by cases as follows:

$$((\lambda x.\,e)[\cdot] :: s\,,\,v) \to_{\mathrm{v}} (s\,,\,e\{v/x\}) \tag{$\to_{\mathrm{v}}1$}$$

$$([\cdot]e :: s\,,\,v) \to_{\mathrm{v}} (v[\cdot] :: s\,,\,e) \tag{$\to_{\mathrm{v}}2$}$$

$$(s\,,\,e\,e') \to_{\mathrm{v}} ([\cdot]e' :: s\,,\,e) \tag{$\to_{\mathrm{v}}3$}$$

$$(s\,,\,e_1 \oplus e_2) \to_{\mathrm{v}} (s\,,\,e_i) \qquad \text{for } i = 1, 2. \tag{$\to_{\mathrm{v}}4$}$$

We write $(s\,,\,e) \downarrow_{\mathrm{v}}^{(n)}$ if for some closed value $v \in V^{\oplus}(\emptyset)$ there exists a sequence of transitions $(s\,,\,e) \to_{\mathrm{v}} \cdots \to_{\mathrm{v}} (\mathtt{nil}\,,\,v)$ of length less than or equal to n; and we write $(s\,,\,e) \downarrow_{\mathrm{v}}$ and say that $(s\,,\,e)$ *may terminate* if $(s\,,\,e) \downarrow_{\mathrm{v}}^{(n)}$ holds for some $n \geq 0$.

The relationship between this termination relation and 'may evaluate to some value in call-by-value', $e \Downarrow_{\mathrm{v}} \overset{\text{def}}{=} \exists v.\ e \Downarrow_{\mathrm{v}} v$, is as follows.

Lemma 5.8.3 *For all closed frame stacks $s \in Stk^{\oplus}(\emptyset)$ and closed $\lambda^{\oplus}$-terms $e \in \Lambda^{\oplus}(\emptyset)$, $(s\,,\,e) \downarrow_{\mathrm{v}}$ iff $E_s[e] \Downarrow_{\mathrm{v}}$. In particular $e \Downarrow_{\mathrm{v}}$ holds iff $(\mathtt{nil}\,,\,e) \downarrow_{\mathrm{v}}$.*

Proof The result can be deduced from the following properties of transition, evaluation and termination, where $\to_{\mathrm{v}}^*$ stands for the reflexive-transitive closure of $\to_{\mathrm{v}}$ and $(\_) @ (\_)$ stands for the operation of appending two lists.

$$(s'\,,\,E_s[e]) \to_{\mathrm{v}}^* (s @ s'\,,\,e) \tag{5.48}$$

$$(s'\,,\,E_s[e]) \downarrow_{\mathrm{v}} \Rightarrow (s @ s'\,,\,e) \downarrow_{\mathrm{v}} \tag{5.49}$$

$$e \Downarrow_{\mathrm{v}} v \Rightarrow (s\,,\,e) \to_{\mathrm{v}}^* (s\,,\,v) \tag{5.50}$$

$$(s\,,\,e) \downarrow_{\mathrm{v}}^{(n)} \Rightarrow \exists v.\ e \Downarrow_{\mathrm{v}} v \wedge (s\,,\,v) \downarrow_{\mathrm{v}}^{(n)}. \tag{5.51}$$

Properties (5.48) and (5.49) are proved by induction on the length of the list s; (5.50) by induction on the derivation of $e \Downarrow_v v$; and (5.51) by induction on n (and then by cases according to the structure of e).

Therefore if $\langle s, e \rangle \downarrow_v$, then $\langle \texttt{nil}, E_s[e] \rangle \downarrow_v$ by (5.48) and hence $E_s[e] \Downarrow_v$ by (5.51). Conversely, if $E_s[e] \Downarrow_v v$, then $\langle \texttt{nil}, E_s[e] \rangle \downarrow_v$ by (5.50) and hence $\langle s, e \rangle \downarrow_v$ by (5.49). □

Definition 5.8.4 (CIU-equivalence) Given $e, e' \in \Lambda^\oplus(\emptyset)$, we define

$$e \leq_v^{\mathrm{ciu}} e' \stackrel{\mathrm{def}}{\Leftrightarrow} \forall s \in Stk^\oplus(\emptyset). \ \langle s, e \rangle \downarrow_v \Rightarrow \langle s, e' \rangle \downarrow_v.$$

This is extended to a $\lambda^\oplus$-term relation, called the (call-by-value) *CIU-preorder*, via closing value-substitutions:

$$\overline{x} \vdash e \leq_v^{\mathrm{ciu}} e' \stackrel{\mathrm{def}}{\Leftrightarrow} \forall v_1, \ldots, v_n \in V^\oplus(\emptyset).$$
$$e\{v_1, \ldots, v_n/x_1, \ldots, x_n\} \leq_v^{\mathrm{ciu}} e'\{v_1, \ldots, v_n/x_1, \ldots, x_n\}$$

(where $\overline{x} = \{x_1, \ldots, x_n\}$). *CIU-equivalence* is the symmetrisation of this relation:

$$\overline{x} \vdash e =_v^{\mathrm{ciu}} e' \stackrel{\mathrm{def}}{\Leftrightarrow} \overline{x} \vdash e \leq_v^{\mathrm{ciu}} e' \wedge \overline{x} \vdash e' \leq_v^{\mathrm{ciu}} e'.$$

It is clear from its definition that the $\lambda^\oplus$-term relation $\leq_v^{\mathrm{ciu}}$ is a preorder (reflexive and transitive) and hence that $=_v^{\mathrm{ciu}}$ is an equivalence relation.

Exercise 5.8.5 Show that β_v-equivalence holds up to $=_v^{\mathrm{ciu}}$:

$$\overline{x} \vdash (\lambda x. e) v =_v^{\mathrm{ciu}} e\{v/x\}.$$

Show that $e_1 \oplus e_2$ is the least upper bound of e_1 and e_2 with respect to the CIU-preorder, $\leq_v^{\mathrm{ciu}}$.

We will use Howe's method to show that $\leq_v^{\mathrm{ciu}}$ is a compatible $\lambda^\oplus$-term relation and deduce that it coincides with the contextual preorder (and hence that $=_v^{\mathrm{ciu}}$ coincides with contextual equivalence). As for previous applications of Howe's method, we know that $(\leq_v^{\mathrm{ciu}})^H$ is a compatible $\lambda^\oplus$-term relation containing $\leq_v^{\mathrm{ciu}}$ (Lemma 5.5.1). So for compatibility of $\leq_v^{\mathrm{ciu}}$, we just need to show $(\leq_v^{\mathrm{ciu}})^H \subseteq \leq_v^{\mathrm{ciu}}$. Since $\leq_v^{\mathrm{ciu}}$ is defined on open terms by taking closing value-substitutions, both it and $(\leq_v^{\mathrm{ciu}})^H$ are closed under value-substitution (Lemma 5.5.3); so it suffices to show for closed $\lambda^\oplus$-terms that

$$\emptyset \vdash e \ (\leq_v^{\mathrm{ciu}})^H \ e' \Rightarrow e \leq_v^{\mathrm{ciu}} e'$$

that is,

$$\emptyset \vdash e \ (\leq_v^{\mathrm{ciu}})^H \ e' \wedge \langle s, e \rangle \downarrow_v \Rightarrow \langle s, e' \rangle \downarrow_v.$$

We do this by proving the following analogue of the key Lemma 5.5.4. It uses an extension of the Howe precongruence candidate construction $(\_)^H$ to (closed) frame stacks: given a $\lambda^\oplus$-term relation $\mathcal{R}$, the relation $s \; \mathcal{R}^H \; s'$ is inductively defined by:

$$\frac{}{\text{nil } \mathcal{R}^H \text{ nil}} \qquad \frac{\emptyset \vdash e \; \mathcal{R}^H \; e' \qquad s \; \mathcal{R}^H \; s'}{[\cdot]e :: s \; \mathcal{R}^H \; [\cdot]e' :: s'}$$

$$\frac{\{x\} \vdash e \; \mathcal{R}^H \; e' \qquad s \; \mathcal{R}^H \; s'}{(\lambda x.e)[\cdot] :: s \; \mathcal{R}^H \; (\lambda x.e')[\cdot] :: s'}. \qquad \text{(How-Stk)}$$

Lemma 5.8.6 (Key lemma, version 3)

$$\forall s, e, s', e'. \; s \; (\leq_v^{\text{ciu}})^H \; s' \wedge \emptyset \vdash e \; (\leq_v^{\text{ciu}})^H \; e' \wedge (s \, , \, e) \downarrow_v^{(n)} \Rightarrow (s' \, , \, e') \downarrow_v. \tag{5.52}$$

Proof The proof is by induction on n. The base case $n = 0$ is straightforward, so we concentrate on the induction step. Assume (5.52) holds and that

$$s_1 \; (\leq_v^{\text{ciu}})^H \; s' \tag{5.53}$$

$$\emptyset \vdash e_1 \; (\leq_v^{\text{ciu}})^H \; e' \tag{5.54}$$

$$(s_1 \, , \, e_1) \to_v (s_2 \, , \, e_2) \tag{5.55}$$

$$(s_2 \, , \, e_2) \downarrow_v^{(n)}. \tag{5.56}$$

We have to show that $(s' \, , \, e') \downarrow_v$ and do so by analysing (5.55) against the four possible cases $(\to_v 1)$–$(\to_v 4)$ in the definition of the transition relation.

Case $(\to_v 1)$: So $s_1 = (\lambda x.e)[\cdot] :: s_2$, $e_1 = \lambda x.e_1'$ and $e_2 = e\{\lambda x.e_1'/x\}$, for some x, e and e_1'. Thus (5.53) must have been deduced by applying (Howe-Stk) to

$$\{x\} \vdash e \; (\leq_v^{\text{ciu}})^H \; e' \tag{5.57}$$

$$s_2 \; (\leq_v^{\text{ciu}})^H \; s_2' \tag{5.58}$$

where $(\lambda x.e')[\cdot] :: s_2' = s'$. Since $e_1 = \lambda x.e_1'$, (5.54) must have been deduced by an application of (How2) to

$$\{x\} \vdash e_1' \; (\leq_v^{\text{ciu}})^H \; e_1'' \tag{5.59}$$

$$\lambda x.e_1'' \leq_v^{\text{ciu}} e' \tag{5.60}$$

for some e_1''. From Lemma 5.5.3 we have that $(\leq_v^{\text{ciu}})^H$ is substitutive; so since (5.59) implies $\emptyset \vdash \lambda x.e_1' \; (\leq_v^{\text{ciu}})^H \; \lambda x.e_1''$, from this and (5.57) we get $\emptyset \vdash e\{\lambda x.e_1'/x\} \; (\leq_v^{\text{ciu}})^H \; e'\{\lambda x.e_1''/x\}$, that is, $\emptyset \vdash e_2 \; (\leq_v^{\text{ciu}})^H \; e'\{\lambda x.e_1''/x\}$. Applying the induction hypothesis (5.52) to this, (5.58) and (5.56) gives $(s_2' \, , \, e'\{\lambda x.e_1''/x\}) \downarrow_v$ and hence also $((\lambda x.e')[\cdot] :: s_2' \, , \, \lambda x.e_1'') \downarrow_v$. From this and

(5.60) we get $((\lambda x. e')[\cdot] :: s_2' , e') \downarrow_v$. In other words $(s' , e') \downarrow_v$, as required for the induction step.

Case $(\rightarrow_v 2)$: So $s_1 = [\cdot]e_2 :: s$, $e_1 = \lambda x. e_1'$ and $s_2 = (\lambda x. e_1')[\cdot] :: s$, for some s, x and e_1'. Thus (5.53) must have been deduced by applying (How-Stk) to

$$s \ (\leq_v^{ciu})^H \ s_2' \tag{5.61}$$

$$\emptyset \vdash e_2 \ (\leq_v^{ciu})^H \ e_2' \tag{5.62}$$

$$\tag{5.63}$$

where $[\cdot]e_2' :: s_2' = s'$. Since $e_1 = \lambda x. e_1'$, (5.54) must have been deduced by an application of (How2) to

$$\{x\} \vdash e_1' \ (\leq_v^{ciu})^H \ e_1'' \tag{5.64}$$

$$\lambda x. e_1'' \leq_v^{ciu} e' \tag{5.65}$$

for some e_1''. By (How-Stk) on (5.61) and (5.64), we get $s_2 \ (\leq_v^{ciu})^H \ (\lambda x. e_1'')[\cdot] :: s_2'$. Applying the induction hypothesis (5.52) to this, (5.62) and (5.56) gives $((\lambda x. e_1'')[\cdot] :: s_2' , e_2') \downarrow_v$ and hence also $([\cdot]e_2' :: s_2' , \lambda x. e_1'') \downarrow_v$. From this and (5.65) we get $([\cdot]e_2' :: s_2' , e') \downarrow_v$. In other words $(s' , e') \downarrow_v$, as required for the induction step.

Case $(\rightarrow_v 3)$: So $e_1 = e_2 e$ and $s_2 = [\cdot]e :: s_1$, for some e. Thus (5.54) must have been deduced by applying (How3) to

$$\emptyset \vdash e_2 \ (\leq_v^{ciu})^H \ e_2'' \tag{5.66}$$

$$\emptyset \vdash e \ (\leq_v^{ciu})^H \ e'' \tag{5.67}$$

$$e_2'' e'' \leq_v^{ciu} e' \tag{5.68}$$

for some e_2'' and e''. Applying (How-Stk) to (5.67) and (5.53) we get $s_2 \ (\leq_v^{ciu})^H$ $[\cdot]e'' :: s'$. Applying the induction hypothesis (5.52) to this, (5.66) and (5.56) gives $([\cdot]e'' :: s' , e_2'') \downarrow_v$ and hence also $(s' , e_2'' e'') \downarrow_v$. From this and (5.68) we get $(s' , e') \downarrow_v$, as required for the induction step.

Case $(\rightarrow_v 4)$: We treat the $i = 1$ subcase of $(\rightarrow_v 4)$, the argument for the $i = 2$ subcase being symmetric. So $s_1 = s_2$ and $e_1 = e_2 \oplus e$, for some e. Thus (5.54) must have been deduced by applying (How4) to

$$\emptyset \vdash e_2 \ (\leq_v^{ciu})^H \ e_2'' \tag{5.69}$$

$$\emptyset \vdash e \ (\leq_v^{ciu})^H \ e'' \tag{5.70}$$

$$e_2'' \oplus e'' \leq_v^{ciu} e'$$

for some e_2'' and e''. Since $s_1 = s_2$, we can apply the induction hypothesis (5.52) to (5.53), (5.69) and (5.56) to conclude that $(s' , e_2'') \downarrow_v$ and hence also that

$\langle s'\, , \, e_2'' \oplus e' \rangle \downarrow_v$. From this and (5.70) we get $\langle s'\, , \, e' \rangle \downarrow_v$, as required for the induction step.   □

Theorem 5.8.7 (CIU-equivalence is contextual equivalence) *For all $\overline{x} \in$ $\wp_{\text{fin}}(\text{Var})$ and $e_1, e_2 \in \Lambda^{\oplus}(\overline{x})$, $\overline{x} \vdash e_1 \leq_v^{\text{ciu}} e_2$ iff $\overline{x} \vdash e_1 \leq_v e_2$ (and hence $\overline{x} \vdash e_1 =_v^{\text{ciu}} e_2$ iff $\overline{x} \vdash e_1 =_v e_2$).*

Proof Since $\leq_v^{\text{ciu}}$ is reflexive, so is the $\lambda^{\oplus}$-term relation $(\leq_v^{\text{ciu}})^H$ and hence so is its extension to closed frame stacks. So we can take $s = s'$ in Lemma 5.8.6 and conclude that $\emptyset \vdash e \,(\leq_v^{\text{ciu}})^H\, e' \;\Rightarrow\; e \leq_v^{\text{ciu}} e'$. As we remarked before the lemma, this is enough to show that $(\leq_v^{\text{ciu}})^H = \,\leq_v^{\text{ciu}}$ and hence that $\leq_v^{\text{ciu}}$ is compatible. It is immediate from Lemma 5.8.3 that it satisfies the adequacy property (v-Adeq) from Remark 5.6.7. So $\leq_v^{\text{ciu}}$ is contained in the largest compatible adequate $\lambda^{\oplus}$-term relation:

$$\overline{x} \vdash e \leq_v^{\text{ciu}} e' \;\Rightarrow\; \overline{x} \vdash e \leq_v e'. \tag{5.71}$$

To prove the converse of this, first note that since the contextual preorder is compatible, if $\emptyset \vdash e \leq_v e'$ then $\emptyset \vdash E_s[e] \leq_v E_s[e']$ (by induction on the length of the list s, using (5.47)); hence by adequacy of $\leq_v$ and Lemma 5.8.3 we have

$$\emptyset \vdash e \leq_v e' \;\Rightarrow\; \emptyset \vdash e \leq_v^{\text{ciu}} e'.$$

So if $\overline{x} \vdash e \leq_v e'$, then by compatibility of $\leq_v$ we have $\emptyset \vdash \lambda \overline{x}.\,e \leq_v \lambda \overline{x}.\,e'$ and hence also $\emptyset \vdash \lambda \overline{x}.\,e \leq_v^{\text{ciu}} \lambda \overline{x}.\,e'$. Then supposing $\overline{x} = \{x_1, \ldots, x_n\}$, for any closed values $v_1, \ldots, v_n$, we can use the compatibility of $\leq_v^{\text{ciu}}$ (established in the first part of this proof) together with the validity of β_v-equivalence (Exercise 5.8.5) to get $\emptyset \vdash e\{v_1, \ldots, v_n/x_1, \ldots, x_n\} \leq_v^{\text{ciu}} e'\{v_1, \ldots, v_n/x_1, \ldots, x_n\}$. Therefore we do indeed have that $\overline{x} \vdash e \leq_v e'$ implies $\overline{x} \vdash e \leq_v^{\text{ciu}} e'$.   □

Remark 5.8.8 Theorem 5.8.7 serves to establish some basic properties of contextual equivalence for the call-by-value $\lambda^{\oplus}$-calculus (such as β_v-equivalence, via Exercise 5.8.5). Nevertheless, in this call-by-value setting its usefulness is somewhat limited.[6] This is because of the presence in frame stacks of evaluation frames of the form $(\lambda x.\,e)[\cdot]$. For closed values v we have $(\lambda x.\,e)v \Downarrow_v$ iff $e\{v/x\} \Downarrow_v$; so testing may-termination with respect to such evaluation frames is essentially the same as testing may-termination in an arbitrary context. In the call-by-name setting the CIU theorem gives a more useful characterisation of contextual equivalence; see Example 5.9.1. Nevertheless, such 'context

---

[6] In fact the properties of $=_v$ for this calculus are rather subtle. For example, it is possible to show that $\lesssim_v \cap \lesssim_v^{op}$ is strictly contained in $=_v$: the untyped nature of the calculus means there are expressions with unbounded non-deterministic behaviour (via the usual encoding of fixpoint recursion and arithmetic), thereby allowing one to encode Lassen's example separating mutual similarity from contextual equivalence [Las98b, pp. 72 and 90].

lemmas' cannot help us with deeper properties that a contextual equivalence may have (such as the extensionality and representation independence results considered in [Pit02]), where bisimilarities, logical relations and related notions come into their own. However, the weakness of CIU theorems is also their strength; because they only give a weak characterisation of contextual equivalence, they seem to hold (and are relatively easy to prove via Howe's method) in the presence of a very wide range of programming language features where other more subtle analyses are not easily available or are more troublesome to develop; see [PS08, appendix A], for example.

5.9 Call-by-name equivalences

In this section we consider briefly the call-by-name version of the results described so far. Apart from changing the evaluation relation and using arbitrary substitutions instead of value-substitutions, the essential features of Howe's method for proving congruence results remains the same.

Syntax We will use the $\lambda^{\oplus}$-calculus from Section 5.7, that is, the untyped λ-calculus extended with erratic choice, $\oplus$. Recall from there that a $\lambda^{\oplus}$-term relation is *compatible* if it satisfies (Com1)–(Com4); is a *precongruence* if it is compatible and satisfies (Tra); and is a *congruence* if it is a precongruence and satisfies (Sym). Howe's 'precongruence candidate' construction is similarly unchanged: it sends a $\lambda^{\oplus}$-term relation $\mathcal{R}$ to the $\lambda^{\oplus}$-term relation $\mathcal{R}^H$ inductively defined by rules (How1)–(How4).

Operational semantics *Call-by-name evaluation* of closed $\lambda^{\oplus}$-terms is the binary relation $\Downarrow_n \subseteq \Lambda^{\oplus}(\emptyset) \times V^{\oplus}(\emptyset)$ inductively defined by the rules

$$\frac{}{v \Downarrow_n v} \tag{Val}$$

$$\frac{e_1 \Downarrow_n \lambda x.e \qquad e\{e_2/x\} \Downarrow_n v}{e_1\, e_2 \Downarrow_n v} \tag{Cbn}$$

$$\frac{e_i \Downarrow_n v}{e_1 \oplus e_2 \Downarrow_n v}. \quad (i=1,2) \tag{Ch}$$

The *call-by-name transition relation*, $(s\,,\,e) \to_n (s'\,,\,e')$, is given by

$$([\cdot]e' :: s\,,\,\lambda x.e) \to_n (s\,,\,e\{e'/x\}) \tag{$\to_n 1$}$$

$$(s\,,\,e\,e') \to_n ([\cdot]e' :: s\,,\,e) \tag{$\to_n 2$}$$

$$(s\,,\,e_1 \oplus e_2) \to_n (s\,,\,e_i) \qquad \text{for } i = 1, 2 \tag{$\to_n 3$}$$

where now s ranges over *call-by-name frame stacks*

$$s ::= \text{nil} \mid [\cdot]e :: s. \tag{5.72}$$

Defining

$$e\Downarrow_n \overset{\text{def}}{=} \exists v \in V^\oplus(\emptyset).\ e\Downarrow_n v \tag{5.73}$$

$$(s\ ,\ e)\downarrow_n \overset{\text{def}}{=} \exists v \in V^\oplus(\emptyset).\ (s\ ,\ e) \to_n \cdots \to_n (\text{nil}\ ,\ v) \tag{5.74}$$

the analogue of Lemma 5.8.3 holds and in particular we have

$$e\Downarrow_n \iff (\text{nil}\ ,\ e)\downarrow_n. \tag{5.75}$$

Applicative (bi)similarity A relation $\mathcal{S} \subseteq \Lambda^\oplus(\emptyset) \times \Lambda^\oplus(\emptyset)$ is a *call-by-name applicative simulation* if for all $e_1, e_2 \in \Lambda^\oplus(\emptyset)$, $e_1\ \mathcal{S}\ e_2$ implies

$$e_1 \Downarrow_n \lambda x. e_1' \implies \exists e_2'.\ e_2 \Downarrow_n \lambda x. e_2' \wedge \forall e \in \Lambda^\oplus(\emptyset).\ e_1'\{e/x\}\ \mathcal{S}\ e_2'\{e/x\}. \tag{n-Sim}$$

We write $\lesssim_n$ for the largest such relation and call it *call-by-name applicative similarity*. A relation $\mathcal{B} \subseteq \Lambda^\oplus(\emptyset) \times \Lambda^\oplus(\emptyset)$ is a call-by-name applicative *bisimulation* if both $\mathcal{B}$ and its reciprocal $\mathcal{B}^{op}$ are call-by-name applicative simulations. We write $\simeq_n$ for the largest such relation and call it *call-by-name applicative bisimilarity*. We extend $\lesssim_n$ and $\simeq_n$ to $\lambda^\oplus$-term relations via closing substitutions:

$$\overline{x} \vdash e \lesssim_n e' \overset{\text{def}}{=} \forall e_1, \ldots, e_n \in \Lambda^\oplus(\emptyset).$$
$$e\{e_1, \ldots, e_n/x_1, \ldots, x_n\} \lesssim_n e\{e_1, \ldots, e_n/x_1, \ldots, x_n\} \tag{5.76}$$

$$\overline{x} \vdash e \simeq_n e' \overset{\text{def}}{=} \forall e_1, \ldots, e_n \in \Lambda^\oplus(\emptyset).$$
$$e\{e_1, \ldots, e_n/x_1, \ldots, x_n\} \simeq_n e\{e_1, \ldots, e_n/x_1, \ldots, x_n\} \tag{5.77}$$

(where $\overline{x} = \{x_1, \ldots, x_n\}$).

With these definitions, the proof that $\lesssim_n$ is a precongruence and that $\simeq_n$ is a congruence proceeds as before, by using Howe's method to show that these $\lambda^\oplus$-term relations are compatible. For $\mathcal{R} = \lesssim_n$ or $\mathcal{R} = \simeq_n$ one proves the key lemma

$$e_1 \Downarrow_n \lambda x. e \wedge \emptyset \vdash e_1\ \mathcal{R}^H\ e_2 \implies \exists e'.\ e_2 \Downarrow_n \lambda x. e' \wedge \{x\} \vdash e\ \mathcal{R}^H\ e' \tag{5.78}$$

by induction on the derivation of $e_1 \Downarrow_n \lambda x. e$. In case $\mathcal{R} = \lesssim_n$, this gives $\lesssim_n = (\lesssim_n)^H$ and so $\lesssim_n$ inherits the compatibility property from $(\lesssim_n)^H$. In case $\mathcal{R} = \simeq_n$, one uses the transitive closure trick from Section 5.7 to deduce from

(5.78) that $\simeq_n = ((\lesssim_n)^H)^+$ and so $\simeq_n$ inherits the compatibility property from $((\simeq_n)^H)^+$.

Contextual equivalence Taking the relational approach outlined in Remark 5.6.7, we can define the *call-by-name contextual preorder*, $=_n$, to be the largest $\lambda^\oplus$-term relation $\mathcal{R}$ that is both compatible and *adequate for call-by-name evaluation*:

$$\forall e.e' \in \Lambda^\oplus(\emptyset). \ \emptyset \vdash e \, \mathcal{R} \, e' \implies (e \Downarrow_n \implies e' \Downarrow_n) \qquad \text{(n-Adeq)}$$

(with the proviso that the existence of a largest such relation is not immediately obvious, but can be deduced as in the remark). *Call-by-name contextual equivalence* is the symmetrisation of this preorder: $=_n \overset{\text{def}}{=} \leq_n \cap \leq_n^{op}$.

CIU-equivalence Two closed $\lambda^\oplus$-terms are in the *call-by-name CIU-preorder*, $e \leq_n^{ciu} e'$, if for all call-by-name frame stacks s we have that $(s \,, e) \downarrow_n$ implies $(s \,, e') \downarrow_n$. This is extended to a $\lambda^\oplus$-term relation via closing substitutions:

$$\overline{x} \vdash e \leq_n^{ciu} e' \overset{\text{def}}{=} \forall e_1, \ldots, e_n \in \Lambda^\oplus(\emptyset).$$
$$e\{e_1, \ldots, e_n/x_1, \ldots, x_n\} \leq_n^{ciu} e'\{e_1, \ldots, e_n/x_1, \ldots, x_n\}$$

(where $\overline{x} = \{x_1, \ldots, x_n\}$). *Call-by-name CIU-equivalence* is the symmetrisation of this relation: $=_n^{ciu} \overset{\text{def}}{=} \leq_n^{ciu} \cap (\leq_n^{ciu})^{op}$.

The proof that $\leq_n^{ciu}$ is compatible is via the key lemma

$$\forall s, e, s', e'. \ s \, (\leq_n^{ciu})^H \, s' \wedge \emptyset \vdash e \, (\leq_n^{ciu})^H \, e' \wedge (s \,, e) \downarrow_n^{(n)} \implies (s' \,, e') \downarrow_n \tag{5.79}$$

which, like Lemma 5.8.6, is proved by induction on the number n of steps of transition in $(s \,, e) \downarrow_n^{(n)}$ and then by cases on the definition of the call-by-name transition relation $\to_n$.

Compatibility of $\leq_n^{ciu}$ gives the call-by-name *CIU-theorem*:

$$\leq_n^{ciu} = \leq_n \qquad \text{and} \qquad =_n^{ciu} = =_n \tag{5.80}$$

as in the proof of Theorem 5.8.7, except that one uses validity of β-equivalence

$$\overline{x} \vdash (\lambda x. e)e' =_n^{ciu} e\{e'/x\} \tag{5.81}$$

rather than β_v-equivalence. Because call-by-name frame stacks have a rather simple form (they are just a list of closed terms waiting to be applied as arguments for a function), this CIU-theorem is more useful than the call-by-value version. The following example illustrates this.

Example 5.9.1 It is not hard to see that $\lambda x_1. \lambda x_2. (x_1 \oplus x_2) \not\lesssim_n (\lambda x_1. \lambda x_2. x_1) \oplus (\lambda x_1. \lambda x_2. x_2)$. However, it is the case that

$$\lambda x_1. \lambda x_2. (x_1 \oplus x_2) \lesssim_n (\lambda x_1. \lambda x_2. x_1) \oplus (\lambda x_1. \lambda x_2. x_2) \qquad (5.82)$$

(indeed the two terms are contextually equivalent). This can be shown by appealing to the CIU-theorem and checking that

$$(s , \lambda x_1. \lambda x_2. (x_1 \oplus x_2)) \downarrow_n \Rightarrow (s , (\lambda x_1. \lambda x_2. x_1) \oplus (\lambda x_1. \lambda x_2. x_2)) \downarrow_n \qquad (5.83)$$

holds for all call-by-name frame stacks s. For if $s = \mathtt{nil}$ or $s = [\cdot]e :: \mathtt{nil}$, then the right-hand side of the implication in (5.83) holds. Whereas if $s = [\cdot]e_1 :: [\cdot]e_2 :: s'$ is a frame stack of length two or more, then the first three transitions of each configuration are

$$(s , \lambda x_1. \lambda x_2. (x_1 \oplus x_2)) \to_n \cdot \to_n (s' , e_1 \oplus e_2) \to_n (s' , e_i)$$
$$(s , (\lambda x_1. \lambda x_2. x_1) \oplus (\lambda x_1. \lambda x_2. x_2)) \to_n (s , \lambda x_1. \lambda x_2. x_i) \to_n \cdot \to_n (s' , e_i)$$

for $i = 1, 2$; and hence

$$([\cdot]e_1 :: [\cdot]e_2 :: s' , \lambda x_1. \lambda x_2. (x_1 \oplus x_2)) \downarrow_n$$
$$\Rightarrow (s' , e_1) \downarrow_n \vee (s' , e_2) \downarrow_n$$
$$\Rightarrow ([\cdot]e_1 :: [\cdot]e_2 :: s' , (\lambda x_1. \lambda x_2. x_1) \oplus (\lambda x_1. \lambda x_2. x_2)) \downarrow_n.$$

Remark 5.9.2 The relationship between the various call-by-name equivalences considered in this section is:

$$(\simeq_n) \subsetneq (\lesssim_n \cap \lesssim_n^{op}) \subsetneq (=_n) = (=_n^{ciu}).$$

The first inclusion is a consequence of the definition of applicative (bi)similarity; it is proper because of Example 5.7.1 (which works the same for call-by-name as for call-by-value). The second inclusion is a corollary of the compatibility property for $\lesssim_n$; and Example 5.9.1 shows that it is strict.

Exercise 5.9.3 Show that unlike for call-by-name contextual equivalence, the terms $\lambda x_1. \lambda x_2. (x_1 \oplus x_2)$ and $(\lambda x_1. \lambda x_2. x_1) \oplus (\lambda x_1. \lambda x_2. x_2)$ are not call-by-value contextually equivalent. [Hint: consider the call-by-value evaluation behaviour of $t(\lambda x_1. \lambda x_2. (x_1 \oplus x_2))$ and $t((\lambda x_1. \lambda x_2. x_1) \oplus (\lambda x_1. \lambda x_2. x_2))$, where $t \overset{\text{def}}{=} \lambda z. z z v_2 v_2 v_1 v_1$ with v_1 and v_2 as in Example 5.7.1.]

5.10 Summary

Having seen Howe's method in action in a few different settings, let us summarise what it involves.

(1) One has a notion $\mathcal{R}$ of program equivalence or preordering that one wishes to show is compatible with the constructs of the programming language:

$$P_1 \mathrel{\mathcal{R}} P_2 \;\Rightarrow\; C[P_1] \mathrel{\mathcal{R}} C[P_2].$$

Higher-order features of the language make a direct proof difficult, often because any proof of compatibility requires a proof of a closely related substitutivity property

$$P_1 \mathrel{\mathcal{R}} P_2 \;\Rightarrow\; P\{P_1/x\} \mathrel{\mathcal{R}} P\{P_2/x\}$$

(maybe with some restriction as to what P_1 and P_2 range over).

(2) Howe's precongruence candidate construction builds a relation $\mathcal{R}^H$ that is easily seen to have the required compatibility and substitutivity properties. In the case when $\mathcal{R}$ is a preorder, we get the desired properties of $\mathcal{R}$ by showing $\mathcal{R} = \mathcal{R}^H$. In the case when $\mathcal{R}$ is an equivalence, we get the desired properties of $\mathcal{R}$ by showing that it is equal to the transitive closure $(\mathcal{R}^H)^+$ of the precongruence candidate. (Use of transitive closure overcomes the inherent asymmetry in the definition of $\mathcal{R}^H$.)

(3) The key step in proving $\mathcal{R} = \mathcal{R}^H$ or $\mathcal{R} = (\mathcal{R}^H)^+$ is to show that $\mathcal{R}^H$ is contained in $\mathcal{R}$. This involves a delicate proof by induction over the operational semantics of programs.

5.11 Assessment

Howe's method was originally developed to prove congruence properties of bisimilarities for untyped functional languages. The method has since been successfully applied to bisimilarities for higher-order languages with types [Gor95, Pit97b], objects [Gor98], local state [JR99] and concurrent communication [FHJ98, Bal98, GH05].

The transfer of the method from functions to process calculi has highlighted a couple of drawbacks of Howe's method, the first more important than the second.

First, the operational semantics of processes is usually specified in terms of transitions labelled with actions, rather than in terms of evaluation to canonical form. Evaluation-based applicative bisimilarities correspond to transition-based *delay bisimilarities* in which externally observable actions are matched by actions preceded by a number of internal ('silent') actions; see [San12, chapter 4]. Howe's method works well for proving congruence properties for such delay bisimilarities; but it does not appear to work for the more common *weak bisimilarities* in which externally observable actions are matched by actions both preceded and followed by a number of internal actions. For these reasons Jeffrey and Rathke [JR00] advocate replacing Howe's method with the use of Sangiorgi's trigger semantics from the higher-order π-calculus [San96]; see also [JR05, appendix A]. Another more recent approach uses the notion of *environment bisimulation* introduced by Sangiorgi, Kobayashi and Sumii [SKS07, Sum09], who show how to obtain congruence (and 'bisimilarity up to') results for higher-order languages without the need to invoke Howe's method.

Secondly, the induction proof in step (3) of the method (that is, 'key lemmas' like Lemma 5.7.2) relies heavily on the syntax-directed nature of the definition of the precongruence candidate $\mathcal{R}^H$; this does not interact well with a quotient by a structural congruence that sometimes forms part of the operational semantics of processes; see [PR98], for example.

Despite these caveats, Howe's method is unusually robust compared with many techniques based on operational semantics, witnessed by the fact that it can be applied to prove congruence properties for a variety of different forms of program equivalence. We believe it deserves a place in the semanticist's tool kit.

Bibliography

[Abr90] S. Abramsky. The lazy λ-calculus. In D.A. Turner, editor, *Research Topics in Functional Programming*, chapter 4, pages 65–117. Addison Wesley, 1990.

[Abr91] S. Abramsky. Domain theory in logical form. *Annals of Pure and Applied Logic*, **51**:1–77, 1991.

[Bal98] M. Baldamus. *Semantics and logic of higher-order processes: Characterizing late context bisimulation*. PhD thesis, Fachbereich 13 – Informatik, Technishen Universität Berlin, 1998.

[CH07] K. Crary and R. Harper. Syntactic logical relations for polymorphic and recursive types. In L. Cardelli, M. Fiore, and G. Winskel, editors, *Computation, Meaning and Logic, Articles dedicated to Gordon Plotkin*, volume 172 of *Electronic Notes in Theoretical Computer Science*, pages 259–299. Elsevier, 2007.

[FH92] M. Felleisen and R. Hieb. The revised report on the syntactic theories of sequential control and state. *Theoretical Computer Science*, **103**:235–271, 1992.

[FHJ98] W. Ferreira, M. Hennessy, and A. Jeffrey. A theory of weak bisimulation for core CML. *Journal of Functional Programming*, **8**(5):447–491, 1998.

[GH05] J.C. Godskesen and T. Hildebrandt. Extending Howe's method to early bisimulations for typed mobile embedded resources with local names. In *FSTTCS 2005: Foundations of Software Technology and Theoretical Computer Science 25th International Conference, Hyderabad, India, December 15–18, 2005. Proceedings*, volume 3821 of *Lecture Notes in Computer Science*, pages 140–151. Springer, 2005.

[Gor95] A.D. Gordon. Bisimilarity as a theory of functional programming. In *Eleventh Conference on the Mathematical Foundations of Programming Semantics, New Orleans, 1995*, volume 1 of *Electronic Notes in Theoretical Computer Science*. Elsevier, 1995.

[Gor98] A.D. Gordon. Operational equivalences for untyped and polymorphic object calculi. In Gordon and Pitts [GP98], pages 9–54.

[GP98] A.D. Gordon and A.M. Pitts, editors. *Higher Order Operational Techniques in Semantics*. Cambridge University Press, 1998.

[How89] D.J. Howe. Equality in lazy computation systems. In *4th Annual Symposium on Logic in Computer Science*, pages 198–203. IEEE Computer Society Press, 1989.

[How96] D.J. Howe. Proving congruence of bisimulation in functional programming languages. *Information and Computation*, **124**(2):103–112, 1996.

[JR99] A. Jeffrey and J. Rathke. Towards a theory of bisimulation for local names. In *14th Annual Symposium on Logic in Computer Science*, pages 56–66. IEEE Computer Society Press, 1999.

[JR00] A. Jeffrey and J. Rathke. A theory of bisimulation for a fragment of concurrent ML with local names. In *Proceedings of the 15th Annual Symposium on Logic in Computer Science*, pages 311–321. IEEE Computer Society Press, 2000.

[JR05] A. Jeffrey and J. Rathke. Contextual equivalence for higher-order π-calculus revisited. *Logical Methods in Computer Science*, **1**:(1), April 2005.

[Las98a] S.B. Lassen. Relational reasoning about contexts. In Gordon and Pitts [GP98], pages 91–135.

[Las98b] S.B. Lassen. *Relational reasoning about functions and nondeterminism*. PhD thesis, Department of Computer Science, University of Aarhus, 1998.

[Mil77] R. Milner. Fully abstract models of typed lambda-calculi. *Theoretical Computer Science*, **4**:1–22, 1977.

[Mil89] R. Milner. *Communication and Concurrency*. Prentice Hall, 1989.

[Mor69] J. Morris. *Lambda calculus models of programming languages*. PhD thesis, MIT, 1969.

[MT91] I.A. Mason and C.L. Talcott. Equivalence in functional languages with effects. *Journal of Functional Programming*, **1**:287–327, 1991.

[MT92] I.A. Mason and C.L. Talcott. Inferring the equivalence of functional programs that mutate data. *Theoretical Computer Science*, **105**:167–215, 1992.

[Pie02] B.C. Pierce. *Types and Programming Languages*. MIT Press, 2002.

[Pit97a] A.M. Pitts. A note on logical relations between semantics and syntax. *Logic Journal of the Interest Group in Pure and Applied Logics*, **5**(4):589–601, 1997.

[Pit97b] A.M. Pitts. Operationally-based theories of program equivalence. In P. Dybjer and A.M. Pitts, editors, *Semantics and Logics of Computation*, Publications of the Newton Institute, pages 241–298. Cambridge University Press, 1997.

[Pit02] A.M. Pitts. Operational semantics and program equivalence. In G. Barthe, P. Dybjer, and J. Saraiva, editors, *Applied Semantics, Advanced Lectures*, volume 2395 of *Lecture Notes in Computer Science, Tutorial*, pages 378–412. Springer, 2002. International Summer School, APPSEM 2000, Caminha, Portugal, September 9–15, 2000.

[PR98] A.M. Pitts and J.R.X. Ross. Process calculus based upon evaluation to committed form. *Theoretical Computer Science*, 195:155–182, 1998.

[PS08] A.M. Pitts and M.R. Shinwell. Generative unbinding of names. *Logical Methods in Computer Science*, 4(1:4):1–33, 2008.

[San96] D. Sangiorgi. Bisimulation for higher-order process calculi. *Information and Computation*, 131(2):141–178, 1996.

[San12] D. Sangiorgi. *An Introduction to Bisimulation and Coinduction*. Cambridge University Press, 2012.

[SKS07] D. Sangiorgi, N. Kobayashi, and E. Sumii. Environmental bisimulations for higher-order languages. In *Twenty-Second Annual IEEE Symposium on Logic In Computer Science (LICS'07)*, pages 293–302. IEEE Computer Society Press, July 2007.

[Sum09] E. Sumii. A complete characterization of observational equivalence in polymorphic lambda-calculus with general references. In *Computer Science Logic, Proceedings of 18th EACSL Annual Conference (CSL 2009)*, volume 5771 of *Lecture Notes in Computer Science*, pages 455–469 Springer, 2009.

[Win93] G. Winskel. *The Formal Semantics of Programming Languages*. Foundations of Computing. The MIT Press, 1993.

6

Enhancements of the bisimulation proof method

DAMIEN POUS AND DAVIDE SANGIORGI

One of the main reasons for the success of bisimilarity is the strength of the associated proof method. We discuss here the method on processes, more precisely, on Labelled Transition Systems (LTSs). However the reader should bear in mind that the bisimulation concept has applications in many areas beyond concurrency [San12]. According to the proof method, to establish that two processes are bisimilar it suffices to find a relation on processes that contains the given pair and that is a bisimulation. Being a bisimulation means that related processes can match each other's transitions so that the derivatives are again related.

In general, when two processes are bisimilar there may be many relations containing the pair, including the bisimilarity relation, defined as the union of all bisimulations. However, the amount of work needed to prove that a relation is a bisimulation depends its size, since there are transition diagrams to check for each pair. It is therefore important to use relations as small as possible.

In this chapter we show that the bisimulation proof method can be enhanced, by employing relations called *'bisimulations up to'*. These relations need not be bisimulations; they are just *contained in* a bisimulation. The proof that a relation is a 'bisimulation up to' follows diagram-chasing arguments similar to those in bisimulation proofs. The reason why 'bisimulations up to' are interesting is that they can be substantially smaller than any enclosing bisimulation; hence they may entail much less work in proofs. Sometimes the benefits of these up-to techniques are spectacular. A 'bisimulation up to' can be finite – even a singleton – whereas any enclosing bisimulation is infinite. Sometimes it may be hard even *to define* an enclosing bisimulation, let alone carry out the whole proof. In certain languages, e.g. languages for mobility such as π-calculus or higher-order languages such as Higher-Order π-calculus [SW01] or Ambients [MN05], the enhancements seem essential to obtain any non-trivial bisimilarity result.

Many enhancements have been studied in the literature, usually referred to as *up-to techniques*. In this chapter, we focus on those that are most fundamental, in that they are very common and can be used on a broad spectrum of languages. Other enhancements exist that exploit peculiarities in the definition of bisimilarity on certain classes of languages. For instance, in name-passing languages such as π-calculus the bisimulation clauses make use of name substitutions, and then up-to-injective-substitution techniques are heavily employed [BS98a, JR99, SW01]. In languages with information hiding mechanisms (e.g. existential types, encryption and decryption constructs [AG98, SP07b, SP07a]) or in higher-order languages [Las98, KW06], bisimulation relations are usually enriched with an environment that collects the observer knowledge on the values exchanged with the processes. The appearance of environments brings up several forms of up-to techniques for manipulating them: e.g. techniques for shrinking or enlarging the environment, and techniques for replacing information in the environment (based, for instance, on subtyping) [SKS07].

The theory of enhancements presented here allows one to derive complex up-to techniques algebraically, by composing simpler techniques by means of a few operators. This is a general theory: while all examples in the chapter deal with processes and bisimulation, the heart of the theory is presented on fixed-point theory, and is therefore applicable to coinductive objects other than bisimilarity. In particular, the theory can be applied to languages whose transition semantics features more sophisticated LTSs than the plain CCS-like LTS used in this chapter (e.g. value passing LTSs), and can be extended to enhancements not examined in this chapter.

A special place in the chapter is occupied by weak bisimilarity. Indeed, the basic theory of weak bisimilarity presents some delicate aspects (e.g. the congruence properties) [San12], and these differences over strong bisimilarity are magnified in theories of enhancements of the bisimulation proof method.

Outline of the chapter Section 6.1 details the motivations for studying enhancements of the bisimulation proof method; concrete examples of enhancements are presented in Section 6.2. Section 6.3 introduces a general theory of enhancements. Section 6.4 focuses on a particular form of enhancements, called 'up-to-context', which is important when the language of processes is defined from a grammar. Section 6.5 treats weak bisimilarity. Section 6.6 gives a summary of the main up-to techniques for strong and weak bisimulation discussed in the chapter.

Solutions to most of the exercises can be found from the Web page for the book given in the preface.

Notation We write id for the identity function, and $f \circ g$ for the composition of two functions f and g: $(f \circ g)(x) \stackrel{\text{def}}{=} f(g(x))$. We also use the notation $x \mapsto f(x)$ to define functions. Given a function f and a natural number n, we define f^n, the n-th iteration of f, by induction on n thus: $f^0 \stackrel{\text{def}}{=}$ id and $f^{n+1} \stackrel{\text{def}}{=} f \circ f^n$.

We let $\mathcal{R}$, $\mathcal{S}$ range over binary *relations* on processes; we often use the infix notation for relations: $P \mathrel{\mathcal{R}} Q$ means $(P, Q) \in \mathcal{R}$; the notation is extended pointwise to vectors, i.e. $\widetilde{P} \mathrel{\mathcal{R}} \widetilde{Q}$ holds if $\widetilde{P}$ and $\widetilde{Q}$ are vectors of the same length and componentwise related by R. The union of relations $\mathcal{R}$ and $\mathcal{S}$ is $\mathcal{R} \cup \mathcal{S}$, their intersection is $\mathcal{R} \cap \mathcal{S}$, and their composition is $\mathcal{R}\mathcal{S}$ (i.e. $P \mathrel{\mathcal{R}\mathcal{S}} P'$ holds if $P \mathrel{\mathcal{R}} Q$ and $Q \mathrel{\mathcal{S}} P'$ for some process Q). We write $\mathcal{I}$ for the identity relation. Like for functions, we define the n-th iteration of a relation $\mathcal{R}$ by induction on the natural number n thus: $\mathcal{R}^0$ is the identity, and $\mathcal{R}^{n+1} \stackrel{\text{def}}{=} \mathcal{R}\mathcal{R}^n$. We moreover write:

- $\mathcal{R}^=$ for the reflexive closure of $\mathcal{R}$: the smallest reflexive relation that contains $\mathcal{R}$, defined as $\mathcal{R} \cup \mathcal{I}$;
- $\mathcal{R}^+$ for the transitive closure of $\mathcal{R}$: the smallest transitive relation that contains $\mathcal{R}$, defined as $\bigcup_{n>0} \mathcal{R}^n$;
- $\mathcal{R}^\star$ for the reflexive and transitive closure of $\mathcal{R}$: the smallest relation that is reflexive and transitive and contains $\mathcal{R}$, defined as $\bigcup_{n\geq 0} \mathcal{R}^n$.

We write $\mathcal{R} \subseteq \mathcal{S}$ for the (set-theoretic) inclusion of relations, whereby $\mathcal{R} \subseteq \mathcal{S}$ if $P \mathrel{\mathcal{R}} Q$ entails $P \mathrel{\mathcal{S}} Q$, for all P, Q.

We extend these operations to *functions over relations* in the expected manner, e.g. if f, g are two functions, then $f \cap g$ denotes the function $\mathcal{R} \mapsto f(\mathcal{R}) \cap g(\mathcal{R})$, and $f \subseteq g$ means that $f(\mathcal{R}) \subseteq g(\mathcal{R})$ for all $\mathcal{R}$. We finally denote by f^ω the *iteration* of a function f over relations, defined as $\bigcup_n f^n$.

6.1 The need for enhancements

6.1.1 The bisimulation game

We recall the definition of bisimilarity, from [San12]:

Definition 6.1.1 (Bisimulation, bisimilarity) A binary relation $\mathcal{R}$ is a *bisimulation* if for all processes P, Q such that $P \mathrel{\mathcal{R}} Q$, and for all labels μ, we have:

- for all P' with $P \xrightarrow{\mu} P'$, there exists Q' such that $P' \mathrel{\mathcal{R}} Q'$ and $Q \xrightarrow{\mu} Q'$;
- the converse on the transitions emanating from Q, i.e. for all Q' with $Q \xrightarrow{\mu} Q'$, there exists P' such that $P' \mathrel{\mathcal{R}} Q'$ and $P \xrightarrow{\mu} P'$.

Bisimilarity ($\sim$) is the union of all bisimulations: $P \sim Q$ if there exists some bisimulation relation $\mathcal{R}$ such that $P \mathcal{R} Q$. □

We sometimes call bisimilarity *strong bisimilarity* (and accordingly, a bisimulation a *strong bisimulation*), as in this chapter we also consider weak bisimilarity (and weak bisimulations).

The bisimulation clauses can be pictorially represented thus:

In clause (1), the diagram should be read from left to right, with a universal quantification in front of P', and an existential one in front of Q'; conversely for clause (2).

Bisimilarity is an equivalence relation. Moreover, bisimilarity itself is a bisimulation and hence it is the largest bisimulation [San12].

6.1.2 Tracking redundancies

In the two clauses of Definition 6.1.1, the same relation $\mathcal{R}$ is mentioned in the hypothesis and in the thesis. In other words, when we check the bisimilarity clause on a pair (P, Q), all needed pairs of derivatives, like (P', Q'), must be present in $\mathcal{R}$. We cannot discard any such pair of derivatives from $\mathcal{R}$, or even 'manipulate' its process components. In this way, a bisimulation relation often contains many pairs strongly related with each other, in the sense that, at least, the bisimilarity between the processes in some of these pairs implies that between the processes in other pairs. For instance, in a process algebra, a bisimulation relation might contain pairs of processes obtainable from other pairs through application of algebraic laws for bisimilarity, or obtainable as combinations of other pairs and of the operators of the language. These redundancies can make both the definition and the verification of a bisimulation relation annoyingly heavy and tedious: it is difficult at the beginning to guess all pairs that are needed; and the bisimulation clauses must be checked on all pairs introduced.

As an example, consider the language defined in Figure 6.1. It is the same CCS language used in [San12], except that *replication* replaces recursively defined constants. We recall from [San12] that: a is a *name*, $\overline{a}$ is a *coname*, the sets of names and conames are disjoint and do not contain the special action τ,

Actions $\mu \ ::= a \mid \overline{a} \mid \tau$

Processes $P, Q ::= \mathbf{0} \mid P \mid P \mid P + P \mid \mu.P \mid (\nu a)P \mid \ !P$

$$\frac{P \xrightarrow{\mu} P'}{P \mid Q \xrightarrow{\mu} P' \mid Q} \qquad \frac{Q \xrightarrow{\mu} Q'}{P \mid Q \xrightarrow{\mu} P \mid Q'} \qquad \frac{P \xrightarrow{\mu} P' \quad Q \xrightarrow{\overline{\mu}} Q'}{P \mid Q \xrightarrow{\tau} P' \mid Q'}$$

$$\frac{P \xrightarrow{\mu} P'}{P + Q \xrightarrow{\mu} P'} \qquad \frac{Q \xrightarrow{\mu} Q'}{P + Q \xrightarrow{\mu} Q'}$$

$$\frac{}{\mu.P \xrightarrow{\mu} P} \qquad \frac{P \xrightarrow{\mu} P'}{(\nu a)P \xrightarrow{\mu} (\nu a)P'}\mu \neq a, \overline{a} \qquad \frac{!P \mid P \xrightarrow{\mu} P'}{!P \xrightarrow{\mu} P'}$$

Fig. 6.1. The calculus of communicating systems (CCS).

and processes are ranged over by P, Q. By convention, $\overline{\overline{a}} = a$, and a trailing $\mathbf{0}$ is often omitted, for instance abbreviating $a.\mathbf{0} + b.\mathbf{0}$ as $a + b$.

The replication of P, written $!P$, intuitively represents

$$P \mid P \mid \ldots \mid P \mid \ldots$$

i.e. an infinite parallel composition of copies of P. In certain process calculi, such as π-calculus, replication is the only form of recursion allowed, since it gives enough expressive power and enjoys interesting algebraic properties [SW01]. In Figure 6.1, as rule for replication, one may have expected the simpler

$$\frac{P \xrightarrow{\mu} P'}{!P \xrightarrow{\mu} !P \mid P'}.$$

This rule is, however, troublesome in the presence of the sum operator, as it would not allow us to derive τ-transitions from processes such as $!(a.P + \overline{a}.Q)$ [SW01].

Exercise 6.1.2 Which bisimulation can be used to prove $!P \mid P \sim !P$? $\square$

Exercise 6.1.3 Suppose that $!P \xrightarrow{\mu} P_0$.

(1) Show that, if $\mu \neq \tau$, then $P_0 = ((((((!P \mid P)\ldots) \mid P) \mid P') \mid P)\ldots) \mid P$, for some P' such that $P \xrightarrow{\mu} P'$. What happens if $\mu = \tau$?

(2) Use the monoidal commutative laws of bisimilarity for parallel composition (laws stating that | is commutative, associative, and admits $\mathbf{0}$ as neutral element) and the law $!P \mid P \sim \ !P$ from the previous exercise to obtain a more concise characterisation of P_0 modulo bisimilarity, namely:

- either $P_0 \sim \ !P \mid P'$, for some P' with $P \xrightarrow{\mu} P'$,
- or $\mu = \tau$ and $P_0 \sim \ !P \mid P' \mid P''$ for some P', P'' and a with $P \xrightarrow{a} P'$ and $P \xrightarrow{\bar{a}} P'$. □

Exercise 6.1.3 brings up the usefulness of bisimilarity laws when reasoning on process transitions. Enhancements of the bisimulation proof method, the *up-to techniques*, allow us to exploit such laws, as well as other means of manipulating the derivatives of process transitions. To illustrate this, suppose we wish to prove $!(a + b) \sim \ !a \mid \ !b$. Intuitively, the two processes are bisimilar because they both provide an infinite amount of a and b transitions, in any order. If we look for a bisimulation candidate, we may consider the following singleton relation as a candidate:

$$\mathcal{R}_0 \stackrel{\text{def}}{=} \{(!(a + b), \ !a \mid \ !b)\}.$$

Unfortunately, $\mathcal{R}_0$ is not a bisimulation. Indeed, for each $n, m \geq 0$, writing P^n for the parallel composition of n copies of P, we have the following a-transitions:

$$!(a + b) \xrightarrow{a} \ !(a + b) \mid (a + b)^n \mid \mathbf{0} \mid (a + b)^m$$

$$!a \mid \ !b \xrightarrow{a} \ !a \mid a^n \mid \mathbf{0} \mid a^m \mid \ !b.$$

The corresponding derivatives are not related by $\mathcal{R}_0$. To obtain a bisimulation, we therefore have to add new pairs to $\mathcal{R}_0$; we may thus try, as a new candidate,

$$\mathcal{R}_1 \stackrel{\text{def}}{=} \bigcup_{n,m,p,q} \{(!(a + b) \mid (a + b)^n \mid \mathbf{0} \mid (a + b)^m, \ !a \mid a^p \mid \mathbf{0} \mid a^q \mid \ !b),$$

$$(!(a + b) \mid (a + b)^n \mid \mathbf{0} \mid (a + b)^m, \ !a \mid \ !b \mid b^p \mid \mathbf{0} \mid b^q)\}.$$

However $\mathcal{R}_1$ is not a bisimulation either: by adding new pairs of processes, we have also added new challenges, which cannot be matched within $\mathcal{R}_1$. For example, in the pair $((!(a + b) \mid \mathbf{0}, \ !a \mid \mathbf{0} \mid \ !b)$, the right-hand side has the transition $!a \mid \mathbf{0} \mid \ !b \xrightarrow{b} \ !a \mid \mathbf{0} \mid \ !b \mid \mathbf{0}$ and the derivative appears nowhere in $\mathcal{R}_1$.

While it is possible to define a bisimulation relation containing the initial pair $(!(a + b), \ !a \mid \ !b)$, the endeavour is much more tedious than what was originally expected. We have to add a lot of 'redundant pairs' to the initial candidate relation $\mathcal{R}_0$. We call the pairs *redundant* because they do not say anything new as far as bisimilarity is concerned: they can be derived from the initial $\mathcal{R}_0$ by means of a few basic bisimilarity laws. For instance, consider the redundant pair $(!(a + b) \mid \mathbf{0}, \; !a \mid \mathbf{0} \mid !b)$; using the law $Q \mid \mathbf{0} \sim Q$ and the congruence laws of bisimilarity, we have

$$!(a + b) \sim \; !(a + b) \mid \mathbf{0}$$

and

$$!a \mid !b \sim \; !a \mid \mathbf{0} \mid !b.$$

Hence, by transitivity, $!(a + b) \sim \; !a \mid !b$ implies $!(a + b) \mid \mathbf{0} \sim \; !a \mid \mathbf{0} \mid !b$. In this example, since the addition of redundant pairs is forced by the bisimulation proof method; the initial singleton relation $\mathcal{R}_0$ turns into an infinite one.

More generally, redundant pairs may make it difficult to guess what is the smallest bisimulation relating two given processes. The resulting bisimilarity may also be difficult to describe succinctly, so that the relation may be awkward to work with.

6.2 Examples of enhancements

The objective of enhancements of the bisimulation proof method is to prove bisimilarity results using relations smaller than bisimulations; that is, relations in which some redundant pairs have been omitted. To write enhancements formally, we first introduce the notion of *progression* and set some terminology.

Definition 6.2.1 (Progression) Given two relations $\mathcal{R}$ and $\mathcal{S}$, we say that $\mathcal{R}$ *progresses to* $\mathcal{S}$, written $\mathcal{R} \rightarrowtail \mathcal{S}$, if $P \; \mathcal{R} \; Q$ implies:

(1) whenever $P \stackrel{\mu}{\rightarrow} P'$, there exists Q' such that $Q \stackrel{\mu}{\rightarrow} Q'$ and $P' \; \mathcal{S} \; Q'$;
(2) whenever $Q \stackrel{\mu}{\rightarrow} Q'$, there exists P' such that $P \stackrel{\mu}{\rightarrow} P'$ and $P' \; \mathcal{S} \; Q'$. □

As for the bisimulation clauses, the two clauses of a progression may be depicted as follows:

$$
\begin{array}{ccc}
P & \mathcal{R} & Q \\
{\scriptstyle\mu}\downarrow & & \downarrow{\scriptstyle\mu} \\
P' & \mathcal{S} & Q'
\end{array}
$$

When $\mathcal{R}$ and $\mathcal{S}$ coincide, the progression clauses are the ordinary clauses in the definition of bisimulation: $\mathcal{R} \rightarrowtail \mathcal{R}$ iff $\mathcal{R}$ is a bisimulation. By 'enhancement of the bisimulation proof method' we refer to a technique that, for a given relation $\mathcal{R}$, allows us to infer $\mathcal{R} \subseteq \sim$ from a progression

$$\mathcal{R} \rightarrowtail \mathcal{R} \cup \{\text{some redundant pairs}\}.$$

That is, in a diagram-chasing we allow the derivative processes to belong to a relation larger than the original one.

The enhancements relieve the work involved with the bisimulation proof method in several ways: first, they make it easier to complete a diagram-chasing; second, they make it possible to work with smaller relations, so that there are fewer diagrams to check; third, they may make it simpler to define such a relation.

The enhancements are called *up-to techniques*, because the relations employed are bisimulations *up to* a certain set of redundant pairs. Before developing a theory of enhancements in Section 6.3, we present some examples.

6.2.1 Diagram-based enhancements

Some up-to techniques were proposed shortly after the discovery of bisimulation. The best-known example is Milner's *bisimulation up to bisimilarity* technique [Mil89], in which bisimilarity can be used to rewrite the derivatives obtained when playing bisimulation games.

Definition 6.2.2 (Bisimulation up to bisimilarity)   A relation $\mathcal{R}$ is a *bisimulation up to* $\sim$ if $\mathcal{R} \rightarrowtail \sim\mathcal{R}\sim$; that is, whenever $P \mathcal{R} Q$, we have:

(1) for all P' with $P \xrightarrow{\mu} P'$, there exist P'', Q', and Q'' such that $P' \sim P''$, $Q \xrightarrow{\mu} Q'$, $Q' \sim Q''$, and $P'' \mathcal{R} Q''$;
(2) the converse, on the transitions emanating from Q.   □

A bisimulation up to bisimilarity is not, in general, a bisimulation: the definition only requires that matching derivatives are *bisimilar to* processes in the relation. However, if $\mathcal{R}$ is a bisimulation up to bisimilarity, then $\mathcal{R}$ is contained in bisimilarity. Intuitively, the technique is sound because bisimilarity is transitive; hence, in clause (1), from the bisimilarity between the processes P'' and Q'' we can also infer the bisimilarity between the derivatives P' and Q'. This is indeed true for bisimilarity. However, in other formulations of bisimilarity, as we shall see, transitivity does not ensure the soundness of the technique.

Lemma 6.2.3 *The up-to-bisimilarity technique is sound; that is, if $\mathcal{R}$ is a bisimulation up to bisimilarity, then $\mathcal{R} \subseteq \sim$.*

Proof If $\mathcal{R}$ is a bisimulation up to bisimilarity then $\sim\mathcal{R}\sim$ (the composition of the three relations) is a bisimulation and $\sim\mathcal{R}\sim \subseteq \sim$. Since $\sim$ contains the identity relation, we also have $\mathcal{R} \subseteq \sim\mathcal{R}\sim$ which allows us to conclude. □

The technique is often used to reason modulo some bisimilarity laws. For instance, the singleton relation $\mathcal{R}_0 \stackrel{\text{def}}{=} \{(!(a + b), \ !a \mid !b)\}$ of the example in Section 6.1.2 is a bisimulation up to bisimilarity; we can prove this by reasoning as in Exercise 6.1.3; we rearrange derivatives using the commutative monoidal laws of parallel composition and the law $!P \mid P \sim !P$, as in this diagram:

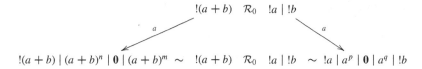

Exercise 6.2.4 Prove $!!a \sim !a$ using a singleton relation. □

An even simpler enhancement gives us the ability to rely on known equalities.

Definition 6.2.5 (Bisimulation up to $\cup$) A relation $\mathcal{R}$ is a *bisimulation up-to* $\cup$ if $\mathcal{R} \rightarrowtail \mathcal{R} \cup \sim$. □

The validity of this technique goes by showing that $\mathcal{R} \cup \sim$ is a bisimulation. For a very simple example, the technique allows us to prove $a \mid a \sim a.a$ using a singleton relation, assuming we already have proved $a \mid 0 \sim a$:

$$
\begin{array}{ccc}
a \mid a & \mathcal{R} & a.a \\
\downarrow a & & \downarrow a \\
a \mid 0 & \sim & a
\end{array}
$$

Yet another possibility is to work modulo transitivity.

Definition 6.2.6 (Bisimulation up to reflexive and transitive closure) A relation $\mathcal{R}$ is a *bisimulation up to reflexive and transitive closure* if $\mathcal{R} \rightarrowtail \mathcal{R}^\star$. □

Exercise 6.2.7 Prove that if $\mathcal{R}$ is a bisimulation up to reflexive and transitive closure, then $\mathcal{R}^\star$ is a bisimulation. □

6.2.2 Context-based enhancements

A different form of enhancement is the *up-to-context* technique [San98, San93, BS98b], that allows us to cut a common context in matching derivatives. This of course applies only when the class of processes is defined from a grammar, so that the notion of context (a process expression with a single occurrence of a hole [·] in it, as a subexpression) makes sense. If C is a context and R is a process, then $C[R]$ is the process obtained by replacing the hole of C with R. In CCS, up-to-context is defined using the following function, acting on relations on processes:

$$\mathcal{C} : \mathcal{R} \mapsto \{(C[P], C[Q]) \mid C \text{ is a context and } P \mathrel{\mathcal{R}} Q\}.$$

Definition 6.2.8 (Bisimulation up to context) A relation $\mathcal{R}$ is a *bisimulation up to context* if $\mathcal{R} \rightarrowtail \mathcal{C}(\mathcal{R})$. That is, whenever $P \mathrel{\mathcal{R}} Q$, we have:

(1) for all P' with $P \xrightarrow{\mu} P'$, there are processes P_0 and Q_0 and a context C such that $P' = C[P_0]$, $Q \xrightarrow{\mu} C[Q_0]$, and $P_0 \mathrel{\mathcal{R}} Q_0$;
(2) the converse, on the transitions emanating from Q. ☐

Pictorially, the diagram-chasing in up-to-context is:

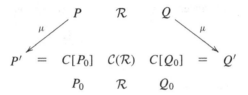

The technique would seem sound whenever bisimilarity is substitutive (i.e. preserved by contexts): from the bisimilarity between P_0 and Q_0 we can infer that the derivatives $P' = C[P_0]$ and $Q' = C[Q_0]$ are bisimilar. The technique is indeed sound in CCS, where bisimilarity is substitutive; however, as we discuss in Section 6.2.5, the connection between substitutivity of a bisimilarity and soundness of the associated up-to-context technique is a delicate issue.

Lemma 6.2.9 *In CCS, the up-to-context technique is sound.*

Proof See Section 6.4. ☐

Exercise* 6.2.10 Prove Lemma 6.2.9 in the replication-free fragment of CCS. (Hint: show that $\mathcal{C}(\mathcal{R})$ is a bisimulation whenever $\mathcal{R} \rightarrowtail \mathcal{C}(\mathcal{R})$.) ☐

The technique can be generalised to *polyadic* contexts; i.e. contexts that may contain an arbitrary number of different holes $[\cdot]_1, \ldots, [\cdot]_n$, and, moreover, each of these holes may appear more than once. In this case, in the bisimulation clause a common context is applied to pointwise related vectors (i.e. in Definition 6.2.8(1), there are $\widetilde{P}_0$ and $\widetilde{Q}_0$ and C such that $P' = C[\widetilde{P}_0]$, $Q \xrightarrow{\mu} Q'$, $Q' = C[\widetilde{Q}_0]$, and $\widetilde{P}_0 \, \mathcal{R} \, \widetilde{Q}_0$). Examples of applications of the technique are presented in Section 6.2.4.

6.2.3 Combining enhancements

It can be useful to compose different techniques to obtain more powerful enhancements. For instance, we may want to combine up-to-bisimilarity and up-to-context.

Definition 6.2.11 (Bisimulation up to bisimilarty and up to context) A relation $\mathcal{R}$ is a *bisimulation up to* $\sim$ *and up to context* if $\mathcal{R} \rightarrowtail \sim\! \mathcal{C}(\mathcal{R})\!\sim$; that is, whenever $P \, \mathcal{R} \, Q$, we have:

(1) for all P' with $P \xrightarrow{\mu} P'$, there are processes Q', $\widetilde{P}_0$ and $\widetilde{Q}_0$ and a context C such that $P' \sim C[\widetilde{P}_0]$, $Q \xrightarrow{\mu} Q'$, $Q' \sim C[\widetilde{Q}_0]$, and $\widetilde{P}_0 \, \mathcal{R} \, \widetilde{Q}_0$;
(2) the converse, on the transitions emanating from Q. $\qquad\square$

Intuitively, the technique is sound because bisimilarity is substitutive and transitive; hence, in clause (1), from the bisimilarity between $\widetilde{P}_0$ and $\widetilde{Q}_0$ we can infer, using substitutivity, that between $C[\widetilde{P}_0]$ and $C[\widetilde{Q}_0]$ and then, using transitivity, also that between the derivatives P' and Q'. We shall see however in Section 6.2.5 that in certain languages, and for certain forms of bisimilarity, transitivity and substitutivity are not sufficient for the soundness of the technique.

We study how to derive the soundness of a composite technique from the soundness of the component techniques in Section 6.3. Without this theory, the soundness of a composite technique has to be proved from scratch.

Lemma 6.2.12 *In CCS, the up-to-bisimilarity-and-context technique is sound.*

Proof See Section 6.3, in particular Proposition 6.3.11. $\qquad\square$

Exercise* 6.2.13 Prove Lemma 6.2.12 in the replication-free fragment of CCS, with monadic contexts. (Hint: show that $\sim \mathcal{C}(\mathcal{R}) \sim$ is a bisimulation, and use the congruence properties of bisimilarity.) $\qquad\square$

Up-to-bisimilarity-and-context can be handy to reason about replications. We give an example here, which is a refinement of the example in Section 6.1.2. Other examples may be found in Section 6.2.4.2.

Lemma 6.2.14 *In CCS, we have* $!(a. P + b. Q) \sim \,!a. P \mid !b. Q$.

Proof We prove that the singleton relation $\mathcal{R}_0 \overset{\text{def}}{=} \{(!(a.\,P + b.\,Q),\ !a.\,P \mid !b.\,Q)\}$ is a bisimulation up to bisimilarity and context.

Consider a transition along a from the left-hand side: $!(a.\,P + b.\,Q) \overset{a}{\to} P_0$. By Exercise 6.1.3, we have $P_0 \sim !(a.\,P + b.\,Q) \mid P$. The right-hand side can answer with $!a.\,P \mid !b.\,Q \overset{a}{\to} Q_0 = (!a.\,P \mid P) \mid !b.\,Q$, and then $Q_0 \sim (!a.\,P \mid !b.\,Q) \mid P$ using associativity and commutativity of parallel composition. Thanks to the up-to-context technique, we can then remove the common parallel context, $[\cdot] \mid P$, to recover the pair from $\mathcal{R}_0$:

$$
\begin{array}{ccccccc}
!(a.\,P + b.\,Q) & & \mathcal{R}_0 & & !a.\,P + !b.\,Q & & \\
& \overset{a}{\swarrow} & & & & \overset{a}{\searrow} & \\
P_0 \quad \sim & !(a.\,P + b.\,Q) \mid P & \mathcal{C}(\mathcal{R}_0) & (!a.\,P \mid !b.\,Q) \mid P & \sim & Q_0 \\
& !(a.\,P + b.\,Q) & \mathcal{R}_0 & !a.\,P \mid !b.\,Q & &
\end{array}
$$

Challenges along b, and from the right-hand side, are handled similarly. $\qquad\square$

6.2.4 Other examples of applications

6.2.4.1 Unique solutions of equations

We apply the previous up-to techniques to prove a useful result of CCS: uniqueness of solutions of equations. This result says that if a context C obeys certain conditions, then all processes P that satisfy the equation $P \sim C[P]$ are bisimilar with each other.

We say that a polyadic context C is *weakly guarded* if each occurrence of each hole of C is within some subexpression of the form $\mu.\,C'$. For instance, $a.\,[\cdot]$ is weakly guarded, but $[\cdot] \mid a.\,[\cdot]$ is not. The transitions performed by weakly guarded contexts are easy to analyse:

Lemma 6.2.15 *If C is weakly guarded and $C[\widetilde{P}] \overset{\mu}{\to} P'$, then there exists a context C' such that $P' = C'[\widetilde{P}]$ and for all $\widetilde{Q}$, $C[\widetilde{Q}] \overset{\mu}{\to} C'[\widetilde{Q}]$.*

Proof Simple induction on the structure of C. Intuitively, since C is weakly guarded, the processes that fill the holes of C do not contribute to the first produced action. $\qquad\square$

Theorem 6.2.16 (Unique solution of equations in CCS) *Let $C_1, \ldots, C_n$ be weakly guarded contexts, and let $\widetilde{P}, \widetilde{Q}$ be processes such that, for all $1 \leq i \leq n$, $P_i \sim C_i[\widetilde{P}]$ and $Q_i \sim C_i[\widetilde{Q}]$ (where P_i and Q_i, respectively, denote the i-th component of vectors $\widetilde{P}$ and $\widetilde{Q}$). Then $\widetilde{P} \sim \widetilde{Q}$.*

Proof Define the following finite relation:

$$\mathcal{R} \stackrel{\text{def}}{=} \{(P_i, Q_i) \mid 1 \leq i \leq n\},$$

and suppose $P_i \stackrel{\mu}{\rightarrow} P_i'$ (the case of a move from Q_i is symmetric). From $P_i \sim C_i[\widetilde{P}]$, we deduce that there is some P_i'' such that $C_i[\widetilde{P}] \stackrel{\mu}{\rightarrow} P_i''$ and $P_i' \sim P_i''$. Using Lemma 6.2.15, we have $P_i'' = C_i'[\widetilde{P}]$ for some context C_i', and $C_i[\widetilde{Q}] \stackrel{\mu}{\rightarrow} C_i'[\widetilde{Q}]$. Since $Q_i \sim C_i[\widetilde{Q}]$ we finally get Q_i' such that $Q_i \stackrel{\mu}{\rightarrow} Q_i'$ and $C_i'[\widetilde{Q}] \sim Q_i'$. This allows us to close the diagram, as depicted below:

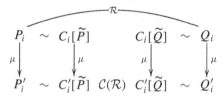

Therefore, $\mathcal{R}$ is a bisimulation up to bisimilarity and up to context and we are done, by Lemma 6.2.12. $\square$

In the proof of Theorem 6.2.16, the cardinality of the relation $\mathcal{R}$ is the same as the cardinality of the vector of given contexts $\widetilde{C}$. In particular, if we are dealing with only one context (i.e. only one equation), then $\mathcal{R}$ consists of only *one* pair. Without the help of up-to techniques the above result would be harder. Using only the up-to-bisimilarity technique, one would need to work with a relation including at least all pairs of the form $(C[\widetilde{P}], C[\widetilde{Q}])$, where C can be *any* context, possibly unguarded. Dealing with these pairs is more complex, for we cannot appeal to Lemma 6.2.15.

6.2.4.2 Replication laws

We now apply the up-to-context technique to the proof of laws involving the replication operator.

Lemma 6.2.17 *For all CCS processes P and Q, we have:*

(1) $!(P \mid Q) \sim\, !P \mid !Q$;
(2) $!(P + Q) \sim\, !P \mid !Q$;
(3) $!P \mid !P \sim\, !P$;
(4) $!!P \sim\, !P$.

Proof We rely on the law $!P \mid P \sim\, !P$, from Exercise 6.1.2; and on the characterisation given in Exercise 6.1.3, about the transitions emanating from a replicated process.

(1) We show that the singleton relation $\mathcal{R} \stackrel{\text{def}}{=} \{(!(P \mid Q), \; !P \mid !Q)\}$ is a bisimulation up to bisimilarity and up to context. We first consider the left-to-right part of the game: suppose that $!(P \mid Q) \stackrel{\mu}{\rightarrow} A$ and find some B such that $!P \mid !Q \stackrel{\mu}{\rightarrow} B$ and $A \sim \mathcal{C}(\mathcal{R}) \sim B$. According to Exercise 6.1.3, we have $A \sim !(P \mid Q) \mid A'$ for some A' with $P \mid Q \stackrel{\mu}{\rightarrow} A'$ or $(P \mid Q) \mid (P \mid Q) \stackrel{\mu}{\rightarrow} A'$ (when $\mu = \tau$). In both cases, since $!P \mid !Q \sim \; !P \mid !Q \mid P \mid Q \sim \; !P \mid !Q \mid P \mid Q \mid P \mid Q$, we deduce that there exists some B such that $!P \mid !Q \stackrel{\mu}{\rightarrow} B \sim \; !P \mid !Q \mid A'$. This allows us to conclude: the up-to-context technique can be used to remove the parallel context $[\cdot] \mid A'$, so as to recover the pair from $\mathcal{R}$:

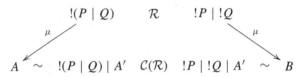

For the right-to-left part of the game, suppose that $!P \mid !Q \stackrel{\mu}{\rightarrow} B$. By analysing the rules for the transitions of a parallel composition, together with Exercise 6.1.3, we have $B \sim \; !P \mid !Q \mid B'$ for some B' with $R \stackrel{\mu}{\rightarrow} B'$ and R in $\{P, Q, P \mid P, Q \mid Q, P \mid Q\}$. Suppose that $R = P$ (the other cases are similar); since $!(P \mid Q) \sim \; !(P \mid Q) \mid P \mid Q$, we find A such that $!(P \mid Q) \stackrel{\mu}{\rightarrow} A \sim \; !(P \mid Q) \mid B' \mid Q$, which allows us to close the diagram, by adding an occurrence of Q on the right-hand side using the law $!Q \sim \; !Q \mid Q$, and removing the parallel context $[\cdot] \mid B' \mid Q$ thanks to the up-to-context technique:

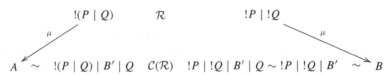

(2) Similar to the previous point.

(3) We can proceed by algebraic reasoning: by using (2) and the fact that $P + P \sim P$, we have:

$$!P \mid !P \; \sim \; !(P + P) \; \sim \; !P \; .$$

(4) By (3) and Exercise 6.1.3, we obtain (†): $!P \stackrel{\mu}{\rightarrow} Q$ entails $Q \sim \; !P \mid Q$. We exploit this property to show that the singleton relation $\mathcal{R} \stackrel{\text{def}}{=} \{(!!P, \; !P)\}$ is a bisimulation up to bisimilarity and up to context. We first consider the right-to-left part of the bisimulation game: if $!P \stackrel{\mu}{\rightarrow} R$, then $!!P \stackrel{\mu}{\rightarrow} \; !!P \mid R$, and

we have to relate $!!P \mid R$ and R by $\sim \mathcal{C}(\mathcal{R}) \sim$. By (†), we have $R \sim \ !P \mid R$, and the latter process can be related to $!!P \mid R$ by removing the common parallel context $[\cdot] \mid R$:

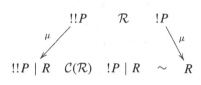

For the left-to-right part of the game, if $!!P \xrightarrow{\mu} Q$, then $Q \sim \ !!P \mid R$, by Exercise 6.1.3, and there are two cases to consider:

- either $!P \xrightarrow{\mu} R$, and we can conclude like previously, since $!!P \mid R \ \mathcal{C}(\mathcal{R})$ $!P \mid R \sim R$,
- or $\mu = \tau$ and $!P \mid !P \xrightarrow{\tau} R$. Here, the interesting case is that of a synchronisation: $R = R_1 \mid R_2$, $!P \xrightarrow{a} R_1$, $!P \xrightarrow{\bar{a}} R_2$. By Exercise 6.1.3 we deduce $!P \xrightarrow{\tau} \sim \ !P \mid R$, which allows to conclude, as in the above case. □

Exercise 6.2.18 Complete the proof for assertion (2) of Lemma 6.2.17. □

Without the up-to-context technique, the bisimulation candidates in the proof of Lemma 6.2.17 would consist of pairs of processes with at least a further component. For instance, the last one would become

$$\mathcal{R}' \stackrel{\text{def}}{=} \{(!!P \mid R, !P \mid R)\}$$

($\mathcal{R}'$ progresses to $\sim \mathcal{R}' \sim$). Having $\mathcal{R}'$ in place of $\mathcal{R}$ does not make the proof conceptually more difficult; it does make it more tedious, however: interactions with the additional process R have to be taken into account, with reasoning similar to that involved in the proof that bisimilarity is preserved by parallel composition. This extra work is not problematic in a simple setting like CCS; it can become a burden, however, in more involved calculi.

6.2.5 What is a redundant pair?

Before moving to Section 6.3, which is devoted to a general theory of enhancements, we come back to the notion of redundant pairs. We said that we would like to infer $\mathcal{R} \subseteq \sim$ from a progression

$$\mathcal{R} \longmapsto \mathcal{R} \cup \{\text{some redundant pairs}\}.$$

The intuition for redundant pairs that we gave at the end of Section 6.1.2 –
a pair is redundant if it can be derived from the remaining pairs using laws
for bisimilarity – is actually not quite right, in the sense that the condition is
important but, in itself, not sufficient. For a simple counterexample, we consider
the relation $\mathcal{R} \stackrel{\text{def}}{=} \{(a.b, a.c)\}$. Since we have $P \sim Q$ whenever $a.P \sim a.Q$,
the pair (b, c) should be redundant in $\mathcal{R} \cup \{(b, c)\}$. However, we have

$$\mathcal{R} \rightarrowtail \mathcal{R} \cup \{(b, c)\} \ ,$$

and yet $a.b \not\sim a.c$.

Even for the techniques discussed in Section 6.2, stating when they are
sound (i.e. for which languages, for which forms of bisimilarity) is difficult.
For instance, consider the up-to-bisimilarity-and-context technique. We hinted
in Section 6.2 that its soundness would seem to derive from the transitivity and
substitutivity of bisimilarity. Again, surprisingly, this condition alone is not
sufficient. For a counterexample, we consider the simple process language

$$P ::= \text{op}(P) \ \big| \ a.P \ \big| \ \mathbf{0}$$

where $a.P$ is a CCS-like prefix, $\mathbf{0}$ is the inactive process and op is an operator
whose behaviour is given by the right-hand side rule below:

$$\frac{}{a.P \xrightarrow{a} P} \qquad \frac{P \xrightarrow{a} P' \quad P' \xrightarrow{a} P''}{\text{op}(P) \xrightarrow{a} P''} \ .$$

That is, in order to release some action, op requires the release of two actions
from its argument. On this language, bisimilarity is transitive and preserved
by all contexts (in fact, we can infer that bisimilarity is a congruence from the
fact that the transition rules of the operators are in the *xyft/tyft* format [GV92]).
Despite this, the up-to-bisimilarity-and-context technique is not sound. Con-
sider the non-bisimilar processes a and $a.a$, and the relation $\mathcal{R} \stackrel{\text{def}}{=} \{(a, a.a)\}$.
The following diagram

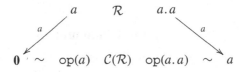

shows that $\mathcal{R} \rightarrowtail \sim\mathcal{C}(\mathcal{R})\sim$ holds: $\mathcal{R}$ is a bisimulation up to bisimilarity and up
to context. However, $\mathcal{R}$ is not contained in bisimilarity.

One can also find examples where the up-to-context technique alone is not
sound, while bisimilarity is a congruence: consider the following language

(syntax and operational rules), where u and v are two constants.

$$P ::= 0 \mid 1 \mid h(P) \qquad \overline{P \xrightarrow{u} h(P)} \qquad \overline{h(0) \xrightarrow{v} 0}.$$

Since $h(1)$ cannot perform a transition labelled by v, we have $h(0) \not\sim h(1)$; hence also $0 \not\sim 1$. In fact, 0 is the only process that is bisimilar to 0, and one can easily prove that $h(P) \sim h(Q)$ whenever $P \sim Q$: bisimilarity is a congruence. However, the up-to-context technique is not sound: the singleton relation $\{(0, 1)\}$ is a bisimulation up to context.

The second rule of the example, for the operator h, does not actually adhere to the usual criteria for rules in Plotkin's Structured Operational Semantics (SOS): the rule looks into the syntax of the argument of h, while only the *transitions* of the argument should matter in a purely semantic rule. Indeed, Exercise 6.4.5 shows that, when the rules of all the operators of a given language are purely semantic, and a few other assumptions are met, then the up-to-context technique is sound. Yet, the general issue of the relationship between the substitutivity property of a bisimilarity and the soundness of the associated up-to-context technique remains largely uncovered, particularly in languages with exchange of values or higher-order features.

6.3 A theory of enhancements

To be able to use an enhancement we first have to prove its soundness. This can be a difficult task, and this difficulty tends to increase as the technique itself, or the language onto which it is applied, becomes more powerful or sophisticated. For instance, the proof of soundness of the technique called 'bisimulation up to bisimilarity and up to context' can be non-trivial. Indeed, it is quite challenging if the language is higher order, meaning that terms of the language can be communicated. Moreover, depending on the considered language, there can be many other forms of up-to techniques, for example, in languages with types [BS98a], security aspects [AG98, SP07a], or store [KW06], we may wish to use up-to-environment, up-to-weakening, up-to-subtyping, and so on.

This motivates the search for a general theory of enhancements that would allow us to understand what an enhancement is, how enhancements can be composed, and how to prove their soundness. We study such a theory in this section.

6.3.1 Bisimulations and bisimilarity as coinductive objects

As there are several variants of bisimulation, including strong, weak, and branching bisimulation [San12], it is useful to define a generic framework for enhancements. For this, we move to the abstract setting of coinduction, viewing coinductive objects such as bisimilarity as the greatest fixed points of monotone functions on complete lattices. We recall [San12] that a complete lattice is a set equipped with a partial-order relation and with all joins (least upper bounds) and meets (greatest lower bounds). The Fixed-point Theorem assures us that any monotone function on a complete lattice has a greatest fixed point, which is the join of all the post-fixed points.

In this chapter, the complete lattice will always be the set of all relations on processes; hence we use $\mathcal{R}, \mathcal{S}$ to range over elements of the lattice, $\subseteq$ for the partial order in the lattice, and $\cup$ and $\cap$ for the join and meet constructs.

In [San12] we studied the characterisation of bisimilarity as the greatest fixed point of a monotone function (the functional of bisimilarity) over process relations. The only difference between the functional for bisimilarity in [San12] and the function **b** below is the presence of clause (3). This clause is required by a technicality explained in Section 6.4 (Remark 6.4.2); it can safely be ignored in the remainder of this section, as it does not affect the results presented here.

Definition 6.3.1 Let **b** be the following function over binary relations:

$\mathbf{b} : \mathcal{R} \mapsto \{\, (P, Q) \mid$

   (1) if $P \xrightarrow{\mu} P'$, then there exists Q' s.t. $Q \xrightarrow{\mu} Q'$ and $P' \, \mathcal{R} \, Q'$; and

   (2) if $Q \xrightarrow{\mu} Q'$, then there exists P' s.t. $P \xrightarrow{\mu} P'$ and $P' \, \mathcal{R} \, Q'$; and

   (3) $P \, \mathcal{R} \, Q \}$.   □

Exercise 6.3.2 Show that $\mathcal{R} \subseteq \mathbf{b}(\mathcal{S})$ iff $\mathcal{R} \subseteq \mathcal{S}$ and $\mathcal{R} \rightarrowtail \mathcal{S}$ (Definition 6.2.1).
                                                                                    □

In other words, using diagrams, $\mathcal{R} \subseteq \mathbf{b}(\mathcal{S})$ iff $\mathcal{R} \subseteq \mathcal{S}$ and the following diagram is satisfied:

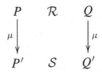

According to the above exercise the post-fixed points of **b** (that is, the relations $\mathcal{R}$ such that $\mathcal{R} \subseteq \mathbf{b}(\mathcal{R})$) are exactly the *bisimulation* relations. Moreover, the function **b** is monotone, so that the fixed-point theorem ensures that it has a greatest fixed point. This greatest fixed point is bisimilarity ($\sim$).

In the sequel, we present both 'concrete' results about (strong) bisimilarity obtained with function **b** above, and 'abstract' results about the coinductive theory of an arbitrary monotone function. The concrete results are given in terms of the function **b** above; in contrast, b indicates a generic monotone function. Accordingly, to have a terminology that drives the intuitions using the bisimulation point of view, we introduce the following synonyms for post-fixed points and greatest fixed points.

Definition 6.3.3 Let b be a monotone function on a complete lattice.

- We call *b-simulation* any post-fixed point of b: any $\mathcal{R}$ such that $\mathcal{R} \subseteq b(\mathcal{R})$.
- We call *b-similarity* the greatest *b*-simulation:

$$\mathtt{gfp}(b) \stackrel{\mathrm{def}}{=} \bigcup \{\mathcal{R} \mid \mathcal{R} \subseteq b(\mathcal{R})\} \ . \qquad \Box$$

Thus, **b**-simulations and **b**-similarity are the ordinary bisimulations and bisimilarity.

The same object may be the greatest fixed point of different functions. In particular, bisimilarity is the greatest fixed point of the bisimilarity functional in [San12], of the function **b** above, and also of the following function **b**′, in which the second clause of **b** is replaced by a clause for 'symmetry':

$\mathbf{b}' : \mathcal{R} \mapsto \{(P, Q) \mid$

    (1) if $P \stackrel{\mu}{\rightarrow} P'$, then there exists Q' s.t. $Q \stackrel{\mu}{\rightarrow} Q'$ and $P' \mathcal{R} Q'$; and

    $(2')$ $Q \mathcal{R} P\}$.

Functions with the same greatest fixed point may however have different sets of post-fixed points, as the exercise below shows.

Exercise 6.3.4

(1) Show that all **b**′-simulations are **b**-simulations, and that the converse does not hold.

(2) Show that the symmetric closure of a **b**-simulation is a **b**′-simulation; conclude that **b**-similarity and **b**′-similarity coincide. $\qquad \Box$

Post-fixed points are used to define the coinduction proof method. Hence a difference between two functions on the post-fixed points is relevant. Comparing **b** and **b**′, for instance, one may prefer **b** because it has a larger set of post-fixed points (there are more **b**-simulations than **b**′-simulations, Exercise 6.3.4(1)). On the other hand, the proof obligations for **b**′ seem milder (only one clause involves transitions). In practice, the difference between **b** and **b**′ is irrelevant, as Exercise 6.3.4(2) reveals. We shall see however that the theory of enhancements allows us to obtain other functions whose greatest fixed point is still bisimilarity and whose post-fixed points are significantly easier to work with than those of **b** or **b**′.

6.3.2 Enhancements as functions

Definition 6.3.5 A function f is *extensive* if $\mathcal{R} \subseteq f(\mathcal{R})$, for all $\mathcal{R}$.   □

All examples of enhancements in Section 6.2 could be expressed in terms of *extensive* functions f on relations for which $\mathcal{R} \longmapsto f(\mathcal{R})$ entails $\mathcal{R} \subseteq \sim$. For instance, 'up-to-bisimilarity' is the function that maps a relation $\mathcal{R}$ onto $\sim\mathcal{R}\sim$, and 'up-to-context' is the function $\mathcal{C}$. To understand these functions, we examine their effect on the function **b** for bisimilarity: by Exercise 6.3.2, we have $\mathcal{R} \longmapsto f(\mathcal{R})$ iff $\mathcal{R} \subseteq \mathbf{b}(f(\mathcal{R}))$, i.e. iff $\mathcal{R}$ is a $(\mathbf{b} \circ f)$-simulation. Therefore, f corresponds to a 'valid' up-to technique if all $(\mathbf{b} \circ f)$-simulations are contained in bisimilarity, $\mathsf{gfp}\,(\mathbf{b})$. Since $\mathsf{gfp}\,(\mathbf{b} \circ f)$ is the largest $(\mathbf{b} \circ f)$-simulation, we obtain the following formulation of up-to techniques.

Definition 6.3.6 (Simulation up to, soundness) Let b, f be two monotone functions.

- A *b-simulation up to f* is a $(b \circ f)$-simulation.
- The function f is *b-sound* if $\mathsf{gfp}\,(b \circ f) \subseteq \mathsf{gfp}\,(b)$.   □

In other words, f is b-sound if all b-simulations up to f are contained in b-similarity, so that f can safely be used as an up-to technique for b. Moreover, in the concrete case of the function **b** for bisimilarity, while a **b**-simulation is a relation satisfying the left-hand side diagram below, a **b**-simulation up to f is a relation satisfying the right-hand side diagram. If $\mathcal{R}$ is smaller than $f(\mathcal{R})$, we may hope that the right-hand side diagram entails less work in proofs.

According to Definition 6.3.6, Lemmas 6.2.3 and 6.2.9, respectively, assert that the functions $\mathcal{R} \mapsto \sim\mathcal{R}\sim$ and $\mathcal{C}$ are **b**-sound. As outlined above, we use two classes of functions in the chapter:

- functions, like **b**, that generate an interesting greatest fixed point (e.g. bisimilarity);
- functions like $\mathcal{R} \mapsto \sim\mathcal{R}\sim$ or $\mathcal{C}$ that are used as up to techniques so as to enhance the coinductive proof method for the functions in the first class.

We use b to range over the functions in the first class, and f, g over the functions in the second class. The functions in the second class, unlike those in the first, are usually extensive.

6.3.3 Compositionality problems

In some of the examples from Section 6.2, we needed different up-to techniques at the same time. For instance, in Lemmas 6.2.14 and 6.2.17, we used a combination of up to contexts and up to bisimilarity.

A natural question is whether it is always possible to compose two up-to techniques or, equivalently, whether the composition of two b-sound functions is still b-sound. The following exercise shows that the answer is negative. The counterexample in the exercise is ad hoc; a more meaningful counterexample will be given in Section 6.5.4.

Exercise 6.3.7 Consider the four-point lattice given by the powerset of $\{0, 1\}$, and define the following (monotone) functions:

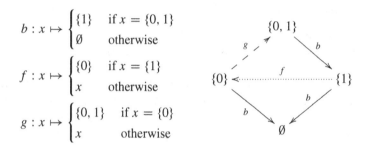

$$b : x \mapsto \begin{cases} \{1\} & \text{if } x = \{0, 1\} \\ \emptyset & \text{otherwise} \end{cases}$$

$$f : x \mapsto \begin{cases} \{0\} & \text{if } x = \{1\} \\ x & \text{otherwise} \end{cases}$$

$$g : x \mapsto \begin{cases} \{0, 1\} & \text{if } x = \{0\} \\ x & \text{otherwise} \end{cases}$$

Compute $\mathtt{gfp}\,(b)$ and show that f and g are b-sound. Show that $g \circ f$ is not b-sound. Notice that $g \cup f = g \circ f$ (where $g \cup f : \mathcal{R} \mapsto g(\mathcal{R}) \cup f(\mathcal{R})$); this shows that in general, there is no 'largest b-sound function'.   □

Thus, up-to techniques, expressed as sound functions, cannot be freely composed. For instance, we cannot appeal to the soundness of the up-to-context function $\mathcal{C}$ and of the up-to-bisimilarity function $\mathcal{R} \mapsto {\sim}\mathcal{R}{\sim}$ to derive the soundness of the up-to-bisimilarity-and-context function $\mathcal{R} \mapsto {\sim}\mathcal{C}(\mathcal{R}){\sim}$. We need to prove the soundness of the composite technique from scratch. The proof is tedious, as it mixes the proofs for up-to-context and for up-to-bisimilarity (the reader who carefully completed Exercise 6.2.13 would agree).

As a solution to the problem, we define a subset of sound functions that has good compositionality properties and that contains most up-to techniques of interest.

Definition 6.3.8 (Compatibility) Let b, f be two functions. The function f is b-compatible if $f \circ b \subseteq b \circ f$.   □

The compatible functions are also sound.

Theorem 6.3.9 *Let b, f be two monotone functions. If f is b-compatible, then f is b-sound.*

Proof Let $\mathcal{R} \stackrel{\text{def}}{=} \text{gfp}\,(b \circ f)$, we have to show that $\mathcal{R} \subseteq \text{gfp}\,(b)$. We first show that $f^n(\mathcal{R}) \subseteq b(f^{n+1}(\mathcal{R}))$, for all n, by induction on n:

- if $n = 0$, since $\mathcal{R}$ is a $(b \circ f)$-simulation, we have $\mathcal{R} \subseteq b(f(\mathcal{R}))$ by definition;
- for $n + 1$, we have

$$
\begin{aligned}
f^n(\mathcal{R}) &\subseteq b(f^{n+1}(\mathcal{R})) && \text{(by induction)} \\
f(f^n(\mathcal{R})) &\subseteq f(b(f^{n+1}(\mathcal{R}))) && \text{(f is monotone)} \\
&\subseteq b(f(f^{n+1}(\mathcal{R}))) && \text{(f is b-compatible)}
\end{aligned}
$$

Let $f^\omega(\mathcal{R}) \stackrel{\text{def}}{=} \bigcup_n f^n(\mathcal{R})$. Since b is monotone, we deduce $f^n(\mathcal{R}) \subseteq b(f^\omega(\mathcal{R}))$ for all n; whence $f^\omega(\mathcal{R}) \subseteq b(f^\omega(\mathcal{R}))$, that is, $f^\omega(\mathcal{R})$ is a b-simulation. This allows us to conclude: we have $\mathcal{R} \subseteq f^\omega(\mathcal{R}) \subseteq \text{gfp}\,(b)$. $\qquad\square$

Remark 6.3.10 Although the terminology differs, the theorem above corresponds to a special case of the 'exchange rule' in fixed-point calculus [DP90] – it suffices to take the identity for the Galois connection, and to work in the dual lattice. $\qquad\square$

The set of functions that are compatible with a given function is closed under composition and union, and contains the identity and other useful constant functions.

Proposition 6.3.11 *Let b be a monotone function; the following functions are b-compatible:*

(1) the identity function;
(2) the constant-to-S function $\widehat{S}$, which maps any relation $\mathcal{R}$ onto S, and where S is any b-simulation;
(3) $f \circ g$, for any b-compatible and monotone functions f and g;
(4) $\bigcup F$, for any set F of b-compatible functions.

Proof The first two items are straightforward; for (3), we have

$$
\begin{aligned}
(f \circ g) \circ b &= f \circ (g \circ b) \subseteq f \circ (b \circ g) \\
&= (f \circ b) \circ g \subseteq (b \circ f) \circ g = b \circ (f \circ g),
\end{aligned}
$$

using the associativity of functional composition, and the two compatibility hypotheses. For (4), we check that for any $\mathcal{R}$,

$$\bigcup F(b(\mathcal{R})) = \bigcup_{f \in F} f(b(\mathcal{R})) \subseteq \bigcup_{f \in F} b(f(\mathcal{R})) \subseteq b\left(\bigcup_{f \in F} f(\mathcal{R})\right)$$

$$= b\left(\bigcup F(\mathcal{R})\right).$$

$\square$

In the remainder of this section, we prove that the functions underpinning the techniques presented in Section 6.2.1 are compatible. The first three points of the above proposition give us the up-to-$\cup$ technique (Definition 6.2.5): the identity function is **b**-compatible by (1), bisimilarity is a bisimulation, so that the function $\mathcal{R} \mapsto \sim$ is **b**-compatible by (2), and the union of these two functions is **b**-compatible by (3). For the other techniques, we give an alternative characterisation of compatible functions, which is easier to work with in concrete proofs.

Lemma 6.3.12 *Let b, f be two monotone functions; f is b-compatible if and only if for all $\mathcal{R}, \mathcal{S}, \mathcal{R} \subseteq b(\mathcal{S})$ entails $f(\mathcal{R}) \subseteq b(f(\mathcal{S}))$.*

Proof Assume that f is b-compatible and $\mathcal{R} \subseteq b(\mathcal{S})$; we have:

$$f(\mathcal{R}) \subseteq f(b(\mathcal{S})) \qquad\qquad (f \text{ is monotone})$$
$$f(\mathcal{R}) \subseteq b(f(\mathcal{S})) \qquad\qquad (f \text{ is } b\text{-compatible})$$

Conversely, assume that $\mathcal{R} \subseteq b(\mathcal{S})$ entails $f(\mathcal{R}) \subseteq b(f(\mathcal{S}))$ for all $\mathcal{R}, \mathcal{S}$. For all $\mathcal{R}$, we have $b(\mathcal{R}) \subseteq b(\mathcal{R})$, whence $f(b(\mathcal{R})) \subseteq b(f(\mathcal{R}))$ by assumption. Thus, we have obtained $f \circ b \subseteq b \circ f$, that is, f is b-compatible. $\square$

In the concrete case of bisimilarity, using the diagrammatic representation of $\mathcal{R} \subseteq \mathbf{b}(\mathcal{S})$, a monotone function f is **b**-compatible if and only if, for all relations $\mathcal{R}, \mathcal{S}$ with $\mathcal{R} \subseteq \mathcal{S}$, we have:

$$
\begin{array}{ccc}
P & \mathcal{R} & Q \\
\mu\downarrow & & \downarrow\mu \\
P' & \mathcal{S} & Q'
\end{array}
\quad \text{implies} \quad
\begin{array}{ccc}
P & f(\mathcal{R}) & Q \\
\mu\downarrow & & \downarrow\mu \\
P' & f(\mathcal{S}) & Q'
\end{array}
$$

In particular, the functions we have used as up-to techniques in the introduction can be shown to be **b**-compatible:

Lemma 6.3.13 *The function $\mathcal{R} \mapsto {\sim}\mathcal{R}{\sim}$ is $\mathbf{b}$-compatible.*

Proof Suppose that $\mathcal{R} \subseteq \mathbf{b}(\mathcal{S})$; we have to show that $\sim\!\mathcal{R}\!\sim\, \subseteq \mathbf{b}(\sim\!\mathcal{S}\!\sim)$. We consider only the left-to-right part of the game: let P, Q, P' such that $P \xrightarrow{\mu} P'$ and $P \sim\!\mathcal{R}\!\sim Q$, i.e. $P \sim P_0\,\mathcal{R}\,Q_0 \sim Q$ for some P_0, Q_0. By definition of bisimilarity, we find P_0' such that $P_0 \xrightarrow{\mu} P_0'$ and $P' \sim P_0'$; using the assumption $\mathcal{R} \subseteq \mathbf{b}(\mathcal{S})$, we then find Q_0' such that $Q_0 \xrightarrow{\mu} Q_0'$ and $P_0'\,\mathcal{S}\,Q_0'$; and again, by definition of bisimilarity, we find Q' such that $Q \xrightarrow{\mu} Q'$ and $Q_0' \sim Q'$. Putting it all together, we have found a Q' such that $Q \xrightarrow{\mu} Q'$ and $P' \sim\!\mathcal{S}\!\sim Q'$, as required. $\qquad\square$

Lemma 6.3.14 *The reflexive and transitive closure function $\mathcal{R} \mapsto \mathcal{R}^\star$ is $\mathbf{b}$-compatible.*

Proof Suppose that $\mathcal{R} \subseteq \mathbf{b}(\mathcal{S})$; we have to show that $\mathcal{R}^\star \subseteq \mathbf{b}(\mathcal{S}^\star)$. Recall that $\mathcal{R}^\star = \bigcup_n \mathcal{R}^n$, where $\mathcal{R}^n$ denotes the n-th iteration of $\mathcal{R}$. We prove by induction that for all n, we have $\mathcal{R}^n \subseteq \mathbf{b}(\mathcal{S}^n)$. The case $n = 0$ is trivial; for $n + 1$ we consider only the left-to-right part of the game: let P, Q, P' such that $P \xrightarrow{\mu} P'$ and $P\,\mathcal{R}\mathcal{R}^n\,Q$, i.e. $P\,\mathcal{R}\,P_0\,\mathcal{R}^n\,Q$ for some P_0. Using the assumption $\mathcal{R} \subseteq \mathbf{b}(\mathcal{S})$, we find P_0' such that $P_0 \xrightarrow{\mu} P_0'$ and $P'\,\mathcal{S}\,P_0'$; and by induction, we then find Q' such that $Q \xrightarrow{\mu} Q'$ and $P_0'\,\mathcal{S}^n\,Q'$. Putting it all together, we have found Q' such that $Q \xrightarrow{\mu} Q'$ and $P'\,\mathcal{S}\mathcal{S}^n\,Q'$, as required. This allows us to conclude, by definition of reflexive and transitive closure. $\qquad\square$

As we shall see in the sequel, the ability to combine up-to techniques becomes essential when we move to more complex enhancements (e.g. up-to-context techniques, or termination-based techniques for weak bisimilarity). The following corollary illustrates this possibility, anticipating Section 6.4 where we show that the closure $\mathcal{C}$ under CCS contexts is $\mathbf{b}$-compatible (Theorem 6.4.12).

Corollary 6.3.15 *The function $\mathcal{R} \mapsto (\mathcal{C}(\mathcal{R}) \cup \sim)^\star$ is $\mathbf{b}$-sound.*

Proof Let $f_1 : \mathcal{R} \mapsto \sim$ and $f_2 : \mathcal{R} \mapsto \mathcal{R}^\star$; these functions are $\mathbf{b}$-compatible by Proposition 6.3.11(2) and Lemma 6.3.14, respectively. By Theorem 6.4.12, so is $\mathcal{C}$. Therefore, $f_2 \circ (\mathcal{C} \cup f_1)$ is $\mathbf{b}$-compatible by Proposition 6.3.11(3,4). Since $(f_2 \circ (\mathcal{C} \cup f_1))(\mathcal{R}) = (\mathcal{C}(\mathcal{R}) \cup \sim)^\star$, we conclude with Theorem 6.3.9. $\qquad\square$

The function in Corollary 6.3.15 represents a powerful technique, which allows one to use either the bisimulation candidate ($\mathcal{R}$) or strong bisimilarity ($\sim$) to rewrite any subterm ($\mathcal{C}$) of the derivatives appearing during the bisimulation game. Moreover, such rewriting can be repeated as many times as needed, thanks to the reflexive and transitive closure.

6.3.4 Symmetry arguments

The definition of bisimilarity (or of the function **b**) has two symmetric clauses, which may sometimes lead to repeating the same argument twice (see for example, Lemmas 6.3.13 and 6.3.14). This can be annoying, most notably when using a proof assistant to formalise the proofs on a computer.

We show in this section how to give a formal account of these symmetries: although the corresponding arguments are straightforward and intuitive in the case of strong bisimilarity, they need to be handled properly when we move to weak bisimilarity, where we sometimes need to work with non-symmetric functions.

This section can be skipped at first reading: we recall the main results and notations when necessary in the remainder of the chapter.

6.3.4.1 Symmetric functions

We first define the function on relations that 'reverses' its argument:

$$i : \mathcal{R} \mapsto \overline{\mathcal{R}} \stackrel{\text{def}}{=} \{(P, Q) \mid Q \mathcal{R} P\}.$$

The function i is a monotone *involution* (in that $i \circ i = \mathrm{id}$). We use it to define two operations on functions: given a function f, we write $\overline{f}$ for the function $i \circ f \circ i$, and $\overleftrightarrow{f}$ for the function $f \cap \overline{f}$:

$$\overline{f}(\mathcal{R}) \stackrel{\text{def}}{=} \overline{f(\overline{\mathcal{R}})} \qquad\qquad \overleftrightarrow{f}(\mathcal{R}) \stackrel{\text{def}}{=} f(\mathcal{R}) \cap \overline{f(\overline{\mathcal{R}})}.$$

Exercise 6.3.16 Give simpler expressions for functions $\overline{f}$ and $\overleftrightarrow{f}$, in the case where f is the function $\mathcal{R} \mapsto {\sim}\mathcal{R}$. □

Lemma 6.3.17 *Let f be a monotone function; the following conditions are equivalent:*

(1) f is i-compatible;
(2) $f = \overline{f}$;
(3) $f \circ i = i \circ f$.

Proof From (1) we have $f = f \circ i \circ i \subseteq i \circ f \circ i \subseteq i \circ i \circ f = f$, hence $f = i \circ f \circ i$, as required in (2), from which we deduce $f \circ i = i \circ f \circ i \circ i = i \circ f$, as required in (3). The entailment from (3) to (1) is straightforward. □

The functions satisfying the conditions of the above lemma are called *symmetric*: they satisfy $f(\overline{\mathcal{R}}) = \overline{f(\mathcal{R})}$, for all $\mathcal{R}$. As the following exercises show, proving the symmetry of a function is usually straightforward, and moreover symmetry smoothly interacts with the notions of simulation, bisimilarity, and compatibility.

Exercise 6.3.18 Among the following functions, which ones are symmetric? (i) $\mathcal{R} \mapsto \sim\mathcal{R}\sim$; (ii) $\mathcal{R} \mapsto \sim\mathcal{R}$; (iii) $\mathcal{R} \mapsto \mathcal{R} \cup \sim$; (iv) $\mathcal{R} \mapsto \mathcal{R}^\star$; (v) $\mathcal{R} \mapsto (\mathcal{R} \cup \sim)^\star$. (Hint: for (v), use Lemmas 6.3.17 and 6.3.11.) □

Exercise 6.3.19 Let s, f be two monotone functions; show that

(1) a relation $\mathcal{R}$ is an s-simulation iff $\overline{\mathcal{R}}$ is an $\bar{s}$-simulation;
(2) a relation $\mathcal{R}$ is an $\overset{\leftrightarrow}{s}$-simulation iff both $\mathcal{R}$ and $\overline{\mathcal{R}}$ are s-simulations;
(3) f is s-compatible iff $\overline{f}$ is $\bar{s}$-compatible. □

6.3.4.2 Symmetric up-to techniques

Take the function **b** for bisimilarity (Definition 6.3.1). If we remove the second clause, which corresponds to the right-to-left part of the bisimulation game, we obtain the function **s** below:

$$\mathbf{s} : \mathcal{R} \mapsto \{(P, Q) \mid$$

(1) if $P \xrightarrow{\mu} P'$, then there exists Q' s.t. $Q \xrightarrow{\mu} Q'$ and $P' \mathcal{R} Q'$; and

(3) $P \mathcal{R} Q\}$.

The function **s** has *(strong) similarity* as its greatest fixed point: only the left-to-right part of the bisimulation game is played. Symmetrically, function $\bar{\mathbf{s}}$ corresponds to the right-to-left part of the bisimulation game. Therefore, to recover bisimulation games, it suffices to consider the function $\overset{\leftrightarrow}{\mathbf{s}}$: we have $\mathcal{R} \subseteq \overset{\leftrightarrow}{\mathbf{s}}(\mathcal{S})$ iff $\mathcal{R} \subseteq \mathbf{s}(\mathcal{S})$ and $\mathcal{R} \subseteq \bar{\mathbf{s}}(\mathcal{S})$.

While we managed to decompose **b** into simpler functions (namely **s** and i, from which $\overset{\leftrightarrow}{\mathbf{s}}$ is derived), an **s**-compatible function is not necessarily $\overset{\leftrightarrow}{\mathbf{s}}$-compatible. Hence we cannot directly obtain up-to techniques for **b** from up-to techniques for **s**, as shown in the following exercise.

Exercise 6.3.20 By Proposition 6.3.11, the constant function $\mathcal{R} \mapsto \mathtt{gfp}(\mathbf{s})$ is **s**-compatible. Show that this function is not **b**-sound and, hence, not **b**-compatible. □

The following proposition gives a simple solution: by restricting ourselves to symmetric functions, one can focus on the left-to-right part of the bisimulation games when studying up-to techniques.

Proposition 6.3.21 *Let s, f be two monotone functions. If f is symmetric and s-compatible, then f is $\overset{\leftrightarrow}{s}$-compatible.*

Proof By Exercise 6.3.19, $f = \overline{f}$ is $\bar{s}$-compatible. We then have $f \circ (s \cap \bar{s}) \subseteq f \circ s \cap f \circ \bar{s} \subseteq s \circ f \cap \bar{s} \circ f = (s \cap \bar{s}) \circ f$. Hence f is $\overset{\leftrightarrow}{s}$-compatible. □

Exercise 6.3.22 Show (again) that functions $\mathcal{R} \mapsto \sim\mathcal{R}\sim$ and $\mathcal{R} \mapsto \mathcal{R}^\star$ are **b**-compatible, by proving that they are symmetric and **s**-compatible. Compare these proofs with the direct ones (Lemmas 6.3.13 and 6.3.14). □

Exercise 6.3.23 We have $\mathbf{b} = \overleftrightarrow{\mathbf{s}} = \mathbf{s} \cap \bar{\mathbf{s}}$. Do we have $\mathrm{gfp}\,(\mathbf{s} \cap \bar{\mathbf{s}}) = \mathrm{gfp}\,(\mathbf{s}) \cap \overline{\mathrm{gfp}\,(\mathbf{s})}$? (The latter relation is *2-similarity*, see [San12].) □

Exercise 6.3.24

- Give a characterisation of the function $\mathbf{b}'$ from Exercise 6.3.4 using $\mathbf{s}$ and i.
- Generalise Exercise 6.3.4 by showing that for any monotone function s, we have $\mathrm{gfp}\left(\overleftrightarrow{s}\right) = \mathrm{gfp}\,(i \cap s)$. □

6.3.4.3 Non-symmetric up-to techniques

For strong bisimilarity, Proposition 6.3.21 is sufficient: all up-to techniques can be obtained as symmetric **s**-compatible functions. This is no longer the case with weak bisimilarity ($\approx$), where we need to consider non-symmetric functions. We briefly explain here how to deal with this situation; we refer to Section 6.5.2.4 for concrete examples, involving weak bisimilarity. We first need to refine the notion of soundness.

Definition 6.3.25 Let s, f, f' be three functions.

- f is *s-sound via* f' if f' is extensive (Definition 6.3.5) and for all relations $\mathcal{R}$, if $\mathcal{R}$ is an s-simulation up to f, then $f'(\mathcal{R})$ is an s-simulation. □

The function f' intuitively keeps track of the 'witness' of the up-to technique: when f is s-sound via f' and $\mathcal{R}$ is an s-simulation up to f, then $\mathcal{R}$ is contained in s-similarity because it is contained in $f'(\mathcal{R})$, which is an s-simulation. For example, the function $f_0 : \mathcal{R} \mapsto \sim\mathcal{R}$ is **s**-sound via itself: if $\mathcal{R}$ is an **s**-simulation up to f_0, then $f_0(\mathcal{R}) = \sim\mathcal{R}$ is an **s**-simulation. More generally, by looking at the proof of Theorem 6.3.9, we obtain that compatible functions are sound via their iteration (recall that f^ω is $\bigcup_n f^n$).

Theorem 6.3.26 *Let s, f be two monotone functions. If f is s-compatible, then f is s-sound via f^ω.* □

The function f_0 is also **s**-sound via the symmetric function $f_1 : \mathcal{R} \mapsto \sim\mathcal{R}\sim$. Indeed, if $\mathcal{R}$ is an **s**-simulation up to f_0, then $f_0(\mathcal{R}) = \sim\mathcal{R}$ is an **s**-simulation, and so is $f_1(\mathcal{R}) = \sim\mathcal{R}\sim$. More generally, the following lemma allows one to extend the witness of a sound function.

Lemma 6.3.27 *Let s, f, f', g be three monotone functions. If f is s-sound via f', then f is s-sound via $g \circ f'$, provided that g is extensive and preserves s-simulations.* □

We finally obtain the following proposition: a function yields a sound up-to technique for bisimilarity ($\overleftrightarrow{s}$), as soon as it is sound for similarity (s) via a symmetric function. In other words, it suffices that the witness of the up-to technique be symmetric.

Proposition 6.3.28 *Let s, f be two monotone functions. If f is s-sound via a symmetric function, then $\mathtt{gfp}\left(\overleftrightarrow{s \circ f}\right) \subseteq \mathtt{gfp}\left(\overleftrightarrow{s}\right)$.*

Proof Assume that f is s-sound via the symmetric function f', and suppose that $\mathcal{R}$ is an $\overleftrightarrow{s \circ f}$-simulation: $\mathcal{R} \subseteq \overleftrightarrow{s \circ f}(\mathcal{R})$. In particular, we have $\mathcal{R} \subseteq s(f(\mathcal{R}))$, from which we deduce that $f'(\mathcal{R})$ is an s-simulation; and we have $\overline{\mathcal{R}} \subseteq s(f(\overline{\mathcal{R}}))$, i.e. $\overline{\mathcal{R}} \subseteq s(f(\overline{\mathcal{R}}))$, from which we deduce that $f'(\overline{\mathcal{R}})$ is an s-simulation. Then, f' being symmetric, we have $f'(\overline{\mathcal{R}}) = \overline{f'(\mathcal{R})}$ and $f'(\mathcal{R})$ is an $\overline{s}$-simulation by Exercise 6.3.19. Together with $f'(\mathcal{R})$ being an s-simulation, this entails $\mathcal{R} \subseteq \mathtt{gfp}\left(\overleftrightarrow{s}\right)$. □

Equivalently, when working with symmetric candidates, we obtain the following up-to technique:

Corollary 6.3.29 *Let s, f be two monotone functions such that f is s-sound via a symmetric function. Any symmetric s-simulation up to f is contained in $\overleftrightarrow{s}$-similarity.*

Proof Let $\mathcal{R}$ be such a symmetric s-simulation up to f: $\mathcal{R} \subseteq s \circ f(\mathcal{R})$. Since $\mathcal{R}$ is symmetric, we also have $\overline{\mathcal{R}} = \mathcal{R} \subseteq \overline{s \circ f}(\mathcal{R})$, so that $\mathcal{R}$ is an $\overleftrightarrow{s \circ f}$-simulation. We conclude with Proposition 6.3.28. □

6.4 Congruence and up to context techniques

In the previous sections we have seen how to derive up-to techniques for bisimilarity in a compositional way, via the notion of compatible function. In particular, we have seen that up-to-bisimilarity and up-to-transitivity correspond to compatible functions. In this section, we show that the function for up-to-context is also compatible. We cover the case of CCS, as defined in Figure 6.1; the methodology can be adapted to other languages.

6.4.1 Contexts

We have introduced contexts, including polyadic contexts, in Section 6.2.2. Each such context C induces a function that manipulates relations on CCS processes, as follows:

$$\lfloor C \rfloor : \mathcal{R} \mapsto \left\{ (C[\widetilde{P}], C[\widetilde{Q}]) \mid \widetilde{P} \, \mathcal{R} \, \widetilde{Q} \right\}.$$

This notation is extended to sets $\mathbb{C}$ of contexts:

$$\lfloor \mathbb{C} \rfloor : \mathcal{R} \mapsto \left\{ (C[\widetilde{P}], C[\widetilde{Q}]) \mid \widetilde{P} \, \mathcal{R} \, \widetilde{Q} \text{ and } C \in \mathbb{C} \right\}.$$

Thus, $\lfloor \mathbb{C} \rfloor(\mathcal{R})$ is the closure of $\mathcal{R}$ under the contexts in $\mathbb{C}$. Also note that the function $\lfloor \mathbb{C} \rfloor$ is always symmetric, independently of the set $\mathbb{C}$. When $\mathbb{C}$ is the set of all (polyadic) CCS contexts, we write $\mathcal{C}$ for $\lfloor \mathbb{C} \rfloor$; we call this function *closure under CCS contexts*.

6.4.2 Up to context techniques

We want to show that $\mathcal{C}$ yields a valid up-to technique for bisimilarity, i.e. that the following diagram is enough to deduce that $\mathcal{R}$ is contained in bisimilarity.

$$
\begin{array}{ccc}
P & \mathcal{R} & Q \\
\mu \downarrow & & \downarrow \mu \\
P' & \mathcal{C}(\mathcal{R}) & Q'
\end{array}
$$

For this, it suffices to show that $\mathcal{C}$ is **b**-sound. However, this would not allow us to combine this up-to technique with other techniques. Therefore, we prove a stronger property, namely that $\mathcal{C}$ is **b**-compatible.

As proposed in the following exercise, compatibility can be proved directly, by a structural induction on contexts. The difficulty comes from the replication operator, which requires us to consider polyadic contexts: the closure function restricted to monadic contexts is not compatible. Moreover, the difficulty increases when we move to the case of weak bisimilarity where one needs to reason modulo unfolding of replications. We propose another proof in Section 6.4.5.

Exercise* 6.4.1 Prove that $\mathcal{C}$ is **b**-compatible, i.e. assume that $\mathcal{R} \subseteq \mathbf{b}(\mathcal{S})$ and prove $\mathcal{C}(\mathcal{R}) \subseteq \mathbf{b}(\mathcal{C}(\mathcal{S}))$ by structural induction on polyadic contexts: show that for all CCS contexts C, if $\widetilde{P} \, \mathcal{R} \, \widetilde{Q}$ and $C[\widetilde{P}] \xrightarrow{\mu} P_0$, then there exists Q_0 such that $C[\widetilde{Q}] \xrightarrow{\mu} Q_0$ and $P_0 \, \mathcal{C}(\mathcal{S}) \, Q_0$. $\square$

Thanks to Proposition 6.3.11, we can combine up-to-context with other up-to techniques expressed as **b**-compatible functions. For example, we can compose functions $\mathcal{C}$, $\mathcal{R} \mapsto \mathcal{R} \cup \sim$, and $\mathcal{R} \mapsto \mathcal{R}^{\star}$, as in the following diagram:

$$
\begin{array}{ccc}
P & \mathcal{R} & Q \\
\mu \downarrow & & \downarrow \mu \\
P' & (\mathcal{C}(\mathcal{R}) \cup \sim)^{\star} & Q'
\end{array}
$$

We have thus derived the function in Corollary 6.3.15.

Remark 6.4.2 If we omit the third clause in the definition of **b** (Definition. 6.3.1), then the function $\mathcal{C}$ remains sound, but it is no longer compatible. To see this, consider the relations $\mathcal{R} \stackrel{\text{def}}{=} \{(!a.\,b,\,!a.\,c)\}$ and $\mathcal{S} \stackrel{\text{def}}{=} \sim\{(!a.\,b \mid b,\, !a.\,c \mid c)\}\sim$. Without the third clause, we would have $\mathcal{R} \subseteq \mathbf{b}(\mathcal{S})$, while $\mathcal{C}(\mathcal{R}) \subseteq \mathbf{b}(\mathcal{C}(\mathcal{S}))$ does not hold. For instance, we have $d.\,!a.\,b \, \mathcal{C}(\mathcal{R}) \, d.\,!a.\,c$, but the only derivatives of these processes, $!a.\,b$ and $!a.\,c$, are not in $\mathcal{C}(\mathcal{S})$. □

6.4.3 Substitutivity

Another consequence of the compatibility of $\mathcal{C}$ is the *substitutivity* of bisimilarity: bisimilarity is preserved by all CCS contexts. This property is a consequence of the following lemma: b-similarity is closed under any b-compatible function (a relation $\mathcal{R}$ is *closed under a function* f if $f(\mathcal{R}) \subseteq \mathcal{R}$).

Lemma 6.4.3 *Let b be a monotone function; for all b-compatible functions f, we have $f(\mathtt{gfp}\,(b)) \subseteq \mathtt{gfp}\,(b)$.*

Proof We have $f(\mathtt{gfp}\,(b)) = f(b(\mathtt{gfp}\,(b))) \subseteq b(f(\mathtt{gfp}\,(b)))$. Hence, $f(\mathtt{gfp}\,(b))$ is a b-simulation, and $f(\mathtt{gfp}\,(b)) \subseteq \mathtt{gfp}\,(b)$. □

Corollary 6.4.4 (Substitutivity of bisimilarity) *Bisimilarity is preserved by all contexts in CCS. That is, we have $\mathcal{C}(\sim) \subseteq \sim$.*

Proof Lemma 6.4.3 applies to $\mathcal{C}$, which is **b**-compatible by Exercise 6.4.1. □

As shown in Section 6.2.5, the converse of Lemma 6.4.3 does not hold: $f(\mathtt{gfp}\,(b)) \subseteq \mathtt{gfp}\,(b)$ does not necessarily entail that f is b-compatible or b-sound.

6.4.4 Rule formats

It is possible to formalise results on up-to-context that are valid for classes of languages, rather for a single language as we have done so far with CCS. It suffices that the semantics of the language is given by means of rules in the style of Structured Operational Semantics (SOS). The results then are expressed in terms of the *format* of such rules. We refer to [San12] and references therein for details on rule formats; we only mention here a few simple facts.

If the LTS adheres to the *de Simone* rule format [dS85], then the context closure function is **b**-compatible [San98], and hence it yields a valid up-to technique.

On the contrary, the more permissive *xyft/tyft* format [GV92] leads to context closure functions which are **b**-sound (see the exercise below), but not necessarily **b**-compatible. Recall the simple process language at the end of Section 6.2.5, which we used to show that the combination of up-to-context and up-to-bisimilarity is not always sound: the rules of the language are in *xyft/tyft* format, but the context closure function is not **b**-compatible. If it were, then it could be combined with the function $\mathcal{R} \mapsto \sim\mathcal{R}\sim$, which is **b**-compatible; but the example showed that the up-to-context-and-bisimilarity technique is not sound, hence also not compatible.

Exercise* 6.4.5 Consider the following syntax of processes: $P ::= \mathbf{0} \mid f(P)$, where f ranges over an arbitrary set of function symbols. Suppose that the LTS is given by a set of rules of the form:

$$\frac{X_0 \xrightarrow{\mu_0} X_1 \xrightarrow{\mu_1} \ldots \xrightarrow{\mu_{n-1}} X_n}{f(X_0) \xrightarrow{\mu} C[X_n]}$$

where μ and μ_i are arbitrary labels, the X_i's are distinct process metavariables, f is a function symbol, and C is an arbitrary context)

Show that the corresponding context closure $\mathcal{C}$ is **b**-sound. (Hint: suppose that $\mathcal{R} \subseteq \mathbf{b}(\mathcal{C}(\mathcal{R}))$; show that $\mathcal{C}(\mathcal{R})$ is a bisimulation, i.e. if $P\ \mathcal{C}(\mathcal{R})\ Q$ and $P \xrightarrow{\mu} P'$, then there exists some Q' such that $Q \xrightarrow{\mu} Q'$ and $P'\ \mathcal{C}(R)\ Q'$, proceeding by induction on the derivation.) $\square$

The result of Exercise 6.4.5 can be generalised to *tree rules* [FvG96], and thus to the *xyft/tyft* format [Pou10].

6.4.5 An alternative method: initial contexts

In certain languages, proving compatibility of up-to context may be delicate: it requires a mix of both induction (on contexts) and coinduction (to define bisimulations). Moreover, naive proof attempts are sometimes deemed to fail. For example, as seen in Section 6.4.2, in CCS with replication, one cannot work with monadic contexts only: we are forced to generalise the technique to polyadic contexts, which results in more tedious case analyses. This is even worse when working with weak bisimilarity, where we need to reason modulo unfolding of replications within the inductive proof (see Section 6.5.3).

In this section, we present a method for deriving the compatibility of up-to-context. The method separates the inductive part of the proof from the coinductive part. Thus proving the compatibility of a context-closure function reduces to checking that each syntactic construction of the language satisfies a simple condition with respect to the function $\mathbf{b}$ of bisimilarity.

The crux of the method is a characterisation of the context closure function $\mathcal{C}$ using a smaller set of contexts, called *initial*, one for each operator of the language.

Definition 6.4.6 (Initial contexts) The following CCS contexts are called *initial*:

$$\mathbf{0} \stackrel{\text{def}}{=} \mathbf{0} \qquad | \stackrel{\text{def}}{=} [\cdot]_1 \mid [\cdot]_2 \qquad ! \stackrel{\text{def}}{=} ![\cdot]_1 \qquad (\nu a) \stackrel{\text{def}}{=} (\nu a)[\cdot]_1$$

$$\mathrm{id} \stackrel{\text{def}}{=} [\cdot]_1 \qquad \mu. \stackrel{\text{def}}{=} \mu.[\cdot]_1 \qquad + \stackrel{\text{def}}{=} [\cdot]_1 + [\cdot]_2.$$

The set of initial CCS contexts is written $\mathbb{C}_i$.   □

Each initial context is a context, so that $\lfloor \mathbb{C}_i \rfloor \subseteq \mathcal{C}$; the containment is strict, however, as $\mathcal{C}(\emptyset)$ is the identity relation while $\lfloor \mathbb{C}_i \rfloor(\emptyset) = \{(\mathbf{0}, \mathbf{0})\}$. Indeed, we have to iterate the function $\lfloor \mathbb{C}_i \rfloor$ to recover the closure under all contexts.

Proposition 6.4.7 *We have* $\mathcal{C} = \lfloor \mathbb{C}_i \rfloor^\omega$.

Proof Since $\mathcal{C}$ is idempotent, $\lfloor \mathbb{C}_i \rfloor \subseteq \mathcal{C}$ entails $\lfloor \mathbb{C}_i \rfloor^\omega \subseteq \mathcal{C}$ by a simple induction. For the converse direction, we fix a relation $\mathcal{R}$, and we show that for all CCS contexts C, we have $\lfloor C \rfloor(\mathcal{R}) \subseteq \lfloor \mathbb{C}_i \rfloor^\omega(\mathcal{R})$, proceeding by structural induction on C. We detail the case of a parallel context $C = C_1 \mid C_2$. Suppose $P_0 \lfloor C \rfloor(\mathcal{R})$ Q_0, that is, $P_0 = C_1[\widetilde{P}] \mid C_2[\widetilde{P}]$ and $Q_0 = C_1[\widetilde{Q}] \mid C_2[\widetilde{Q}]$, with $\widetilde{P} \mathcal{R} \widetilde{Q}$. By induction, $C_i[\widetilde{P}] \lfloor \mathbb{C}_i \rfloor^\omega(\mathcal{R}) C_i[\widetilde{Q}]$ for $i = 1, 2$, i.e. $C_i[\widetilde{P}] \lfloor \mathbb{C}_i \rfloor^{n_i}(\mathcal{R}) C_i[\widetilde{Q}]$ for some n_i ($i = 1, 2$). By letting $n = max\{n_0, n_1\}$, we deduce

$$P_0 = C[\widetilde{P}] \ \lfloor | \rfloor(\lfloor \mathbb{C}_i \rfloor^n(\mathcal{R})) \ C[\widetilde{Q}] = Q_0$$

(since the identity context belongs to $\mathbb{C}_i$, we have $\lfloor \mathbb{C}_i \rfloor^m \subseteq \lfloor \mathbb{C}_i \rfloor^{m+k}$ for all m, k) whence $P_0 \lfloor \mathbb{C}_i \rfloor^{n+1}(\mathcal{R}) Q_0$, and $P_0 \lfloor \mathbb{C}_i \rfloor^\omega(\mathcal{R}) Q_0$.   □

The advantage of this characterisation of contextual closure in terms of initial contexts is that we can reason on such contexts without the need of inductive proofs. The proof of the proposition essentially captures the inductive part of the proof of correctness of up-to-context as formulated in Section 6.4.2, so that we are then left with the coinductive part alone.

Some initial contexts directly yield compatible functions. For example, the functions corresponding to the parallel context, $\lfloor \mid \mid \rfloor$, and to the restriction contexts, $\lfloor (\nu a) \rfloor$, are **b**-compatible (Lemma 6.4.11 below). Since compatible functions are stable under union and composition (Proposition 6.3.11), we deduce the validity of techniques such as 'up-to-restriction-and-parallel-context'.

In contrast, some contexts do not yield compatible functions by themselves. Typically, the replication context spawns parallel compositions along reductions, so that the correctness of 'up-to-replication' inherently depends on the correctness of 'up-to-parallel-contexts'. Similarly, in the π-calculus, where the SOS rules for parallel composition involve also the restriction operator, we cannot prove up-to-parallel-contexts and up-to-restriction independently.

We handle these inter-dependencies using coinduction at the level of compatible functions. For instance, the replication-context function is not compatible by itself; it is however compatible up to the compatibility of the parallel-context function. More formally, we introduce the following technical notion, which generalises the notion of compatibility (Definition 6.3.8):

Definition 6.4.8 Let b, f, g be three functions; f *evolves into g through b*, written $f \overset{b}{\rightsquigarrow} g$, if $f \circ b \subseteq b \circ g$. $\qquad\square$

As we shall see below, in the concrete case of bisimilarity, we have that f evolves into g if the left-hand side diagram below entails the right-hand side one:

Intuitively, while a b-compatible function is a function which evolves to itself (through b), the notion of evolution allows us to consider functions that are 'almost' compatible: they evolve to a larger function. This is reminiscent of the difference between bisimulations and progressions: $\mathcal{R}$ is a bisimulation if $\mathcal{R}$ progresses to itself, but progressions allow us to consider relations that are 'almost' bisimulations: relations that progress to some possibly larger relation. Thus, we get a notion of 'compatibility up to': when $f \overset{b}{\rightsquigarrow} \phi(f)$, where ϕ is a function from functions to functions, we say that f *is b-compatible up to ϕ*.

The following lemma provides a simple characterisation of evolutions.

Lemma 6.4.9 *Let b, f, g be three monotone functions.*

(1) f *is b-compatible iff* $f \overset{b}{\leadsto} f$;

(2) $f \overset{b}{\leadsto} g$ *iff for all relations* $\mathcal{R}, \mathcal{S}$:

$$\mathcal{R} \subseteq b\,(\mathcal{S}) \text{ entails } f(\mathcal{R}) \subseteq b\,(g(\mathcal{S})).$$

Proof The first point is straightforward; we consider the second one.

- If $f \overset{b}{\leadsto} g$ and $\mathcal{R} \subseteq b\,(\mathcal{S})$, then we have $f(\mathcal{R}) \subseteq f(b(\mathcal{S})) \subseteq b(g(\mathcal{S}))$.
- Conversely, for all $\mathcal{R}$, we have $b(\mathcal{R}) \subseteq b\,(\mathcal{R})$, from which we deduce $f(b(\mathcal{R})) \subseteq b\,(g(\mathcal{R}))$. $\qquad\qquad\square$

We finally obtain the following proposition: compatible functions 'up to iteration' yield compatible functions. We will see another example of 'compatibility up to' in Section 6.5.3. See [Pou07, Pou08a] for more details on up-to techniques for compatibility.

Proposition 6.4.10 *Let b, f be two monotone functions, and suppose that f^{ω} is idempotent. If $f \overset{b}{\leadsto} f^{\omega}$, then f^{ω} is b-compatible.*

Proof We show that for all i, $f^i \overset{b}{\leadsto} f^{\omega}$ by induction on i:

- if $i = 0$, we have $f^0 \circ b = b \subseteq b \circ f^{\omega}$, i.e., $f^0 \overset{b}{\leadsto} f^{\omega}$;
- for $i + 1$, we have:

$$
\begin{aligned}
f^i \circ b &\subseteq b \circ f^{\omega} && \text{(by induction)}\\
f^{i+1} \circ b &\subseteq f \circ b \circ f^{\omega}, && \text{(f is monotone)}\\
&\subseteq b \circ f^{\omega} \circ f^{\omega}, && \text{(by assumption)}\\
&= b \circ f^{\omega} && \text{(f^{ω} is idempotent)}
\end{aligned}
$$

$\square$

Our characterisation of contextual closure ($\mathcal{C} = \lfloor \mathbb{C}_i \rfloor^{\omega}$) was guided by the above proposition. Indeed, with $f = \lfloor \mathbb{C}_i \rfloor$, proving that $\mathcal{C}$ is **b**-compatible amounts to proving that $\lfloor \mathbb{C}_i \rfloor$ is **b**-compatible 'up to iteration', i.e. that for all initial contexts $C \in \mathbb{C}_i$ we have $\lfloor C \rfloor \overset{\mathbf{b}}{\leadsto} \mathcal{C}$. This, expanding the notation, means that for all initial contexts C,

$$\mathcal{R} \subseteq \mathbf{b}\,(\mathcal{S}) \quad \text{entails} \quad \lfloor C \rfloor(\mathcal{R}) \subseteq \mathbf{b}\,(\mathcal{C}(\mathcal{S})). \qquad (*)$$

In other words, for the **b**-compatibility of $\mathcal{C}$ we need not analyse the effect of all contexts (as in Exercise 6.4.1): by the compositionality properties of compatible functions, it suffices to analyse initial contexts. Moreover, the appearance of $\mathcal{C}(\mathcal{S})$ on the right-hand side indicates that we can use all contexts when answering the challenges produced by the initial contexts ($\lfloor C \rfloor(\mathcal{R})$).

For CCS, we perform this analysis in the following technical lemma: for each initial context, we give the smallest contextual closure it evolves to, through **b**. As mentioned above, the functions corresponding to parallel composition and restriction are **b**-compatible 'by themselves', while the function associated to the replication operator depends on parallel composition. The functions associated to *dynamic* operators (prefix and sum) evolve into the identity, as these operators disappear after a single transition.

Lemma 6.4.11 *The following evolutions hold:*

- $\lfloor \mu. \rfloor \overset{\mathbf{b}}{\rightsquigarrow} \mathrm{id}$
- $\lfloor + \rfloor \overset{\mathbf{b}}{\rightsquigarrow} \mathrm{id}$
- $\lfloor (\nu a) \rfloor \overset{\mathbf{b}}{\rightsquigarrow} \lfloor (\nu a) \rfloor$
- $\lfloor \mathbf{0} \rfloor \overset{\mathbf{b}}{\rightsquigarrow} \lfloor \mathbf{0} \rfloor$
- $\lfloor \vert \rfloor \overset{\mathbf{b}}{\rightsquigarrow} \lfloor \vert \rfloor$
- $\lfloor ! \rfloor \overset{\mathbf{b}}{\rightsquigarrow} \lfloor \vert \rfloor^{\omega} \circ (\lfloor ! \rfloor \cup \mathrm{id})$.

Proof Take $\mathcal{R}, \mathcal{S}$ such that $\mathcal{R} \subseteq \mathbf{b}(\mathcal{S})$; we study each context of $\mathbb{C}_i$ separately: for all $C \in \mathbb{C}_i$, we show $\lfloor C \rfloor(\mathcal{R}) \subseteq \mathbf{b}(f(\mathcal{S}))$ (where f is the right-hand side function in the assertion of the lemma); that is, we suppose $U \lfloor C \rfloor(\mathcal{R}) V$ and $U \overset{\mu}{\rightarrow} U'$, and we find some V' such that $V \overset{\mu}{\rightarrow} V'$ and $U' f(\mathcal{S}) V'$.

$\lfloor \mu. \rfloor$: $U = \mu'. P \overset{\mu}{\rightarrow} U'$, $V = \mu'. Q$ with $P \mathcal{R} Q$. Necessarily, $\mu = \mu'$ and $U' = P$. We hence have $V = \mu. Q \overset{\mu}{\rightarrow} Q$, with $P \mathrm{id}(\mathcal{S}) Q$ (recall that $\mathcal{R} \subseteq \mathbf{b}(\mathcal{S})$ entails $\mathcal{R} \subseteq \mathcal{S}$ – see Remark 6.4.2).

$\lfloor + \rfloor$: $U = U_1 + U_2$, $V = V_1 + V_2$ with $U_i \mathcal{R} V_i$ for $i \in 1, 2$, and $U_i \overset{\mu}{\rightarrow} U'_i = U'$ for some i. We deduce that there exists some V'_i such that $V_i \overset{\mu}{\rightarrow} V'_i$, and $U'_i \mathcal{S} V'_i$. Finally, $V \overset{\mu}{\rightarrow} V'_i$ with $U' \mathrm{id}(\mathcal{S}) V'_i$.

$\lfloor (\nu a) \rfloor$: $U = (\nu a)P \overset{\mu}{\rightarrow} U'$, $V = (\nu a)Q$ with $P \mathcal{R} Q$. Inference rules impose $U' = (\nu a)P'$ where $P \overset{\mu}{\rightarrow} P'$ and $\mu \neq a, \overline{a}$. Since $P \mathcal{R} Q$, we obtain Q' such that $Q \overset{\mu}{\rightarrow} Q'$ and $P' \mathcal{S} Q'$, and we check that $V \overset{\mu}{\rightarrow} V' = (\nu a)Q'$, with $U' \lfloor (\nu a) \rfloor(\mathcal{S}) V'$.

$\lfloor \mathbf{0} \rfloor$: straightforward.

$\lfloor\mid\rfloor$: $U = P_1 \mid P_2 \xrightarrow{\mu} U'$, $V = Q_1 \mid Q_2$ with $P_1 \mathcal{R} Q_1$ and $P_2 \mathcal{R} Q_2$. According to the inference rules for parallel composition, there are three cases:

- $U' = P_1' \mid P_2$ with $P_1 \xrightarrow{\mu} P_1'$. Since $\mathcal{R} \subseteq \mathbf{b}(\mathcal{S})$, $Q_1 \xrightarrow{\mu} Q_1'$ with $P_1' \mathcal{S} Q_1'$. We check that $V \xrightarrow{\mu} V' = Q_1' \mid Q_2$ and $U' \lfloor\mid\rfloor(\mathcal{S}) V'$ (again we use the property that $\mathcal{R} \subseteq \mathbf{b}(\mathcal{S})$ entails $\mathcal{R} \subseteq \mathcal{S}$).

- $U' = P_1 \mid P_2'$ with $P_2 \xrightarrow{\mu} P_2'$, which is identical to the previous case.

- $U' = P_1' \mid P_2'$ with $P_1 \xrightarrow{a} P_1'$, $P_2 \xrightarrow{\bar{a}} P_2'$, and $\mu = \tau$. We have $Q_1 \xrightarrow{a} Q_1'$ $Q_2 \xrightarrow{\bar{a}} Q_2'$ with $P_1' \mathcal{S} Q_1'$ and $P_2' \mathcal{S} Q_2'$; so that $V \xrightarrow{\tau} V' = Q_1' \mid Q_2'$ and $U' \lfloor\mid\rfloor(\mathcal{S}) V'$.

$\lfloor!\rfloor$: $U = \,!P \xrightarrow{\mu} U'$, $V = \,!Q$ with $P \mathcal{R} Q$. By induction on the derivation, there are two cases:

- $U' = \,!P \mid P^k \mid P' \mid P^{k'}$ with $P \xrightarrow{\mu} P'$ (we recall that P^n indicates the parallel composition of n copies of P). We deduce $Q \xrightarrow{\mu} Q'$ with $P' \mathcal{S} Q'$, and $V \xrightarrow{\mu} V' = \,!Q \mid Q^k \mid Q' \mid Q^{k'}$ and $U' \lfloor\mid\rfloor^{k+k'+1} \circ (\lfloor!\rfloor \cup \mathrm{id})(\mathcal{S}) V'$.

- $U' = \,!P \mid P^k \mid P_0 \mid P^{k'} \mid P_1 \mid P^{k''}$ with $P \xrightarrow{a} P_0$, $P \xrightarrow{\bar{a}} P_1$ and $\mu = \tau$. We deduce $Q \xrightarrow{a} Q_0$ and $Q \xrightarrow{\bar{a}} Q_1$ with $P_0 \mathcal{S} Q_0$ and $P_1 \mathcal{S} Q_1$. We then have $V \xrightarrow{\tau} V' = \,!Q \mid Q^k \mid Q_0 \mid Q^{k'} \mid Q_1 \mid Q^{k''}$, where $U' \lfloor\mid\rfloor^{k+k'+k''+1} \circ (\lfloor!\rfloor \cup \mathrm{id})(\mathcal{S}) V'$.

$\square$

Note that at several places in the proof, we need the property that $\mathcal{R} \subseteq \mathbf{b}(\mathcal{S})$ entails $\mathcal{R} \subseteq \mathcal{S}$. This holds thanks to clause (3) in the definition of $\mathbf{b}$ (Definition 6.3.1); as explained in Remark 6.4.2, this clause is necessary for $\mathcal{C}$ to be $\mathbf{b}$-compatible.

Putting it all together, since each of the the right-hand side functions in Lemma 6.4.11 is contained in $\mathcal{C}$, we can conclude:

Theorem 6.4.12 *The contextual closure $\mathcal{C}$ is $\mathbf{b}$-compatible.*

Proof By Proposition 6.4.10, it suffices to show $\lfloor \mathbb{C}_i \rfloor \xrightarrow{\mathbf{b}} \mathcal{C}$, i.e. for all $C \in \mathbb{C}_i$, $\lfloor C \rfloor \xrightarrow{\mathbf{b}} \mathcal{C}$. These evolutions are guaranteed by Lemma 6.4.11. $\square$

The proof of the above lemma may seem lengthy. It is nonetheless substantially simpler than a direct proof (Exercise 6.4.1), where the corresponding case analysis is performed within a larger induction on arbitrary polyadic contexts. We will see that the approach scales to the weak case (Section 6.5.3) where, in contrast, a direct proof is even more clumsy.

Another advantage of the approach is modularity: when adding a new syntactic construction, it suffices to analyse its evolutions to deduce whether it can be included in the up-to-context technique. In particular, Lemma 6.4.11 makes the dependencies between the various operators explicit (e.g. parallel composition can be proved on its own, while replication relies on parallel composition).

6.5 The case of weak bisimilarity

Strong bisimilarity is often too restrictive: it does not abstract over the internal behaviour of processes. Weak bisimilarity ($\approx$) addresses this problem by allowing processes to play the bisimulation game modulo silent transitions. We refer to [San12, chapter 4] for more details on the motivations for weak bisimilarity. Since the process transitions are more involved and the equivalence itself is coarser, the enhancements of the proof method for weak bisimilarity are even more important than those for strong bisimilarity.

The coinductive proof method for weak bisimilarity is the subject of this section. There are other 'weak' notions of bisimilarity, among which *coupled similarity* and *branching bisimilarity*, see [San12]. The results presented here can be adapted to handle these variations.

As we shall see, the theory of enhancements for weak bisimilarity is not as smooth as in the strong case; there are several reasons to this:

- the weak versions of some important diagram-based techniques are not sound (for example, the weak version of the up-to-bisimilarity technique – Definition 6.2.2);
- there is a canonical function admitting strong bisimilarity as its greatest fixed point (**b**), and all enhancements can be obtained by using **b**-compatible functions; in contrast, in the weak case we will need at least three functions for weak bisimilarity ($\mathbf{wb}, \mathbf{wb}_1, \mathbf{w}_t$), each of them admitting different sets of up-to techniques;
- some enhancements of weak bisimilarity correspond to non-symmetric functions, so that formulating the up-to techniques and factorising the symmetry arguments require the notions we introduced in Section 6.3.4.3;
- some useful enhancements of weak bisimilarity cannot be expressed as compatible functions.

The remainder of this section is organised as follows. We study diagram-based techniques in Section 6.5.2; this requires defining the three above-mentioned functions ($\mathbf{wb}, \mathbf{wb}_1, \mathbf{w}_t$). Then we treat up-to-context enhancements in Section 6.5.3, using the methodology presented in Section 6.4.5.

6.5.1 Weak bisimilarity

To define weak bisimilarity we have to introduce *weak transitions*, written $P \stackrel{\mu}{\Longrightarrow} Q$ and $P \stackrel{\widehat{\mu}}{\Longrightarrow} Q$:

- $P \stackrel{\widehat{\tau}}{\Longrightarrow} P'$ holds if there are $n \geq 0$ and processes $P_0, \ldots, P_n$ with $P = P_0$, $P' = P_n$, and $P_0 \stackrel{\tau}{\rightarrow} P_1 \stackrel{\tau}{\rightarrow} \ldots \stackrel{\tau}{\rightarrow} P_n$;
- $P \stackrel{\mu}{\Longrightarrow} P'$ holds if there are Q, Q' with $P \stackrel{\widehat{\tau}}{\Longrightarrow} Q \stackrel{\mu}{\rightarrow} Q' \stackrel{\widehat{\tau}}{\Longrightarrow} P'$;
- $P \stackrel{\widehat{\mu}}{\Longrightarrow} P'$, for $\mu \neq \tau$, is the same as $P \stackrel{\mu}{\Longrightarrow} P'$.

The following function is the analogue for weak bisimilarity of the function **b** for strong bisimilarity (Definition 6.3.1):

wb $: \mathcal{R} \mapsto \{ (P, Q) \mid$

$$\text{(1) if } P \stackrel{\widehat{\mu}}{\Longrightarrow} P', \text{ then there is } Q' \text{ s.t. } Q \stackrel{\widehat{\mu}}{\Longrightarrow} Q' \text{ and } P' \mathcal{R} Q'; \text{ and}$$

$$\text{(2) if } Q \stackrel{\widehat{\mu}}{\Longrightarrow} Q', \text{ then there is } P' \text{ s.t. } P \stackrel{\widehat{\mu}}{\Longrightarrow} P' \text{ and } P' \mathcal{R} Q'\}.$$

As expected, we have $\mathcal{R} \subseteq \textbf{wb}\,(\mathcal{S})$ if the diagram below is satisfied:

$$
\begin{array}{ccc}
P & \mathcal{R} & Q \\
\widehat{\mu}\Big\Vert & & \Big\Vert\widehat{\mu} \\
P' & \mathcal{S} & Q'
\end{array}
$$

Weak bisimilarity ($\approx$) is the greatest fixed point of **wb**, and the largest **wb**-simulation.

6.5.2 Diagram-based techniques

The above definition of weak bisimilarity corresponds to playing strong bisimilarity games over the 'weak' LTS ($\stackrel{\widehat{\mu}}{\Longrightarrow}$). It is however not satisfactory in proofs: when examining the challenges from a process in a pair, one has to take into account all weak transitions emanating from the processes. This can be tedious, as shown in the following exercise.

Exercise 6.5.1 Describe the weak derivatives of the process $!a.\,b \mid \,!\overline{a}$. Prove that $!a.\,b \mid \,!\overline{a} \approx \,!a \mid \,!b \mid \,!\overline{a}$ using a **wb**-simulation.   □

We saw in [San12], as a solution to this, an alternative definition of weak bisimilarity in which the challenger plays only strong transitions. We thus obtain the two following weak-bisimulation diagrams. In these two diagrams, as well as in the diagrams in the remainder of the section, an existential quantifier in front of a derivative indicates that the diagram should be read only in one direction, the existential marking the responder side. For instance, the second of the two diagrams below reads thus: whenever $P \mathrel{\mathcal{R}} Q$, for all μ and Q' such that $Q \xrightarrow{\mu} Q'$ there is P' with $P \xRightarrow{\widehat{\mu}} P'$ and $P' \mathrel{\mathcal{S}} Q'$.

$$
\begin{array}{ccc}
P & \mathcal{R} & Q \\
\mu \downarrow & & \Downarrow \widehat{\mu} \\
P' & \mathcal{S} & \exists Q'
\end{array}
\qquad\qquad
\begin{array}{ccc}
P & \mathcal{R} & Q \\
\widehat{\mu} \Downarrow & & \downarrow \mu \\
\exists P' & \mathcal{S} & Q'
\end{array}
$$

We define the function that corresponds to these two diagrams:

$\mathbf{wb_1} : \mathcal{R} \mapsto \{ (P, Q) \mid$

    (1) if $P \xrightarrow{\mu} P'$, then there is Q' s.t. $Q \xRightarrow{\widehat{\mu}} Q'$ and $P' \mathrel{\mathcal{R}} Q'$; and

    (2) if $Q \xrightarrow{\mu} Q'$, then there is P' s.t. $P \xRightarrow{\widehat{\mu}} P'$ and $P' \mathrel{\mathcal{R}} Q'$; and

    (3) $P \mathrel{\mathcal{R}} Q \}$.

As in the strong case, clause (3) is needed to obtain the up-to-context technique as a compatible function – Remark 6.4.2. The function $\mathbf{wb_1}$ has weak bisimilarity as its greatest fixed point (see the exercise below, or [San12, lemma 4.2.10]).

Exercise 6.5.2 Show that a relation is a $\mathbf{wb_1}$-simulation if and only if it is a $\mathbf{wb}$-simulation; deduce that $\mathrm{gfp}(\mathbf{wb_1}) = \mathrm{gfp}(\mathbf{wb})$. $\qquad\qquad\square$

While $\mathbf{wb_1}$-simulations and $\mathbf{wb}$-simulations coincide and therefore have the same number of pairs, establishing a $\mathbf{wb_1}$-simulation generally involves fewer diagrams to prove. Moreover, the differences between $\mathbf{wb_1}$ and $\mathbf{wb}$ have important consequences on up-to techniques.

6.5.2.1 The problem with weak bisimilarity

The function $\mathbf{wb}$ for weak bisimilarity yields a rather smooth theory of up-to techniques: it is the standard bisimulation game, just played on a different LTS ($\xRightarrow{\widehat{\mu}}$). In particular, functions $\mathcal{R} \mapsto \approx$ and $\mathcal{R} \mapsto \mathcal{R}^\star$ are $\mathbf{wb}$-compatible, hence also $\mathcal{R} \mapsto (\mathcal{R} \cup \approx)^\star$ is $\mathbf{wb}$-compatible.

The same is not true for the function $\mathbf{wb}_1$, whose definition uses two different LTSs. Indeed, the functions $\mathcal{R} \mapsto \approx\mathcal{R}\approx$, $\mathcal{R} \mapsto \mathcal{R}^\star$, or $\mathcal{R} \mapsto (\mathcal{R} \cup \approx)^\star$ are not $\mathbf{wb}_1$-sound [SM92]: to see this, consider the singleton relation $\{(\tau.a, \mathbf{0})\}$; although $\mathcal{R} \not\subseteq \approx$, we have $\mathcal{R} \subseteq \mathbf{wb}_1 (\approx\mathcal{R}\approx)$:

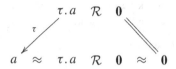

(To obtain a counterexample for function $\mathcal{R} \mapsto \mathcal{R}^\star$, it suffices to include the pair $(a, \tau.a)$ in the bisimulation candidate.) This situation is troublesome, since $\mathbf{wb}_1$ is the function that we wish to use in practice. In the following subsections we look at different ways of circumventing this limitation. The solutions in Sections 6.5.2.2–6.5.2.4 are the most basic. Those in Sections 6.5.2.5 and 6.5.2.6 are more powerful, but also technically more involved.

6.5.2.2 Up to strong bisimilarity

Let us go back to the counterexample in Section 6.5.2.1, and consider an attempt at proving that the function $\mathcal{R} \mapsto \approx\mathcal{R}\approx$ is $\mathbf{wb}_1$-compatible. Assuming $\mathcal{R} \subseteq \mathbf{wb}_1 (\mathcal{S})$, we have to show $\approx\mathcal{R}\approx \subseteq \mathbf{wb}_1 (\approx\mathcal{S}\approx)$. Thus, suppose $P \approx P_0 \mathcal{R} Q_0 \approx Q$ and $P \xrightarrow{\mu} P'$; we have to find some Q' such that $P' \approx\mathcal{S}\approx Q'$ and $Q \overset{\widehat{\mu}}{\Rightarrow} Q'$. Since $\approx$ is a $\mathbf{wb}_1$-simulation, there is some P_0' with $P' \approx P_0'$ and $P_0 \overset{\widehat{\mu}}{\Rightarrow} P_0'$. There are now several cases, depending on the number of steps between P_0 and P_0':

- $P_0 = P_0'$ (and $\mu = \tau$): we can choose $Q' = Q$, and we are done, since $\mathcal{R} \subseteq \mathcal{S}$;
- $P_0 \xrightarrow{\mu} P_0'$: since $\mathcal{R} \subseteq \mathbf{wb}_1 (\mathcal{S})$, we find some Q_0' such that $P_0' \mathcal{S} Q_0'$ and $Q_0 \overset{\widehat{\mu}}{\Rightarrow} Q_0'$; and since $\approx$ is a weak bisimulation, we find Q' such that $Q_0' \approx Q'$ and $Q \overset{\widehat{\mu}}{\Rightarrow} Q'$; thus the diagram is closed;
- $P_0 \xrightarrow{\tau} P_0'' \overset{\mu}{\Rightarrow} P_0'$: as in the previous case, we find Q_0'', Q'' such that $P_0'' \mathcal{S} Q_0'' \approx Q''$, $Q_0 \overset{\widehat{\tau}}{\Rightarrow} Q_0''$, and $Q \overset{\widehat{\tau}}{\Rightarrow} Q''$. The situation is summarised in the diagram below, where we can see where we get stuck: we have not enough

conditions on $\mathcal{S}$ with respect to transitions, so that we are unable to close the remaining parts of the diagram.

$$
\begin{array}{ccccccc}
P & \approx & P_0 & \mathcal{R} & Q_0 & \approx & Q \\
\Big\downarrow \mu & & \Big\downarrow \tau & & \Big\Downarrow \widehat{\tau} & & \Big\Downarrow \widehat{\tau} \\
& & P_0'' & \mathcal{S} & Q_0'' & \approx & Q'' \\
& & \Big\Downarrow \mu & & & & \\
P' & \approx & P_0' & & ? & & ?
\end{array}
$$

A first obvious remedy consists in using strong, rather than weak, bisimilarity.

Exercise 6.5.3 Prove that function $\mathcal{R} \mapsto \sim\mathcal{R}\sim$ is $\mathbf{wb}_1$-compatible.   □

Exercise 6.5.3 tells us that a relation $\mathcal{R}$ satisfying the following diagrams is contained in weak bisimilarity:

$$
\begin{array}{ccc}
P & \mathcal{R} & Q \\
\Big\downarrow \mu & & \Big\Downarrow \widehat{\mu} \\
P' & \sim\mathcal{R}\sim & \exists Q'
\end{array}
\qquad
\begin{array}{ccc}
P & \mathcal{R} & Q \\
\Big\Downarrow \widehat{\mu} & & \Big\downarrow \mu \\
\exists P' & \sim\mathcal{R}\sim & Q'
\end{array}
$$

For example, this technique offers a simple solution to Exercise 6.5.1:

Example 6.5.4 In CCS, we have $!a.b \mid !\overline{a} \approx !a \mid !b \mid !\overline{a}$.

Proof Setting $P \stackrel{\text{def}}{=} !a.b \mid !\overline{a}$ and $Q \stackrel{\text{def}}{=} !a \mid !b \mid !\overline{a}$, we can use the relation $\{(P \mid b^n, \ Q) \mid n \geq 0\}$:

- for the left-to-right part of the game, we note that all transitions from $P \mid b^n$ can be written as

$$
\begin{array}{lll}
P \mid b^n \xrightarrow{a} \sim P \mid b^{n+1}, & & P \mid b^{n+1} \xrightarrow{b} \sim P \mid b^n, \\
P \mid b^n \xrightarrow{\tau} \sim P \mid b^{n+1}, & \text{or} & P \mid b^n \xrightarrow{\overline{a}} \sim P \mid b^n \ ;
\end{array}
$$

therefore, it suffices to check that $Q \xrightarrow{\mu} \sim Q$ for $\mu \in \{a, \overline{a}, \tau, b\}$;
- for the right-to-left part of the game, we note that $Q \xrightarrow{\mu} Q'$ entails $Q \sim Q'$; such transitions can be matched by the above transitions from $P \mid b^n$, except when $\mu = b$ and $n = 0$ in which case we use a sequence of transitions $P \xrightarrow{\tau} \xrightarrow{b} \sim P$.

          □

6.5.2.3 The expansion preorder

In the up-to-strong-bisimilarity technique of Exercise 6.5.3, the appearance of strong bisimilarity is sometimes too constraining. We obtain a more powerful technique using an asymmetric variant of weak bisimilarity called *expansion*, written $\gtrsim$. In practice, it is often possible to show that processes that one expects to be bisimilar are related by expansion. The idea underlying expansion is roughly that if Q expands P, then P and Q are weakly bisimilar, and in addition, during the bisimulation game P never performs more τ transitions than Q. Expansion is not an equivalence (it is not symmetric). To define it, we need some notation:

(1) $\xrightarrow{\hat{\tau}}$ is the reflexive closure of $\xrightarrow{\tau}$; that is, $P \xrightarrow{\hat{\tau}} P'$ if $P \xrightarrow{\tau} P'$ or $P' = P$.
(2) $\xrightarrow{\hat{a}}$ is $\xrightarrow{a}$.   □

Definition 6.5.5 (Expansion relation)
  A relation $\mathcal{R}$ is an *expansion* if whenever $P \mathcal{R} Q$,

(1) $P \xrightarrow{\mu} P'$ implies $Q \xRightarrow{\mu} Q'$ and $P' \mathcal{R} Q'$ for some Q';
(2) $Q \xrightarrow{\mu} Q'$ implies $P \xrightarrow{\hat{\mu}} P'$ and $P' \mathcal{R} Q'$ for some P'.

Q *expands* P, written $Q \gtrsim P$ or $P \lesssim Q$, if $P \mathcal{R} Q$ for some expansion $\mathcal{R}$. We call $\gtrsim$ the *expansion relation*.   □

  The diagrams for the expansion game are:

$$
\begin{array}{ccc}
P & \lesssim & Q \\
\mu\downarrow & & \big\Vert\,\hat{\mu} \\
P' & \lesssim & \exists Q'
\end{array}
\qquad\qquad
\begin{array}{ccc}
Q & \gtrsim & P \\
\mu\downarrow & & \downarrow\,\hat{\mu} \\
Q' & \gtrsim & \exists P'
\end{array}
$$

The expansion preorder lies in between strong and weak bisimilarity (we have $\sim \subsetneq \gtrsim \subsetneq \approx$). Like weak bisimilarity, expansion is preserved by all CCS operators except choice. Expansion was investigated by Arun-Kumar and Hennessy [AKH92] as a preorder giving information about the 'efficiency' of processes. Its use in up-to techniques was proposed in [SM92].

Exercise 6.5.6 Consider the following processes. Which pairs are in the expansion preorder?

(1) $\mathbf{0}$, τ, and $\tau.\tau$.
(2) a, $\tau.a + a$, and $\tau.\tau.a + a$.
(3) $a.b$, $\tau.a.b$, $a.\tau.b$, $a.b.\tau$, $\tau.\tau.a.b$, and $\tau.a.\tau.b$.   □

Expansion leads to an up-to technique for weak bisimilarity called 'up to expansion', formalised by means of the following function on relations.

Lemma 6.5.7 *The function* $\mathcal{R} \mapsto \gtrsim \mathcal{R} \precsim$ *is* **wb**$_1$-*compatible.*

Proof Similar to the proof of Exercise 6.5.3 (since the left-to-right part of the expansion game requires the right-hand side process to answer with at most one step, the faulty diagram-chasing discussed in Section 6.5.2.2 does not arise).

□

Up-to expansion is frequently used to get rid of 'administrative' steps (that is, internal transitions $P \xrightarrow{\tau} P'$ where the initial and final processes P and P' are bisimilar) during weak-bisimulation games. The following exercise illustrates the phenomenon.

Exercise 6.5.8 Prove that $(\nu a)(a.\, P \mid \overline{a}.\, Q) \gtrsim (\nu a)(P \mid Q)$. Use this law to prove $!(\nu a)(b.\, a \mid \overline{a}.\, P) \approx !b.\, (\nu a)P$, using a weak bisimulation up to expansion. What other up-to technique would make the proof even easier?   □

The expansion preorder, being coinductively defined, admits up-to techniques as well. We propose some of them as an exercise, below; we refer to [Pou07, Pou08a] for a systematic treatment.

Exercise* 6.5.9 Define a function **e** on process relations for the expansion game: the greatest fixed point of **e** should be the expansion preorder. Then derive a technique of 'expansion up to strong bisimilarity' by showing that the function $\mathcal{R} \mapsto \sim\mathcal{R}\sim$ is **e**-compatible. Is the 'expansion up to transitivity' technique sound? Propose an 'expansion up to expansion' technique.   □

6.5.2.4 Non-symmetric up-to techniques
An inspection of the soundness proof for the 'up-to-expansion' technique reveals that expansion is not required on the responder side: we can work with the following weaker diagrams:

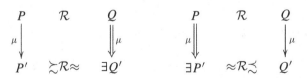

These diagrams involve the non-symmetric function $\mathcal{R} \mapsto \gtrsim\mathcal{R}\approx$. As we shall see in the sequel, there are other enhancements that are best expressed using non-symmetric functions. We explained in Section 6.3.4 how to handle these techniques: we can decompose the map **wb**$_1$ for weak bisimulations, so to focus on the left-to-right part of weak bisimulation games. Hence, let $\mathbf{w}$ be the following function, obtained from $\mathbf{wb}_1$ by removing the second clause:

$$\mathbf{w} : \mathcal{R} \mapsto \{ (P, Q) \mid P \; \mathcal{R} \; Q \text{ and}$$

$$\text{if } P \xrightarrow{\mu} P', \text{ then there exists } Q' \text{ s.t. } Q \xLongrightarrow{\hat{\mu}} Q' \text{ and } P' \; \mathcal{R} \; Q' \}.$$

The converse of $\mathbf{w}$, namely $\overline{\mathbf{w}}$, corresponds to the right-to-left part of the weak bisimulation game, and one can take the conjunction of these two functions, $\overleftrightarrow{\mathbf{w}}$, to recover the whole weak bisimulation game. Indeed, we have $\mathbf{wb}_1 = \overleftrightarrow{\mathbf{w}}$. Therefore, according to Proposition 6.3.28, it suffices to find functions that are $\mathbf{w}$-sound via a symmetric function to obtain up-to techniques for weak bisimilarity. As a typical example, the up-to technique corresponding to the above two diagrams can be obtained as follows:

Lemma 6.5.10   *The function $\mathcal{R} \mapsto \gtrsim\mathcal{R}\approx$ is $\mathbf{w}$-compatible, and $\mathbf{w}$-sound via the symmetric function $\mathcal{R} \mapsto \approx\mathcal{R}\approx$.*

Proof Let $f_0 : \mathcal{R} \mapsto \gtrsim\mathcal{R}\approx$. One shows that f_0 is $\mathbf{w}$-compatible, proceeding as in the proof of Lemma 6.5.7. By Theorem 6.3.26, we then deduce that f_0 is $\mathbf{w}$-sound via f_0^ω, and $f_0^\omega = f_0$ since f_0 is idempotent. We conclude using Lemma 6.3.27 with $g : \mathcal{R} \mapsto \approx\mathcal{R}$: we have $g(f_0(\mathcal{R})) = \approx\gtrsim\mathcal{R}\approx = \approx\mathcal{R}\approx$. $\qquad\square$

6.5.2.5 Distinguishing between silent and visible transitions

In Section 6.5.2.1, the counterexample to the soundness of 'weak bisimulation up to weak bisimilarity' relies on the possibility of implicitly ignoring the derivatives of certain silent transitions in the 'up-to-weak-bisimilarity' (specifically, the transition whose derivative is ignored was $\tau . a \xrightarrow{\tau} a$). The problem, in contrast, does not show up when the challenge is on a visible action. It is indeed possible to restrain the use of the up-to-weak-bisimilarity technique (or equivalently, up-to-transitivity) to visible actions. In the sequel, we let α range over visible actions (i.e. a or $\overline{a}$).

Lemma 6.5.11   *Suppose $\mathcal{R}$ is a relation that satisfies the diagrams below:*

Then $\mathcal{R}^+$ is a $\mathbf{w}$-simulation.

Proof (Sketch) We prove that the following diagrams hold, by three successive inductions on the natural number n (recall that $\mathcal{R}^n$ and $\overset{\tau}{\to}^n$, respectively, denote the n-th iterations of $\mathcal{R}$ and $\overset{\tau}{\to}$):

$$
\begin{array}{ccc}
P & \mathcal{R} & Q \\
\tau\big\downarrow & & \big\Vert\hat{\tau} \\
P' & \mathcal{R} & \exists Q'
\end{array}
\qquad
\begin{array}{ccc}
P & \mathcal{R}^n & Q \\
\hat{\tau}\big\Vert & & \big\Vert\hat{\tau} \\
P' & \mathcal{R}^n & \exists Q'
\end{array}
\qquad
\begin{array}{ccc}
P & \mathcal{R}^n & Q \\
\mu\big\downarrow & & \big\Vert\hat{\mu} \\
P' & \mathcal{R}^+ & \exists Q'
\end{array}
$$

(with τ on the left arrow n and $\hat{\tau}$ on the middle) $\qquad\square$

In order to integrate the technique in Lemma 6.5.11 with previous enhancements, it suffices to define the following function, where, on visible actions, up to transitivity is built-in:

$\mathbf{w}_t : \mathcal{R} \mapsto \{(P, Q) \mid P \, \mathcal{R} \, Q$ and

if $P \overset{\tau}{\to} P'$, then there is Q' such that $Q \overset{\hat{\tau}}{\Rightarrow} Q'$ and $P' \, \mathcal{R} \, Q'$;

if $P \overset{\alpha}{\to} P'$, then there is Q' such that $Q \overset{\alpha}{\Rightarrow} Q'$ and $P' \, \mathcal{R}^+ \, Q'\}$.

By Lemma 6.5.11, this function agrees with weak bisimilarity.

Lemma 6.5.12 *We have* $\mathtt{gfp}(\mathbf{w}_t) = \mathtt{gfp}(\mathbf{w})$, *and* $\mathtt{gfp}\left(\overset{\leftrightarrow}{\mathbf{w}_t}\right) = \mathtt{gfp}\left(\overset{\leftrightarrow}{\mathbf{w}}\right)$.
$\qquad\square$

Exercise 6.5.13 Show that the functions $\mathcal{R} \mapsto \succsim\mathcal{R}$, $\mathcal{R} \mapsto \mathcal{R}\approx$, and $\mathcal{R} \mapsto \mathcal{R}^=$ are $\mathbf{w}_t$-compatible. Why did we use transitive closure rather than reflexive and transitive closure in Lemma 6.5.11 and in the definition of $\mathbf{w}_t$? $\qquad\square$

We finally obtain the following technique.

Corollary 6.5.14 *Let $\mathcal{R}$ be a symmetric relation that satisfies these diagrams:*

$$
\begin{array}{ccc}
P & \mathcal{R} & Q \\
\tau\big\downarrow & & \big\Vert\tau \\
P' & \succsim\mathcal{R}^=\approx & \exists Q'
\end{array}
\qquad\qquad
\begin{array}{ccc}
P & \mathcal{R} & Q \\
\alpha\big\downarrow & & \big\Vert\alpha \\
P' & (\mathcal{R} \cup \approx)^\star & \exists Q'
\end{array}
$$

Then $\mathcal{R}$ is contained in weak bisimilarity.

Proof According to Exercise 6.5.13 and Proposition 6.3.11, the function $f : \mathcal{R} \mapsto \succsim\mathcal{R}^=\approx$ is $\mathbf{w}_t$-compatible, and hence $\mathbf{w}_t$-sound via $f^\omega = f$, by Theorem 6.3.26. As in the proof of Lemma 6.5.10, this witness can be extended to a symmetric function, so that Proposition 6.3.28 applies. We finally check that $f(\mathcal{R})^+ = (\mathcal{R} \cup \approx)^\star$. $\qquad\square$

6.5.2.6 Beyond expansion: termination hypotheses

In the up-to-expansion technique, for $P \succsim Q$ to hold, Q need to be as fast as P at *every* transition along the expansion game. This kind of property may fail to hold, for example, on process optimisations whose benefits are obtained through an amortised analysis, i.e. when Q is globally faster than P at the cost of some bookkeeping steps at the beginning (where Q may be slower than P).

An alternative to the expansion preorder consists in using termination hypotheses. Recall the counterexample against weak bisimilarity up to transitivity:

$$\mathcal{R} \overset{\text{def}}{=} \{(a, \tau.a), \ (\tau.a, \mathbf{0})\} \qquad \mathbf{0} \xleftarrow{\ a\ } a \overset{\mathcal{R}}{\underset{\tau}{\rightleftarrows}} \tau.a \xrightarrow{\ \mathcal{R}\ } \mathbf{0}.$$

$\mathcal{R}$ is a weak bisimulation up to transitivity, although it is not contained in weak bisimilarity. The diagram on the right shows the transitions of the processes in $\mathcal{R}$, together with the pairing given by $\mathcal{R}$. If we forget the labelling of the arrows in the graph, we obtain a standard example of a relation which is locally confluent but not confluent: from the vertex labelled by a, one can reach in several steps the two vertices labelled by $\mathbf{0}$, which are not joinable (so that the relation is not confluent), while following two edges starting from a single vertex always leads to joinable vertices (the relation is locally confluent). In rewriting theory [TeR03], this problem is commonly resolved by resorting to Newman's lemma [New42]: any locally confluent and terminating relation is confluent. By adding a similar hypothesis, we now show how to recover soundness for weak bisimulation up to transitivity.

Looking at the above counterexample, it appears that the problem comes from the ability to cancel silent transitions in weak bisimilarity: when $\tau.a$ does a silent transition to a, transitivity (or up to $\approx$) makes it possible to come back to the initial process: $a \approx \tau.a$. The termination hypothesis we propose in the following theorem prevents this situation: the relation $\mathcal{S}^+ \overset{\tau}{\rightarrow}^+$ terminates if and only if there is no infinite sequence of processes related by $\mathcal{S}$ or $\overset{\tau}{\rightarrow}$ that alternates infinitely often between $\mathcal{S}$-steps and $\overset{\tau}{\rightarrow}$-steps. In particular, cycles like the one from the above counterexample, between processes a and $\tau.a$, are not allowed.

Theorem 6.5.15 *Let $\mathcal{R}, \mathcal{S}$ be two relations with $\mathcal{S} \subseteq \mathcal{R}$, such that the relation $\mathcal{S}^+ \overset{\tau}{\rightarrow}^+$ terminates and the following diagrams are satisfied:*

$$
\begin{array}{ccc}
P & \mathcal{R} & Q \\
\tau \downarrow & & \parallel \tau \\
P' & \mathcal{S}^\star \mathcal{R} & \exists Q'
\end{array}
\qquad\qquad
\begin{array}{ccc}
P & \mathcal{R} & Q \\
\alpha \downarrow & & \parallel \alpha \\
P' & \mathcal{R}^\star & \exists Q'
\end{array}
$$

*Then $\mathcal{R}^\star$ is a **w**-simulation.*   □

The proof is rather involved; it can be found in [Pou07, Pou08a].

This technique can be used in places where up-to-expansion is not sufficient. We need however non-trivial process behaviours to illustrate the situation, and therefore we do not report examples here. The interested reader may consult [Pou08b], where the technique is used to reason about an optimisation for a distributed abstract machine.

We conclude by showing how the above technique can be combined with other techniques, like, e.g. up-to-context. Indeed, since proving the soundness of each technique separately is already quite involved, this is a situation where we need the theory of compatible functions: it would be really hard to prove the soundness of the combined technique from scratch.

First we have to formalise the technique of Theorem 6.5.15 as a function on relations. For this, we use the following function:

$$t_\succ : \mathcal{R} \mapsto (\mathcal{R} \cap \succ)^* \mathcal{R},$$

where $\succ$ is a given transitive relation. This relation $\succ$ allows us to 'control' the pairs that are used to rewrite the derivatives of the challenger transitions. Using this function, and taking $\mathcal{S} = \mathcal{R} \cap \succ$ in Theorem 6.5.15, we obtain:

Corollary 6.5.16 *If* $\succ \xrightarrow{\tau}{}^+$ *terminates, then function* $t_\succ$ *is* **w**- *and* $\mathbf{w}_t$-*sound.*

Unfortunately, function $t_\succ$ is not **w**- or $\mathbf{w}_t$-compatible, which prevents us from combining it freely with other compatible functions. We solve this problem with the next theorem, which allows us to combine a sound function g and a compatible function f into a sound function, by relying on an additional compatibility property between f and g.

Theorem 6.5.17 *Let* b, f, g *be three monotone functions. If* g *is* b-*sound and* f *is both* b- *and* g-*compatible, then* $g \circ f$ *is* b-*sound.*

Proof We first prove that f is $(b \circ g)$-compatible: we have $f \circ b \circ g \subseteq b \circ f \circ g \subseteq b \circ g \circ f$, by the b- and g-compatibility of f, and the monotonicity of b.

Therefore f is $(b \circ g)$-sound: $\mathrm{gfp}\,(b \circ g \circ f) \subseteq \mathrm{gfp}\,(b \circ g)$. We can now conclude, since $\mathrm{gfp}\,(b \circ g) \subseteq \mathrm{gfp}\,(b)$ by b-soundness of g. $\qquad\square$

The theorem tells us that if we wish to combine the sound function $t_\succ$ with some compatible functions, we have to show that these functions are $t_\succ$-compatible. In practice, this is easy to do, thanks to the compositionality properties of compatibility. An example is Corollary 6.5.19 below; the compatibility properties needed in the corollary are summarised in the following lemma, whose proof is straightforward.

Lemma 6.5.18 *The following functions are $t_\succ$-compatible:*

- $\mathcal{R} \mapsto \mathcal{R}S$ *where S is a reflexive relation;*
- *any context closure $\mathcal{C}$, provided that $\mathcal{C}(\succ) \subseteq \succ$, i.e. that $\succ$ is closed under these contexts.*   □

We show in Section 6.5.3.1 that up-to-context is a valid up-to technique for weak bisimulation in CCS, the corresponding function $\mathcal{C}$ being **w**-compatible. We can thus combine up-to-context and other compatible techniques with the termination-based technique, so as to obtain the following very powerful up-to technique. The result illustrates the benefits of the abstract and modular theory of enhancements we presented: proving the soundness of the final up-to technique from scratch (as opposed to deriving it from the soundness of its component techniques) would be hard. The technique so derived corresponds to the powerful technique we had for strong bisimilarity (the function $\mathcal{R} \mapsto (\mathcal{C}(\mathcal{R}) \cup \sim)^\star$ of Corollary 6.3.15); it is however constrained using a termination hypothesis.

Corollary 6.5.19 *If $\succ\overset{\tau}{\rightarrow}^+$ terminates and $\succ$ is closed under CCS contexts, then the function $\mathcal{R} \mapsto ((\mathcal{C}(\mathcal{R}) \cup \approx) \cap \succ)^\star \mathcal{C}(\mathcal{R})\approx$ is **w**-sound.*

Proof By Proposition 6.3.11 and Lemma 6.5.18, the function $f : \mathcal{R} \mapsto \mathcal{C}(R)\approx$ is **w**- and $t_\succ$-compatible; and $t_\succ$ is **w**-sound by Corollary 6.5.16. We can thus apply Theorem 6.5.17, and we check that $t_\succ(f(\mathcal{R})) = ((\mathcal{C}(\mathcal{R}) \cup \approx) \cap \succ)^\star \mathcal{C}(\mathcal{R})\approx$.   □

Corollary 6.5.19 shows that any symmetric relation $\mathcal{R}$ that satisfies the following diagram is contained in weak bisimilarity, provided that the relation $\succ$ is transitive, closed under contexts, and satisfies the termination hypothesis.

$$
\begin{array}{ccc}
P & \mathcal{R} & Q \\
\mu \downarrow & & \downarrow\!\!\downarrow \hat{\mu} \\
P' & ((\mathcal{C}(\mathcal{R}) \cup \approx) \cap \succ)^\star \; \mathcal{C}(\mathcal{R}) \approx & \exists Q'
\end{array}
$$

In applications of the technique, one usually proceeds as follows:

(1) find a weak bisimulation up to context, up to transitivity, and up to weak bisimilarity, without worrying about the termination guarantee;

(2) collect the pairs that were used to rewrite the derivatives of each challenge, and call ▷ such a relation;

(3) define $\succ$ as the closure of $\rhd$ under contexts and transitivity (i.e. $\succ \stackrel{\text{def}}{=} \mathcal{C}\rhd^+$), and check that it satisfies the termination hypothesis (i.e. $\succ\stackrel{\tau}{\rightarrow}^+$ terminates).

We shall see in Section 6.5.3.2 that in CCS with sum, we actually have to restrict the function $\mathcal{C}$ from Corollary 6.5.19 to *non-degenerate* CCS contexts, referred to with the function $\mathcal{C}^{nd}$. Moreover, if we use replication in contexts, then the congruence requirement about the relation $\succ$ is slightly stronger, since the actual **w**-compatible function is not $\mathcal{C}^{nd}$ itself, but an extension of it (Theorem 6.5.24).

Exercise 6.5.20 Show that the function $\mathcal{R} \mapsto ((\mathcal{R} \cup \approx) \cap \succ)^\star \mathcal{R}^= \approx$ is $\mathbf{w}_t$-sound whenever $\succ\stackrel{\tau}{\rightarrow}^+$ terminates. Draw the diagrams corresponding to the associated up-to technique. □

Exercise* 6.5.21 Corollary 6.5.19 actually gives an up-to technique for weak similarity only: it still needs to be extended to weak bisimilarity, using symmetry arguments. Extend Theorem 6.5.17 and Corollary. 6.5.16 using the notion of soundness 'via' introduced in Section 6.3.4.3. Deduce that Corollary 6.5.19 actually gives an up-to technique for weak bisimilarity. (A detailed answer can be found in [Pou07, Pou08a].) □

6.5.3 Up-to context and congruence

We now move to the analysis of the up-to-context technique for weak bisimilarity. Like in the strong case (Section 6.4), we focus on CCS with replication.

Weak bisimilarity is not a congruence in CCS: we have $a \approx \tau.a$, but $b + a \not\approx b + \tau.a$. (The right-hand side process is able to silently evolve into a; this transition cannot be matched by the left-hand side process.) As a consequence, there is no hope of proving that the function $\mathcal{C}$ is **w**-compatible, i.e. that up to context is valid for weak bisimilarity in CCS. This problem is however orthogonal to the theory of up-to techniques, so we shall ignore it at first, by working in the sum-free fragment of CCS: in this fragment, weak bisimilarity is a congruence, and the up-to-context technique is valid.

6.5.3.1 The case of sum-free CCS

Recall the notations from Sections 6.4.1 and 6.4.5: we use the method based on initial contexts to obtain the up-to-context technique. Let $\mathbb{C}_i^- \stackrel{\text{def}}{=} \mathbb{C}_i \setminus \{+\}$ be the set of initial CCS contexts (Definition 6.4.6), without the initial context for sum. We call *closure under sum-free CCS contexts* the function $\mathcal{C}^- \stackrel{\text{def}}{=} \lfloor \mathbb{C}_i^- \rfloor^\omega$.

Unfortunately, the function $\mathcal{C}^-$ is not **w**-compatible: we need to slightly extend it so that it becomes **w**-compatible. The problem comes from replication: consider for example the relation $\mathcal{R} \stackrel{\text{def}}{=} \{(\tau.a, a)\}^=$; we have $\mathcal{R} \subseteq \mathbf{w}(\mathcal{R})$, but, as depicted below, $\mathcal{C}^-(\mathcal{R}) \subseteq \mathbf{w}(\mathcal{C}^-(\mathcal{R}))$ does not hold: the right-hand side process cannot answer within $\mathcal{C}^-(\mathcal{R})$ since $!a$ cannot move; we would need to rewrite $!a$ into $!a \mid a$.

$$
\begin{array}{ccc}
!\tau.a & \lfloor ! \rfloor(\mathcal{R}) & !a \\
\Big\downarrow {\scriptstyle \tau} & & \\
!\tau.a \mid a & & ?
\end{array}
$$

However, we can still follow the methodology we presented in the strong case (Section 6.4.5): we have to analyse the effect of each syntactic construction on transitions. The problematic case above can be resolved by working up to unfolding of replications, which is contained in strong bisimilarity. For the other operators, we obtain the same properties we had in Lemma 6.4.11 in the strong case.

Lemma 6.5.22 *The following evolutions hold:*

- $\lfloor \mu. \rfloor \stackrel{\mathbf{w}}{\leadsto} \mathrm{id}$
- $\lfloor (\nu a) \rfloor \stackrel{\mathbf{w}}{\leadsto} \lfloor (\nu a) \rfloor$
- $\lfloor 0 \rfloor \stackrel{\mathbf{w}}{\leadsto} \lfloor 0 \rfloor$
- $\lfloor | \rfloor \stackrel{\mathbf{w}}{\leadsto} \lfloor | \rfloor$
- $\lfloor ! \rfloor \stackrel{\mathbf{w}}{\leadsto} (\mathcal{R} \mapsto \sim \mathcal{C}^-(\mathcal{R}) \sim)$.

Proof We only prove the last case, for the replication operator. Consider $\mathcal{R}, \mathcal{S}$ such that $\mathcal{R} \subseteq \mathbf{w}(\mathcal{S})$; we have to show $\lfloor ! \rfloor(\mathcal{R}) \subseteq \mathbf{w}(\sim \mathcal{C}^-(\mathcal{S}) \sim)$. Suppose that $P \mathcal{R} Q$ and $!P \stackrel{\mu}{\rightarrow} P'$; there are two cases (we recall that P^n denotes the parallel composition of n copies of P):

- $P' = !P \mid P^k \mid P_0 \mid P^{k'}$ with $P \stackrel{\mu}{\rightarrow} P_0$. Since $\mathcal{R} \stackrel{\mathbf{w}}{\leadsto} \mathcal{S}$, we deduce $Q \stackrel{\mu}{\Rightarrow} Q_0$ with $P_0 \mathcal{S} Q_0$. There are two cases:
  - $Q \stackrel{\mu}{\Rightarrow} Q_0$, and we have $!Q \stackrel{\mu}{\Rightarrow} Q' \stackrel{\text{def}}{=} !Q \mid Q^k \mid Q_0 \mid Q^{k'}$, with $P' \mathcal{C}^-(\mathcal{S}) Q'$;
  - $Q = Q_0$ (and $\mu = \tau$); in this case, $!Q$ cannot move. This is where we have reason modulo $\sim$: we have $!Q \sim Q' \stackrel{\text{def}}{=} !Q \mid Q^{k+1+k'}$, and $P' \mathcal{C}^-(\mathcal{S}) Q' \sim !Q$.
- $P' = !P \mid P^k \mid P_0 \mid P^{k'} \mid P_1 \mid P^{k''}$ with $P \stackrel{a}{\rightarrow} P_0$ and $P \stackrel{\bar{a}}{\rightarrow} P_1$ ($\mu = \tau$). Since $\mathcal{R} \stackrel{\mathbf{w}}{\leadsto} \mathcal{S}$, we deduce $Q \stackrel{a}{\Rightarrow} Q_0$ and $Q \stackrel{\bar{a}}{\Rightarrow} Q_1$ with $P_0 \mathcal{S} Q_0$ and

$P_1 \, S \, Q_1$. We then have $!Q \overset{\tau}{\Rightarrow} Q' \overset{\text{def}}{=} !Q \mid Q^k \mid Q_0 \mid Q^{k'} \mid Q_1 \mid Q^{k''}$, where $P' \, C^-(S) \, Q'$.

□

Due to this use of 'up-to-strong-bisimilarity', the compatibility up to iteration technique we used in the strong case (Proposition 6.4.10) is no longer sufficient: the function $\mathcal{R} \mapsto {\sim}C^-(\mathcal{R}){\sim}$ we used for the replication context is not contained in C^-. Instead, we rely on the 'compatibility up to iteration and a compatible map' technique, formalised below in Theorem 6.5.23. The main hypotheses in the theorem are the evolution $f \overset{s}{\rightsquigarrow} g \circ f^\omega$ and the s-compatibility of g: they indicate that f is s-compatible 'up to iteration and up to the compatible function g'; the remaining hypotheses make it possible to obtain a simple expression for the produced s-compatible map $(g \circ f^\omega)$. We recall that f is extensive if $\mathcal{R} \subseteq f(\mathcal{R})$, for all $\mathcal{R}$.

Theorem 6.5.23 *Let s, f, g be three monotone functions such that:*

(1) g is s-compatible, extensive, and idempotent;
(2) f is g-compatible and f^ω is idempotent.

If $f \overset{s}{\rightsquigarrow} g \circ f^\omega$, then $g \circ f^\omega$ is s-compatible.

Proof By Lemma 6.3.11, and with a simple induction, we obtain that f^ω is g-compatible. We then show, for all i, that $f^i \overset{s}{\rightsquigarrow} g \circ f^\omega$, by induction on i:

- if $i = 0$, we have $f^0 \circ s = s \subseteq s \circ f^\omega \subseteq s \circ g \circ f^\omega$, i.e., $f^0 \overset{s}{\rightsquigarrow} g \circ f^\omega$;
- for $i + 1$, we have:

$$
\begin{array}{ll}
f^i \circ s \subseteq s \circ g \circ f^\omega & \text{(by induction)} \\
f^{i+1} \circ s \subseteq f \circ s \circ g \circ f^\omega, & (f \text{ is monotone}) \\
\subseteq s \circ g \circ f^\omega \circ g \circ f^\omega, & \text{(by assumption)} \\
\subseteq s \circ g \circ g \circ f^\omega \circ f^\omega, & (f^\omega \text{ is } g\text{-compatible}) \\
= s \circ g \circ f^\omega & (f^\omega \text{ and } g \text{ are idempotent})
\end{array}
$$

From this, we deduce $f^\omega \overset{s}{\rightsquigarrow} g \circ f^\omega$, whence

$$
\begin{array}{ll}
g \circ f^\omega \circ s \subseteq g \circ s \circ g \circ f^\omega & \\
\subseteq s \circ g \circ g \circ f^\omega & (g \text{ is } s\text{-compatible}) \\
\subseteq s \circ g \circ f^\omega & (g \text{ is idempotent})
\end{array}
$$

i.e. $g \circ f^\omega$ is s-compatible. □

The validity of up to context for weak bisimilarity follows: although the closure C^- is not **w**-compatible by itself, it is contained in a larger function that is **w**-compatible.

Theorem 6.5.24 *The symmetric function* $\mathcal{R} \mapsto {\sim}C^-(\mathcal{R}){\sim}$ *is* **w**-*compatible.*

Proof Take $g : \mathcal{R} \mapsto {\sim}\mathcal{R}{\sim}$. The function g is **w**-compatible, extensive, and idempotent; moreover, strong bisimilarity is a congruence in CCS, so that, in particular, $C^-({\sim}) \subseteq {\sim}$, which leads to the g-compatibility of C^-. Hence, by Theorem 6.5.23, it suffices to show $\lfloor \mathbb{C}_i^- \rfloor \overset{\mathbf{w}}{\rightsquigarrow} g \circ C^-$, i.e. that for all $C \in \mathbb{C}_i^-$, we have $\lfloor C \rfloor \overset{\mathbf{w}}{\rightsquigarrow} g \circ C^-$. This follows from Lemma 6.5.22. $\qquad\square$

6.5.3.2 The sum operator

We now briefly show how to deal with the sum operator. We have to consider *guarded sums*; correspondingly we use *non-degenerate* contexts [SW01], i.e. contexts in which each hole is underneath a prefix. In order to obtain the corresponding closure under contexts, we introduce the following family of (initial) contexts, where R is any process, $n \geq 0$, and μ_i is any prefix:

$$R + \Sigma_{i=1}^n \mu_i.[\cdot]_i.$$

Accordingly, we denote by $\mathbb{C}_i^{nd}$ the set obtained from $\mathbb{C}_i^-$ by adding the above contexts, and we define the *closure under non-degenerate CCS contexts* as the function $C^{nd} \overset{\text{def}}{=} \lfloor \mathbb{C}_i^{nd} \rfloor^\omega$. Like for Theorem 6.5.24, we obtain:

Theorem 6.5.25 *The closure under non-degenerate CCS contexts is contained in the* **w**-*compatible function:* $\mathcal{R} \mapsto {\sim}C^{nd}(\mathcal{R}){\sim}$.

Proof It suffices to check that $\lfloor R + \Sigma_{i=1}^n \mu_i.[\cdot]_i \rfloor \overset{\mathbf{w}}{\rightsquigarrow} C^{nd}$; we can then conclude with Lemma 6.5.22 and Theorem 6.5.23. $\qquad\square$

As a consequence, we also obtain that weak bisimilarity is closed under non-degenerate CCS contexts.

Corollary 6.5.26 *We have* $C^{nd}(\approx) \subseteq {\approx}$.

Proof By Lemma 6.4.3 and Theorem 6.5.25, we have ${\sim}C^{nd}(\approx){\sim} \subseteq {\approx}$, whence $C^{nd}(\approx) \subseteq {\approx}$, since strong bisimilarity is reflexive. $\qquad\square$

6.5.4 Combining contexts and transitivity

Recall the function $\mathbf{w}_t$ we introduced in Section 6.5.2.5, to obtain an up-to-transitivity technique for weak bisimulation, restricted to challenges on visible actions. Surprisingly, C^- is not $\mathbf{w}_t$-sound: a counterexample is depicted below,

Table 6.1.

up to	**b**	**wb**	**wb₁**	**ws**ₜ
transitivity	compatible	compatible	with constraints	on visible actions
context	compatible	sound	compatible	unsound
both	compatible	unsound	with constraints	unsound

where $\mathcal{R}$ is not contained in weak bisimilarity while $\mathcal{R}$ is a $\mathbf{w}_t$-simulation up to context:

$$\mathcal{R} \stackrel{\text{def}}{=} \left\{ \big(a, (\nu b)(b.\, a \mid \overline{b})\big), (b.\, a, b), \big((\nu b)(b \mid \overline{b}), \mathbf{0}\big), ((\nu b)\mathbf{0}, \mathbf{0}) \right\}$$

$$C \stackrel{\text{def}}{=} (\nu b)([\cdot]_1 \mid \overline{b})$$

In comparison with the previous **w**-compatibility proof, the point is that the evolution $\lfloor\rfloor \stackrel{\mathbf{w}_t}{\leadsto} C^-$ does not hold: since parallel composition is able to aggregate two visible actions into a silent action, up to transitivity is lifted from visible challenges (where it is allowed by $\mathbf{w}_t$) to silent challenges (where it is not).

This counterexample also shows that the composition of a sound function with a compatible function is not necessarily sound: the above relation $\mathcal{R}$ is also a **wb**-simulation up to transitivity and up to context, so that this combination of techniques cannot be **wb**-sound. However, $\mathcal{R} \mapsto \mathcal{R}^\star$ is **wb**-compatible, and C^- is **wb**-sound (since it is **wb₁**-sound, and $\mathcal{R} \subseteq \mathbf{wb}(C^-(\mathcal{R})$ entails $\mathcal{R} \subseteq \mathbf{wb}_1(C^-(\mathcal{R}))$). Here, the additional hypothesis of Theorem 6.5.17 is not satisfied: we do not have $C(\mathcal{R})^\star \subseteq C(\mathcal{R}^\star)$ for all $\mathcal{R}$, even for the small part C of C^- that is required by the counterexample.

More importantly, the above discussion shows that functions with the same greatest fixed point may yield rather different sets of up-to techniques. Therefore, one has to carefully select the function depending on the kind of coinductive techniques needed. In the case of weak bisimilarity, for example, there is a trade-off between the ability to use up to context or up to transitivity. Table 6.1 summarises the situation about these two up-to techniques in CCS: while they can be safely combined in the strong case, this is no longer possible in the weak case, unless one uses termination guarantees (e.g. Corollary 6.5.19).

6.6 A summary of up-to techniques for bisimulation

We conclude the chapter by recalling some of the most powerful up-to techniques examined. As hinted in the introduction, other techniques can be found in the literature; they are usually more specific to a given setting, however, so that they are not included in this summary.

6.6.1 Strong bisimilarity

One of the most powerful up-to techniques that we have derived for strong bisimilarity is illustrated by the following diagram, where $\mathcal{C}$ is the closure under arbitrary CCS contexts:

$$
\begin{array}{ccc}
P & \mathcal{R} & Q \\
\mu \downarrow & & \downarrow \mu \\
P' & (\mathcal{C}(\mathcal{R}) \cup \sim)^\star & Q'
\end{array}
$$

Any relation $\mathcal{R}$ that satisfies this diagram is contained in strong bisimilarity. According to this technique, when answering a challenge, one can use either the bisimulation candidate ($\mathcal{R}$) or strong bisimilarity ($\sim$) to rewrite any subterm of the derivatives (using $\mathcal{C}$ to select subterms); moreover, such rewriting can be repeated as many times as needed, thanks to the reflexive and transitive closure.

6.6.2 Weak bisimilarity

The situation with weak bisimilarity is more diverse. A common technique is 'up-to-expansion-and-context': any symmetric relation $\mathcal{R}$ that satisfies the following diagram is contained in weak bisimilarity (where $\mathcal{C}^{nd}$ is the closure under non-degenerate CCS contexts, and $\gtrsim$ is the expansion preorder we defined in Section 6.5.2.3):

$$
\begin{array}{ccc}
P & \mathcal{R} & Q \\
\mu \downarrow & & \Downarrow \hat{\mu} \\
P' & \gtrsim \mathcal{C}^{nd}(\mathcal{R}) \approx & \exists Q'
\end{array}
$$

Other techniques allow one to reason up to transitivity, with different constraints. We summarise the main ones.

- We can employ up-to-transitivity if we play challenges on weak transitions and renounce to up-to-context, as summarised in this diagram:

$$
\begin{array}{ccc}
P & \mathcal{R} & Q \\
\widehat{\mu}\Big\downarrow\!\!\Big\| & & \Big\|\!\!\Big\downarrow\widehat{\mu} \\
P' & (\mathcal{R} \cup \approx)^{\star} & Q'
\end{array}
$$

- We can also restrict the use of up-to-transitivity to challenges along visible transitions, so that it suffices to consider challenges along strong transitions. One can use up-to-expansion on silent challenges, but up-to-context is not allowed:

$$
\begin{array}{ccccccccc}
P & \mathcal{R} & Q & \qquad & P & \mathcal{R} & Q \\
\tau\Big\downarrow & & \Big\|\!\!\Big\downarrow\widehat{\tau} & & \alpha\Big\downarrow & & \Big\|\!\!\Big\downarrow\alpha \\
P' & \gtrsim \mathcal{R}^{=} \approx & \exists Q' & & P' & (\mathcal{R} \cup \approx)^{\star} & \exists Q'
\end{array}
$$

- We can finally use up-to-transitivity-and-context, under an additional termination hypothesis. This is illustrated in the following diagram, where relation $\succ$ must be transitive, closed under contexts, and must satisfy a termination criterion related to silent transitions ($\succ\!\xrightarrow{\tau}\!^{+}$ has to terminate):

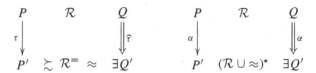

$$
\begin{array}{ccc}
P & \mathcal{R} & Q \\
\mu\Big\downarrow & & \Big\|\!\!\Big\downarrow\widehat{\mu} \\
P' & \big((\mathcal{C}^{nd}(\mathcal{R}) \cup \approx) \cap \succ\big)^{\star}\, \mathcal{C}^{nd}(\mathcal{R}) \approx & \exists Q'
\end{array}
$$

The termination constraint can be restricted to silent challenges; we have however to renounce to up-to context:

$$
\begin{array}{ccccccccc}
P & \mathcal{R} & Q & \qquad & P & \mathcal{R} & Q \\
\tau\Big\downarrow & & \Big\|\!\!\Big\downarrow\widehat{\tau} & & \alpha\Big\downarrow & & \Big\|\!\!\Big\downarrow\alpha \\
P' & ((\mathcal{R} \cup \approx) \cap \succ)^{\star}\, \mathcal{R}^{=} \approx & \exists Q' & & P' & (\mathcal{R} \cup \approx)^{\star} & \exists Q'
\end{array}
$$

Bibliography

[AG98] M. Abadi and A.D. Gordon. A bisimulation method for cryptographic protocols. *Novdic Journal of Computing*, **5**(4):267, 1998.

[AKH92] S. Arun-Kumar and M. Hennessy. An efficiency preorder for processes. *Acta Informatica*, **29**(9):737–760, 1992.

[BS98a] M. Boreale and D. Sangiorgi. Bisimulation in name-passing calculi without matching. In *Proceedings of the 13th LICS Conference* IEEE Computer Society Press, 1998.

[BS98b] M. Boreale and D. Sangiorgi. A fully abstract semantics for causality in the π-calculus. *Acta Informatica*, **35**(5):353–400, 1998.

[DP90] B. Davey and H. Priestley. *Introduction to Lattices and Order*. Cambridge University Press, 1990.

[dS85] R. de Simone. Higher-level synchronising devices in Meije-SCCS. *Theoretical Computer Science*, **37**:245–267, 1985.

[FG98] C. Fournet and G. Gonthier. A hierarchy of equivalences for asynchronous calculi. In *Proceedings of the 25th ICALP*, volume 1443 of *LNCS*, pages 844–855. Springer Verlag, 1998.

[FvG96] W. Fokkink and R.J. van Glabbeek. Ntyft/ntyxt rules reduce to ntree rules. *Information and Computation*, **126**(1):1–10, 1996.

[GV92] J.F. Groote and F.W. Vaandrager. Structured operational semantics and bisimulation as a congruence. *Information and Computation*, **100**(2):202–260, 1992.

[JR99] A. Jeffrey and J. Rathke. Towards a theory of bisimulation for local names. In *Proceedings LICS*, pages 56–66, 1999.

[KW06] V. Koutavas and M. Wand. Small bisimulations for reasoning about higher-order imperative programs. In *Proceedings of the 33rd POPL*, pages 141–152. ACM, 2006.

[Las98] S.B. Lassen. *Relational reasoning about functions and nondeterminism*. PhD thesis, Department of Computer Science, University of Aarhus, 1998.

[Mil89] R. Milner. *Communication and Concurrency*. Prentice Hall, 1989.

[MN05] M. Merro and F. Zappa Nardelli. Behavioural theory for mobile ambients. *Journal of the ACM*, **52**(6):961–1023, 2005.

[New42] Maxwell H.A. Newman. On theories with a combinatorial definition of 'equivalence'. *Annals of Mathematics*, **43**(2):223–243, 1942.

[Pou07] D. Pous. Complete lattices and up-to techniques. In *Proceedings APLAS '07*, volume 4807 of *LNCS*, pages 351–366. Springer Verlag, 2007.

[Pou08a] D. Pous. *Techniques modulo pour les bisimulations*. PhD thesis, École Normale Supérieure de Lyon, February 2008.

[Pou08b] D. Pous. Using bisimulation proof techniques for the analysis of distributed algorithms. *Theoretical Computer Science*, **402**(2–3):199–220, 2008.

[Pou10] D. Pous. Up-to context for the xyft/tyft format, 2010. Handwritten notes, available on request.

[San93] D. Sangiorgi. Locality and non-interleaving semantics in calculi for mobile processes. *Theoretical Computer Science*, **155**:39–83, 1996.

[San98] D. Sangiorgi. On the bisimulation proof method. *Journal of Mathematical Structures in Computer Science*, **8**:447–479, 1998.

[San12] D. Sangiorgi. *An Introduction to Bisimulation and Coinduction*. Cambridge University Press, 2012.

[SKS07] D. Sangiorgi, N. Kobayashi, and E. Sumii. Environmental bisimulations for higher-order languages. In *Proceedings LICS '07*, pages 293–302. IEEE Computer Society, 2007.

[SM92] D. Sangiorgi and R. Milner. The problem of 'weak bisimulation up to'. In *Proceedings 3rd CONCUR*, volume 630 of *LNCS*, pages 32–46. Springer Verlag, 1992.

[SP07a] E. Sumii and B.C. Pierce. A bisimulation for dynamic sealing. *Theoretical Computer Science*, **375**(1–3):169–192, 2007.

[SP07b] E. Sumii and B.C. Pierce. A bisimulation for type abstraction and recursion. *Journal of the ACM*, **54**(5), 2007.

[SW01] D. Sangiorgi and D. Walker. *The π-Calculus: A Theory of Mobile Processes*. Cambridge University Press, 2001.

[TeR03] TeReSe. *Term Rewriting Systems*. Cambridge University Press, 2003.

[vG93] R.J. van Glabbeek. The linear time – branching time spectrum II: The semantics of sequential systems with silent moves. In *Proceedings 4th CONCUR*, volume 715 of *LNCS*, pages 66–81. Springer Verlag, 1993.

7

Probabilistic bisimulation

PRAKASH PANANGADEN

7.1 Introduction

The history of bisimulation is well documented in earlier chapters of this book. In this chapter we will look at a major non-trivial extension of the theory of labelled transition systems: probabilistic transition systems. There are many possible extensions of theoretical and practical interest: real-time, quantitative, independence, spatial and many others. Probability is the best theory we have for handling uncertainty in all of science, not just computer science. It is not an idle extension made for the purpose of exploring what is theoretically possible. Non-determinism is, of course, important, and arises in computer science because sometimes we *just cannot do any better* or because *we lack quantitative data from which to make quantitative predictions*. However, one does not find any use of non-determinism in a quantitative science like physics, though it appears in sciences like biology where we have not yet reached a fundamental understanding of the nature of systems.

When we do have data or quantitative models, it is far preferable to analyse uncertainty probabilistically. A fundamental reason that we want to use probabilistic reasoning is that if we merely reported what is *possible* and then insisted that no bad things were possible, we would trust very few system designs in real life. For example, we would never trust a communication network, a car, an aeroplane, an investment bank nor would we ever take any medication! In short, only very few idealised systems ever meet purely logical specifications. We need to know the 'odds' before we trust any system.

Typically probabilistic systems come in two guises: discrete and continuous. We understand discrete systems intuitively.[1] Even in school one is taught to compute the odds of obtaining Egg Foo Yong together with Chicken Chow

---

[1] At least, we think we understand them!

Mein if one orders at random in a Chinese restaurant. Even this subject has many tricky twists and turns[2] but the overall mathematical principles are based on elementary principles. By contrast, the theory of probability on continuous spaces is based on advanced ideas from analysis and measure theory; in fact a great deal of analysis was invented to cater to the needs of probability.

One might take the view that any automated analysis or logical reasoning must be inherently discrete in character. In particular, even if one is interested in reasoning about a physical system, one has to first discretise the system. In fact, this point of view actually provides a good argument for retaining the continuous view of the system. A given system may well be described in continuous terms. Without formalising the continuous system – and having a notion of equivalence between discrete and continuous systems – how does one argue that the discretised system is a faithful model of the underlying continuous system? Even supposing one is willing to treat a discrete model as given, what if one needs to refine the model? For example, a given discretisation may arise from some type of approximation based on a given *tolerance*; how does one refine the tolerance or discretise *adaptively*? Clearly the underlying continuous model has to be retained and used if we want to construct different discrete approximations. A systematic study of approximation is beyond the scope of the present chapter, but it is the subject of present activity and is discussed in the literature [Pan09].

From an immediate practical point of view, bisimulation can be used to reason about probabilistic, continuous-state-space discrete-time systems (henceforth Markov processes) in the following simple way. One often 'discretises' a continuous system by partitioning the state space into a few equivalence classes. Usually one has some intuition that the resulting discrete system 'behaves like' the original continuous system. This can be made precise by our notion of bisimulation. It is also the case that some systems cannot be discretised, and once again, one can formalise what this means via bisimulation.

In this chapter, we cannot review all the mathematical background so the treatment will be more detailed for the discrete case and somewhat more in the spirit of an overview for the continuous case. There is, however, a serious conceptual reason for looking at the continuous case even in this expository article. The powerful tools that we are forced to use establish *much more powerful results, even for the discrete case*. Indeed, the first results on logical characterisation of bisimulation for continuous state-space systems were

---

[2] Consider the following puzzle: You have three cards of the same size and shape, one is red on both sides, one is green on both sides and one is red on one side and green on the other side. One card is picked at random and one of its two sides is shown to you and it is green. What is the probability that the other side is green?

treated with scepticism because they seemed to violate all the intuitions that we had gained from non-deterministic systems. In particular, the results show that purely probabilistic systems are 'almost' as well behaved as *deterministic* systems: there is a logical characterisation of simulation, two-way simulation is the same as bisimulation and bisimulation can be characterised by a purely positive logic. Rather than shy away from the continuous case, I would like to tempt the reader to learn the relevant mathematics and plunge into it.

In the theory of probabilistic transition systems one has a precursor of the idea of bisimulation called 'lumpability' known since the early days of queueing theory [KS60] and well before the study of concurrency. Lumpability is aptly named: it gives conditions under which the states of a transition system can be identified, or 'lumped' together. What was missing was the notion of labels, but the important ideas were anticipated. Unfortunately, these ideas had to be rediscovered in computer science because this literature was not known and the definitions were given in a way that made it very hard to recognise as being connected to bisimulation.

The modern study of probabilistic bisimulation was initiated in a very influential paper by Larsen and Skou [LS91]. In this paper they introduced *reactive* discrete probabilistic labelled transition systems, defined bisimulation, related it to testing equivalences and proved a logical characterisation theorem for probabilistic bisimulation.

The important idea here was to focus on reactive systems. In these systems the 'internal' non-determinism is fully probabilistic and the 'external' non-determinism, i.e. the choice of labels, in unquantified. There is no attempt to ascribe probabilities for what the environment might choose to do. Other models studied included generative probabilistic systems [vGSST90], where there are probabilities over environment actions, and so-called *probabilistic automata* [SL94, SL95], where there is a mixture of probability and non-determinism. Bisimulation for probabilistic automata is particularly fruitful and is being actively pursued by Segala and his collaborators and students. In the present article I will focus on reactive systems.

In the mid-1990s, I and my then student, Josée Desharnais began studying probabilistic transition systems on continuous state spaces. The intention was to apply the theory to stochastic hybrid systems. We were quickly mired in mathematics that we did not understand well at the time and could not even prove that bisimulation was an equivalence relation! We had tried to generalise ideas from modal logic (zig-zag morphisms); see, for example, *First Steps in Modal Logic* by Sally Popkorn [Pop94]. We were also influenced by the categorical treatment of bisimulation in terms of open maps due to Joyal, Nielsen and Winskel [JNW93]. This led to the idea of defining bisimulation as spans of zig-zags, but we could not compose them. Eventually with Edalat's help we were able to compose these spans [BDEP97] using a new construction called a *semi-pullback* [Eda99]. Independently, de Vink and Rutten [dVR97, dVR99] developed a theory along coalgebraic lines but they used ultrametric spaces where they could compose spans.

The semi-pullback construction was intricate and rather ad hoc. Later it was put on a much firmer footing by Doberkat [Dob03] who used more sophisticated techniques like measurable selection theorems [Sri98]. We were seeking a more tractable definition of bisimulation and eventually realised that a simple generalisation of the Larsen–Skou definition could be given [DGJP00]. It is this version that I will present in this chapter.

The biggest surprise, for us at any rate, was the discovery that the logical characterisation of bisimulation [DEP98] could be given with a *much simpler logic than was used for the discrete case*. The logic used only binary conjunction – even when the branching was uncountable – and had no negation, in fact it had no negative constructs whatsoever. This turned out to hold for the modified definition of bisimulation as well [DGJP00] which showed that the two definitions were equivalent. The proof of logical characterisation used special properties of analytic spaces. Thus the results do not apply to all measure spaces but to a very general class that includes any that are likely to come up in applications.

If one reconsiders the problems that we faced when defining bisimulation initially, a new point of view emerges. Instead of working with spans one should work with cospans. Stated less categorically, one should think of the bisimulation equivalence classes rather than of the relation *per se*. This leads to a wholly new conception of bisimulation which was developed by Danos, Desharnais, Laviolette and me [DDLP06]. A very similar view emerged in the work of Bartels, Sokolova and de Vink [BSdV04] who were working in an explicitly coalgebraic framework and who called it a 'cocongruence'. We were able to establish the logical characterisation theorem in general measurable spaces with this version of bisimulation, which again shows that *on analytic spaces* this coincides with the traditional view.

In the end one has to say that probabilistic bisimulation has a fundamental flaw. It is unreasonable to work with an equivalence relation that requires exact matching of real numbers. If two states are bisimilar and one were to perturb the transition probabilities slightly the states would end up not being bisimilar. One would like to say that they are 'close'. Jou and Smolka [JS90] argued that one should work with metrics rather than equivalences. There were several proposed metrics on offer but they did not correspond well with the notion of bisimulation. One needed a pseudo-metric whose kernel was bisimulation. This first appeared independently in work by Desharnais, Gupta, Jagadeesan and me [DGJP99] and by Rutten [Rut98]. The theory of metric analogues of bisimulation was pursued by van Breugel and Worrell [vBW01b, vBW01a] who gave, among other things, a polynomial-time decision procedure for the metric. These and related metrics for Markov decision processes have proved useful in AI applications [FPP04, FPP05].

This book is focussed on bisimulation, so I have not included many topics in the theory of labelled Markov processes. A book-length treatment is available in my recent book, *Labelled Markov Processes* [Pan09] which covers approximation, metrics, the category of stochastic relations and other topics. It does not give the treatment of cocongruences given here and for a reader primarily interested in bisimulation this chapter contains information on this topic that is not found in the book. The book discusses the analysis background in some depth, whereas the present chapter is rather brief. The detailed proof of the logical characterisation of bisimulation (even for discrete systems) requires some of this advanced analysis and thus, a complete understanding of that proof will require material that is given in my book. A more advanced book which stresses the coalgebraic point of view and the connections with logic is called *Stochastic Coalgebraic Logic* by Doberkat [Dob10]. It gives an overview of some mathematical topics not covered in my book, especially the use of descriptive set theory and more powerful treatments of semi-pullbacks.

The structure of this chapter is as follows. The next section deals with discrete systems and requires only elementary mathematics. The next section is a quick introduction to measure theory. The first half should be accessible to students with no background beyond calculus but the second half is rather more sophisticated. In that section we give the definitions of labelled Markov processes using the mathematics from the preceding section. The next section defines a monad due to Giry which is used for the subsequent coalgebraic treatments. It can be skipped and the category theoretic parts following can be skimmed without losing the basic message. However, I believe that one should learn to think coalgebraically, especially about any kind of bisimulation. The next section gives the definition of probabilistic bisimulation for continuous-state-space systems; it gives both categorical and relational versions. The next section gives the proof of the logical characterisation and shows why all the exotic mathematics is useful. The following section presents a new concept dual to the usual notion of bisimulation. I believe that this notion will replace traditional bisimulation; it needs the coalgebraic viewpoint in an essential way.

The next section is on Kozen's coinduction principle. It does not require any explicit knowledge of category theory and extracts the useful essence of the coalgebra viewpoint. Everyone can and should read it. The chapter ends with a brief summary.

7.2 Discrete systems

The first breakthrough in the study of probabilistic bisimulation was the paper of Larsen and Skou [LS91] where bisimulation for discrete reactive systems was studied and shown to correspond to a kind of testing. A key contribution of that paper was a Hennessy–Milner like theorem giving a logical characterisation of probabilistic bisimulation. We review this here and give a very nice, hitherto unpublished, proof of the logical characterisation result due to James (Ben) Worrell.

Definition 7.2.1 A **labelled Markov chain** is a quadruple $(S, \mathsf{L}, C_l, P_l)$, where S is a countable set of states, L is a set of labels, and for each $l \in \mathsf{L}$, we have a subset C_l of S, a function, P_l, called a **transition probability matrix**,

$$P_l : C_l \times S \to [0, 1]$$

satisfying the normalisation condition

$$\forall l \in \mathsf{L}, s \in C_l.\, \Sigma_{s' \in S} P_l(s, s') = 1.$$

Why the restriction to C_l rather than just defining $P_l : S \times X \to [0, 1]$? This is done to allow some actions to be *rejected* in certain states. If we insisted that P_l be defined on all states then it would turn out that every labelled Markov chain would be bisimilar to the one-state process with a probability 1 self-loop for every label. This is entirely analogous to the situation with a non-deterministic transition system where if every state can make a transition on every label we get a system bisimilar to the trivial one-state system. This is because we are only distinguishing states on the basis of their ability to accept or reject actions. So, if we want some interesting structure we should have some states rejecting some actions. A more interesting way to achieve the same effect is to allow *subprobability* distributions: distributions where the sum of all the probabilities is *bounded by* 1 rather than being equal to 1. I shall follow this approach when I discuss continuous-state systems later on.

Here are two simple examples

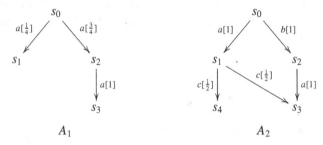

The numbers in square brackets are the probabilities. The system A_1 has only a actions. The set C_a in this case is $\{s_0, s_2\}$: the a action is not defined on s_1 and s_3. In the system A_2 we have three actions a, b and c. Here $C_a = \{s_0, s_2\}$, $C_b = \{s_0\}$ and $C_c = \{s_1\}$. Note that in s_0 we have two different actions enabled and *each* one has a total probability of 1. Thus, the probabilities are conditioned on a specific action; we do not have a probability distribution measuring the relative probabilities of different actions.

In the paper of Larsen and Skou [LS91] there was a restriction called the 'minimum deviation assumption'. This said that all the probabilities appearing were multiples of some real number ε. This is a strong finite-branching assumption. It was important for their proof of the logical characterisation of bisimulation. It turns out that such restrictions are not needed and we dispense with them. The purely probabilistic situation is better behaved than the non-deterministic situation. As we shall see later, one does not need any kind of finite branching assumption for the continuous case but one still gets a logical characterisation result *without infinitary connectives*.

When are two states to be considered bisimilar? Consider the two systems below.

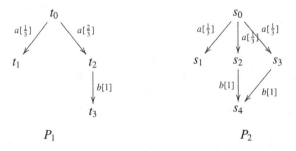

Should we consider s_0 and t_0 to be equivalent? Clearly all the dead states should be bisimilar: t_1, t_3, s_1, s_4. Then t_2, s_2 and s_3 should all be viewed as bisimilar: they can all do a b transition to a dead state with probability 1, and nothing else. Now when we try to match the transitions out of s_0 and t_0 we see that there is nothing in system P_2 that corresponds to the transition $t_0 \xrightarrow{a, \frac{2}{3}} t_2$ of system P_1. On the other hand, this transition does correspond to the transition from s_0 to the states s_2, s_3 *taken together*. Thus, in order to get a reasonable notion of probabilistic bisimulation one cannot just match transitions as one does in the non-deterministic case: it is necessary to *add* the transition probabilities to bisimilar states.

We need some basic notation pertaining to relations. If R is an equivalence relation on a set S, we write S/R for the set of equivalence classes. If R is any binary relation on a set S, we say that a subset A is R-closed, if $a \in A$ and aRb implies that $b \in R$. If R is an equivalence relation an R-closed set is just a union of equivalence classes. If X is any subset of S we write $R(X)$ for the set $\{y \in S \mid \exists x \in X, \ xRy\}$; we call this the R-*closure* of X. A final notational point: we write $P_l(s, E)$ for $\sum_{x \in E} P_l(s, x)$.

Definition 7.2.2 Given a labelled Markov chain $\mathcal{S} = (S, \mathsf{L}, C_l, P_l)$ we define **a probabilistic bisimulation relation** to be an equivalence relation R on S such that sRt implies that

(1) $\forall l \in \mathsf{L}, \ s \in C_l \iff t \in C_l$, and
(2) $\forall l \in \mathsf{L}, E \in S/R, \ P_l(s, E) = P_l(t, E)$.

The second condition gives the addition over bisimilar states that we need.

Definition 7.2.3 We say that s is **(strongly) probabilistically bisimilar to** t if there is *some* probabilistic bisimulation relation R with sRt. As is commonly done for (non-probabilistic) strong bisimulation, we write $s \sim t$ for this relation.

Henceforth we will just say 'bisimulation' and 'bisimilar to.'

Exercise 7.2.4 Show that if we dropped C_l and defined labelled Markov chains to have transition probability distributions from every state for every label, then every system would be bisimilar to a one-state system.

The logic introduced by Larsen and Skou is the following:

$$\mathcal{L} : \mathsf{T} \mid \phi \wedge \phi \mid \phi \vee \phi \mid \Delta_a \mid \langle a \rangle_q \phi.$$

Here $s \models \Delta_a$ means that s cannot perform the a action and $s \models \langle a \rangle_q \phi$ means that from s one can perform an a action and with probability at least q the resulting state will satisfy ϕ. More precisely, there is a set A such that $P_a(s, A) \geq q$ and $\forall x \in A, \ x \models \phi$.

There are many variations that one can imagine. Perhaps the simplest is to have negation and dispense with Δ and disjunction. All the variations considered by Larsen and Skou have some negative construct. The striking fact – first discovered in the context of continuous state spaces [DEP98, DEP02] – is that one can get a logical characterisation result with purely positive formulas. The discrete case is covered by these results. Surprisingly no elementary proof for the discrete case – i.e. one that avoids the measure theory machinery – is known.

I now present Worrell's proof of the logical characterisation theorem. It is very short and perspicuous and completely avoids the use of the minimal deviation assumption. It uses a very original idea: the extension of the notion of bisimulation to relations that are not necessarily equivalences.

Definition 7.2.5 A **dynamic relation** on $\mathcal{S} = (S, \mathsf{L}, C_l, P_l)$ is a binary relation R on S, such that $s\,R\,t$ implies

(1) $\forall l \in \mathsf{L},\ s \in C_l \iff t \in C_l$, and
(2) $\forall l \in \mathsf{L}, X \subseteq S,\ P_l(s, X) \leq P_l(t, R(X))$.

Note the inequality in clause (2) and the use of the R-closure.

If R happens to be an equivalence relation then a dynamic relation is just a bisimulation relation. This is not completely obvious. First, if R is an equivalence relation and E is an equivalence class of R then $R(E) = E$. Thus $P_l(s, E) \leq P_l(t, E)$. But the sum across all equivalences classes must be 1 so in fact we get an equality. Clearly any bisimulation relation is a dynamic relation.

Proposition 7.2.6 *The composition of two dynamic relations is a dynamic relation. The union of a family of dynamic relations is a dynamic relation. The converse of a dynamic relation is a dynamic relation.*

Proof Only the last claim is not routine. Suppose $s\,R^c\,t$. Then for $X \subseteq X$ we have $R(S \setminus R^{-1}(X)) \subseteq (S \setminus X)$ from elementary set theory. We have assumed that $t\,R\,s$ so using the fact that R is a dynamic relation we get $P_l(t, S \setminus R^{-1}(X)) \leq P_l(s, R(S \setminus R^{-1}(X)))$. From the fact that $P_l(s, \cdot)$ is monotone we get

$$P_l(t, S \setminus R^{-1}(X)) \leq P_l(s, R(S \setminus R^{-1}(X))) \leq P_l(s, S \setminus X).$$

Now, taking complements $P_l(s, X) \leq P_l(t, R^{-1}(X))$, which shows that R^{-1} is a dynamic relation. $\square$

It follows that the union of all dynamic relations is an equivalence relation and is thus the same as probabilistic bisimulation. This means that if we want to show that s is bisimilar to t it suffices to find a dynamic relation R with $s\,R\,t$; this may be easier than finding a bisimulation relation since there is only one direction to check.

The logical characterisation of bisimulation by $\mathcal{L}$ has two directions.

Proposition 7.2.7 *If s is bisimilar to t they obey all the same formulas of $\mathcal{L}$.*

This can be proved by a routine induction on the structure of formulas. The interesting direction is the converse. It is established by showing that logical 'simulation' is a dynamic relation. It is usually established by showing that logical equivalence is a bisimulation, but this way we only have to deal with one direction.

Exercise 7.2.8 Give the 'routine' proof of the proposition above.

We write $s \prec t$ to mean that for all formulas ϕ of $\mathcal{L}$, $s \models \phi$ implies that $t \models \phi$.

Proposition 7.2.9 *The relation $\prec$ is a dynamic relation.*

Proof Suppose that $s \prec t$ and l is some fixed label with $s \in C_l$. It suffices to show that for each *finite* $O \subseteq S$, $P_l(s, O) \leq P_l(t, \prec (O))$, where, as usual, $\prec (O) = \{y \in S \mid \exists x \in S,\ x \prec y\}$; we will call this set O'. Suppose that $P_l(s, O) = \lambda > 0$ and t makes transitions to $\{t_1, t_2, \ldots\}$ in O' and to $\{t_1', t_2', \ldots\}$ in $S \setminus O'$. Now for any $i \in \mathbb{N}$ we can find a formula ϕ_i such that every state in O satisfies ϕ_i and which t_i' does not satisfy. This follows from the definition of O', in order for t_i' not to be in O' there must be some formula that is satisfied by a state in O but not by t_i'. Since O is finite we can construct ϕ_i by forming a finite conjunction. Now we have

$$s \models \langle l \rangle_\lambda \bigwedge_{i=1}^{n} \phi_i.$$

Now since $s \prec t$, t must satisfy the same formula. Thus $P_l(t, O') \geq \lambda$. This shows that $\prec$ is a dynamic relation. $\qquad \square$

Exercise 7.2.10 Consider the systems shown below.

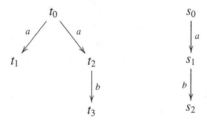

These are non-deterministic systems and not probabilistic systems. They are
clearly not bisimilar, thus there must be a formula in Henessy–Milner logic
that distinguishes s_0 from t_0. Find such a formula. Prove by induction on the
structure of formulas that a purely positive formula (constructed from diamond
and conjunction only) cannot distinguish s_0 and t_0.

Exercise 7.2.11 Consider the systems described in the previous exercise. Show
that if one assigns any probabilities to the two non-deterministic branches and
any subprobability to the a-transition from s_0 the systems are not bisimilar
unless we assign zero probability to the transtion from t_0 to t_1. Show that, in
contrast to the exercise above, there is a purely positive formula that distinguishes t_0 and s_0.

Exercise* 7.2.12 The last exercise showed an example illustrating why the
probabilistic case does not require negation. Give an example and similar
analysis showing why we don't need infinite conjunctions even when we have
infinite branching. This example appears in [DEP02].

7.3 A rapid survey of measure theory

This section can be omitted if the reader is familiar with the basics of measure
and probability theory on arbitrary measurable spaces. Such a background can
be obtained by reading books such as *Probability and Measure* by Billingsley [Bil95] or *Real Analysis and Probability* by Ash [Ash72] or the book with
the same title by Dudley [Dud89] or *Introduction to Measure and Probability*
by Kingman and Taylor [KT66]. I have recently written a book called *Labelled
Markov Processes* [Pan09] which covers this material from scratch. I have also
written a survey paper [Pan01] which gives the intuition behind the mathematics
without going into proofs.

In measure theory one tries to associate a numerical notion of 'size' to
sets. This notion is intended to generalise the familiar notion of length of
an interval to more intricate sets. The basic inspiration is geometric, but the
concept makes sense even on spaces that have no familiar geometric structure.
For probability theory it is clear that such a notion is crucial if one wants to
talk about probabilities of events that may be subsets of some continuum. It
is important to recognise that the cardinality concept, which is so successful
in the discrete case, is completely inappropriate in the continuous case. For
example, there are uncountable sets of 'length' 0.

In formulating the notion of Markov processes, we need to refine two concepts that were used in the discrete case. We cannot simply define transition

probabilities between states; except in rare cases, such transition probabilities are zero. Accordingly, first we have to define transition probabilities between a state and a set of states. Second, we cannot define transition probabilities to any arbitrary set of states; we need to identify a family of sets for which transition probabilities can be sensibly defined. These are the *measurable sets*.

Why cannot we define 'sizes' of arbitrary sets? Well of course we can if we want, but the notion of size will violate one basic point that we would be loath to give up. If we take a subset of the reals and 'slide it along without distortion' its length should not change. The notion of sliding (translation) is easily formalised. If S is a subset of the reals then we define $1 + S \stackrel{\text{def}}{=} \{1 + x \mid x \in S\}$ to be the set obtained by sliding S one unit in the positive direction. Consider the unit interval; clearly its length should be 1. It is possible – using the axiom of choice – to find a countable family of sets such that any one is obtained by sliding *any* of the others, and such that they *do not overlap*, and together they *exactly* cover the unit interval. Now all these sets should have the same size, say ε, and they must add up to 1, but that is not possible. We have constructed[3] a set for which no reasonable notion of size that generalises the notion of length of an interval is possible.

What can we do? We can try to pick out a family of sets for which the theory of size works sensibly. What do we want from such a family. We want to be able to add up the sizes of *countable families* of non-overlapping sets. If we try to work with larger families everything goes wrong; for example every subset of the reals is a union of singleton sets and these should surely have size 0, but then every set would have size 0! This motivates the following definition.

Definition 7.3.1 A σ-**algebra** on a set X is a family of subsets of X which includes X itself and which is closed under complementation and countable unions.

A set equipped with a σ-algebra is called a *measurable space*.

The definition of σ-algebra does not force any sets (other than X itself and the empty set $\emptyset$) to be included. We would like to say that some familiar sets must be measurable. For example, with the real numbers we would like the intervals to be measurable. Given any family of sets we can look at the smallest σ-algebra containing it; we call this the σ-algebra *generated* by the given family. Even with a family of easily understood sets, like the intervals, the family of measurable sets generated contains sets that are very difficult to describe explicitly.

---

[3] This construction uses the axiom of choice. One can argue that one should not use this axiom in mathematics and there are models of set theory without choice where all subsets of the reals are measurable; but then even worse things happen!

Most of the time we are working with $\mathbb{R}^n$ or a subset but it is nevertheless worth formulating the theory on an arbitrary topological space. Given a topological space $(X, \mathcal{T})$, we can define the σ-algebra, often written $\mathcal{B}$, generated by the open sets (or, equivalently, by the closed sets). This is usually called the *Borel algebra* associated with the topology. When there is no confusion about the topology, it is usually just called 'the Borel algebra'.

Definition 7.3.2 Given a σ-algebra (X, Σ), a **subprobability measure** on X is a $[0, 1]$-valued set function, μ, defined on Σ such that

- $\mu(\emptyset) = 0$,
- for a pairwise disjoint, countable collection of sets, $\{A_i \mid i \in I\}$, in Σ, we require

$$\mu(\bigcup_{i \in I} A_i) = \sum_{i \in I} \mu(A_i).$$

In addition, for probability measures we require $\mu(X) = 1$.

I will always be talking about subprobability measures. Any measure which assigns a finite value to the whole space is called a *finite measure*. Subprobability measures are, of course, finite. Sometimes one comes across the concept of a σ-finite measure. This means that the whole space X can be expressed as the countable union of sets of finite measure. The real line with the usual (Lebesgue) measure is σ-finite.

It is worth clarifying how the word 'measurable' is used in the literature. Given a σ-algebra Σ on a set X one says 'measurable set' for a member of Σ. Suppose that one has a measure μ. One can have the following situation. There can be sets of measure zero which contain non-measurable subsets. Because these sets are not measurable one cannot say that they have measure zero. This happens with Lebesgue measure on the Borel sets in the real line, for example. There is a 'completion' procedure[4] which produces a larger σ-algebra and an extension of the original measure in such a way that all subsets of sets of measure zero are measurable and have measure zero.

The completion works by adding to the σ-algebra all sets X such that there exist measurable sets Y, Z having the same measure, with $Y \subseteq X \subseteq Z$. When applied to the Borel subsets of the real line we get the *Lebesgue measurable* sets. One often uses the phrase 'measurable set' to mean a set which belongs to the completed σ-algebra rather than the original σ-algebra.

---

[4] This is an unfortunate name because it gives the mistaken impression that the result cannot be further extended.

Definition 7.3.3 A function $f : (X, \Sigma_X) \to (Y, \Sigma_Y)$ between measurable spaces is said to be **measurable** if $\forall B \in \Sigma_Y.\ f^{-1}(B) \in \Sigma_X$.

I will not use the Lebesgue measurable sets nor the once-popular notion of measurable function as defined by, for example, Halmos [Hal74]. That definition leads to an awkward situation: the composition of two measurable functions is not measurable.

To take stock so far, it is worth keeping the following intuitions in mind:

- A measurable set is one that is not too 'jagged' so that we can sensibly measure its size.
- A measure on a collection of sets is a numerical measure of size of each set.
- A measurable function is one that varies 'slowly enough' that we can compute its integral.

The rest of this section gets increasingly technical.

A very useful uniqueness result is the Π lemma.

Definition 7.3.4 A Π system is a family of sets closed under finite intersections.

Suppose that we have a Π system P that generates a σ-algebra, $\Sigma(P)$. We have the following result.

Proposition 7.3.5 *If two measures on* $\Sigma(P)$, μ_1 *and* μ_2, *agree on* P, *then they agree on all of* $\Sigma(P)$.

This allows one to work with Π systems rather than with the σ-algebras that they generate. The sets in a Π system are much simpler than the sets in a σ-algebra. For example, in the real line a nice Π system is the set of closed intervals, which are much simpler sets than all the Borel sets. In this case if two measures agree on intervals then they must agree on all the Borel sets. It is extremely pleasant to have such results: it would be extremely awkward to verify that two measures agree without such a result.

A key ingredient in the theory is the transition probability function.

Definition 7.3.6 A **transition probability function** on a measurable space (X, Σ) is a function $\tau : X \times \Sigma \to [0, 1]$ such that for each fixed $x \in X$, the set function $\tau(x, \cdot)$ is a (sub)probability measure, and for each fixed $A \in \Sigma$ the function $\tau(\cdot, A)$ is a measurable function.

One interprets $\tau(x, A)$ as the probability of the system starting in state x making a transition into one of the states in A. The transition probability is a *conditional probability*; it gives the probability of the system being in one of the states of the set A after the transition, *given* that it was in the state x before the transition. In general the transition probabilities could depend on time, in the sense that the transition probability could be different at every step (but still independent of past history); we will only consider the time-independent case.

How do we know that we can construct such functions? It turns out that such functions always exist on certain topological spaces called *Polish spaces*. These, however, are not quite general enough for our purposes so we will need a broader class of spaces called *analytic spaces*.

The next several definitions and results pertain to analytic spaces.

Definition 7.3.7 A **Polish** space is the topological space underlying a complete, separable metric space; i.e. it has a countable dense subset.

Definition 7.3.8 An **analytic** space is the image of a Polish space under a continuous function from one Polish space to another.

The following proposition [Dud89] gives equivalent definitions of analytic set.

Proposition 7.3.9 *Suppose that X and Y are Polish spaces and f is a function from X to Y. The following are equivalent:*

- *f is continuous and A is the image of X under f,*
- *f is measurable and A is the image of X under f,*
- *f is continuous and A is the image of a Borel subset B of X,*
- *f is measurable and A is the image of a Borel subset B of X,*
- *$g : \mathbb{N}^\infty \to Y$ is continuous and A is the image of $\mathbb{N}^\infty$ and*
- *$g : \mathbb{N}^\infty \to Y$ is measurable and A is the image of $\mathbb{N}^\infty$.*

Thus in this definition it turns out to be equivalent to say 'measurable' image and it makes no difference if we take the image of the whole Polish space or of a Borel subset of the Polish space.

Analytic spaces are more general than Polish spaces but they also have the basic property that the transition probability functions that we want can be defined on them.

It is worth noting that the space $\mathbb{N}^\infty$ captures both continuous aspects – for example, every open set in $\mathbb{R}^n$ is the continuous image of it – and discrete aspects since it is, for example, totally disconnected. The surprising fact is that there are non-Borel analytic sets. The construction is rather complicated but it does not require the axiom of choice. We say that a measurable space is *an analytic space* if it is measurably isomorphic to an analytic set in a Polish space.

The next theorem states that analytic sets, though not always Borel, are always measurable.

Theorem 7.3.10 *In a Polish space any analytic set is measurable in the σ-field constructed by completing any probability measure.*

Such sets are called *universally measurable*. It is very hard to find non-analytic universally measurable sets.

The next lemmas are theorem 3.3.5 of [Arv76] and one of its corollaries. We say that two sets in a Polish space are *separated* if there are disjoint Borel sets which contain them. The following result is needed later.

Proposition 7.3.11 *Two disjoint analytic sets in a Polish space are separated.*

We say that a σ-field *separates points* if, whenever $x \neq y$, there is a measurable set, E, for which $\chi_E(x) \neq \chi_E(y)$. The following powerful theorem and its consequences play a key role in our treatment of the logic. The first theorem is a very strong 'rigidity' property: it says that if one has a sub-σ-algebra, say Λ of an analytic space Σ and Λ separates points (so it is not too small) and countably generated (so it is not too large) then Λ is all of Σ.

Theorem 7.3.12 *Let (X, Σ) be an analytic space and suppose that Σ_0 is a countably generated sub-σ-field of Σ that separates points in X. Then $\Sigma_0 = \Sigma$.*

It is perhaps a bit misleading to think of countably generated as being a 'size' condition. The σ-algebra consisting of the countable and cocountable subsets of the reals is a sub-σ-algebra distinct from the usual Borel algebra; it is not, of course, countably generated.

Analytic spaces can be quotiented by 'nice' equivalence relations. We know of no such property for Polish spaces.

Proposition 7.3.13 *Let X be an analytic space and let $\sim$ be an equivalence relation on X. Assume that there is a sequence $f_1, f_2, \ldots$ of real-valued measurable functions on X such that for all x, y in X we have $x \sim y$ iff for all f_i we have $f_i(x) = f_i(y)$. Then $X/\sim$ is an analytic space.*

Doberkat calls these relations 'smooth' which is a nice name but I prefer to avoid it since it clashes with the notion of smoothness in geometry.

This long digression into analytic spaces would be pointless if we did not have the following result.

Theorem 7.3.14 *Regular conditional probability densities exist on analytic spaces.*

This result can be found in the textbook of J. Hoffman-Jørgensen [HJ94]. These regular conditional probability densities are exactly the Markov kernels that one needs to define labelled Markov processes.

7.4 Labelled Markov processes

In this section we give the formal definitions of labelled Markov processes (LMPs).

7.4.1 Some examples

We begin with a simple example, more for introducing terminology and concepts than for any practical interest. Consider a system with two labels $\{a, b\}$. The state space is the real plane, $\mathbb{R}^2$. When the system makes an a-move from state (x_0, y_0), it jumps to (x, y_0), where the probability distribution for x is given by the density $K_\alpha \exp(-\alpha(x - x_0)^2)$, where $K_\alpha = \sqrt{\alpha/\pi}$ is the normalising factor. When it makes a b-move it jumps from state (x_0, y_0) to (x_0, y), where the distribution of y is given by the density function $K_\beta \exp(-\beta(y - y_0)^2)$. The meaning of these densities is as follows. The probability of jumping from (x_0, y_0) to a state with x-coordinate in the interval $[s, t]$ under an a-move is $\int_s^t K_\alpha \exp(-\alpha(x - x_0)^2)dx$. Note that the probability of jumping to any given point is, of course, 0. In this system the interaction with the environment controls whether the jump is along the x-axis or along the y-axis but the actual extent of the jump is governed by a probability distribution.

Interestingly, this system is indistinguishable from a one-state system that can make a or b moves. Thus, from the point of view of an external observer, this system has an extremely simple behaviour. The more complex internal behaviour is not externally visible. All that an observer can see is that the process always accepts an a-transition or a b-transition with probability 1. The point of a theory of bisimulation that encompasses such systems is to say when systems are equivalent. Of course this example is already familiar from the non-probabilistic setting; if there is a system in which all transitions are always enabled, it will be bisimilar (in the traditional sense) to a system with one state. Bisimulation, like most other process equivalences, abstracts from the structure of the internal state space and records only the interaction with the environment. This example shows that it is possible for a system presented as a continuum state system to be in fact reducible to a simple finite-state system.

Now we consider a system which cannot be reduced to a discrete system. There are three labels $\{a, b, c\}$. Suppose that the state space is $\mathbb{R}$. The state gives the pressure of a gaseous mixture in a tank in a chemical plant. The environment can interact by (a) simply measuring the pressure, or (b) it can inject some gas into the tank, or (c) it can pump some gas from the tank. The pressure fluctuates according to some thermodynamic laws depending on the reactions taking place in the tank. With each interaction, the pressure changes according to three different probability density functions, say $f(p_0, p)$, $g(p_0, p)$ and $h(p_0, p)$ respectively, with non-trivial dependence on p_0. In addition, there are two threshold values p_h and p_l. When the pressure rises above p_h the interaction labelled b is disabled, and when the pressure drops below p_l the interaction labelled c is disabled. It is tempting to model this as a three-state system, with the continuous state space partitioned by the threshold values. Unfortunately one cannot assign unique transition probabilities to these sets of states for arbitrary choices of f, g and h; only if very implausible uniformity conditions are obeyed can one do this. These conditions require, for example, that for any pressure value, p say, between p_l and p_h the probability of jumping to a pressure value above p_h is independent of the actual value of p. This is very implausible given the intuition that if the value of p is close to p_h the pressure fluctuations in the system are much more likely to carry the value of the pressure above p_h than if the initial pressure p is far below p_h.

These two examples show that systems presented as continua may or may not be 'equivalent' to discrete systems. In particular if one wants to work with a discrete model one will need some precise definition of what it means for the discrete model to be equivalent to the original system.

Here is an example from aircraft control. Imagine that there is a flying device, say a drone aircraft, that has three control actions: **a** – turn left, **b** – turn right and **c** – straight. The response to these controls is not perfect owing to wind turbulence and other random factors. The actions **a** and **b** move the craft sideways with some probability distributions on how far it moves. The craft may 'drift' even with **c**. The aircraft must stay within a certain corridor. The regions near the edges of the corridor are designated as dangerous and too close to the boundary. The action **a** (**b**) must be disabled when the craft is too near the left (right) boundary because it has to stay within the corridor. One might think that one has a nice four or five state system but this is not the case. The probability of drifting into the dangerous border regions depends on how close the aircraft is to the border and varies continuously with distance. Unless very special (and unlikely) uniformity conditions hold, this cannot be compressed into a finite-state system.

7.4.2 Formal definitions

When we define labelled Markov processes, instead of an arbitrary σ-algebra structure on the set of states, I will require that the set of states be an analytic space and the σ-algebra be the Borel algebra generated by the topology.

Definition 7.4.1 A **labelled Markov process** with label set L is a structure $(S, \Sigma, \{\tau_a \mid a \in L\})$, where S is the set of states, which is assumed to be an analytic space, and Σ is the Borel σ-algebra on S, and

$$\forall a \in L, \tau_a : S \times \Sigma \longrightarrow [0, 1]$$

is a transition subprobability function.

We will fix the label set to be some L once and for all. We will write (S, Σ, τ_a) for labelled Markov processes, instead of the more precise $(S, \Sigma, \{\tau_a \mid l \in L\})$ and often refer to a process by its set of states.

In order to define a category of labelled Markov processes, we define simulation morphisms between processes.

Definition 7.4.2 A **simulation morphism** f between two labelled Markov processes, (S, Σ, τ_a) and (S', Σ', τ'_a), is a measurable function $f : (S, \Sigma) \to (S', \Sigma')$ such that

$$\forall a \in L. \forall s \in S. \forall A' \in \Sigma'. \tau_a(s, f^{-1}(A')) \leq \tau'_a(f(s), A').$$

Suppose that the system being simulated can make a transition from the state s to the set of states A with a certain probability, say p. Then the simulating system will simulate it in the following sense: the transition probability from $f(s)$ to any measurable set B such that $f(A) \subseteq B$ is greater than p. This is equivalent to the statement in the definition. We cannot directly talk about the transition probability from $f(s)$ to $f(A)$ since the latter may not be measurable. We require simulation to be measurable for the definition to make sense. If f were not measurable we would not be guaranteed that $f^{-1}(A')$ is measurable.

Definition 7.4.3 The objects of the category **LMP** are labelled Markov processes, having a fixed set L as the set of labels, with simulations as the morphisms.

7.5 Giry's monad

This section is rather categorical in nature and can be omitted by those averse to this subject. It is needed to understand the section on cocongruences.

It has been recognised that coalgebras provide a sweeping universal[5] picture of 'systems' [Rut95]. This section sets up the categorical framework needed to understand LMPs coalgebraically. The nicest categorical way to look at LMPs

---

[5] Perhaps I should say 'couniversal?'

is as *coalgebras* of a suitable monad. The monad for this coalgebra was defined by Giry [Gir81] following suggestions of Lawvere.

We start with the category **Mes** of measurable spaces: (X, Σ_X) where X is a set and Σ_X is a σ-algebra on X, with measurable functions. Recall that a function $f : (X, \Sigma_X) \to (Y, \Sigma_Y)$ is measurable if $f^{-1}(B) \in \Sigma_X$ for all $B \in \Sigma_Y$. We define the functor $\Pi : \textbf{Mes} \to \textbf{Mes}$ as follows. On objects

$$\Pi(X) =_{df} \{\nu \mid \nu \text{ is a subprobability measure on } X\}.$$

For any $A \in \Sigma_X$ we get a function $p_A : \Pi(X) \to [0, 1]$ given by $p_A(\nu) =_{df} \nu(A)$. The σ-field structure on $\Pi(X)$ is the least σ-field such that all the p_A maps are measurable. A measurable function $f : X \to Y$ becomes $\Pi(f)(\nu) = \nu \circ f^{-1}$. Clearly Π is a functor.

We claim that Π is a monad. We define the appropriate natural transformations $\eta : I \to \Pi$ and $\mu : \Pi^2 \to \Pi^6$ as follows:

$$\eta_X(x) = \delta(x, \cdot), \mu_X(\Omega) = \lambda B \in \Sigma_X. \int_{\Pi(X)} p_B \Omega.$$

The definition of η should be clear but the definition of μ needs to be explained. First, note that Ω is a measure on $\Pi(X)$. Recall that p_B is the measurable function, defined on $\Pi(X)$, which maps a measure ν to $\nu(B)$. The σ-field on $\Pi(X)$ has been defined precisely to make this a measurable function. Now the integral $\int_{\Pi(X)} p_B \Omega$ is meaningful. Of course one has to verify that $\mu_X(\Omega)$ is a subprobability measure. The only slight subtlety is checking that countable additivity holds.

Theorem 7.5.1 *[Giry] The triple* (Π, η, μ) *is a monad on* **Mes**.

The Kleisli category of this monad is called **SRel**, for *stochastic relations*. Just as the category of binary relations is the Kleisli category of the powerset monad so the stochastic relations are the Kleisli morphisms for Giry's 'fuzzy' powerset monad. In Giry's paper she worked with the set of probability distributions rather than with subprobability distributions as I am doing here. This gives **SRel** some additional structure (partially additive structure) but it is not important for our purposes.

Here is the explicit description of **SRel**. The objects are the same as in **Mes**. An **SRel** morphism $h : X \to Y$ is a measurable function from X to $\Pi(Y)$. In other words $h : X \to (\Sigma_Y \to [0, 1])$, and applying some curry powder we get $h : X \times \Sigma_Y \to [0, 1]$. Now $h(x, \cdot)$ is clearly a measure on Y for each fixed x and, for each fixed $B \in \Sigma_Y$, $h(\cdot, B)$ is a measurable function. We see that an

---

[6] Try not to confuse μ with a measure.

LMP is just a Kleisli morphism from X to itself. In other words, an LMP is a coalgebra of the functor Π. Composition is given as follows. Suppose that h is as above and $k : (Y, \Sigma_Y) \to (Z, \Sigma_Z)$. Then we define $k \circ h : (X, \Sigma_X) \to (Z, \Sigma_Z)$ by the formula $(k \circ h)(x, C) = \int_Y k(y, C)h(x, dy)$. Note how, in this formula, the measurability conditions on h and k are just right for the integral to make sense.

Exercise 7.5.2 Show, using the monotone convergence theorem, that composition of kernels is associative.

7.6 Probabilistic bisimulation

We define probabilistic bisimulation coalgebraically but later in this section we give a purely relational version.

7.6.1 Categorical definition

There is a standard categorical treatment of bisimulation, due to Aczel and Mendler [AM89], which can be applied immediately to labelled Markov processes. If we look at the category of coalgebras of Π as being *the* category of labelled Markov processes we have the following notion of morphism.

Definition 7.6.1 A **zig-zag** morphism between two LMPs S and S' is a measurable function $f : S \to S'$ such that

$$\forall a \in \mathsf{L}, x \in S, B \in \Sigma' \ \tau_a(x, f^{-1}(B)) = \tau_a(f(x), B).$$

The term 'zig-zag' comes from the modal logic literature [Pop94]. It captures the 'back-and-forth' condition that one sees in the usual definitions of bisimulation. A zig-zag morphism is the functional analogue of bisimulation. In order to get the relational version one needs to introduce *spans*.

Definition 7.6.2 A **span** in a category $\mathcal{C}$ between $\mathcal{C}$-objects A and B is an object R and a pair of morphisms f, g from R to A and B, respectively.

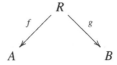

Now we just define probabilistic bisimulation as a span of zig-zags.

Definition 7.6.3 A **probabilistic bisimulation** between (S_1, Σ_1, τ_1) and (S_2, Σ_2, τ_2) is a span of zig-zags f, g

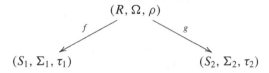

In order to show that one has an equivalence relation it is necessary to establish transitivity. With spans this means that when one has

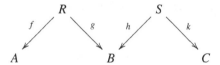

there should be a way of 'completing' the picture in order to obtain

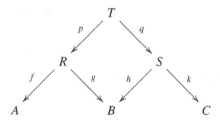

If the category in question has pullbacks then one can indeed use the pullback construction to compose spans. The category of LMPs with zig-zag morphisms unfortunately does not have pullbacks. One can use a weaker construction: the *weak pullback*. Here – as with pullbacks – one requires that there is a way of completing the square but the construction need not be universal: any other way of completing the square must factor through the weak pullback but not uniquely. In order to get a category of coalgebras that has weak pullbacks it is sufficient that Π preserve weak pullbacks. Unfortunately this does not hold and the category of LMPs with zig-zags does not have weak pullbacks.

Exercise 7.6.4 Show, with a simple discrete example, why we need spans of zig-zags. More precisely, give two simple discrte systems that are clearly bisimilar (i.e. we can find a span of zig-zags) but there is no zig-zag between them in either direction.

In [dVR97, dVR99] de Vink and Rutten showed that in a related category, namely ultrametric spaces, the analogue of Giry's monad does preserve weak pullbacks. Ultrametric spaces are, however, unlike the common continuous spaces that one wants to work with. Thus, for example, familiar spaces like the reals, or any manifold, are not ultrametric spaces. Indeed, one can make the case that ultrametric spaces are closer to being discrete than being continuous!

The problem of showing that spans can be composed was solved by a construction due to Edalat [Eda99] called the 'semi-pullback.' This was used in the theory of bisimulation for LMPs developed by Desharnais *et al.* [BDEP97, DEP02]. Edalat's construction was ingenious and intricate and involved moving between two closely related categories. A cleaner construction was given later by Doberkat [Dob03] where powerful techniques like measurable selection theorems were used.

7.6.2 Relational definition

A much simpler approach was developed by Desharnais, Gupta, Jagadeesan and the present author in [DGJP00, DGJP03]. Here the categorical approach was abandoned in favour of a return to the relational definition of Larsen and Skou [LS91].

Definition 7.6.5 If R is a binary relation we say that a set X is R-**closed** if

$$X = R(X) := \{u \mid \exists x \in X, \ x R u\}.$$

If R is an equivalence relation, then an R-closed set is just a union of equivalence classes.

We will define a bisimulation relation on a single LMP; it is clear that we could define it between two different LMPs by taking the disjoint union of the LMPs.

Definition 7.6.6 Given an LMP $\mathcal{S} = (S, \Sigma, \tau_a)$ a **probabilistic bisimulation** is a binary relation R defined on the state space S, such that if $s R t$ then, for every *measurable* R-closed set C,

$$\forall a \in \mathsf{L}, \ \tau_a(s, C) = \tau_a(t, C).$$

As before, we say that two states are bisimilar if we can find a bisimulation relation that relates them.

Exercise* 7.6.7 Show that the relational definition is equivalent to the span definition for discrete systems. This is worked out in [DEP02].

7.7 Logical characterisation

The proof of the logical characterisation theorem for the continuous case is full of surprises. It is not obvious that one should expect an analogue of the Hennessy–Milner theorem without a very rich logic. The reason for this is that in the non-deterministic case one needs image-finiteness. If one does not have image-finiteness one needs infinite conjunctions. All the studies in the literature that consider infinite branching are restricted to the countable case. In the continuous case one has *uncountable* branching and one certainly does not have the kind of minimal deviation assumption considered by Larsen and Skou.

As it turned out, not only is there a logical characterisation theorem, it does not need infinite conjunctions, *even when the underlying system has uncountable branching*. Furthermore, the logic that characterises bisimulation turns out to be simpler than the logics used for the discrete case, it does not even need disjunction or *any* negative constructs. Of course, these results, once established for the continuous case, do apply to the discrete case. As of this writing, no direct proof that avoids the measure-theoretic machinery is known for the discrete case.

As before we assume that there is a fixed set of 'actions' L. The logic is called $\mathcal{L}$ and has the following syntax:

$$\mathsf{T} \mid \phi_1 \wedge \phi_2 \mid \langle a \rangle_q \phi$$

where a is an action and q is a rational number. This is the basic logic with which we establish the logical characterisation of bisimulation.

The semantics for this logic are given in terms of a satisfaction relation $s \models \phi$ between states and formulas of $\mathcal{L}$:

$$s \models \mathsf{T} \quad \text{for all } s \in S$$
$$s \models \phi_1 \wedge \phi_2 \quad \text{if } s \models \phi_1 \text{ and } s \models \phi_2$$
$$s \models \langle a \rangle_q \phi \quad \text{if there is a measurable set } A \text{ such that}$$
$$\tau_a(s, A) \geq q \text{ and } \forall u \in A, \ u \models \phi.$$

We write $[\![\phi]\!] = \{s \mid s \models \phi\}$. The following is an easy proof by induction on the structure of formulas.

Proposition 7.7.1 *For all formulas ϕ of $\mathcal{L}$, the set $[\![\phi]\!]$ is measurable.*

In view of this we can write $s \models \langle a \rangle_q \phi$ as meaning $\tau_a(s, [\![\phi]\!]) \geq q$.

Exercise 7.7.2 Give the induction proof for the above proposition.

It is straightforward to show that bisimilar states satisfy the same formulas.

Proposition 7.7.3 *Let R be a bisimulation on S. If $s\,R s'$ then s and s' satisfy the same formulas.*

Proof We proceed by induction on the structure of formulas. The cases of T and conjunction are trivial. Now assume the implication is true for ϕ, i.e. for every pair of R-related states either both satisfy ϕ or neither of them does. This means that the set $[\![\phi]\!]$ is R-closed, and by Proposition 7.7.1 is measurable.

Since R is a bisimulation transition probabilities to R-closed measurable sets must agree, $\tau_a(s, [\![\phi]\!]) = \tau_a(s', [\![\phi]\!])$ for all $a \in \mathsf{L}$.   □

We introduce a *logical* equivalence relation between states.

Definition 7.7.4 Let $S = (S, \Sigma, \tau_a)$ be an LMP and s and t be states of S. We say that $s \approx t$ if

$$\forall \phi \in \mathcal{L}\ s \models \phi \iff t \models \phi.$$

Our main goal is to show that $\approx$ is a bisimulation relation.

We first show that there is a zig-zag from any system S to its quotient under $\approx$. If (S, Σ) is a measurable space, the quotient $(S/_\approx, \Sigma_\approx)$ is defined as follows. $S/_\approx$ is the set of all equivalence classes. Then the function $q : S \to S/_\approx$ which assigns to each point of S the equivalence class containing it maps onto $S/_\approx$, and thus determines a σ-algebra structure on $S/_\approx$: by definition a subset E of $S/_\approx$ is a measurable set if $q^{-1}(E)$ is a measurable set in (S, Σ).

Proposition 7.7.5 *Let (S, Σ, τ_a) be an LMP. We can define ρ_a so that the canonical projection q from (S, Σ, τ_a) to $(S/_\approx, \Sigma_\approx, \rho_a)$ is a zig-zag morphism.*

In order to prove this proposition we need a couple of lemmas in addition to Theorem 7.3.12 and Proposition 7.3.13.

The first lemma just says that the transition probabilities to sets of the form $[\![\phi]\!]$ are completely determined by the formulas.

Lemma 7.7.6 *Let (S, Σ, τ_a) and (S', Σ', τ'_a) be two LMPs. Then for all formulas ϕ and all pairs (s, s') such that $s \approx s'$, we have $\tau_a(s, [\![\phi]\!]_S) = \tau'_a(s', [\![\phi]\!]_{S'})$.*

Proof Suppose that the equation does not hold. Then, say, for some ϕ, $\tau_a(s, [\![\phi]\!]_S) < \tau'_a(s', [\![\phi]\!]_{S'})$. We choose a rational number q between these values. Now it follows that $s' \models \langle a \rangle_q \phi$ but $s \not\models \langle a \rangle_q \phi$, which contradicts the assumption that s and s' satisfy all the same formulas.   □

The final result that we need is Proposition 7.3.5 which tells us that when two measures agree on a π-system they will agree on the generated σ-algebra.

This is just what we need; the formulas are closed under conjunction so the collection of sets $[\![\phi]\!]$ is a π-system.

Proof of Proposition 7.7.5: We first show that $S/_\approx$ is an analytic space. Let $\{\phi_i \mid i \in \mathbf{N}\}$ be the set of all formulas. We know that $[\![\phi_i]\!]_S$ is a measurable set for each i. Therefore the characteristic functions $\chi_{\phi_i} : S \to \{0, 1\}$ are measurable functions. Moreover we have

$$x \approx y \text{ iff } (\forall i \in \mathbf{N}.\ x \in [\![\phi_i]\!]_S \iff y \in [\![\phi_i]\!]_S) \text{ iff } (\forall i \in \mathbf{N}.\ \chi_{\phi_i}(x) = \chi_{\phi_i}(y)).$$

It now follows by Lemma 7.3.13 that $S/_\approx$ is an analytic space.

Let $\mathcal{B} = \{q([\![\phi_i]\!]_S) : i \in \mathbf{N}\}$. We show that $\sigma(\mathcal{B}) = \Sigma_\approx$. We have inclusion since $\mathcal{B} \subseteq \Sigma_\approx$: indeed, for any $q([\![\phi_i]\!]_S) \in \mathcal{B}$, $q^{-1}q([\![\phi_i]\!]_S) = [\![\phi_i]\!]_S$ which is in Σ by Lemma 7.7.1. Now $\sigma(\mathcal{B})$ separates points in $S/_\approx$, for if x and y are different states of $S/_\approx$, take states $x_0 \in q^{-1}(x)$ and $y_0 \in q^{-1}(y)$. Then since $x_0 \not\approx y_0$, there is a formula ϕ such that x_0 is in $[\![\phi]\!]_S$ and y_0 is not. This means that

$$\forall s \in q^{-1}(x), s \in [\![\phi]\!]_S \text{ and } \forall t \in q^{-1}(y), t \notin [\![\phi]\!]_S$$

so that x is in $q[\![\phi]\!]_S$, whereas y is not. Since $\sigma(\mathcal{B})$ is countably generated, it follows by Theorem 7.3.12, that $\sigma(\mathcal{B}) = \Sigma_\approx$.

We are now ready to define $\rho_a(t, \cdot)$ over $\Sigma_\approx$ for $t \in S/_\approx$. We define it so that $q : S \to S/_\approx$ is a zig-zag (recall that q is measurable and surjective by definition), i.e. for any $B \in \Sigma_\approx$ we put

$$h_a(t, B) = \tau_a(s, q^{-1}(B)),$$

where $s \in q^{-1}(t)$. Clearly, for a fixed state s, $\tau_a(s, q^{-1}(\cdot))$ is a subprobability measure on $\Sigma_\approx$. We now show that the definition does not depend on the choice of s in $q^{-1}(t)$ for if $s, s' \in q^{-1}(t)$, we know that $\tau_a(s, q^{-1}(\cdot))$ and $\tau_a(s', q^{-1}(\cdot))$ agree over $\mathcal{B}$, again by the fact that $q^{-1}q([\![\phi_i]\!]_S) = [\![\phi_i]\!]_S$ and by Lemma 7.7.6. So, since $\mathcal{B}$ is closed under the formation of finite intersections we have, from Proposition 7.3.5, that $\tau_a(s, q^{-1}(\cdot))$ and $\tau_a(s', q^{-1}(\cdot))$ agree on $\sigma(\mathcal{B}) = \Sigma_\approx$.

It remains to prove that for a fixed Borel set B of $\Sigma_\approx$, $\rho_a(\cdot, B) : S/_\approx \to [0, 1]$ is a Borel measurable function. Let A be a Borel set of $[0, 1]$. Then $\rho_a(\cdot, B)^{-1}(A) = q[\tau_a(\cdot, q^{-1}(B))^{-1}(A)]$; we know that $\sigma = \tau_a(\cdot, q^{-1}(B))^{-1}(A)$ is Borel since it is the inverse image of A under a Borel measurable function. Now we have that $q(\sigma) \in \Sigma_\approx$, since $q^{-1}q(\sigma) = \sigma$: indeed, if $s_1 \in q^{-1}q(\sigma)$, there exists $s_2 \in \sigma$ such that $q(s_1) = q(s_2)$, and we have just proved above that then the $\tau_a(s_i, q^{-1}(\cdot))$'s must agree, so if $\tau_a(s_i, q^{-1}(B)) \in A$ for $i = 2$, then it is also true for $i = 1$, so $s_1 \in \sigma$ as wanted. So $\rho_a(\cdot, B)$ is measurable. This concludes the proof that $S/_\approx$ is an LMP and q a zig-zag. $\qquad\square$

Theorem 7.7.7 *Let (S, i, Σ, τ) be a labelled Markov process. Two states $s, s' \in S$ are bisimilar if and only if they satisfy the same formulas of $\mathcal{L}$.*

Proof One direction has been done already. For the other direction we will use Proposition 7.7.5 to show that the relation $\approx$ defined on the states of S is in fact a bisimulation relation. The key facts are

(1) $B \in \Sigma_\approx$ if and only if $q^{-1}(B) \in \Sigma$,
(2) $\forall s \in S, B \in \Sigma_\approx . \rho(q(s), B) = \tau(s, q^{-1}(B))$.

Let $X \in \Sigma$ be $\approx$-closed. Then we have $X = q^{-1}(q(X))$ and hence $q(X) \in \Sigma_\approx$. Now if $s \approx s'$, then $q(s) = q(s')$, and $\tau_a(s, X) = \rho_a(f(s), f(X)) = \tau_a(s', X)$, and hence $\approx$ is a bisimulation.   □

It is worth noting the measure theory ideas that went into the proof. We were able to leverage the property of Π systems to get a long way without negation. We did not need disjunction. The use of Theorem 7.3.12 is crucial, but it is not easy to pinpoint what exactly it replaces in the classical case. Finally the use of the quotienting construction depends on having analytic spaces.

7.8 Probabilistic cocongruences

We have seen that the logical characterisation of bisimulation depends on properties of analytic spaces. Though analytic spaces are general enough for almost every conceivable application there is something troubling about the fact that these topological ideas were needed for what should have been a purely measure theoretic situation.

It was noted that the composition of spans in the category of coalgebras required that the Π functor preserve weak pullbacks; this was a major source of all the technical problems that were ultimately solved by using properties of analytic spaces. What if we worked with cospans instead of spans? Perhaps the Π functor should have to preserve pushouts? In fact this is not needed at all! One can construct pushouts in the category of coalgebras *for free.*

Usually bisimulation is defined as a span in the coalgebra category as shown below.

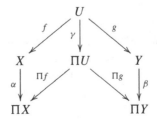

Here α and β define Π-coalgebras on X and Y, respectively; in other words they define LMPs. The span of zig-zags given by f and g – with f and g both surjective – define a bisimulation relation between (X, α) and (Y, β). We assume that there is only one label for simplicity. We have seen how this span concept is the categorical generalisation of the notion of binary relation.

If we think in terms of equivalence relations then one can switch to thinking in terms of the equivalence classes instead of the relation as a set of pairs. The categorical version of this is exactly the cospan.

An important observation is that with cospans one can compose using pushouts and *this does not require Π to preserve anything*. We consider the situation shown below, where we have omitted labels for some of the arrows, for example $\Pi f : \Pi X \to \Pi U$, where they can be inferred by functoriality. The arrows f, g, h and k are zig-zags.

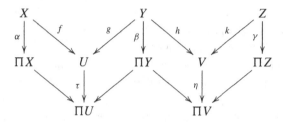

One way to construct a cospan from $\mathcal{X}$ to $\mathcal{Z}$ is to construct a pushout in the coalgebra category. In **Mes** we can construct a pushout for the arrows g and f to obtain the situation shown below.

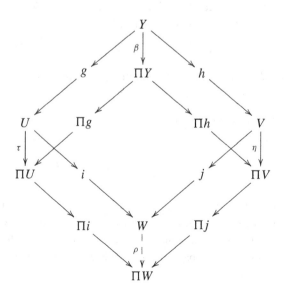

Here W is the object constructed as the tip of the pushout in **Mes**. In order
to have a pushout in the category of coalgebras we need to put a coalgebra
structure on W, i.e. we need to construct a morphism $\rho : W \to \Pi W$, shown
dotted in the diagram. This is exactly what the couniversal property of the
pushout promises. Consider the following calculation:

$$
\begin{aligned}
&g; \tau; \Pi i \\
=\quad &\beta; \Pi g; \Pi i \qquad && g \text{ is a zig-zag,} \\
=\quad &\beta; \Pi(g; i) \qquad && \text{functoriality,} \\
=\quad &\beta; \Pi(h; j) \qquad && \text{pushout,} \\
=\quad &\beta; \Pi h; \Pi j \qquad && \text{functoriality,} \\
=\quad &h; \eta; \Pi j \qquad && h \text{ is a zig-zag.}
\end{aligned}
$$

Thus, the outer square formed by Y, U, V and ΠW commutes and couniver-
sality implies the existence of the morphism ρ from W to ΠW. It is a routine
calculation that this gives a pushout in the category of coalgebras. This does
not require any special properties of Π; it holds in the most general case, i.e.
in **Mes**. We call this dual concept a *cocongruence*.

This concept was independently discovered by Danos, Desharnais, Laviolette and the present author [DDLP06] and by Bartels, Sokolova and de
Vink [BSdV04]. In the paper by Danos *et al.* the concept being explored was
a new kind of bisimulation relation called, in that paper, 'event bisimulation'.
I do not like this terminology very much but I will stick with it. The idea is to
have a concept that does not refer to the 'points' of the space as much as to the
measurable sets.

Definition 7.8.1 An **event bisimulation** on an LMP (S, Σ, τ) is a sub-σ-
algebra Λ of Σ such that (S, Λ, τ) is an LMP.

An almost immediate consequence of this definition is the following.

Lemma 7.8.2 *If Λ is an event bisimulation, then the identity function on S
defines a zig-zag morphism from (S, Σ, τ) to (S, Λ, τ).*

In fact event bisimulations fit much better with the concept of zig-zags than
ordinary bisimulations do.

Lemma 7.8.3 *If $f : (S, \Sigma, \tau) \to (S', \Sigma', \tau')$ is a zig-zag morphism, then
$f^{-1}(\Sigma')$ is an event bisimulation on S.*

In [DDLP06] the relation between this notion and the more traditional notion
of bisimulation is discussed at length. In the discrete case the two coincide;
perhaps this explains why the concept did not emerge earlier. In [DDLP06]
we proved that for analytic spaces the concepts coincide. In fact this proof is

'implicit' in the proof of the logical characterisation of bisimulation presented in the last section.

With event bisimulation we have logical characterisation in the most general context. Given our logic $\mathcal{L}$ we define $\sigma(\mathcal{L})$ to be the σ-algebra generated by sets of the form $[\![\phi]\!]$ for $\phi \in \mathcal{L}$. An important property of sub-σ-algebras is stability.

Definition 7.8.4 Let (S, Σ, τ) be an LMP and $\Lambda \subseteq \Sigma$. We say that Λ is **stable** with respect to (S, Σ, τ) if for all $A \in \Lambda, r \in [0, 1], a \in \mathcal{A}$,

$$\{s : \tau_a(s, A) > r\} \in \Lambda.$$

Note that Λ is an event bisimulation if and only if it is stable and that the condition of measurability of a kernel $\tau(\cdot, A)$ is exactly that Σ be stable.

Theorem 7.8.5 *If $S = (S, \Sigma, \tau)$ is an LMP with Σ an arbitrary σ-algebra defined on it, then $\sigma(\mathcal{L})$ is the smallest stable σ-algebra included in Σ.*

From this the logical characterisation result follows.

Corollary 7.8.6 *The logic $\mathcal{L}$ characterises event bisimulation.*

Proof From Theorem 7.8.5, stability tells us that $\sigma([\![\mathcal{L}]\!])$ is an event bisimulation and the fact that it is the smallest implies that any event bisimulation preserves $\mathcal{L}$ formulas. □

What is the connection between event bisimulation and cocongruence? We can redefine event bisimulation in coalgebraic terms as follows.

Definition 7.8.7 An **event bisimulation** on $S = (S, \Sigma, \tau)$ is a surjection in the category of coalgebras of Π to some $\mathcal{T}$.

We have already noted that such arrows are zig-zags and that a zig-zag induces an event bisimulation on its source. For the case of an event bisimulation between two different LMPs we have

Definition 7.8.8 An **event bisimulation** between S and S' is a cospan of surjections in the category of coalgebras to some object $\mathcal{T}$.

This can be viewed as ordinary event bisimulation on $S + S'$.

7.9 Kozen's coinduction principle

In order for probabilistic bisimulation – or any kind of bisimulation – to be used in practice, one needs a coinduction principle. Kozen [Koz06, Koz07] has formulated a beautiful and simple coinduction principle for stochastic processes that provides just the tool one needs. The hard analysis that goes into the study of bisimulation is packaged inside the proof of the coinduction principle and one can use it for reasoning without needing to master the analytic arguments.

The following example is taken from Kozen's paper [Koz07]. Consider the following program that describes a stochastic process for simulating a coin that gives heads with probability q using a coin that gives heads with probability p. It is natural to think of this as a recursive procedure. We have a procedure $Q(\cdot)$ which return true or false, which we think of as *head* and *tails*, respectively. $Q(q)$ has to be programmed to return true with probability q. We are given $P()$ which returns true with probability p.

```
Q(q) {
    if ( q > p) {
        if (P()) then true else Q((q-p)/(1-p)) }
    else {
        if (P()) then Q(q/p) else false }}
```

It is an easy calculation to see that the probability of halting is 1. The probability that the procedure halts and gives true on input q satisfies the recurrence.

$$H(q) = \begin{cases} p \cdot H(\frac{q}{p}) & \text{if } q \le p, \\ p + (1-p) \cdot H(\frac{q-p}{1-p}), & \text{if } q > p. \end{cases}$$

The only *bounded* solution to this recurrence is $H(q) = q$ which is what we wanted. Similarly, one can calculate the expected time (in terms of the number of calls to P) as $\frac{q}{p} + \frac{1-q}{1-p}$. These arguments are elementary. However, the following 'optimised' version of the program also does the right simulation.

```
Q(q) {
    if ( q >= (1-p)) then {
        if (P()) then Q((q-(1-p))/p) else true }
    else if ( q > p) then {
        if (P()) then true
        else Q((q-p)/(1-p)) }
    else {
        if (P()) then Q(q/p) else false}}
```

In this case, there is no simple algebraic expression that one can write down for the running time in order to compare it with the previous expected running time. One would normally expect to have to analyse the series solutions to the recurrence and use some kind of convergence argument.

Kozen's coinduction principle allows one to avoid having to analyse series and their convergence properties. Roughly speaking the principle says that if one has a 'nice' operator τ on a suitable linear space B and a closed subspace ϕ of B then if there is some element in ϕ and if for every element in ϕ the action of τ keeps it in ϕ then the fixed point of τ is also in ϕ. This fixed-point principle can be written in the logical form:

$$\frac{\exists e \in \phi \quad \forall e, \ \phi(e) \Rightarrow \phi(\tau(e))}{\phi(e^*)}$$

where e^* is the fixed point of τ.

Kozen shows how this coinduction principle can be used to argue that the expected running time of the modified program is better than the expected running time of the original program. The calculations are purely algebraic in this case. This line of research is highly suggestive and should be a main focus of research in probabilistic bisimulation.

7.10 Conclusions

In this chapter I have focused on strong probabilistic bisimulation for fully probabilistic systems. This is a somewhat conservative view, there are many variants of bisimulation to consider and there are more general models. On the other hand, I have addressed systems with continuous state spaces. My own belief is that the latter will become more and more important and it is worthwhile keeping the other aspects simple in order to focus on this. As the relevant mathematics is assimilated by the community I expect to see all the other variations of probabilistic bisimulation extended to the continuous case: indeed, this has already started to happen.

The first major extension of these ideas begins with a critique of the relevance of equivalence relations in the first place [JS90]. The argument runs as follows. If one considers two bisimilar systems (or two bisimilar states in one system), a small perturbation of the transition probabilities will render them inequivalent, even though they are still very similar. If the systems depend on real-valued parameters then these parameters cannot be known exactly and requiring an *exact* match as is commonly done for bismulation is problematic. What one needs instead is a metric.

The first idea that one can try is to allow the probabilities to match up to some small real parameter ϵ. Unfortunately this does not give a transitive relation. A reasonable thing to shoot for is a pseudo-metric, i.e. a metric that allows two distinct points to be at zero distance. One would then require that the states at zero distance would be bisimilar. The first definition of such a pseudo-metric is due to Desharnais, Gupta, Jagadeesan and Panangaden [DGJP99]. The subject was subsequently explored at length by van Breugel and Worrell [vBW01b, vBW01a] who developed polynomial-time algorithms for computing some of the metrics. Applications to AI and MDPs were explored by Ferns *et al.* [FPP04, FPP05].

A very important concept to be explored is weak bisimulation. The case of fully probabilistic processes was considered by Baier and Hermann [BH97]. Of course when one considers weak bisimulation it is inevitable that one will have to consider the interplay between non-determinism and probability. The most satisfactory definition is the one due to Philippa, Lee and Sikorsky [PLS00]. A metric analogue for this concept was developed [DGJP02a] and a logical characterisation theorem was proved [DGJP02b]. This was worked out for the alternating model, i.e. for models where the probabilistic transitions and non-deterministic choices alternate. In effect, one is able to name probability distributions. In the non-alternating model the situation is somewhat different.

This model has been introduced by Segala and Lynch [SL94] under the name of probabilistic automata and has been extensively studied by Segala and his students ever since then. Two important recent papers are [ST05, Seg06] where these notions are compared.

Finally I would like to mention the theory of real-time systems. This is of great importance in applications to performance evaluation. Jane Hillston [Hil94] has developed a process algebra geared to reasoning about performance issues, and bisimulation of real-time systems plays an important role. As I have remarked before, the queueing theory community anticipated the key idea of bisimulation when they defined lumpability. The systems of greatest interest are continuous-time Markov chains. Model checking algorithms for such systems have been developed [BHHK00, HCH$^+$02]. Bisimulation for such systems can be defined and in fact a logical characterisation theorem for CTMCs was proved with respect to continuous stochastic logic [DP03]. When one loses the Markov property bisimulation cannot really be defined on the states since the behaviour will depend on how much time the system has already spent in the state. One can define a *uniformity* on such systems [GJP04, GJP06], a concept that fits somewhere between a metric and an equivalence.

The theory of probabilistic systems is undergoing active development with a rapidly increasing sophistication of the mathematical tools being used. There are many fruitful directions to explore: efficient algorithms to compute metrics, logical characterisation theorems, approximation results and extension of various kinds. I hope that some of the readers of this chapter will be inspired to work on this fascinating topic.

Bibliography

[AM89] P. Aczel and N. Mendler. A final-coalgebra theorem. In *Category Theory and Computer Science*, number 389 in *Lecture Notes in Computer Science*, pages 357–365. Springer-Verlag, 1989.

[Arv76] W. Arveson. *An Invitation to C^*-Algebra*. Springer-Verlag, 1976.

[Ash72] R.B. Ash. *Real Analysis and Probability*. Academic Press, 1972.

[BDEP97] R. Blute, J. Desharnais, A. Edalat, and P. Panangaden. Bisimulation for labelled Markov processes. In *Proceedings of the 12th IEEE Symposium On Logic In Computer Science, Warsaw, Poland*, 1997.

[BH97] C. Baier and H. Hermanns. Weak bisimulation for fully probabilistic processes. In *Proceedings of the 1997 International Conference on Computer Aided Verification*, number 1254 in *Lecture Notes in Computer Science*. Springer-Verlag, 1997.

[BHHK00] C. Baier, B. Haverkort, H. Hermanns, and J.-P. Katoen. Model checking continuous-time Markov chains by transient analysis. In *CAV 2000: Proceedings of the 12th Annual Symposium on Computer-Aided Verification*, number 1855 in *Lecture Notes in Computer Science*, pages 358–372. Springer-Verlag, 2000.

[Bil95] P. Billingsley. *Probability and Measure*. Wiley-Interscience, 1995.

[BSdV04] F. Bartels, A. Sokolova, and E.P. de Vink. A hierarchy of probabilistic system types. *Theoretical Computer Science*, **327**:3–22, 2004.

[DDLP06] V. Danos, J. Desharnais, F. Laviolette, and P. Panangaden. Bisimulation and cocongruence for probabilistic systems. *Information and Computation*, **204**(4):503–523, 2006.

[DEP98] J. Desharnais, A. Edalat, and P. Panangaden. A logical characterization of bisimulation for labelled Markov processes. In *Proceedings of the 13th IEEE Symposium on Logic in Computer Science, Indianapolis*, pages 478–489. IEEE Press, June 1998.

[DEP02] J. Desharnais, A. Edalat, and P. Panangaden. Bisimulation for labeled Markov processes. *Information and Computation*, **179**(2):163–193, 2002.

[DGJP99] J. Desharnais, V. Gupta, R. Jagadeesan, and P. Panangaden. Metrics for labeled Markov systems. In *Proceedings of CONCUR99*, number 1664 in *Lecture Notes in Computer Science*. Springer-Verlag, 1999.

[DGJP00] J. Desharnais, V. Gupta, R. Jagadeesan, and P. Panangaden. Approximation of labeled Markov processes. In *Proceedings of the 15th Annual IEEE Symposium on Logic in Computer Science*, pages 95–106. IEEE Computer Society Press, June 2000.

[DGJP02a] J. Desharnais, V. Gupta, R. Jagadeesan, and P. Panangaden. The metric analogue of weak bisimulation for labelled Markov processes. In *Proceedings of the 17th Annual IEEE Symposium on Logic in Computer Science*, pages 413–422, July 2002.

[DGJP02b] J. Desharnais, V. Gupta, R. Jagadeesan, and P. Panangaden. Weak bisimulation is sound and complete for $pCTL^*$. In L. Brim, P. Jancar, M. Kretinsky, and A. Kucera, editors, *Proceedings of 13th International Conference on Concurrency Theory, CONCUR02*, number 2421 in *Lecture Notes in Computer Science*, pages 355–370. Springer-Verlag, 2002.

[DGJP03] J. Desharnais, V. Gupta, R. Jagadeesan, and P. Panangaden. Approximating labeled Markov processes. *Information and Computation*, **184**(1):160–200, 2003.

[Dob03] E.-E. Doberkat. Semi-pullbacks and bisimulations in categories of stochastic relations. In J.C.M. Baeten, J.K. Lenstra, J. Parrow, and G.J. Woeinger, editors, *Proceedings of the 27th International Colloquium On Automata Languages And Programming, ICALP'03*, number 2719 in *Lecture Notes in Computer Science*, pages 996–1007. Springer-Verlag, July 2003.

[Dob10] E.-E. Doberkat. *Stochastic Coalgebraic Logic*. Springer-Verlag, 2010.

[DP03] J. Desharnais and P. Panangaden. Continuous stochastic logic characterizes bisimulation for continuous-time Markov processes. *Journal of Logic and Algebraic Progamming*, **56**:99–115, 2003. Special issue on Probabilistic Techniques for the Design and Analysis of Systems.

[Dud89] R.M. Dudley. *Real Analysis and Probability*. Wadsworth and Brookes/Cole, 1989.

[dVR97] E. de Vink and J.J.M.M. Rutten. Bisimulation for probabilistic transition systems: A coalgebraic approach. In *Proceedings of the 24th International Colloquium on Automata Languages and Programming*, 1997.

[dVR99] E. de Vink and J.J.M.M. Rutten. Bisimulation for probabilistic transition systems: A coalgebraic approach. *Theoretical Computer Science*, **221**(1/2):271–293, June 1999.

[Eda99] A. Edalat. Semi-pullbacks and bisimulation in categories of Markov processes. *Mathematical Structures in Computer Science*, **9**(5):523–543, 1999.

[FPP04] N. Ferns, P. Panangaden, and D. Precup. Metrics for finite Markov decision precesses. In *Proceedings of the 20th Conference on Uncertainty in Artificial Intelligence*, pages 162–169, July 2004.

[FPP05] N. Ferns, P. Panangaden, and D. Precup. Metrics for Markov decision processes with infinite state spaces. In *Proceedings of the 21st Conference on Uncertainty in Artificial Intelligence*, pages 201–208, July 2005.

[Gir81] M. Giry. A categorical approach to probability theory. In B. Banaschewski, editor, *Categorical Aspects of Topology and Analysis*, number 915 in *Lecture Notes in Mathematics*, pages 68–85. Springer-Verlag, 1981.

[GJP04] V. Gupta, R. Jagadeesan, and P. Panangaden. Approximate reasoning for real-time probabilistic processes. In *The Quantitative Evaluation of Systems, First International Conference QEST04*, pages 304–313. IEEE Press, 2004.

[GJP06] V. Gupta, R. Jagadeesan, and P. Panangaden. Approximate reasoning for real-time probabilistic processes. *Logical Methods in Computer Science*, **2**(1):paper 4, 2006.

[Hal74] P. Halmos. *Measure Theory*. Number 18 in Graduate Texts in Mathematics. Springer-Verlag, 1974. Originally published in 1950.

[HCH+02] B.R. Haverkort, L. Cloth, H. Hermans, J.-P. Katoen, and C. Baier. Model checking performability properties. In *Proceedings of the International Conference on Dependable Systems and Networks 2002*, pages 102–113. IEEE Computer Society, June 2002.

[Hil94] J. Hillston. *A compositional approach to performance modelling.* PhD thesis, University of Edinburgh, 1994. Published as a Distinguished Dissertation by Cambridge University Press in 1996.

[HJ94] J. Hoffman-Jørgenson. *Probability With a View Towards Applications - Two volumes.* Chapman and Hall, 1994.

[JNW93] A. Joyal, M. Nielsen, and G. Winskel. Bisimulation and open maps. In *Proceedings of 8th Annual IEEE Symposium on Logic in Computer Science*, pages 418–427, 1993.

[JS90] C.-C. Jou and S.A. Smolka. Equivalences, congruences, and complete axiomatizations for probabilistic processes. In J.C.M. Baeten and J.W. Klop, editors, *CONCUR 90 First International Conference on Concurrency Theory*, number 458 in *Lecture Notes in Computer Science.* Springer-Verlag, 1990.

[Koz06] D. Kozen. Coinductive proof principles for stochastic processes. In R. Alur, editor, *Proceedings of the 21st Annual IEEE Symposium on Logic in Computer Science LICS'06*, pages 359–366, August 2006.

[Koz07] D. Kozen. Coinductive proof principles for stochastic processes. *Logical Methods in Computer Science*, 3(4:8):1–14, 2007.

[KS60] J.G. Kemeny and J.L. Snell. *Finite Markov Chains.* Van Nostrand, 1960.

[KT66] J.F.C. Kingman and S.J. Taylor. *Introduction to Measure and Probability.* Cambridge University Press, 1966.

[LS91] K.G. Larsen and A. Skou. Bisimulation through probablistic testing. *Information and Computation*, **94**:1–28, 1991.

[Pan01] P. Panangaden. Measure and probability for concurrency theorists. *Theoretical Computer Science*, **253**(2):287–309, 2001.

[Pan09] P. Panangaden. *Labelled Markov Processes.* Imperial College Press, 2009.

[PLS00] A. Philippou, I. Lee, and O. Sokolsky. Weak bisimulation for probabilistic processes. In C. Palamidessi, editor, *Proceedings of CONCUR 2000*, number 1877 in *Lecture Notes in Computer Science*, pages 334–349. Springer-Verlag, 2000.

[Pop94] S. Popkorn. *First Steps in Modal Logic.* Cambridge University Press, 1994.

[Rut95] J.J.M.M. Rutten. A calculus of transition systems (towards universal coalgebra). In A. Ponse, M. de Rijke, and Y. Venema, editors, *Modal Logic and Process Algebra, A Bisimulation Perspective*, number 53 in CSLI Lecture Notes, 1995. Available electronically from www.cwi.nl/~janr.

[Rut98] J.J.M.M. Rutten. Relators and metric bisimulations. In *Proceedings of Coalgebraic Methods in Computer Science*, volume 11 of *ENTCS*, 1998.

[Seg06] R. Segala. Probability and nondeterminism in operational models of concurrency. In *Proceedings of the 17th International Conference on Concurrency Theory CONCUR '06*, number 4137 in *Lecture Notes in Computer Science*, pages 64–78, 2006.

[SL94] R. Segala and N. Lynch. Probabilistic simulations for probabilistic processes. In B. Jonsson and J. Parrow, editors, *Proceedings of CONCUR94*, number 836 in *Lecture Notes in Computer Science*, pages 481–496. Springer-Verlag, 1994.

[SL95] R. Segala and N. Lynch. Probabilistic simulations for probabilistic processes. *Nordic Journal of Computing*, **2**(2):250–273, 1995.

[Sri98] S.M. Srivastava. *A Course on Borel Sets*. Number 180 in Graduate Texts in Mathematics. Springer-Verlag, 1998.

[ST05] R. Segala and A. Turrini. Comparative analysis of bisimulation relations on alternating and non-alternating probabilistic models. In *Proceedings of the Second International Conference on the Quantitative Evaluation of Systems (QEST)*, pages 44–53. IEEE Press, September 2005.

[vBW01a] F. van Breugel and J. Worrell. An algorithm for quantitative verification of probabilistic systems. In K.G. Larsen and M. Nielsen, editors, *Proceedings of the Twelfth International Conference on Concurrency Theory – CONCUR'01*, number 2154 in *Lecture Notes in Computer Science*, pages 336–350. Springer-Verlag, 2001.

[vBW01b] F. van Breugel and J. Worrell. Towards quantitative verification of probabilistic systems. In *Proceedings of the Twenty-eighth International Colloquium on Automata, Languages and Programming*. Springer-Verlag, 2001.

[vGSST90] R. van Glabbeek, S. Smolka, B. Steffen, and C. Tofts. Reactive generative and stratified models for probabilistic processes. In *Proceedings of the 5th Annual IEEE Symposium on Logic in Computer Science*, 1990.